Migration and Development

Migration and Development: Factoring Return into the Equation

By

Savina Ammassari

CAMBRIDGE SCHOLARS
PUBLISHING

Migration and Development: Factoring Return into the Equation, by Savina Ammassari

This book first published 2009

Cambridge Scholars Publishing

12 Back Chapman Street, Newcastle upon Tyne, NE6 2XX, UK

British Library Cataloguing in Publication Data
A catalogue record for this book is available from the British Library

ISBN (10): 1-4438-1352-4, ISBN (13): 978-1-4438-1352-5

CONTENTS

List of Tables

ABBREVIATIONS AND ACRONYMS

BEPC	*Brevet d'étude du premier cycle*
CPP	Convention People's Party
DFID	Department for International Development
ENSEA	Ecole Nationale Supérieure de Statistique et d'Economie Appliquée
ESRC	Economic and Social Research Council
GDP	Gross Domestic Product
GNI	Gross National Income
GNP	Gross National Product
IDS	Institute of Development Studies
IMF	International Monetary Fund
IOM	International Organisation for Migration
ISSER	Institute for Statistical, Social and Economic Research
OECD	Organization for Economic Cooperation and Development
PDCI	*Parti Démocratique de Côte d'Ivoire*
PNDC	Provisional National Ruling Council
PNP	Peoples National Party
RDA	*Ressemblement Démocratique Africain*
SCMR	Sussex Centre for Migration Research
SNA	System of National Accounts
TOKTEN	Transfer of Knowledge through Expatriate Nationals
TRANSREDE	Transnational Migration, Return and Development in West Africa
UGCC	United Gold Coast Convention
UN	United Nations
UNDP	United Nations Development Program
UNECA	United Nations Economic Commission for Africa
UNESCO	United Nations Economic, Social and Cultural Organisation
UNICEF	United Nations International Childrens' Emergency Fund
US	United States of America
US$	United States Dollars

ACKNOWLEDGEMENTS

I started writing this book in 2001 while I was doing a doctorate at the University of Sussex on "International Migration and Return of Elites to Ghana and Côte d'Ivoire" that in part was sponsored by the United Kingdom Economic and Social Research Council (ESRC). My original research idea and project developed into a collaborative effort to study "Transnational Migration, Return and Development in West Africa" (Transrede Project) directed by the Sussex Centre for Migration Research (SCMR) with the Ecole Nationale Supérieure de Statistique et d'Economie Appliquée (ENSEA) in Côte d'Ivoire and the Institute for Statistical, Social, and Economic Research (ISSER) in Ghana. It was funded by the United Kingdom Department for International Development (DFID).

I personally have worked on the Transrede Project, which lasted from 2001 to 2003, as coordinator of the study regarding higly skilled migrants. The Transrede study was larger in scope than my own doctoral research project because it focused on migration and return of both highly skilled and less skilled migrants. The two projects' central aim was the same. They sought to explore the role of migration abroad and to assess the benefits of return in view of the dual contexts of poverty alleviation and of sustainable development in the sending countries. I personally have coordinated the research on highly-skilled return migrants within my own doctoral research and the Transrede Project.

My investigations of the topic of highly-skilled, élite return migration and the empirical research findings regarding the two West-African countries have resulted in a doctoral thesis and in several papers, but the encompassing evidence is contained in this book.

I wish to thankfully acknowledge the encouragement and support offered by Margaret Grieco without which this volume would not have seen the light. I am also grateful to Pat FitzGerald who took on the final editing task. To both I am indebted for their very precious help in publishing this book.

Special thanks go to Richard Black and Russell King, the supervisors of my doctoral thesis and my work at SCMR – for their valuable advice and continued support in a long and challenging research effort. I also would like to acknowledge the collaboration of Richmond Tiemoko who under the Transrede Project coordinated the complementary research on less skilled migrants.

Several people have taken part in the research project and deserve acknowledgement: Benjamin Zanou, Raïmi Fassassi, Edouard Talnan and Dossina Yeo in Côte d'Ivoire; Clement Ahiadeke, Kudjoe Dovlo, Ekow Coleman, Peter Ofori, Angela Thoemke, Mathilda Folly and Francesca Soto in Ghana; Nalu Binasia and her collaborators at Sussex University.

Thanks also go to Robyn Iredale and her team at the Centre for Asia-Pacific Social Transformation Studies, University of Wollongong in Australia, who made questionnaires available that were used for a similar study funded by the Ford Foundation on the return of skilled and business migrants to Bangladesh, China, Taiwan and Vietnam. Some questions have been borrowed or adapted from that questionnaire because it seemed desirable to achieve a certain overlap in order to allow for future comparative analyses.

The help of the persons and institutions mentioned above was very important but in addition I am particularly grateful to all the highly-skilled Ivorian and Ghanaian migrants who have participated in this study and provided valuable additional contacts. Without their interest in the issues explored and their availability to respond to the many questions raised, this study would not have been possible. This book is largely dedicated to them and to their families.

Finally, I owe profound gratefulness to my family, friends and colleagues who have supported me in many ways during the fieldwork in Abidjan, Accra, London and Paris, including those who during my frequent trips have invited me home and sometimes, on top of that, have cared for my then very young children. In particular, I would like to thank Aby Ndiaye, Giulia Maura and Shaun Househam, Isabel and Miguel Empis, Jenny Money and Micaela Vicinanza.

Most of all I wish to express gratitude to my husband Frédéric Bernard who has always been a great source of inspiration and assistance and to my daughters Lilia and Lara who were born while I was working on this research project. Lilia participated in most of the fieldwork in Africa and Europe, and before she was born, Lara assisted in most of the writing up of the book. I thank my sister Adriana Ammassari for her valuable suggestions and advice. Most of all I am grateful to my mother, Elke Koch-Weser Ammassari, who has provided continued support and encouragement, and who along with my father, has been an example to follow.

This book is dedicated to my late father – Paolo Ammassari.

Chapter One

General Introduction

At the beginning of this century the World Bank (2000: 38) stressed that "cross-border migration, combined with the 'brain drain' from developing to industrial countries, will be one of the major forces shaping the landscape of the 21st century". In 2000, more than 176 million persons lived outside the countries of their birth or nationality, and this number grew to 191 million in 2005 which was more than the double recorded in 1980 (UN Population Division, 2009). Since then, international migration flows have further expanded, especially those involving highly-skilled migrants (IOM, 2008a; OECD, 2007). In the context of late capitalism and globalisation, human mobility is likely to assume even greater significance in the future. With increased transnational flows of goods, services and capital, people too will move across national boundaries with greater frequency than ever before in what has been called "the age of migration" (Castles and Miller, 1998). In particular, this will be the case with highly-skilled persons as there is a strong selectivity of migration in their favour (Jonkers, 2008; Solimano, 2006, 2008; UN Economic and Social Council, 2006).

The total volume of South to North migration has grown very fast in the past forty years because of the growing gap in living standards between developing countries and economically more advanced countries. The most important shares of this increase have been accounted for by Southern Asia, Western Asia and North Africa. But sub-Saharan Africa is also increasingly affected by emigration to wealthier countries in the North, due to the widening gap in the latters' economic, social and political situation and that of the migrants' countries of origin (Sander and Maimbo, 2005; Adepoju, 1991a, 1995a, 2003). Western Europe and North America are the preferred destinations, along with some oil-rich countries in the Persian Gulf. Overall, there is a clear trend showing that international migration flows originating in Africa are becoming more diversified (Bardouille et al., 2008; Bakewell and de Haas, 2007; Robin, 1996a, 1996b; Stalker, 2000).

Research Aims and Objectives

Within the population of migrants, people belonging to the élite generally have a greater propensity to move because they have more skills and education, technical means and financial resources, networks and connections, information and better chances to draw benefits from their migration experience. With improved and more accessible transportation and communications, highly-qualified migrants cross borders more freely, favouring the circulation of knowledge and technology. This has broad implications because the movement of highly skilled people from the developing world affects low-income countries and recipient countries alike" (World Bank, 2000: 39).

South to North migration has been the focus of much controversial debate since the 1960s. One central question has been whether it has a positive or a negative impact on developing countries. Migration studies conducted in different parts of the world have produced quite contradictory results, making it difficult to draw any meaningful general conclusions. The problem is partly due to the fact that the theoretical base for understanding these forces remains weak and that migration studies often fail to incorporate the necessary variety of perspectives, levels and assumptions (Castles, 2008, 2007; De Haas, 2007).[1] The contradictory nature of empirical findings also results from the fact that only a few studies have distinguished between highly-skilled, élite migrants and unskilled, non-élite migrants. Yet, the nature of their mobility differs significantly and so do the development implications for both the emigration and immigration country.

It has been argued that emigration can alleviate some of the problems developing countries are facing (Beine et al., 2001).[2] Emigration may relieve labour market pressures and generate remittances which constitute an important source of foreign exchange at the national level and of income for migrant families. Financial and human capital transfers occurring through return migration can be hypothesised to have a positive impact in that they help in improving the quality of life back home and in promoting socio-economic development. On the other hand, it has been stressed that emigration can also hamper development of the

1 See also Brettell and Hollifield (2000), Bakewell (2008), Massey et al. (1993, 1998) and Portes (2008).

2 This perspective has already been adopted in the past by authors such as Grubel and Scott (1977).

sending country because the most dynamic and ambitious people have a greater propensity to go abroad (IOM 2008a; Boussaid, 1998; Johry, 1995; Korner, 1997).[3] The loss of skilled people – the so-called "brain drain" – may have detrimental effects as it weakens human capacity to harness modern agricultural and industrial technology. Also, migrant remittances do not necessarily have a positive developmental impact on the sending country as they may be used for consumption rather than investment purposes, or they may generate dependency, inequalities and a problem of inflation. This long-standing debate is yet to be settled (De Haas, 2007; Hernandez-Coss, 2006; Ellerman, 2003).

Intercontinental mobility of the élite – to which people having a higher status in terms of education, occupation, wealth and power belong by definition – without return, has been and remains a major concern for development policy makers (OECD, 2008; IOM, 2003). In fact, apart from concerns related to the permanent loss of individuals with technical knowledge and skills that are crucially needed for development, élite return migrants assume key significance in a dynamic developmental context as they can be seen not only as a source of global interconnection but also as agents of national and local development (Mayr and Peri, 2008). However, a more thorough knowledge of the linkages between migration, return and development is essential for properly informed policy decisions. Such knowledge can help in alleviating the costs of human capital transfers and can ensure that the benefits are both maximised and more fairly distributed

Hence, return is another aspect of the migration process that has to be studied in order to determine its consequences for the development of the emigration country. Attention focused on return migration has so far been limited, and again there is little agreement regarding its impact (Agunias, 2006; IOM, 2008b; King, 2000). Emphasis has been placed on the positive consequences of financial and human capital transferred back home by returning migrants. The first is brought back in the form of savings, whereas the second materialises through the training and work experience that migrants acquire in the host country. On the other hand, it has been argued that many migrants gain very little of the latter, because they mainly perform unskilled work which teaches them very little. It is, moreover, claimed that even if migrants were to acquire new skills abroad, it is unlikely that these can easily be used productively back home.

3 See also Glaser (1978) and Mundende (1989).

The existing body of theoretical and empirical evidence shows that the impact of international migration and return on development varies considerably, depending, among other things, on the volume, type and timing of migration flows. The characteristics of migrants, degree and direction of selectivity, and situation of the countries involved in migration are critical factors which need to be taken into consideration. The consequences of migration also vary according to the level of analysis that is selected. There can be very different implications for individual migrants, their families, kinship or close social environments, and their home countries. The short-term effects of international migration may, moreover, differ significantly from its long-term effects.

Empirical evidence concerning migration and return gathered so far is too fragmentary to allow us to draw clear conclusions and devise concrete policy measures aimed, in particular, at a maximisation of the benefits stemming from the mobility of the highly skilled, an objective that ranks high on the policy agenda of OECD countries (OECD, 2001, 2007). It is therefore crucial to examine, by means of the most appropriate methodological strategies, the implications of migration and return for the meeting of international development targets in specific country settings, possibly allowing for regional comparisons – as in this research on West Africa – to gain a clearer and more comprehensive picture. While empirical evidence from southern Europe, Asia and the Pacific, the Middle East and the Caribbean is accumulating, very little is known about the developmental impact of international migration and return in sub-Saharan Africa, despite the urgent need to alleviate poverty and foster sustainable development in this part of the world (Ammassari, 2008; Findlay and Stewart, 2002; Lowell, 2002b).

The present research is aimed at returning élite migrants who, compared to "average" migrants, seem to have far better chances to assume a critical role back home and to contribute to the socio-economic, cultural and political development of their country of origin (Lowell, 2002a). They are more prone to access positions allowing them to acquire additional human, financial and social capital whilst abroad, and with this "added value" they have greater capabilities and resources to effect change on their permanent or temporary return(s). The élite concurrently has better chances to be socially mobile, i.e. to gain key positions of responsibility and authority in public and private sectors on return, and therefore its members are in a more strategic position to influence the course of events in their country of origin. Beyond capital assets in the form of financial remittances and/or accumulated savings and accrued knowledge, work skills and experience which translate into human capital, migrants coming home can also transfer social capital in the form of productive human relationships (Faist, 1997). These manifold capital gains represent a major potential for the country of origin, provided of course that migrants do return home.

Beyond possible family reasons there are social, cultural and political factors determining migrants' decisions to return or not to return back home. Certainly economic prospects and employment opportunities play an important role, but so do traditionally-rooted and newly-acquired values and political allegiances. Age, level of education, professional expertise, occupational status and monetary resources represent important independent variables; as eventually also might religion and ethnicity. In association with the cultural matrix and the nature and shape of the migration experience, such variables are expected to influence occupational initiative, social status and lifestyle, gender relations and role definitions in family life, social mobility aspirations for offspring, social relationships and networks, and the propensity to stay permanently on return or to emigrate again.

Return migration does not always imply an easy reintegration into the original context; migrants who come back usually encounter difficulties in readapting and dealing with contradictory feelings concerning their place of origin and their chosen country(ies) of emigration. Return migrants can be seen as innovators in the context of traditional modes of social, economic and political organisation and of long-established value systems.

The following general working hypothesis guides this research. Although after return élite migrants face several challenges of readjustment and reintegration, it seems likely that they play an important role in the development of their home country. Such a role manifests itself in terms of the human, financial and social capital transfers they operate. The present research chooses a multi-level analytical perspective to assess the implications of return migration at different levels. This means that improvements which have occurred after return in the migrants' personal sphere are explored along with changes that they have engendered in their family environment and the workplace as well as transformations they have provoked in the wider socio-economic and political sphere. With the objective of contributing to a better understanding of these complex processes, this research critically delves into the following three key aspects and raises specific corresponding questions in interviews and questionnaires:

1) The élite migrants' experience abroad: where, when and why did they migrate? How often and for how long did they stay away? What were their educational achievements and professional activities before departure and then abroad? What did they experience and learn while away? What was their lifestyle and status abroad? Which linkages did they establish with the host country? Which ties did they keep with the home country? Whilst abroad, what was their attitude towards return?
2) The return and transfer of resources: when and why did highly-skilled migrants return? Who made the decision of their return? Who participated in the return move and what was the reaction of friends in the host country? How permanent or temporary did they consider their return? Which linkages did they maintain with the host country(ies)? What kinds of human, social and financial capital did they transfer, if any? How was this capital used or invested? To what extent were these processes pre-planned, or did they occur spontaneously?
3) The élite migrants' experience back home: how did highly-skilled migrants readjust and reintegrate? What obstacles did they encounter in utilising the newly-acquired capital in their home economies and societies? What resistance did they face in the workplace, family and social environments? What is the potential role and impact of human, financial and social capital transfers? What implications are there at the micro, meso and macro level?

A Brief Outline of the Book's Structure

The book is structured into eleven chapters. After this general introduction, in Chapter Two, the linkage between migration, return and development is considered in detail. The aim is to summarise past and present debates around this issue and to review previous empirical research findings on this subject. The chapter argues that, although less or low skilled return migrants have rarely been found to be agents of change, highly-skilled return migrants have more chances to assume such a meaningful role in their home country. This particular group of migrants is in a better position to acquire capital abroad and effect changes back home. A distinction is made between financial, human and social capital that returning migrants transfer from abroad and each contributes to boost their development potential after return. However, the review also raises some major conceptual issues. The chapter therefore considers the need to distinguish between different types of migrants and addresses the problem of definition and measurement of return migration. It also evokes some of the most important assumptions forwarded in the literature to illuminate the migration-development nexus. The chapter concludes with a discussion of the contemporary trends in migration in West Africa, a region where return migration of the highly skilled and its implications have so far been disregarded.

Chapter Three describes the comparative multi-method research approach that was adopted in this study. It places special emphasis on the need to link the more conventional micro and macro perspectives used in the research on return migration through a greater focus on the meso level of analysis. This is a useful approach which makes it possible to conduct an inquiry into the impact of return migrants in the workplace and family environment. Using both qualitative and quantitative methodologies seemed a suitable way to assess not only if returnees introduce any change, but also to detect the kinds of change they provoke in different spheres. This chapter moreover explains that no strictly reliable sampling frame could be established and describes the strategies that were chosen to overcome this problem.

In Chapter Four, background information on Ghana and Côte d'Ivoire is provided. It shows that there are some major commonalities in their demographic and social characteristics. But there also are fundamental dissimilarities in their colonial backgrounds, recent history and contemporary politics as well as in their economic profile and key development indicators. For a long time Côte d'Ivoire has provided potential migrants and return migrants with a politically more stable and economically more advanced environment than Ghana. Only at the end of the 1990s has Côte d'Ivoire started to experience a period of political and social turmoil and plunged into a civil war following coups d'état in 1999 and in 2001.

The first results of the research are presented in Chapter Five, which offers background information on the samples of migrants who were interviewed in the different study sites. After furnishing a brief profile of the participants in in-depth interviews, the socio-demographic characteristics of the two country samples of returned migrants are presented. It emerges that Ivorian participants in the study are somewhat more highly educated and work mostly as employees in the public sector, while Ghanaians tend to be less educated and are more frequently self-employed with or without employees. The chapter acknowledges that this difference may be due to the snowball sampling procedure that was adopted to identify respondents. But these differences can in part be explained when the profile of the two countries is considered and the migration experiences of their populations are taken into account.

The findings presented in Chapter Six confirm that Ivorian and Ghanaian highly-skilled return migrants who were surveyed in this study have acquired and transferred home relevant human, financial and social capital. These migrants return home with considerable savings, skills, knowledge and ideas, as well as with personal and professional contacts. All this equips them with the necessary means to operate meaningful changes after return. A key distinction is, however, drawn between the ideology of return among the older and the younger generation, and this has an impact on the type of capital transfers that are made.

Chapter Seven enquires further into the conditions under which migrants can become agents of change. It focuses on the experience of Ivorian and Ghanaian highly skilled in Europe and North America and concludes that the migrants' experience abroad is particularly determinant for their acquisition of different types of capital. Most significant in this respect is their duration of absence and length of work abroad. The experiences abroad of Ghanaian and Ivorian highly-skilled migrants are described in some detail to foster a better understanding of the conditions that enable them to acquire a special development potential.

The eighth chapter is devoted to the dynamics of return migration to Côte d'Ivoire and Ghana. It investigates how the decision to go back home was made, who had a say in the process and who participated in the return move. It is argued that, as far as the migrants' change potential is concerned, this process and its determinants are of somewhat less importance in framing migrants' return decision-making. Yet, it shows how return was planned and organised in the light of specific expectations. The chapter also looks at the benefits that migrants derived from return incentive programmes and policies, which however in this context of investigation were found to be rather limited.

The challenges of readjustment and reintegration that migrants encounter back home are the subject of Chapter Nine. In terms of professional opportunities, returning migrants found what they were expecting but they also faced problems in adjusting to local working conditions. Similarly their living conditions after return and general readaptation proved more problematic than they had foreseen. For some, these problems remained sufficiently large so that they opted to remain abroad or re-emigrate. The extent to which such problems influenced the willingness of migrants to effect change was also explored.

Taking as evidence the understanding and assessment of their own experiences, Chapter Ten assesses migrants' and returnees' impact at different levels. The findings show that, at the micro level, many migrants had achieved their objectives, improving relative income levels, expressing satisfaction with their working conditions and, more generally, appreciating a higher quality of life back home. At the meso level migrants provided support to their family and kin in line with traditionally prevailing expectations and pressures. They also introduced many kinds of new knowledge, skills and ideas in the workplace. At the macro level, return migrants can also be seen to have promoted major socio-economic and political transformations. This included the creation of new businesses and the promotion of various community development initiatives.

Chapter Eleven deals with the policy implications of this study. It concludes that the developmental impact of highly-skilled return migrants is more important when these have acquired not only educational qualifications, but also relevant work experience abroad. However, there seems to be an optimal duration of absence of about five years, after which the acquisition of capital becomes constant. Also, from a certain point onwards, the likelihood increases that migrants may not return home or might lose the willingness to implement change after return. This important finding supports arguments and ideas favouring the circulation of highly-skilled migrants. Some recommendations are formulated in this respect, and with regards to the need to facilitate the reintegration of migrants back home. In conclusion, the chapter dwells once more on the strengths and weaknesses of this study before it provides some directions for further research aimed at harnessing the development potential of highly-skilled migrants in developing countries.

CHAPTER TWO

REVISITING THE LINKAGE BETWEEN MIGRATION AND DEVELOPMENT

The purpose of this chapter is to provide an overview of the relationship between migration, return and development. Regardless of its importance for the understanding of the migration-development linkage, return migration has always been somewhat disregarded in the migration literature (Cassarino, 2004; King, 2000). Even a superficial review of this literature shows that relatively few articles and books deal with this critical issue. While empirical studies on return migration have started to accumulate, theoretical approaches and models to study development implications of return migration and more precisely of highly-skilled migrants, are still lacking.

In the following sections, first the consequences that international migration can have on domestic labour markets, the effects of migrant remittances and the "brain drain" phenomenon are discussed. The return of migrants is addressed in a separate section because this part of the migration process deserves special attention if a better understanding of the migration-development linkage is sought. Then the developmental impacts of potential capital transfers occurring with return, and particularly the transfer of financial, human, and social capital, are examined. The chapter concludes by looking at the contemporary migration trends in West Africa.

Consequences of International Migration

Studies regarding the interrelations between international migration and development (Castles, 2008; De Haas, 2008; Nyberg-Sørensen et al. 2002a, 2002b) suggest that migration effects can be examined at three main levels: the individual level; the family, household, kin group or local community level; and the wider regional, district or national level. The nature of the eventual effects may be contradictory. For example, emigration of the highly skilled may have direct positive returns for individual migrants and their families (e.g. remittances and better standards of living), but may concurrently cause adverse effects for the national economy (e.g. loss of skilled human capital).

The consequences of migration may vary considerably according to the time perspective that is chosen. Certain consequences that appear positive in the short run may turn out to be negative in the medium or long run. Most important, however, is that the consequences of migration differ depending on its volume and type. The macro level consequences are obviously quite different when only a few people migrate, or in the case of mass migration. But migration effects also vary considerably according to different types of migration such as internal and international migration, temporary and permanent migration, regular and illegal migration.[1] The characteristics of migrants and the degree and direction of selectivity are also important determinants of variations in migration impacts. Variations in the consequences of migration do not only depend on the socio-economic situation in the areas or countries involved in the migration but also on the political and cultural situation. This broad range of factors influencing the nature of migration impacts is rarely taken into due consideration.

A review of the literature shows that the consequences of migration for the sending countries have generally been assessed at three levels: the effects of the departure of workers on labour markets; the impact of remittances on the national economy and on the living standards of migrants' family members; and the implications of the loss of highly-skilled migrants on the availability of human capacity necessary to harness development. Diverging views and contradictory findings concerning these issues will be discussed in the following sections.

Labour Market Effects

There has always been a heated debate regarding the effects of emigration on labour markets in sending countries. This issue is obviously of particular importance in the West African context which is characterised by rapid population growth and increasing unemployment. Some demographic forecasts suggest that the regional labour force in the year 2025 (477 million) will nearly match the region's population in 1990 (483 million) (Adepoju, 1998: 302).

1 Migration types can be distinguished using spatial, temporal, administrative, and legal criteria. See for example Boyle et al. (1998) and Lewis (1982).

Neoclassical economic theory expects out-migration to bring about a positive impact on labour markets under such pressure, by diminishing un- and underemployment (Solimano, 2001).[2] In these countries labour is generally abundant and capital is relatively scarce. Wages are lower here than in the more advanced industrial countries. Higher wages in the industrial countries attract labour migrants from the developing world. International migration, deriving from these imbalances, results in increased labour supply in immigration countries and decreased labour demand in emigration countries. As a result, wage levels rise in the emigration country and drop in the immigration country until an equilibrium is reached. At that point, one might expect return migration to be initiated. This model has been criticised because the decision to migrate is not influenced by economic factors alone. It is also determined by social, political, and even cultural factors. It also has been stressed that its underlying assumptions, such as the homogeneity of labour as a production factor and the conviction that markets normally reach a stable equilibrium, are too rigid (Fischer et al., 1997).

More specifically, some studies have shown that emigration can itself produce labour shortages in certain sectors of the economy. Adepoju (1991b) reports that in sub-Saharan Africa this has occurred mainly in agriculture and stresses that development may be obstructed as the young and enterprising adult males migrate while the older and more conservative members of the population stay home. Others, though, have demonstrated that labour shortages resulting from emigration can induce technological change encompassing a more rational use of resources. For example, Findley and Sow's (1998) longitudinal study on rural emigration in Mali shows that labour shortages have produced favourable changes in farming practices. Households with migrants in France had to take on outside labour to replace absent labour. This strategy has had positive effects because it has allowed them to extend their cultivation by using part of the production to pay the labourers in kind.

Migrant Remittances

It is often emphasised that while emigration countries lose manpower – and particularly the "best and brightest", in the words of Papademetriou

2 See for example Ranis and Fei (1961), Harris and Todaro (1970), Todaro (1976).

and Martin (1991) – they also get something in return. Migrants who work abroad usually send part of their income to their family, relatives or friends in the home country. The economic impact of these remittances has been considered beneficial at both the micro and macro levels at least in the short term.[3] Remittances represent an important source of income for families and households and the importance of the total volume of remittances is undeniable (World Bank, 2008).

In 2008 migrant remittances received by developing countries through formal channels were estimated at US$ 283 billion, up from US$265 billion in 2007 and US$72 in 2001 (Ratha, 2008).[4] Unrecorded remittances which are transferred through informal channels such as the migrants themselves or other people, for example, are estimated at about half the total volume of officially recorded remittances (World Bank, 2006). They are presumed to be particularly high in sub-Saharan Africa where they could correspond to 75 per cent of officially recorded remittances (Freund and Spatafora, 2005), or even to as much as 2.5 times the recorded flows (Sander and Maimbo, 2005).

Remittance data are today much more comprehensive and reliable, revealing that the aggregate value of migrant remittances has grown strongly over several years (World Bank, 2008).[5] Already, back in 2001, Gammeltoft (2002) had compiled data showing that these flows doubled between 1989 and 1999 and can significantly exceed that of other external financial flows. Globally, migrant remittances have surpassed official development assistance since the mid-1990s and presently represent the largest source of external finance to developing countries after foreign direct investment (World Bank, 2008). But in certain countries remittances can even significantly exceed foreign direct investment flows and also

---

3 See also Adams (2007, 2005), Adams and Page (2003), De Haas (2007), Özden and Schiff (2006), and Bardouille et al. (2008) and Adams and Page (2008) and Quartey (2006) with a focus on Africa and on Ghana respectively.

4 Officially recorded remittances are calculated as the sum of workers' remittances, compensation of employees and migrant transfers. See www.worldbank.org/prospects/migrationandremittances for remittance data definitions and datasets.

5 Despite measurement of migrant remittances has improved there remain problems to comprehensively record these financial flows because remittances are transferred through both formal and informal channels. There also remain challenges related to the definition of remittances and to ensure remittance data quality and availability (IOM, 2008a).

national export earnings. It also has long been stressed that remittances have a positive impact on the balance of payments of sending countries as they help to narrow the trade gap, control external debt, facilitate debt servicing and produce much-needed foreign exchange (Appleyard, 1989a, 1992, 1995).

The drawback of such conspicuous monetary transfers is that developing countries may become dependent on earnings that are nonetheless uncertain and remain vulnerable due to changes in migration policies and to economic or political crises (Hernandez-Coss, 2005; Appleyard, 1989a; Ghosh, 1992). For example, remittance flows dropped significantly following the political and economic crisis in 1999 in Côte d'Ivoire, which hosts migrants from many West African countries (Bardouille et al., 2008). This had also occurred during the first Gulf War (1990–1991) because it produced sudden returns of migrants to their home countries (Skeldon, 1997; Van Hear, 2002).

Yet Ratha (2008) established that remittances are a more stable source of external development finance when compared to some other sources and has stressed their counter-cyclical nature. In fact, it is especially in times of crisis in their country of origin that migrants start sending home more remittances to help their families, friends and communities. In addition, this author's remittance data analyses found that poor countries receive relatively larger remittances and these are more evenly distributed among countries than are flows of private capital (Ratha, 2007).

Migrant remittance flows to sub-Saharan Africa have steadily increased since the mid-1990s. They grew from US$ 3.2 billion in 1995 to US$ 9.3 billion in 2005 and to US$ 10.3 billion in 2006 (Ratha, 2008b). Although their growth has lagged behind that recorded in other regions of the world and increases in these flows have overall decelerated in the past two years, migrant remittances remain a very important source of foreign revenue. They exceed official development assistance in Côte d'Ivoire (Ratha et al., 2008b) as well as in Ghana, where they also significantly surpass direct foreign investment (Quartey, 2006).

The amounts that migrants remit vary depending, among other things, on their income, propensity to save and to some extent on the length of stay abroad. Institutional arrangements for money transfers, exchange rates and risk factors, as well as the strength of social ties, also influence the amount of remittances (Sanders and Maimbo, 2004; Barro et al., 2003; Maimbo, 2008). King (1986) showed that remittances increase proportionally with the income of migrants, while they decrease with the length of stay abroad. He also found that remittance money is likely to be more important when migrants plan to return than if they intend to settle for good in the host country. The amounts remitted tend to increase with the distance and the costs of migration. This seems to confirm that migrant families expect a monetary return on the investment in migration of one or more family members who have been sent abroad. Studies conducted in West Africa show that remittances are part of an "implicit contractual arrangement" between emigrants and their families (Black et al., 2003a). De Haan and Rogaly (2002) found that remittances increase in periods of crisis as they are an integral component of risk diversification strategies pursued by families to ensure support in moments of need. Russell et al. (1990) also detected in this region a positive correlation between amounts remitted and per capita household income from other sources.

The impact of remittances has been the focus of considerable debate (De Haas, 2007). Some scholars have argued that remittances fail to enhance development because they are not spent on investment goods but rather on basic consumer goods. Hermele (1997: 136) describes how this argument goes: "Remittances are not put to productive use, but mostly spent for unproductive purposes – housing, land purchase, transport, repayment of debt – or, to a smaller degree, wasted on conspicuous consumption, or simply saved as insurance and old-age pension funds". This argument is contradicted by the findings of Adams and Page (2008), who used a nationally representative household survey in Ghana to demonstrate that households use remittances in the same way as any other source of income.

The debate hinges on the definition of "productive" and "unproductive" uses of remittances. Expenditures on food (particularly in conditions of undernourishment), shelter, land and especially education may have a positive development effect and mainly, but certainly not exclusively, in the long run. For example, Taylor (1999) points out that building a house has an impact on family health and village infrastructural construction activities, whilst Lowell and Findlay (2001) note that the "induced effect" of emigration on increasing demand for education, and on the growth of private funds to support it, do have a highly beneficial developmental effect. Quartey (2006) found that remittances in Ghana improve household welfare and help households to minimise the effects of economic shocks.

Other scholars have emphasised other aspects. For example, Looney (1990) has shown how remittances can cause inflation because they create a demand without concomitant production capacity, whilst Böhning (1984) emphasised that remittances increase the demand for imported goods, producing a negative effect on the balance of payments. Thomas-Hope's (1999) findings from Jamaica confirm this view, showing that migrants were charged higher prices for houses and services. Some scholars laid emphasis on the "remittance multiplier effect" arguing that expenditures of remittance-receiving households may create a positive demonstration effect on households that do not receive any (Appleyard, 1989b).

Increasing social inequalities have been seen as another negative effect of remittances. Lipton (1980, 1982), for instance, has argued that remittances sharpen income inequality because the better-off parts of communities are more likely to send migrants abroad and thus are also more likely to draw greater benefits from migration.[6] A study by Rodriguez (1998) in the Philippines and research done by Adams (1991) in rural Egypt confirm this negative impact of remittances on income distribution.

On the contrary, through analysis of data covering 71 developing countries, Adams and Page (2005) confirmed that remittances can significantly reduce poverty and empirical evidence from different African countries also contradicts pessimistic views regarding the use of remittances. For instance, Gustafsson and Makounen (1994) have found for Lesotho that migrant remittances actually decrease inequality. From their study on sub-Saharan Africa, Russell et al. (1990) concluded that "once subsistence needs are met, migrants do use remittances for investment purposes including education, livestock, farming, and small scale enterprise".[7] Findley and Sow (1998) report from Mali that remittances not only covered basic food and cash needs but also allowed recipients to pay for irrigation in agriculture. Remittances have also been a significant source of financing for agricultural inputs in Zambia (Chilivumbu, 1985). Research in Somaliland has highlighted investment of remittances in productive ventures even in highly unfavourable economic and political conditions (Ahmed, 2000; Gundel, 2002; Maimbo, 2008).

Caldwell (1969), in a much earlier study on internal migration in Ghana, had already found that migrants spent remittances to pay for schooling and wages of farm labourers and to develop small businesses. In other instances remittances have been used to finance social and economic development projects in the home country. In their study on Senegal, Diatta and Mbow (1999) found that remittances were a substantial source of revenue for migrant families and were also used to

---

6 See also Ammassari (1994).

7 It should be noticed that some differences were found in the use of remittances by sex (Russell et al., 1990) and by educational status (Athukorala, 1990).

promote development in migrants' home communities. Similarly, a quite extensive literature in French reports that Sahelian migrants in France financed community development initiatives, such as the construction of schools, health centres and post offices or the provision of clean water. Other initiatives comprised the development of trade and handicraft, improvements in public transportation and the organisation of adult literacy and vocational training courses.[8] Even the salaries of teachers or health workers are sometimes financed by migrant remittances.

The Brain Drain

Migration of the educated and skilled from African countries to industrial countries in the North has reached significant proportions, and there is little evidence that these flows will decrease in the near future (ECA, 2006a, 2006b). This trend is the result of changes in government policies and in the nature of global labour demand and supply. About one in ten highly-skilled people born in the developing world are today estimated to live in either North America or Europe (IOM, 2008a).[9] It also has been suggested that as much as 30 to 50 per cent of those originating from developing countries and who were trained in science and technology have settled in developed countries (Lowell and Gerova, 2004). These figures raise the issue of "brain drain" which constitutes a major challenge to the development of their countries of origin.

Docquier and Marfouk (2004, 2006) have, for the first time, thoroughly documented international migration by educational attainment. They produced valuable statistics on the volume and increases in highly-skilled migration from African to OECD countries in the 1990s. Emigration rates were calculated by dividing the number of emigrants at each level of education by the number of people with the same level of education at home, including the emigrants themselves. This has helped to demonstrate that not only did migration from African to OECD countries increase

8 See for example Cissé (1993), Condé et al. (1986), Daum (1993, 1994, 1997), Dembele (1993), Diombéra (1993), Fadé (1993), Kane (2001), Lavigne Delville (1991), Nédélec (1998), Panos (1998) and Quiminal (1991, 1993).

9 The definition of highly skilled is not always clear. Typically, a combination of both education and occupation is used to select the highly skilled. But often the group that is referred to as "the highly skilled" comprises only adult people with tertiary education (IOM, 2008a).

from 1990 to 2000, but the magnitude and trend were also much more pronounced among highly-skilled African emigrants. The most significant increase was registered in West Africa (6 per cent), followed by that recorded in Central Africa (3.5 per cent) and in Eastern Africa (2.9 per cent). Emigration rates of the highly skilled from Northern and Southern Africa were much lower and declined slightly during the 1990–2000 period. Meanwhile, emigration rates among unskilled and medium-skilled workers were much lower and remained almost constant. These increases can be attributed to the poor working and living conditions in their home countries as well as to many other factors, including conflict and political unrest which push people out of their countries.

The brain drain inevitably raises a great deal of concern among African governments who continue calling for effective policy measures to enhance the return of highly-skilled migrants or encourage them to maintain links with their home country (ECA, 2006b; ILO, 2002). The much needed human resource pool in Africa is shrinking because the educated with various specialisations and skills (e.g., medical doctors, nurses, engineers, university professors, and researchers) are leaving to work and live abroad. This has major implications in the health sector for example, where African countries are facing increasing demand as a result of HIV/AIDS and other diseases.[10] In 2006, 926 Ghanaian doctors practiced in the OECD alone, representing 29 per cent of doctors practicing in Ghana (ECA, 2006a).

It is estimated that in the year 2000 about one third of the most highly qualified African nationals lived outside their country of origin, mainly in Western Europe and North America (World Bank, 2000). Carrington and Detragiache (1998) showed that at that time in Africa more than one third of individuals with a university degree had left the continent toward the end of the 1990s. According to these two authors, Ghana was among the countries which were the most affected by the brain drain since 26 per cent of its highly-skilled people had emigrated.[11] The data

---

10 See Marchal and Kegels (2003), OECD (2007), Pond and McPake (2006) and WHO (2006).

11 Logan (1992) published data on US immigration showing that the proportion of Africa's total migrant pool which is made up of professionals is larger than that concerning the rest of the world and that the rate of growth of the professional migrant flow from Africa is generally higher. UNCTAD estimates that, between 1960 and 1987, about 70,000 highly-skilled Africans left the continent to access the West (quoted in Russell et al., 1990). This corresponds to approximately 30

compiled by Docquier and Marfouk (2004) reconfirmed the magnitude of the brain drain in this country. They found that emigration rates of highly-skilled Ghanaian nationals aged 25 or more to OECD countries was 33.7 per cent in 1990 and increased to 42.9 per cent in 2000, while that of highly-skilled Ivorian nationals belonging to the same age group was 6.1 per cent and 7.8 per cent respectively.

The brain drain has been the subject of controversial debates since the 1960s.[12] The "divergence theory" sets emphasis on the highly detrimental effects of these flows, claiming that developing countries are losing their best people, thereby weakening human capacity to harness development. The emigration country loses critical human capital in which it has invested through education and training and for which it is not adequately compensated.[13] Some authors, such as Ojo (1990), already concluded at the beginning of the 1990s that this kind of brain drain produces negative effects on the development of sending countries. He concluded that these difficulties relate less to the loss of great numbers of highly-skilled people, and more to the loss of a few key highly qualified individuals in strategic sectors.

On the other hand, representatives of the "convergence school" argue that the problem of the brain drain is less critical than is usually portrayed. They tend to emphasise the beneficial consequences of migration for the receiving and sending countries and especially the positive effects of emigration on (un)employment.[14] It is argued that if highly educated and skilled people were not to emigrate they would be under-utilised at home due

---

per cent of the high-level manpower stock available within the continent at that time, an estimate confirmed in 2000 by the World Bank (2000: 39).

12 See Attafi (1994), Danso (1995), Mahroum (2000), Stark et al. (1997; 1998) and Wickrasemakara (2002). For earlier publications see Bennell and Godfrey (1980), Das (1979) and Gardiner (1968) for a special focus on Africa; Bhagwati (1976) and Glaser (1978) for more general overviews.

13 A major aspect of the brain drain controversy is whether high-level skills are drawn off unfairly.

14 A survey conducted in 1985 in Côte d'Ivoire shows that 37.5 per cent of people with a university diploma in Abidjan, and more than 50 per cent of such people in other cities, were economically inactive or unemployed (Russell et al., 1992). More than half of these people had been in that situation continually for the year preceding the survey. Among those with vocational and technical diplomas, 33 per cent were lacking employment in Abidjan and 26 per cent in other cities. The results also showed that about 10 per cent of graduates had started working in the informal sector as self-employed entrepreneurs.

to unemployment or poor working conditions which may suffocate their inventive and creative abilities that can better be used abroad (Lowell and Findlay, 2002). It is also stressed that human capital investments made in such high-level migrants are partly recovered through remittances. Furthermore, more recent literature has shown that the departure of highly educated migrants produces a "schooling incentive" acting on people who remain in the emigration country (Batista et al., 2007; Docquier and Rapoport, 2008).

Although the brain drain dilemma remains largely unresolved, some suggestions to solve the problem have been put forward. Already in the early 1990s, Obia (1993) devised a model with the aim of assisting developing countries to identify problem areas caused by the brain drain and find potential solutions. He argued that highly-skilled migrants should be seen as development assets, whether they return or stay abroad. The contribution of migrants can in his view be enhanced through consulting activities and by utilising grant monies to tackle research and development needs.

More recently, the issues of "brain drain" and "brain regain" have been studied more in depth with a focus on different sectors and on human capital loss and accumulation especially with emphasis on the information technology sector (Kapur and McHale, 2005; Saxenian, 2005).[15] In particular, the brain drain in the health sector of developing countries has started to be more comprehensively documented (Bhargava and Docquier, 2006). According to Docquier (2006) a certain level of highly-skilled emigration, between 5 to 10 per cent, is beneficial for developing countries. But he also acknowledges that brain drain occurs at much higher rates in many sub-Saharan African and Central American countries, and this is detrimental for their development.

Several policy initiatives have been put forward to foster the return of highly educated and skilled migrants and to encourage their support in the development of their home country (Ghosh, 2000b; De Haas, 2006; Lowell and Gerova, 2004).[16] "Return of talent" programmes were implemented in a number of sub-Saharan Africa countries such as Ghana,

---

15 See Agunias (2006) for a literature review on circular migration.

16 Not only has the support of highly-skilled migrants been sought but also that of unskilled migrants. Both can act as "partners in development cooperation" (Libercier and Schneider, 1996) and become involved in "co-development" initiatives. On this last topic see Ammassari (2003a), Bathily (2003), Grillo and Riccio (2003) and Weil (2002).

Mali and Senegal, with some sponsored directly by governments and other civil society institutions through bilateral and multilateral organisations (Ammassari, 2003a).[17]

The importance of return migration of highly-skilled migrants is now better acknowledged. Mayr and Peri (2008) recently published evidence confirming that return migration of the highly skilled is not a marginal phenomenon. The evidence shows that one fourth of all migrants return home, and an even greater proportion among the highly educated. It also suggests that those who plan to migrate and return invest more in schooling and that the return of migrants with international work experience enhances human capital in the emigration country.

Nonetheless, there is a growing recognition that many highly-skilled migrants may not return home. Attention has therefore shifted to the role and contributions of the "diaspora", a term employed to denominate expatriate populations and communities who can transfer knowledge, technology and capital back home without return migration (IOM, 2008, Kutznetsov, 2006; Sami and Guchteneire, 2006).[18] De Haas (2006) reported in detail how governments and developing agencies can support diaspora involvement in the development of origin countries. This question raised considerable interest in recent years among those whose aim is that of maximising the benefits of international migration for the sending countries.

The Study of Return Migration: Some Theoretical Issues

The return of migrants, with its human capital implications, is one of the most commonly cited benefits of migration for the sending country, along with remittance and labour market effects. But this is not the only form of capital transfer involved with return migration. Financial and social capital can also be mobilised through migrants' return. Migrants may accumulate savings while living and working abroad and bring them back once they return. They may also make professional and personal contacts,

17 See also De Haas (2006) and Koser (2000) on different types of policy frameworks and operational programmes, Logan (1990) and Ardittis (1985) on the UNDP-sponsored TOKTEN Programme, Pires (1992) and Ardittis (1991) on IOM's Return of Qualified Nationals Programme, and Strachan (1980) and Abraham (1968) for examples of return supported by government.

18 See also Brown (2000), Fibbi and Meyer (2002) and Meyer (2001).

which prove useful and productive for their endeavours back home. Here it is argued that the acquisition and transfer of different forms of capital are influenced by migrants' experiences abroad and the situation to which they return. But more generally speaking the implications of return migration vary also according to the level of analysis that is chosen and are based on several critical factors. These include the volume of return migration, characteristics of migrants, migration selectivity, types of migration and return, reasons of emigration and return, and conditions of the countries involved in the migration.

The relatively short history of return migration scholarship can be traced in three main generations of migration studies. The first generation focused on the push and pull factors of migration in the context of industrialisation. Flows were mostly seen as distinct movements from emigration to immigration areas, but the existence of "counter-streams", including migrants who return home, was acknowledged. Lee (1966: 54–6), for instance, argued that some migrants return because they have acquired new attributes in their destination countries which promise to be advantageous in their countries of origin (e.g. skills or wealth).

The second generation of migration studies emphasised the nature of structured relationships between the emigration areas (periphery) and the immigration areas (core) (see, for example, Mabogunje, 1970; Portes and Walton, 1981). Both areas were seen as tied into a general migration system. It was not only migration flows that linked these areas together, but also flows of information, capital, goods and services. Historical power constellations and cultural linkages facilitated these flows and nurtured the reciprocal relationships. In extensions of this perspective, return migration was considered as a form of feedback from the area of destination to the area of origin. Social network theory, for example, has posited that information provided by returnees and their post-return behaviour may either stimulate or deter further emigration (Boyd, 1989; Fawcett, 1989; Gurak and Caces, 1992).

The third generation of studies on contemporary international migration has developed in more recent times. The new conceptual framework suggests that in the context of globalisation, areas of origin and of destination are linked together in transnational spaces by migrants who build and maintain simultaneous and multi-stranded relations that span boundaries (Abella and Ducanes, 2008; Glick-Schiller et al., 1995; Smith and Guarnizo, 1998). In this view, return migration is a central part of ongoing migration processes. It is no longer seen as the "closure" of the migration cycle, but rather as one of the multiple steps of a continued movement (King, 2000).

Evidently the three perspectives are not mutually exclusive and each one can contribute to enriching a research approach which intends to capture the changing dynamics of migration in the face of modern globalisation tendencies.

Problems of Definition and Measurement

Defining return migration and other closely related concepts in the present context characterised by accelerating and increasingly multifaceted migration processes is a difficult task. But it is of course necessary to clarify some of these notions to allow for measurements and comparisons within the framework of an empirical study. King (2000: 8) has elaborated on the early work of Bovenkerk (1974) to define return migration as a "process whereby people return to their country or place of origin after a significant period in another country or region". However, although useful, this definition suffers from the problem that it is not clear what is meant by "significant period". Indeed, the time dimension is an essential aspect that needs to be clarified in operational terms if an empirical investigation is to be conducted on the ground. This study followed the UN Recommendations on Statistics of International Migration and only migrants having spent at least one year abroad were considered.[19] Another selection criterion was their presence back home for at least six months,

19 The need to elucidate the concept of return migration to allow for a reliable measurement of this phenomenon and sound understanding of its implications has long been stressed by UN agencies. See IOM (2008a) and Bilsborrow et al. (1997). The UN Recommendations on Statistics of International Migration suggest that the category of "short-term emigrants returning" includes "persons (excluding border workers) who have entered the country, who had previously been in the country at least once for more than a year and not away continuously for more than one year, and whose last departure was to work abroad at an occupation remunerated from a foreign country or to accompany or join such a person as a dependant or domestic employee". Return migrants who have been abroad for more than a year would figure among the "long-term immigrants" provided that they intend to stay in their home country for at least a year. Return migrants who plan to stay for a shorter period or do not intend to work for a year would be included in the category "other immigrants". It is clear that the application of this definition does not easily allow identification of return migrants.

because they needed to have had enough time to effect some change and to readapt, or not, to their original context.

UN guidelines for improving and harmonising data collection systems are useful to produce information that is in a readily comparable format. But unfortunately they are not always followed (IOM, 2008a; Bilsborrow et al., 1997). Even more regrettable is the fact that most migration statistics do not systematically operate a distinction between different types of migrants based on their level of education, qualifications or skills. For a study like this one existing data derived from administrative sources is therefore of relatively little use. More can be expected from censuses, but here again there are some limitations.

Censuses have the advantage of providing information from which one can draw general conclusions. But their disadvantages are that at best they produce data every ten years and that they collect few indicators on migration. Specialised household surveys regarding demographic, social and economic issues tend to have the same limitation, in addition to that related to their high cost. These are some of the reasons why more circumscribed surveys, like this one, are sponsored to assess the implications of migration and return flows.

However, even in smaller surveys the problem of definition arises. In this case it seemed important to define two main concepts: what is meant by highly-skilled élite migrants and how development is interpreted in this particular context. Regarding the first issue, "highly-skilled migrants" in this study are defined as those who, in their country of origin, belong to the élite which represents a minority and includes people of relatively high education, occupational status, wealth and power. When these people return they tend to get into top positions in the public and private sector and therefore should have a fair ability to make an impact. "Low- or unskilled migrants", instead, comprise those persons who have little or no formal education or training. They usually come from the lower strata of society, but may of course become socially mobile through migration.[20]

20 The sociological term "élite" refers to an hierarchically stratified organisation of society where a relatively small number of people occupy the positions at the top. While the term has lost some of its cogency in postmodern democratic societies where social inequality shows up more and more in horizontal terms (in particular, according to differences in life-style), in West African countries it aptly identifies minorities whose privilege, among others, it is to have greater chances in moving from and to their country of origin. See Bottomore (1993) for a discussion of the role of élites in developing countries.

The second issue was already raised some time ago by Bovenkerk (1974: 45), one of the fathers of return migration studies. He stressed the importance of defining what is meant by the terms innovation, change, and development and revealed his disappointment with the fact that:

> In almost all the literature in which the influence of returned migrants on the social and economic development has been studied, development and the various innovative stages that lead to it, is implicitly defined in terms of the model presented by the rich Western countries of the world. This is supposedly the viewpoint of most returnees themselves, because they bring back influences from these very countries. There may, in these sources, be some discussions about the way Western ideas are to be translated by the returnees in the context of their home countries, but the usefulness of these ideas themselves are never questioned.

This raises an important issue, recently reiterated by other migration scholars including Castles (2008) and De Haas (2008), which deserves attention on two levels: on the one hand, scientific discourse and interpretative schemes and, on the other, migrants' life history reports and self-definitions. For the purposes of this study "development" is not only conceived in terms of its economic dimension but just as much in terms of its socio-cultural and political dimensions. It consists of highly dynamic and multifaceted complex processes tending towards the reduction of poverty and the achievement of widespread well-being. Development, sustained by technological innovation, is not limited to economic growth but involves enriching changes in human thought and activity which encompass important social, mental and even spiritual elements whose relative worth is best defined by the people themselves. As Bovenkerk has already highlighted, migrants often return with a Western model of development in their minds because they bring back influences from countries located in this part of the world. However, this does not mean that they do not challenge the appropriateness and usefulness of the knowledge, skills and ideas that they have acquired abroad and find creative ways to adapt them to their local home context (Kessy, 1998).

Characteristics of Migrants and Migration Selectivity

Migration selectivity deserves a central focus in studies concerned with the implications of migration for the areas of destination and the areas of origin, as well as for the migrants themselves. Migrants are not a random sample of the population living in the country of origin.[21] Schooling and training increase the propensity to migrate, and so does wealth as it provides the resources to move. The better-off and more educated migrants are more likely to migrate and to do so more frequently and for longer distances (Lowell, 2002).[22] This is particularly true in the sub-Saharan context where legal routes of migration are accessible almost exclusively to the relatively rich and highly skilled, and illegal pathways often involve high costs which are difficult to bear for poorer, low or unskilled migrants. Yet, as an apparent paradox, high propensities to migrate also tend to be associated with low education and illiteracy (Lipton, 1982).[23]

Some authors have stressed that migrants tend to be more ambitious, entrepreneurial and capable than those who decide not to move. It is argued that the more migrants are favourably selected, the more successful will be their adjustment at destination, and the greater their positive impact on the host country's economy and society (Chiswick, 2000). Conversely, the more migrants are favourably selected, the more important, in general, will be the loss for their home country. Migration selectivity therefore has important policy implications for both sending and receiving countries (Özden and Schiff, 2006).

This is why policies and programmes for managing migration at the national, regional and international levels have attracted increasing attention. There is a growing interest from receiving countries in admitting highly-skilled workers and such countries adjust their immigration laws accordingly (IOM, 2008a, Iredale, 1999, 2001; Mahroum, 2001; OECD,

21 Migration is selective also with regards to age and sex. Young adult males are generally thought more likely to migrate, as are single persons – although there is growing evidence that the movement of single women migrants has been under-emphasised (IOM, 2003). From her analysis of global migration trends, Zlotnik (2003) concludes that female labour migration has increased faster in Africa than in other parts of the world. On the feminisation of migration see also Brydon, (1979, 1992) and Moreno-Fuentes Chammartin (2002).

22 Rose (1970) studied the relationship between the number of migrants and distance and concluded that lower-class people migrate for shorter distances as they find many more intervening opportunities in a given distance than upper-class people.

23 Studies of international migration from rural areas in the Sahel show that a very important role in this respect is played by migration networks (Blion and Rigoni, 2001; Quiminal and Timera, 2002).

2002). Meanwhile, more careful thought is given by sending countries to the need to devise more effective policy measures to harness the development potential of their citizens abroad, through return or various "diaspora options" (Castles and Wise, 2008; Lowell and Findlay, 2002; Martin, 2003).

An overview of European migration policies towards highly-skilled foreign workers at the turn of the century, when the data for this study were collected, is provided in a report prepared by McLaughlan and Salt (2002). It shows that both France and the United Kingdom, which remained the primary destinations of Ghanaian and Ivorian élites, had developed "skilled entry routes". These included the work permit system and specific highly-skilled migrant programmes. The duration of an initial work permit was a maximum of five years in the United Kingdom. It could normally be extended for another five years. After a stay of four years it was possible to change status. In France there were two types of work permit at that time. "Temporary" work permits were valid for nine months and renewable, and "permanent" work permits were valid for one year and renewable indefinitely.[24]

Iredale (1999) has elaborated on the distinction between types of migrants and proposes four categories of skilled migrants. Her classification is based on the following criteria: (1) migration motive (e.g. brain drain, government induced, industry led); (2) nature of source and destination (e.g. originating in developing or advanced countries, and moving to an advanced or developing country); (3) channel or mechanism used for migration (e.g. international recruitment agencies, rotation in multinational companies or international organisations); and (4) length of stay abroad (e.g. permanent, circulatory or temporary). Similarly, Gould (1988a, 1988b) had, much earlier, classified circulatory flows into contract workers moving between developing countries, trainees and self-employed professionals migrating from developing to economically more advanced countries, and personnel of multinational corporations moving between more advanced countries or between these latter and developing countries. Later work by Findlay and Salt (1989) and Findlay (1990) has helped in elaborating this typology and in analysing migration implications by the type of movement. But the problem of these later efforts is that they tend to focus almost exclusively on highly-skilled

24 A more recent overview of migration policies targeted at the highly skilled is provided by Agunias (2006).

transient migrants, that is highly-skilled migrants moving in well-defined multinational corporate settings.

Types of Migration and Return

As there are different forms of migration, so there are also varying types of return. These differentials are claimed to be important factors influencing the impact of migration and return on development (Ammassari and Black, 2001; Cassarino, 2004). A very common distinction is the one between temporary and permanent returns, which is based on the intention of the returning migrant to go abroad again or to settle for good back home. Two more categories can be established on the basis of the temporal criterion: occasional returns and seasonal returns. The first consist of short-term visits to see the family or to conduct business, for example.[25] The second involve temporary stays, which are determined by the seasonal character of the activities conducted as, for example, agricultural work in the home country that requires significant labour inputs.

Another classification that is important in order to discern the consequences of return is the one conceived by Bovenkerk (1974) and later refined by Gmelch (1980) and King et al. (1983). This is based on two main criteria: the lengths of time that migrants intended to stay abroad and their return orientation. It encompasses four categories: (1) intended temporary migration with return; (2) intended temporary migration without return; (3) intended permanent emigration with return; and (4) intended permanent emigration without return.[26] This classification is useful as empirical studies have shown that capital transfers in the form of remittances, for example, are more significant when migrants intend to return home. However, typologies using the intentions of migrants as criteria for classification usually present some problems. Firstly, migrants do not necessarily have definite plans at the time of their departure to

25 Asiedu (2003) illustrates the benefits of migrant return visits to Ghana.

26 Anwar (1979) has introduced the discussion about "the myth of return", a term that describes the contradictory feelings that migrants nurture vis-à-vis their home country and the country where they live. A return remains always envisaged, no matter how settled migrants are in the host country. But the return is constantly postponed although remittances are sent regularly and close contacts are maintained with home.

stay abroad or to return (Gmelch, 1980). Secondly, migrants' intentions may change over time depending also on opportunities and constraints arising abroad and back home, their own and their family members' stage in the life-course, and various professional or personal motives. Indeed, it has been argued that the intentions of migrants are a poor indicator of actual migration behaviour.[27]

King (2000: 9–10) has suggested another typology of return migration, based on the level of development of the countries involved in the migration. Three forms of return are contemplated in this respect: (1) return from developing to industrial countries that were linked by colonial ties; (2) return from countries which have achieved a relatively similar economic development level; and (3) return from industrial to developing countries whether linked by colonial ties or not. It is the absence, within this last type of return, of the highly skilled which is the subject of much concern and controversy.

Cerase (1974) developed a typology of return migration based on a study on return migration from the United States to rural areas in southern Italy.[28] Focusing on the length of time the emigrants spent abroad and the degree of their acculturation in the host society, Cerase proposed four different categories of return.

1) The *return of failure* includes migrants who have failed to overcome the "traumatic shock" on arrival and who were not able to adapt to the new environment. These "failures" represent only a minority and readapted quite easily to their home context because they return quickly before starting their integration into the host society.
2) The *return of conservatism* involves those migrants who have migrated to pursue a specific objective and thus save a significant portion of their income. These migrants tend to stay longer abroad and during their absence transfer remittances or save some money to realise their plans

27 See also Bovenkerk (1974: 18) who argues that "migrants do not always have a clear idea about their intentions and, moreover, tend to rationalize their reasons into motives that are accepted by the community as legitimate standard-motives".

28 It is important to note that the great majority of the returned migrants that Cerase interviewed originated in rural communities, but settled and lived during their period overseas in an urban area. This means that they "experienced an abrupt passage from a rural world to an urban and industrial one" (Cerase, 1974: 249).

back home. This means that the values of the home society continue to prevail as a reference for measuring success and achievement.

3) The *return of innovation* concerns migrants who stay in the host society long enough to start referring to its value system, but who eventually return home. These migrants are the ones who bring back new ideas and values and are ready to apply the skills they have acquired abroad in their home context.
4) The *return of retirement* involves migrants who have terminated their working lives abroad and go back home to retire. The third type is the form of return that has most "positive" implications on the sending country. Cerase is however quite sceptical that returnees can successfully assume the role of "agents of change". He argues that this is only possible if their actions can affect the economic structure and power relations of the home communities.

Return Motives and Readjustment Problems

Existing empirical evidence also suggests that the influence of return migration on socio-economic change in the emigration country varies depending on the motives for return and the problems that returnees encounter. Return motives include a variety of economic, social and family-related, as well as political, reasons (King, 2000).[29] Social and family-related reasons seem of particular importance. Strong family ties, the wish to rejoin family and friends, homesickness, problems of adjustment in the host country, racial harassment and the aim to enjoy an improved social status back home are significant reasons for return, according to the literature. Other factors are related to migrants' stage in the life-course, as age brings changing needs and preferences. Migrants may, for instance, wish to raise their children back in their home country. They may return to get married, to care for elderly parents, or to take on particular family-related responsibilities.

Some migration scholars have examined the relationship between integration and assimilation and return (Hoffmann-Nowotny, 1973; Esser, 1980). They have claimed that return occurred because migrants were unable to integrate or assimilate into the host society. Rogers (1984: 233) has argued that "Returns may indeed indicate failure to become integrated

29 See also Bovenkerk (1974: 20–25), Gmelch (1980: 138–41) and King et al. (1983: 25–31).

and assimilated into the host country, but they may not do so. For some migrants they may be 'new' decisions, arrived at on a basis of changed personal and societal circumstances".[30] She has proposed a typology that distinguishes between eight types of reasons for return which depend on events classified according to three dichotomous variables: (1) events taking place in or having reference to either the home or the host country; (2) events which are related or unrelated to the motives of migration; and (3) events which are assessed at the aggregate or individual level. More specifically these eight return reasons are the following:

1) migrants return because they perceive that positive changes have occurred in those situations in their home countries that brought about or contributed to their original migration;
2) migrants return because events in their home countries unrelated to their original migratory intentions necessitate, in their view, their presence in the country;
3) migrants return because the host country no longer satisfies the needs that they came to satisfy, or satisfies them less well than earlier;
4) migrants return because events in the host countries unrelated to their motives for migration make it less desirable for them to remain there than it had been before;
5) migrants return because they have satisfied the goals that they or their families had set for them or, if they had no specific targets, because they feel that they can now change their original situation in the home country;
6) migrants return because their families at home need them and they agree to follow their call;
7) migrants return because they erred in their assessment that the needs that motivated their migration could be satisfied better in the host country than at home;
8) migrants return because, although the specific needs that motivated their migration are fulfilled in the host country, they feel that the costs involved are too high. (Rogers 1984: 288–90).

---

30 In her research on Yugoslavian migrants in Austria, Rogers (1984) found that migrants' attachments to home and host countries co-exist. The attachment of migrants to their host country was mainly instrumental, whereas the attachment to the home country was often sentimental.

There are also various studies of the difficulties that migrants face on return (Arowolo, 2000; King, 2000; Lepore, 1986). Gmelch (1980) has distinguished two perspectives from which this question may be approached. On the one hand, the actual economic and social situation of returnees can be examined, looking at employment and housing, participation in associations, and so on. On the other hand, the migrants' own perceptions can be measured based on the degree of "satisfaction" or "dissatisfaction" with regard to their expectations nurtured vis-à-vis the home country on return.

Readjustment problems have been considered as an indicator of social change brought about by return migrants. Cerase (1974), for instance, has postulated that, the greater the conflict of re-adaptation due to the changed value structure of the return migrants, the greater the probability that they will provoke social change. Conversely, the more traditional their value orientation on return, the less likely they are to bring about innovation and social change. King (2000) has indicated that these hypotheses find confirmation in much existing empirical evidence. But he has also emphasised the ambivalence that accompanies migrants' return. Migrants are often relieved to be back home in a familiar context, but they are also quite disappointed after return and easily irritated with how things are done at home. Also, the relationship between returnees and non-migrants is generally often ambiguous (Gmelch, 1980).

Development Implications of Different Forms of Capital Transfer

The factors determining personal success and societal development include, *inter alia*, not only the magnitude of migration flows, migrant selectivity, migration types and motives, and the characteristics of emigration and immigration countries. In an early bibliographical essay, Bovenkerk (1974) suggested nine factors that may influence the potential of migration and return as a development force:

1) the *number of returnees*, in absolute and relative terms;
2) the *concentration of returnees in time*, because when migrants' returns are concentrated in a shorter time span, the critical mass exists that is needed to bring about change;

3) the *duration of absence*, because when it is too short, not enough may be learned to transfer anything meaningful, and when it is too long, migrants' may become too detached from home or too old to translate new ideas into practice;
4) the *social class of the migrants*, as skilled elite migrants seem more likely to assume the role of agents of change than unskilled labour migrants;
5) the *motives for return*, because the more return migrants have responded to pull-factors in their home countries the greater the chance for innovation, whereas the more they have reacted to push-factors the less the chance for innovation;
6) the *degree of difference between the country of emigration and the country of immigration*, because if this is too great the skills and experiences that migrants acquire abroad may not be useful back home;
7) the *nature of the acquired training and skills*, as it seems that the more general the training received abroad the greater the chances for innovation, whereas the more specific the training the less transferable it is to the home setting;
8) the *organisation of return*, because the better the return is planned and organised the greater the chance for change;
9) the *political relationship between the countries of emigration and return*, as the definition of progress in the home country may influence returnees' impacts.

The inconclusive nature of empirical findings on the developmental impacts of return migration which emerges from what has been discussed so far, results in part from the fact that few studies distinguish impacts according to all these critical variables (King, 2000). This was already in fact pointed out by Bovenkerk (1974: 46), who concluded that such accumulated evidence was "too little, too unreliable, too unspecific, too fragmentary and too partial, to make possible comparisons of the conditions under which innovation by return migrants succeeded and in which attempted innovation became failure". He put emphasis on the difficulties associated with weighing up the relative importance of various factors.

For Ghosh (2000b) there are two key factors which condition developmental effects: (a) the aptitude of the returning migrant and the degree of preparation of return; and (b) the socio-economic and institutional situation existing in the home country. The returnee's preparedness is also seen by Cassarino (2004) as one of the most important factors influencing the propensity of migrants to turn into agents of development in their home country. With regard to this factor, and in particular with reference to what equips migrants to make a development impact after return, a further distinction needs to be made between resources that migrants accumulate abroad in the form of financial, human and social capital (Ammassari, 2008; Ammassari and Black, 2001).

Financial Capital

The review of the existing body of literature reveals that development implications of return migration have so far been explored along two major lines: financial capital in terms of savings accumulated by migrants while working in the host country, and human capital acquired abroad in the form of education, training, and working experience. The transfer of social capital, which is equally important for development, has been considered much less. This materialises, among other mechanisms, through professional and personal contacts and participation in networks and organisations.

Financial capital is the best quantifiable, and thus visible, form of capital brought back by returning migrants. Migrants who live and work abroad may indeed save money, which they may transfer to the home country on return. These transfers of savings are different from the money that migrants send back home to their families or relatives while they are still living abroad. The impact of savings has raised a very similar controversy to the one concerning the effects of remittances outlined earlier. While some scholars have stressed the positive implications of migrants' savings for migrants themselves, their families and their countries, others have argued that the impact of savings generally is insignificant and sometimes even negative.

Overall, the empirical evidence concerning the uses to which migrant savings are put is quite limited and contradictory. But there seems to be a certain consensus that an important proportion of savings goes for constructing a house or to purchase a plot of land. This also seems to be quite a common finding in West Africa (Smith and Mazzucato, 2003; Tall, 1994). However, some recent studies show that migrants' savings are also invested in the development of small and medium size enterprises (Black et al., 2002; Black and Tiemoko, 2003). Tall (2003) reports from

Senegal, that important resources are invested into new information and communication technology, including the launch of cyber bars and internet cafés.

A quite common finding in different parts of the world is the preference of returning migrants for self-employment (Arif and Irfan, 1997; Black and Castaldo, 2008; Black et al., 2003c; Murphy, 1999; Nambiar, 1998; Zachariah et al., 2000). Ilahi (1999) found that migrants who accumulated a greater amount of savings while abroad are more likely to opt for self-employment after return. Research conducted by McCormick and Wahba (2003) and Mesnard (2004) confirm this finding by showing that migrants who undertake investments after return are those who saved more while abroad. Cassarino (2000) showed that social and business contacts were an important asset for migrants who embarked in self-employment after return. Black and Castaldo (2009) demonstrated that migrants' work experience abroad is the most significant predictor of entrepreneurial activity after return; accumulated savings, reasons for return and return visits are important too, but to a somewhat lesser extent.

Some return migration scholars have stressed that returning migrants transfer substantial amounts on their return as they usually earn more abroad than what they would earn at home and try to limit consumption. This was emphasised by King (1986: 24), for example, who found that "the greater the wealth and general well-being on return, the greater are likely to have been the sacrifice, self-denial and deprivation of the migrants during the 'other existence' abroad".[31] He also indicated that the amount which migrants save depends among other things on the level of their wage and necessary expenses for subsistence, accommodation and transport.

Human Capital

One of the most debated issues has been that of human capital gains for emigration countries through the return of migrants. It has often been claimed that migrants acquire valuable training and work experience when they study and/or work in more industrialised countries. New skills, ideas and attitudes of returned migrants are expected to have a positive impact on the development of their home country. Much empirical evidence has

31 A relatively extensive body of evidence concerning social mobility of migrants as compared to non-migrants was produced in the 1960s and 1970s. See for instance Dahya (1973); Gmelch (1979); Krane (1973; 1976).

however contradicted this optimistic view. Various studies from southern Europe, especially from the 1970s, have found that only a minority of migrants had gained new skills while working abroad (Gmelch, 1980; King, 1986). The majority did not learn anything new because they were only able to access unskilled work. Work on migration to Europe from Africa and the Middle East has also identified "deskilling" of migrants as a major problem (Al-Rasheed, 1992; Brydon, 1992).

But even among those migrants who are able to acquire new skills and experiences, few may be able to apply them in practice back home. It is obviously difficult for migrants who have acquired technical or industrial skills to apply them in rural settings lacking the infrastructure needed to make an effective use of their new skills (Castles and Kosack, 1973; Gmelch, 1980).[32] Also, many labour migrants are unskilled and get to do unskilled work whilst abroad, which does not teach them anything new. Unskilled labour migrants often get very little training (Bovenkerk, 1982). Böhning (1972), for example, studied the social and occupational apprenticeship of Mediterranean workers in West Germany and found very little evidence in support of the hypothesis that migrants return home equipped with new skills and the desire to introduce change. Migrants had been largely engaged in low-grade positions in industry and worked mainly on mass-production lines. They were often frustrated and this hampered their learning. Abadan-Unat (1976) stressed that labour migrants with real industrial know-how tended to stay on in West Germany. Their expertise can hardly be used back home. Migrants who returned were those with very limited skills who tended to avoid industrial jobs back home. These migrants have learned very little beyond, for example, how to empty dustbins in Munich or wash dishes in Zürich.

There is also empirical evidence gathered in other regions which contradicts the conventional view of human capital theory considering labour market experience in industrial countries as an asset. Muschkin (1993), for example, has researched the consequences of return migrant status for employment in Puerto Rico. When she compared return migrants with non-migrants, she found that the former had higher

32 See also Piore (1979), who takes a critical standpoint, stressing that returnees are not a significant source of industrial skills. The most skilled remain abroad whereas the failures tend to return. But returnees are not willing to go back to the agricultural work they did before leaving. This work is usually performed by immigrants from less developed countries.

unemployment rates and lower mean earnings.[33] A longer duration of stay was, moreover, associated with negative employment outcomes. These findings led her to postulate that the longer migrants were absent from home, the weaker their network ties and the greater the difficulties of finding employment. Moreover, a greater length of absence also seemed to prolong migrants' work in jobs with skill requisites that do not transfer well back home. On the other hand, when studying the return of Pakistanis from the Middle East, Arif and Irfan (1997) found that migrants had been able to move out of production-service occupations into business and agriculture occupations on their resettlement back home. This advancement was largely due to their experience abroad with the length of stay in the Middle East influencing occupational mobility.

There is also an important body of empirical evidence that seriously challenges empirical findings that return migrants produce only very little change. Returnees may not only bring back new skills and capacities, but also innovative ideas and changed attitudes and behaviours (Gmelch, 1980).[34] The question is obviously whether they have succeeded in introducing the foreign-acquired ideas and practices into their home communities. Murphy (1999; 2000) found in rural China that return migrants are introducing a capitalistic dynamic into their communities. This has repercussions on the local institutional and political environment and infrastructure. Returnees play a major role in the development of small-scale enterprises. But they also contribute to enhancing the integration of local markets into the national economy and help in establishing links for the transfer of information. Saloutos (1956), in a much earlier study, already stressed the benefits of migration and return for Greece, arguing that returnees brought back new ideas on democracy, health standards, and social behaviour. They introduced liberal business practices, and pro-US and pro-Western values.

The results of research conducted in the Caribbean support the hypothesis that return migrants can act as agents of change under certain circumstances. In their study of a Barbadian village, Sutton and Makiesky (1975) found that returnees not only had acquired new values and beliefs, but also a greater racial and political consciousness. Comparing skilled and unskilled return migrants in Barbados, Gmelch (1987) found a

33 That return migrants had problems finding employment on return or were occupationally downwardly mobile was also detected by Arif (1998), Athukorala (1990) and Kazi (1991).

34 See also Ammassari (2003b).

significant proportion of student-migrants entering professional or white-collar occupations at home who were more likely to introduce new ideas and techniques acquired while abroad. Unskilled migrants had less impact because they went back to jobs that did not exploit their overseas work experience. They also lacked the necessary positions of authority and power enabling them to induce change.[35]

Studies of return migration in Jamaica confirm that returnees can play a meaningful role in the development of the home country. Taylor (1976) reported that Jamaican migrants return home with accrued skills and experience. This has been confirmed by Thomas-Hope (1999) in a recent study showing that the majority of returnees from North America and Europe have gained additional skills and capacities as well as changed the way they were functioning in the workplace. Most importantly, however, returnees have an impact due to the leadership roles that they assume in their home communities.[36]

Social Capital

While financial and human capital transfers have received attention in the migration literature, the transfer of social capital, consisting of a set of specific resources that can be mobilised within groups, networks and organisations, has largely been ignored. Social capital designates the potential wealth that can be drawn from social relations. Thus Bourdieu and Wacquant (1992: 11) define it as "the sum of the resources, actual or virtual, that accrue to an individual or a group by virtue of possessing a durable network of more or less institutionalized relationships of mutual acquaintance and recognition". It is built on mutual obligations and expectations, norms of reciprocity, trust and solidarity.

A review of the literature shows that studies concerned with social capital have almost exclusively dealt with the extent of participation in formally established organisations networkslike associations and

35 Gmelch (1980) also examined the impact of return migrants outside the workplace and has stressed that it is hard to draw any meaningful conclusions as it is difficult to separate the role of return migrants as agents of change from other foreign influences such as films and television or tourism.

36 In this respect it is interesting to study the return of the élite person who traditionally goes abroad to study (and, sometimes, to work) and the lives of leading individuals such as political leaders or successful businessmen.

cooperatives and with the resources that derive from such participation. For the study of the transfer of social capital, however, another kind of resource assumes particular significance. This is the competence that people acquire in building and nurturing interpersonal relations and social ties in varied socio-economic, cultural and political contexts. Such networking competence is to be conceived as a subjective variable corresponding to the product of a formal and informal learning process that helps in achieving "wider horizons". Language skills, the ability to interact and work with people of different cultures, and familiarity with norms, customs and values are among the benefits that migrants acquire abroad. As a subjective resource social capital can indeed be transferred, whereas as an objective resource, as Meyer (2002) stresses, it is locally embedded and therefore more difficult to transfer.[37]

Migrants can tap into social capital in both the sending and the receiving country. Benefits derived from such social capital include information on jobs, social services, and housing abroad. But they also include information on these critical issues back home, and knowledge about business and investment opportunities, or loans to finance private enterprises. The more migrants have developed networking competencies, and have invested in maintaining social capital back home and in establishing social capital abroad, the more they have the freedom of choice to return, to stay away, or to shuttle back and forth.[38] But also, the more successful they should be in achieving their goals at both ends, because not only do they have improved information, but also greater access to resources, and increased control and authority within the community. The return of this type of migrant has a greater likelihood to effect positive changes in the sending country.

On arrival in the receiving country, migrants establish social ties with people or groups from their home country, who can provide

37 It has long been acknowledged that there is a territorial restriction of certain assets, a phenomenon that Da Vanzo (1981: 118) has denominated "location specific capital". For Faist (1997: 204) the fact that social capital is difficult to transfer abroad raises the expectation that "potential migrants prefer those forms of movement that allow them to keep their social ties intact (circular migration), to interrupt them only briefly (seasonal migration) or to transfer the whole set of important social ties abroad (e.g. family migration in the context of chain migration)".

38 Faist (2000) notes that all three forms of capital can enhance the autonomy of individuals and enlarge their freedom of choice.

material support, help in making new social connections and and assist the newcomers to overcome their ignorance about the new community (Brettell, 2000).[39] But then migrants gradually establish new webs of ties involving local and other foreign people and start building corresponding social capital. In the sending country, social capital is maintained by migrants through visits, contacts by mail or telephone, remittances, marriage with a compatriot, or membership in associations linking receiving and sending countries. Presumably, both forms of social capital play a critical role because it is assumed that social capital is used to transfer and re-transfer back other forms of capital, e.g. financial and human capital (Faist, 1997). Interfacing both forms of social capital helps migrants develop transnational identities and loyalties.

However, as stressed by Ghosh, besides the different aptitudes and resources of the returning migrant, the other key factor, that is the socio-economic and institutional situation existing in the home context, also has to be taken into account if one is to assess the development impact of highly-skilled return migration.

Contemporary Trends in Migration in West Africa

From what has been said so far it appears crucial not only to distinguish between different types of migrants, but also to consider their impact in each specific context. In West Africa, where intercontinental migration and return of the highly skilled has yet to be properly studied, spatial mobility has always been a key feature of people's lives. It has often been observed that there are few other regions in the world where the population is so mobile (Ricca, 1989). The highest concentration of migrants and refugees is registered in this part of the world, including a growing proportion of women and children (Adepoju, 1998). The region is well-known for its extensive migration systems, some of which reach far beyond the African continent.[40]

Although the quantity and quality of data on migration in sub-Saharan Africa have started to improve, there still is a considerable

39 See also Boyd (1989) and Choldin (1973).

40 For internal and intra-regional migration see, for example, Appleyard (1998), Baker and Aina (1995), Cordell et al. (1996), Gould (1974) and Makinwa-Adebusoye (1992). An overview of South-North migration regarding sub-Saharan Africa can be found in Adepoju (1991a).

scarcity of reliable migration data. It is therefore difficult to determine the exact volume of different types of migration. According to Zlotnik (2003) the number of international migrants in the countries of the Economic Community of West African States (ECOWAS) increased from 2.5 million in 1960 to 6.8 million in 2000.[41] Statistics published at the beginning of the current decade by the UN Population Division (2002) show that in eleven ECOWAS countries Ghana, Guinea, Guinea Bissau, Mali, Niger, Nigeria, Senegal and Sierra Leone the number of migrant exits exceeded the number of entries. However, these figures are quite difficult to interpret because a distinction is neither made between nationals and foreigners, nor between migrants and refugees. Furthermore, these statistics do not tell us anything about the destination of the flows.

Internal forms of migration, and particularly rural to rural and rural to urban migration, continue to account for most migratory movements in West Africa (Bakewell and De Haas, 2007; Traoré and Bocquier, 1998). International migration remains predominantly intra-regional and occurs mainly between neighbouring countries. Meanwhile, intercontinental migration to economically more advanced countries located in the northern hemisphere has grown in importance due to the deteriorating socio-economic conditions affecting the region since the 1960s (Adepoju 1998; 1991a). The number of documented migrants from sub-Saharan Africa to the North has expanded from 17,259 in 1960–1964 to 77,636 in 1985–1989.[42] These migration flows are mainly directed to Western Europe and North America. They remain male dominated, although the number of women who migrate over longer distances and for longer periods has steadily increased (Adepoju 1995b; Zlotnik, 2003). Highly-skilled migrant flows from West African to industrialised countries in the North have also expanded along historical links between countries of origin and of destination. Data published by Docquier and Marfouk (2006) show that 34 per cent and 21 per cent of tertiary educated foreign-born adults in France and the United Kingdom respectively were originally coming from Africa.

In West Africa, as elsewhere, it is possible to distinguish between "forced" and "voluntary" migration flows. The former include refugees

41 Altogether 16 countries belong to the Economic Organisation of West African States (ECOWAS): Benin, Burkina Faso, Cape Verde, Côte d'Ivoire, the Gambia, Ghana, Guinea, Guinea-Bissau, Liberia, Mali, Mauritania, Niger, Nigeria, Senegal, Sierra Leone and Togo.

42 Zlotnik (1993 cited in Awusabo-Asare 1995: 156).

and asylum seekers, whereas the latter can be classified into two main groups. On the one hand, there are the poorer (though not poorest) low or unskilled people for whom migration represents a survival strategy. This group of people often has little choice other than to migrate. The Soninké people coming from the Senegal River Valley, situated between Mali, Mauritania and Senegal, are probably the most well-known example. This group has been the subject of much research because its members, most of whom are poor and illiterate, started to go overseas early on as a strategy to diversify income and find alternative ways to satisfy basic needs (Blion and Rigoni, 2001; Daum, 2000; De Haan, 2000; Keita, 1996; Quiminal and Timera, 2002).

On the other hand, there are the educated and wealthier people who usually come from the urban élite and who choose migration as a strategy for advancement. For them migration represents an effective way to improve their own and their family status and to be upwardly mobile. These highly-skilled migrants are generally pulled out by the greater training and work opportunities existing in the wealthier countries in the region or in the North. An increasing numbers of young people go abroad to study because of the degradation of local higher education systems and better study opportunities abroad (IOM, 2008). Blaud (2001) documented this trend in African countries and explained why many expatriate students may decide not to return home for political as well as economic reasons. Some may return only much later on after having gained significant work experience abroad. The brain drain in this region is therefore likely to develop further in the coming years. IOM (2008) published data showing that 45 per cent of Ghanaian graduates live in an OECD country.

Côte d'Ivoire has long remained the main country of immigration in the region.[43] But with the military coup of 1999 and the ensuing political and economic crisis it has started losing its appeal.[44] The main countries of emigration are the Sahelian countries, including Burkina Faso, Mali, Niger and Senegal.[45] Some countries on the coast, such as Ghana, for example, have also developed into major emigration countries, although

43 Côte d'Ivoire has also been an important country of transit for migrants who plan to move on to other regions (Barros et al., 2002; Bredeloup, 1995).

44 See Brossard (2003) and Dozon (2000) on the rising xenophobia that characterised Côte d'Ivoire in the early 2000s.

45 Senegal has actually been a major country of both emigration and immigration (Ammassari, 2003a).

they originally used to be important countries of immigration. Ghana's transition to an emigration country started after the 1966 military coup. It is estimated that two million workers left the country between 1974 and 1981, with many of them settling in Nigeria and Côte d'Ivoire (Bakewell and De Haas, 2007). In the mid-1980s, an increasing number of Ghanaians started migrating to European and North American destinations (Anarfi and Kwankye, 2003).

Intra-regional migration flows continue to be directed primarily towards coastal areas, whereas those outside the region were until recently determined by historical and cultural ties. In the past migration occurred principally between former colonies and past colonial powers because of their linguistic, administrative, political, investment and transportation links. More recently, however, migration flows outside the region are becoming more diversified and are increasingly directed towards a broader array of countries in the North as well as in the South (Bakewell and De Haas, 2007; Robin, 1996). This can be related to the introduction of more restrictive immigration policies in the North, but more generally to accelerating processes of globalisation.

The contemporary causes of emigration in West Africa are multiple and complex, including overall deteriorating socio-economic conditions, declining standards of living and spreading poverty (Bakewell and De Haas, 2007; Adepoju, 1995a, 1995b). A series of demographic, economic, social, political and even cultural factors determine the volume and the composition of intercontinental migration flows. A rapid growth in the population and labour force, sharp rises in un- and underemployment, decreasing real incomes and growing costs of living, low agricultural production and ecological disasters triggering food shortages, and political instability are only a few of the more critical causes of out-migration. The expansion of education and training systems after independence (Brydon and Gould, 1984) and the economic reforms and structural adjustment programmes promoted during the 1980s and 1990s also represent important determinants of emigration because they have enhanced unemployment in both public and private sectors (Adepoju, 1995b).

The decision to migrate is rarely made by individuals acting on their own. Much more often migration decision-making involves entire families as well as wider social structures and networks. Cordell et al. (1996) have stressed that in West Africa migration results from a complex series of implicit and explicit negotiations occurring within the household. This has also been confirmed by other studies emphasising the role of traditional hierarchies in decisions on who should move, where, when, and the mode of behaviour at destination (Adepoju, 1995a; Findley and Sow, 1998).[46] Similarly, remittance behaviour is influenced by mutual obligations and expectations, and norms of reciprocity and solidarity (Grubert, 2002).

It is clear that usually migration not only concerns those who go, but also those who stay (Hammer et al., 1997). Social ties between emigrants and their families and kin back home are particularly strong in the African context (Russell et al., 1990). Migrant families and kin bear part or all the costs of migration. In return they expect migrants to send home remittances and gifts, to visit regularly, and to remain in contact by mail or phone. Migrants may also be encouraged to marry locally to guarantee that eventually they will return home (Findley and Sow, 1995).

Migration is an integral component of African families' survival and mobility strategies which often culminate in return (Oucho, 1995b). Decisions to stay, to leave, or to return are closely related to the nature of the household economy and domestic and social power structures. But personal abilities and ambitions as well as structural and institutional factors operating at the local, regional and global levels also play a highly critical role.

Migrant remittances to sub-Saharan African countries have significantly increased over time (see Table 2-1). However, it is difficult to evaluate the total volume of these financial flows because in this part of the world significant amounts are transferred through informal channels (Bardouille et al., 2008; Barro et al., 2003). Moreover, even when focusing exclusively on officially transferred remittances, a glance at the migration literature and official reports reveals that quite different figures are used to describe trends and discuss remittances behaviour. One reason is that data on remittances are not available for all countries and years.[47] Time series therefore include estimations which are calculated in different ways.

Data on official remittances compiled by Tiemoko (2003) from IMF's Balance of Payment publications show that net remittances in

46 See also Makinwa-Adebusoye (1995) and Oucho (1995b).

47 Another problem related to the evaluation of the volume of migrant remittances is that different countries collect information using different definitions. As a result it is not always clear what exactly is included in the different categories which are commonly used in the IMF Statistical Yearbook, including "worker remittances", "migrant remittances" as well as "compensation of employees". Moreover, these figures do not reveal where these remittances are coming from (Black and Tiemoko, 2003).

Table 2-1 Migrant remittances to sub-Saharan Africa, 1995–2007 (US$ billion)

Remittances	1995	2000	2001	2002	2003	2004	2005	2006	2007
Inward remittance flows	3.2	4.6	4.7	5.0	6.0	8.0	9.3	10.3	10.8
Outward remittance flows	2.0	2.5	2.3	2.5	2.8	3.0	3.3	2.9	

Source: Ratha and Xu (2008).

countries belonging to the Economic Community of West African States (ECOWAS) increased from US$589 in 1995 to US$1,511 in 1999. Empirical evidence from the region confirms the importance of remittances for migrant households and communities, particularly in times of crisis (De Haan and Rogaly, 2002; Lachaud, 2002).[48] Since remittances are seen as a more stable source of foreign development finance, governments are studying ways to enhance these flows which represent an important source of public revenue, especially in the context of diminishing foreign aid and investment.

In 2000 officially reported remittances in several West African countries, for example Benin, Burkina Faso, Côte d'Ivoire, Nigeria, Senegal and Togo, considerably exceeded foreign direct investment flows (Ammassari, 2003a). Nigeria received about seven times more money through remittances than through foreign aid. For a traditional emigration country such as Cape Verde migrant remittances represented more than one third of the export earnings and more than 13 per cent of its gross national product (GNP). If officially transferred remittances in 2000 constituted a relatively small portion of the GNP of Ghana and Côte d'Ivoire, they nevertheless represented a little less than a third of foreign direct investment in Ghana and a little more than one third of foreign aid in Côte d'Ivoire.

Officially recorded remittance flows to Ghana and Côte d'Ivoire have increased very significantly over the past 20 years (Table 2-2). In Ghana remittances have grown from US$6 million in 1989 to US$105 million in

48 Daum (1994) has estimated that in the Senegal River Valley (Mali) remittances represented 80 per cent of the income of households.

Table 2-2 Migrant remittances to Ghana and Côte d'Ivoire, 1989–2007

Year	Migrant remittances (US$ million)	
	Ghana	Côte d'Ivoire
1989	6	36
1990	6	40
1991	6	42
1992	7	–
1993	10	58
1994	16	110
1995	17	151
1996	27	147
1997	26	136
1998	30	142
1999	31	138
2000	32	119
2001	46	116
2002	44	120
2003	65	142
2004	82	159
2005	99	163
2006	105	164
2007	105	176

Source: Black et al. (2003a) and Ratha and Xu (2008).

2007 and in Côte d'Ivoire from US$36 million to US$ 176 million. In 2006 inward remittance flows represented 0.9 per cent of Ghana's and 0.8 per cent of Côte d'Ivoire's gross domestic product (GDP). While remittance outflows have remained constant in Ghana since 2000 at US$6 million, these have steadily increased in Côte d'Ivoire representing US$597 million in 2006 (or 3.4 per cent of GDP) up from US$390 million in 2000.

Remittances, the way they are transferred, their use and impact have been dealt with quite extensively in the migration literature concerning

West Africa.[49] Meanwhile, in this regional context, little is known about international migration and return and their implications for the acquisition and employment of financial, human and social capital. Few scholars have focused on this specific issue in this particular context and those who have done so, have dealt exclusively with low or unskilled migrants.[50] This study addresses this shortcoming by focusing attention on the international migration and return of highly-skilled élite migrants. The purpose is to demonstrate that this specific group can make a difference when they return home.

49 See for example, Barro et al. (2003), Blion (2001), Blion and Verrière (1998), Yatera et al. (2000) and Verrière (2000).

50 See Blion (1995), Diatta and Mbow (1999), Kambiré (1994), Petit (2002), Twum-Baah et al. (1995) and Quiminal (2002). Growing attention has been driven to policies and programmes favouring return in West Africa. Parant (2000) and Petek-Salom (2002) represent an example.

CHAPTER THREE

ADOPTING A COMPARATIVE MULTIMETHOD RESEARCH APPROACH

In this comparative study, which sets special emphasis on the connectivity of migrants and migration streams in the wider context of population groups and socio-economic, political and cultural processes, it is important to link micro and macro research perspectives (Ammassari and Black, 2001). Such an approach, which introduces both individual and societal factors into the analytical scheme, helps to overcome traditional divisions that persist in much migration research and continue to hamper a more extensive and thorough understanding of the complexity of these processes and their dynamics.

Micro and macro perspectives can best be linked if a multimethod research approach involving qualitative and quantitative methodologies is adopted. This has several advantages because it allows the researcher to conduct cross-sectional and longitudinal inquiries into particularly intricate issues. In this study, as to the longitudinal perspective, emphasis was given to in-depth interviews based on open-ended questions regarding individual migration, return experiences or plans, and expectations for the future. Narratives reconstructing family and personal life histories and direct observation to deepen and enrich the understanding of the role of return migration were also employed in each contextual setting. Concurrently, choosing a cross-sectional perspective, a questionnaire survey was conducted to obtain more general data concerning the socio-demographic characteristics of the returnees, the nature of their migration behaviour, their post-return development impacts, and the organisation of their daily lives.

Linking Micro and Macro Perspectives

Past theoretical and empirical migration studies have generally taken either a macro- or a micro-level analytical perspective. Macro theory and empirical research have focused on migration flows and chiefly on their volume, direction, composition and persistence. The structural characteristics of the areas of origin and destination have been emphasised as well as their socio-economic and political characteristics. This approach has paid particular attention to aspects that are common to some segments of the population that share some economic, social or cultural attribute. Micro-level analyses have instead focused on the normative and psycho-social factors that determine individual behaviours and influence decision-making processes. From this perspective, personal and subjective aspects, in particular, perceptions, motivations, aspirations, expectations and values, assume primary importance.

Both micro- and macro-level determinants and consequences of migration and return should of course be carefully examined. Additional attention deserves, however, to be focused on the meso level, which provides crucial means to link these more conventional levels of analysis (Faist, 1997; 2000). At the meso level, not only families and households, but also webs of kinship and other social clusters help to influence migrants' decisions to move, stay or return. These decisions are rarely made by isolated individuals. Rather, they are embedded in a complex web of interpersonal relationships and social ties where overarching economic, political and cultural institutions shape opportunities and constraints. In this context, social capital, consisting of a set of specific resources that can be mobilised within groups, networks and organisations, can become an essential element for the analysis of migration trends.

In comparison with the other two approaches, the meso-level approach to migration has emerged in two strands of literature. Firstly, the processes of immigrant incorporation have been studied in economic sociology (Castles, 2004; Portes, 1995, 2008). Here immigrants are not seen simply as isolated individuals, but rather as members of groups and participants in broader social structures that affect their mobility in various ways. Secondly, migrant networks conceived as "sets of interpersonal ties that connect migrants, former migrants and non-migrants in origin and destination areas through ties of kinship, friendship, and shared community origin" (Massey et al., 1993: 448) have been studied in order to identify the ways by which they facilitate the achievement of shared goals.

Looking at all three levels of analysis is important to explore the implications for development of migration and return as these depend to a great extent on the experiences that migrants acquire abroad and the conditions they encounter back home after return. The opportunities and obstacles they face in each of these contexts influence their acquisition of capital and development potential, as do their personal attributes. Another important hypothesis this study addresses is that migration and return motivations affect outcomes for the migrants themselves, their families as well as their countries.

Determinants of Migration and Return

Migrant decision-making – that is, why people move – has always been a paramount question in migration studies, although multiple reasons are generally involved in explaining a specific move. Fundamental at the macro level are, in addition to basic demographic and ecological characteristics of the countries of origin and destination, the structural and economic opportunities and constraints which are generally assumed to be the result of differences in the supply and demand for labour. There is no doubt that wage and employment differentials play an important role, but there are other critical variables influencing migration and return. In addition to other economic determinants, such as access to capital and credit for example, various political and social factors include for instance the availability and quality of basic infrastructure and social services but also the presence or absence of conflict and rule of law. National and international policies and laws governing mobility represent important deterrents or incentives for migration and return. Those migrants who have acquired permanent residence status or citizenship abroad may be more likely to return than those who fear to be stuck if ever they fail to reintegrate back home. This was highlighted in some of the migration literature focusing on Sahelian migrants in France (Blion and Rigoni, 2001). Blion (2002) also describes how the remittance behaviour of this group has changed since the introduction of restrictive immigration policies in France with decreases in money transfers because fewer migrants planned to return home.

At the micro level, rational choice theories have most commonly been used to explain why people migrate.[1] Their main assumption is that a person is able to weigh the different advantages and disadvantages of the current place of residence and those of potential alternative residences. Such cost-benefit calculations are not always made with reference to realistic parameters but are instead based on perceived opportunities and constraints at origin and destination. Thus, information acquired through different communication channels such as the media or the internet,

1 See, for example, Harris and Todaro (1970), Todaro (1969, 1976), Sjaastad (1962) and Wolpert (1965).

relatives or friends and through other migrants or personal visits play a vital role. Indeed, although some generalisations are possible, the decision to move or to return remains a fairly subjective and not always a rational exercise. Through moving, people may strive to improve or secure any, all or a combination of the following: wealth (e.g., income), social status (e.g., prestigious job, authority and power), comfort (e.g., satisfactory working and living conditions), stimulation (e.g., possibilities for professional growth), autonomy (e.g., high degree of personal freedom), affiliation (e.g., joining family and friends), meaningful life (e.g., opportunities to improve society) and better life for one's children (e.g., quality education) (Faist 1997: 189–90).

It seems quite reasonable to believe, in line with the value-expectancy model of De Jong and Fawcett (1981), that migration decisions are made on the basis of values (goals and preferences) and expectancies (subjective probabilities). Both can vary considerably based on people's specific circumstances, beliefs, aspirations and obligations which are subjective by their very nature. For example, past empirical studies focusing mainly on unskilled migrants have found that economic factors are more important for those going abroad, whereas family reasons assume greater significance for those returning home. Whether this applies also to highly skilled élite migrants returning to West Africa, remains an open question.

If emigration decisions can be characterised by a continuum along different "degrees of freedom" (Faist, 1997: 196), the same can be done for decisions to go back home. At one extreme, there is very little or no choice to stay in the host country. Migrants may be repatriated against their will because their residency or working permit has expired. Similarly, certain migrants may not be able to consider return simply because they lack the necessary means to pay for the return trip or transfer of personal belongings. Or, they may not have saved enough money to secure suitable accommodation on return. Such a situation can discourage return because it implies that migrants have to go back and live with their parents or other family members. At the other extreme, there is an important level of autonomy in people's decision-making. This is likely to depend among other things on the availability of resources. The more money, qualifications and skills, information and connections, the migrant has, the greater the freedom of choice to go abroad or to return. The greater are also the chances to reintegrate into the home context without too many difficulties. That is why social capital is assumed to play an equally important role abroad and back home. Its role in the mobilisation of other forms of capital makes it an essential ingredient for a satisfactory and successful return move.

The decision to stay, to move or to return is made more or less freely by individuals considering that these are always embedded in collectives and social networks, a reality which needs to be examined at the meso-level. As a result, micro-level rational choice theories have widened their perspective to consider families and households as migration decision-making units But also migration system theories, mainly dealing with macro-level forces and factors, have increasingly focused on networks which are held together by social or even by only symbolic ties such as ethnic or religious bonds (De Haas, 2008; Portes, 2006).

The above discussion links migration and return decision-making to the three levels of analysis and shows that:

- at the macro level demographic, ecological, political, socio-economic and cultural conditions produce particular, more or less favourable, opportunity structures;
- at the meso level interactive relationships constitute collective bonds and create facilitating social networks; whereas
- at the micro level the degree of freedom of choice to migrate is influenced by personal and collective means as well as reference schemes and aspirations regarding the future.

Along these conceptual lines, sets of structural, relational and personal variables were identified in view of their incorporation into the research instruments. It was expected that, in various combinations, these would contribute to explain the heterogeneity of migration and return choices.

Migration Patterns and Return Experiences

What migrants learn abroad and what they acquire in terms of human, social and financial capital is crucial in influencing potential development impact. In this context, personal attributes of the returnees such as age and gender assume particular relevance. Mostly considering growing levels of education, it can be expected that the experiences of migrants belonging to different age groups or generations would vary significantly. Some important variations based on gender differences are anticipated as well. But there are also other variables which are worthwhile to consider, especially those related to the migrants' life-course (e.g., marital status and the eventual presence of offspring).

The migrants' geographical and social origins are expected to influence their activities and experiences before departure and then abroad. Some of them may have already belonged to the élite before they went abroad. For others migration may have represented an effective advancement strategy that has allowed them to climb the societal ladder and to become part of the élite following return. In this context, it is helpful to compare migrants' occupation and migration history with those of their parents.

Some significant variations are also to be expected based on the migrants' destination. The most important differences are likely to emerge between experiences made in Anglophone and Francophone settings because their cultural contexts to which migrants are exposed differ considerably. Similarly, having studied and/or worked in Europe or alternatively in North America may influence a migrant's experience because of the significant differences of their educational systems and business practices. Also, whether migrants have been to only one place or to two or more is likely to affect what they did learn whilst away, as those who have been more mobile and have lived in more, perhaps also more heterogeneous, places may return with a wider spectrum of experiences and broadened perspectives.

In general, the duration of absence seems – from the literature – to be the most critical variable influencing the ability and willingness of migrants to make a contribution on return. It is hypothesised that the more time migrants spend abroad, the more they are exposed to situations potentially different to the ones they are used to back home, the more they can benefit from opportunities that may be lacking at home, and the more opportunities they have to learn new things and acquire new ideas, and to make new contacts. But also, the more chances they have to work and earn money and accumulate savings. In sum, the migrants' acquisition of financial, human and social capital is expected to be directly correlated with their duration of absence.

Yet, as already suggested by Bovenkerk (1974), there may be an optimum length of absence for migrants to assume a meaningful role after return. If the time spent away is too short, they may not have acquired enough human, financial and social capital to transfer back home. If the absence is too long, returning migrants may no longer know their home country, and make important miscalculations in the way they invest these various forms of capital.

To understand the foreign experiences of returning migrants better – and the "added value" with which they go back – not only their education and work experience needs to be examined. Other factors may help in shaping their capital acquisition abroad, such as, for instance, their residence status. Migrants who only had a temporary status may have "integrated" less in the host society than those with a permanent status or others who have acquired local citizenship. For example, a student whose aim is to stay abroad only for the time it takes to get a degree may have less time, opportunities and even willingness to mix with local people or to get involved with local institutions. An investigation into the migrants' lifestyles and social interaction, as well as their feelings in the host community, therefore seems useful.

These factors are expected to influence not only return propensities and post-return adjustments. Two other factors assume importance: the linkages migrants may have established in the host country (e.g., marriage with a native, naturalisation or the purchase of a house), and the ties they have kept back home while living abroad (e.g., correspondence and particularly visits). These are seen to influence the migrants' attachments and allegiances to the home and host countries, or to both, as these may co-exist in the present context. The migrants' attitudes regarding return and expectations concerning the home country are anticipated to be key variables affecting their reintegration experience, and thus change potential, back home. In fact, if the expectations of returning migrants are too high, they may easily get disappointed after return. How realistic migrants' expectations are depends in part on whether they visited their country of origin before they returned home. Exploring the problems that migrants encounter after return is important because these are expected to affect the development potential of return migrants.

Research Design and Methodological Approach

Justification for choosing one particular research approach instead of another can be sought in alternative philosophical standpoints and particularly through ontological and epistemological considerations which are concerned with what scientific knowledge is about and with its nature and validity. Reflecting on these issues, the basic question is whether it is possible to obtain knowledge about the social world by means of empirical data. Assuming that this is possible, the next question to be asked is how it is possible to obtain satisfactory knowledge; what do we want to know and which would be the most appropriate procedures to study social rather than physical phenomena? Here, of course, more specific methodological and technical considerations become important.

Fundamentally in the social sciences, two different aims of knowledge production can be distinguished. On the one hand, there is the attempt, going back to the founding father Auguste Comte, to emulate the natural sciences by trying to explain complex issues by means of a minimum of observable variables and without speculating about unobservable processes. On the other hand, there is the Weberian conviction that human conduct cannot be understood without taking into account the subjective meaning attached by those concerned to the conduct we are observing (Weber, 1949). According to the former point of view, theory and method are distinct from each other and *a priori* derived hypotheses must be tested in order to expand nomological knowledge. In contrast, according to the latter position, method and theory cannot so clearly be separated. Here hypothesis generation and concept formation tend to be intertwined with data gathering (Ammassari, 1991; Bailey, 1987).

Most social scientists today would admit that both approaches – the quantitatively oriented positivist one and the more qualitatively oriented interpretivist one – have valid aspects. In quantitative research, the replicability of research findings and the public control of procedures are major concerns, whilst in qualitative research the exploration of meaning and the discovery of its social organisation constitute the central task. These traditionally opposed philosophies can be reconciled by adopting a multimethod approach that encompasses both qualitative and quantitative methodologies. Such an approach is also well suited to overcoming the classical micro-macro divide and to integrating different theoretical perspectives regarding migration phenomena.

In the present study, qualitative methods such as focused interviewing and life histories have allowed a thorough analysis of the subjective experiences of individuals. Since these may or may not be shared by others, it was deemed important to gain an understanding of these experiences and to discern their value not only for the migrants themselves, but also for their families and wider social networks. The use of qualitative methodologies has permitted the exploration of a series of aspects that are very difficult to quantify, such as the perceptions attitudes and aspirations of migrants.

Hence much more detailed information was obtained concerning certain qualitative indicators than would have been possible to achieve through the exclusive employment of quantitative data collection techniques. At the same time, the questionnaire survey has enabled the generation of two quantitative data sets, one on each of the countries surveyed. This information was used to elucidate the characteristics of the migrants, the attributes of their migration and return experiences and the impacts of their return. Additional quantitative data, in aggregate form and regarding the macro level, was derived from various official data sources such as national statistical services, the World Bank and the United Nations.

Limitations Regarding the Adopted Multimethod Approach

In principle, it would have been desirable to interview a much larger number of return migrants in both of the two African research sites, to administer a questionnaire also to Ghanaian and Ivorian migrants who were still (or again) living abroad in Europe, as well as to a "control group" of non-migrants. However, due to the limited time and resources available this was not possible. The study also faced some major methodological constraints. An experimental research design for a rigorous assessment of migration effects could not be selected because of the impossibility of forming correctly matched experimental and control groups. Furthermore, given the absence of returnee listings, probabilistic sampling procedures could not be used. Instead, a non-probabilistic sampling procedures based on sex by age quota estimations was adopted in order to identify the people to be interviewed.

Qualitative and quantitative and methodologies were used in this study in a complementary way across the three phases of the fieldwork. During the first phase, after an extensive review of documentary evidence, a pilot study involving a series of preliminary focused interviews was conducted to explore migration and return in Ghana and Côte d'Ivoire. An open-ended, unstructured questioning method was considered important at this early stage to gain a good initial grasp of the processes in these two contexts. However, qualitative information was also sought at this time to assist with the design of the quantitative research instrumentation.

The quantitative survey was put in place during the second phase of the fieldwork. A large number of semi-structured interviews were conducted with returned migrants in Ghana and Côte d'Ivoire with the help of a questionnaire. An unstructured interviewing method was instead adopted for the individual and group interviews that were undertaken during the third phase of the fieldwork in the two European destinations with Ghanaian and Ivorian migrants who at that time remained abroad.

The comparative approach targeting two countries appeared, on the other hand, especially useful to gather empirical evidence that could help to increase the understanding of the differential consequences of migration and return on development. Such a double focus allows expanding the knowledge base by exploring the commonalities and dissimilarities existing between the two study sites. In addition survey information was also collected in London and Paris, the two most important European destinations. Focusing on both origin and destination seemed essential to better understand the patterns and effects of contemporary international migration because this mobility is far more dynamic, multidirectional and complex than it used to be in the past. Information obtained from the European interviews in particular has helped to understand why certain migrants prefer to remain abroad and not to return to their country of origin. It has allowed a better grasp as to how return is envisioned, and sometimes practically planned and organised, by those who are abroad. Moreover, in the case they opted not to return home, or at least not to do so in permanent terms, the role of these migrants in the development of their home countries was explored.

Strategies to Overcome Research Design Constraints

To assess the developmental impact of migration, returned migrants have sometimes been compared with non-migrants by using a quasi-experimental research design. Whether this is an adequate way to proceed depends largely on the specific questions that guide a particular piece of research. But here attention was focused more on the kinds of contribution that highly-skilled return migrants make in their home context and on the conditions under which they can make such contributions, than on what distinguishes these contributions from the ones of non-migrants. It could be argued, however, that a control group of non-migrants is needed if the "value added" of international migration and return are to be properly assessed. In this case there were several problems associated with the adoption of such a procedure.

Firstly, a comprehensive and reliable sampling frame was lacking. While it would have been possible to develop such a sampling frame, for example, on the grounds of records kept in the public service or in professional associations, the use of such a strategy would have entailed too narrow a focus on either civil servants or on specific professions (e.g., health workers, architects or lawyers). Information collected during the preliminary pilot study, however, had revealed the existence of very different kinds of contributions made by returnees and suggested the need to look at both public and private sectors as well as at different fields of professional activity. Using records of professional associations would also have introduced another bias because not all returnees or non-migrants become members of such institutions.

Secondly, a rigorous experimental design can only be adopted if the sample of returnees and non-migrants are identical as regards their background characteristics. It requires the adoption of a quota sampling procedure based on the control of a series of key indicators (e.g., sex, education and occupational development) so that the effects of the independent variables on the dependent ones can properly be assessed. Translating a quota sampling scheme into practice is usually a difficult task, even more so when seeking to interview people belonging to the élite, and still more so again when surveying in a developing country context. For example, there are real problems in reaching the élite and in obtaining agreements to interviews. Not only are people who belong to the élite very busy, but they are also reluctant to reveal their "stories". A rolling sampling procedure helps in easing these difficulties because contacts between the researcher and potential respondents are made by those who were already interviewed.

Thirdly, as in most studies, there were limited resources available. Since only a limited number of questionnaires could be administered, some strategic decisions needed to be taken. The more questionnaires administered to non-migrants, the less could have been administered to returnees, thereby reducing the database for a meaningful statistical data analysis of both samples. An alternative option would have been to focus only on one country, but it was felt that a comparative approach was a particularly useful strategy through which to explore the conditions under which return migrants can assume a developmental role.

Because of the above-mentioned problems, a "rolling sampling" procedure was adopted to identify and select respondents in each study site. In this approach, a limited number of return migrants were contacted through personal connections. These people were interviewed and at the end of the interview they were asked to provide the names and contact numbers of other migrants who had returned. In this way a list of potential respondents could be established, including the name and position, company or institution, phone numbers and some additional comments (e.g., who had made the contact). There is no answer to the question as to how comprehensive this list is. But it can be mentioned that in the two countries under study everybody tends to know everybody else in the élite, and that some contacts were provided over and over again, suggesting that some of its members are better known and connected.

Various shortcomings of the snowball sampling technique were, of course, kept in mind. A special effort was made to determine and concurrently to diversify as much as possible the composition of the sample. Towards this aim a series of selection criteria was developed and communicated to the research assistants. The criteria of selection were aimed at including both men and women,[2] from both the public (academic and non-academic) and the private sector, and belonging to different age groups. Furthermore, research assistants and returnees who provided contacts were told that no more than one person from the same family, working in the same firm or institution, belonging to the same association or club should be interviewed, in order to diversify as much as possible the sample.

A number of concepts and issues needed, of course, to be clearly defined before the start of the fieldwork. "Migration" was in this context defined as a process whereby people leave their home countries to go and live in another country or in several other countries for a period exceeding one year. The "home country" or "country of origin" corresponds to the country of birth and citizenship. There could, however, be a few exceptions. For example, a Ghanaian or Ivorian who was born abroad but who grew up in the country of origin and later emigrated could be covered by this study. The same could happen with migrants who had given up their original citizenship following a naturalisation in the host country.

"Return migration" was defined as a process whereby people come back to their country of origin after having lived for more than one year abroad. "Élite migrants" were defined as those migrants who belong to the élite in their country of origin, which means that they can, but need not necessarily, belong to the élite in the host society. The "élite" represents the most influential and prestigious stratum in society. It consists of a minority, a group of people of relatively high status in terms of education/qualifications, occupation, wealth and power. In the Ivorian and Ghanaian contexts, "éliteness" comprises a combination of

2 Efforts were also made to include a suitable number of women in the samples but not necessarily 50 per cent of the sample, because Ghanaian and Ivorian women still have a lower propensity to embark on intercontinental migration.

some or all of the following: family background; high levels of education/qualifications which could have been acquired at home or abroad, or a mixture of both; exercise of power, through occupation/employment, class or whatever; wealth; and finally also a self-perception as being part of an élite – a sort of "élite consciousness".

For this study returned élite migrants were sought exclusively in the capital cities of Accra and Abidjan and mainly in top positions of responsibility and authority in both the private and the public sector. Unemployed or retired returnees were not included in the samples. Mainly senior government officials, chief executive officers, managers, owners of firms, professors, political party leaders, medical doctors, lawyers, judges, heads of non-governmental organisations, architects and engineers were targeted by the research. These types of people are assumed to possess a fair ability to influence the course of events in different spheres of society (Bottomore, 1993).

At this point it needs to be repeated that this study presents certain limits. Without a statistically representative sample no strictly rigorous generalisations are possible. Likewise, in the absence of an experimental design involving also non-migrants or not returned migrants in the quantitative survey, not much can be said about different propensities to migrate or to return. Also, the development role of returned migrants was mainly assessed on the basis of their own evaluation and judgements. This leaves open the possibility that some interviewees and respondents to the questionnaires might have embellished answers regarding their developmental impact.

Gathering information from a variety of sources has helped to overcome some of these constraints. Furthermore, a few special measures were adopted to increase the reliability and validity of the research findings. The strategy of "member verification" was adopted. This consisted in feeding back some preliminary findings to a few participants in the study so that they could evaluate the adequacy of the accounts and provide additional elements of clarification if needed. Something similar to the principle of "audit trails" was also followed. This has involved a situation whereby the supervisors of the research were regularly asked to check and control the clarity and consistency of the work at different stages of the research project. Moreover, colleagues working on the Transrede project have been involved in the monitoring; for instance they were asked to review and validate the coding of answers to open-ended questions.

Organisation of the Fieldwork

Before the first phase of the fieldwork was started, documentary evidence and existing data were collected and reviewed in libraries, on the web and in the field. This comprehensive review helped the researcher to gain some preliminary insights into the issues of intercontinental migration and return as related to development and the related theoretical models and conceptual assumptions. The review of information from secondary sources also yielded some useful information that facilitated the development of the research instrumentation. First an interview guide encompassing open-ended questions was designed to be used for exploratory in-depth interviews with returnees in the two West African capital cities. The questions contained in this tool concern the migrants' experiences abroad, the decision to return and the migrants' experiences back home (see Annex One). Their sequence was conceived in this way to reconstruct the life and migration histories of the respondents.

A total of 18 and 17 preliminary interviews were conducted with return migrants in Abidjan and Accra respectively during the pilot phase of the fieldwork. In this latter research site two additional interviews were conducted with the spouses of returned migrants who had participated in the study. The snowball sampling procedure worked well in practice, particularly in Accra. The identification of respondents represented a greater challenge in Abidjan. Several reasons can be listed to explain this difference including the following: a) proportionally speaking there are fewer people going abroad and returning to Côte d'Ivoire; b) return migration is less of a publicly debated issue in Côte d'Ivoire and therefore attracts less attention; and c) the politically unstable situation in Côte d'Ivoire following the coup d'état of 1999 created a climate of suspicion where people were (and still are) hesitant to reveal personal and professional information.

Preliminary interviews lasted anything between 45 and 120 minutes. In Abidjan most of them were conducted in quiet corners of hotel lounges, whereas in Accra respondents were mainly interviewed in their offices. Although the matter of confidentiality was raised at the beginning of every interview, it turned out that this was not a major issue for the majority of the respondents. This is probably due to the fact that those who are in positions of authority and responsibility are often considered "public" people. Only one Ghanaian required a written statement that the information provided would not be used in an improper way. All in-depth interviews were tape-recorded with the consent of the respondents, but notes were taken as well. Interview guides were used with much flexibility, following the need to adopt an exploratory, open-ended questioning approach. This strategy proved an effective means of discovering the unexpected. Some questions also appeared pertinent in some instances, but not necessarily in others, as personal experiences are highly diversified.

The second phase of the fieldwork consisted of the main questionnaire survey. A semi-structured, partially standardised and largely pre-coded questionnaire was designed, taking particular themes into consideration. The questionnaire had, of course, to reflect the objectives of this study and be well adapted to the West African context. An effort was made to reduce as much as possible the number of open-ended questions in order to ensure speedy questionnaire administration. This was not to exceed one hour, because élite respondents usually have very limited time. In addition, an attempt was made to facilitate and, at the same time, improve the speed and accuracy of multiple choice responses by adopting a procedure whereby a series of cards presenting the alternative propositions were developed to be handed to the respondents. These cards proved very effective in helping to choose and to rank alternative responses.

However, the most important feature of this questionnaire is that it was designed specifically to capture the great complexity and dynamics of contemporary migratory movements (see Annex Two). These are increasingly accelerated and multi-directional, as Castles and Miller (1998) have noted, and thus migration in current times no longer represents a once-in-a-lifetime experience. People may have moved at different times to the same or different places. They may have accumulated highly diversified experiences at each destination or in the course of subsequent stays. This heterogeneity existing in current migration patterns and experiences was given due consideration in the design of the questionnaire. The questionnaire was conceived to capture the specificity of particular migration histories and experiences appropriately. As such it allows us to record different subsequent migrations and, for every migration, information is recorded concerning its timing, duration, main reason, migration decision-making, feelings and resident status at destination.

After its conception the main survey questionnaire was piloted with a limited number of people in both sites. This pre-test involved eight returnees in Accra and five in Abidjan. Special thought was given not only on the pertinence of the questions and pre-coded answers, but also to the specific formulation used in each language. The questionnaire was originally designed in English and subsequently translated into French.

Particular attention was paid in this respect to matching concepts and meanings rather than to translating the questionnaire literally.

A total of 304 élite return migrants were interviewed during this quantitative phase of the study, 150 in Abidjan and 154 in Accra.[3] Ideally even more questionnaires could have been foreseen, but there were some time constraints and finite financial resources. The questionnaires were administered to respondents with the help of research assistants who were trained within the framework of the Transrede project and closely supervised in their work. The research assistants were given a manual for questionnaire administration in English and in French outlining in detail the procedure that they needed to follow to conduct interviews with élite migrants in the two survey locations. Supervision and quality control of the data collection process was challenging at times; regular briefings and de-briefings, especially at the beginning, ensured that the research team was able to achieve good standards. More problematic was the data coding and entry of quantitative data done in Ghana and Côte d'Ivoire. Different data entry frameworks were originally elaborated, making it difficult to combine the two data sets and several errors and mistakes were detected during subsequent data cleaning. Also, many variables had to be re-coded to merge the two data sets into the single file needed for the multivariate analyses.

Questionnaires were all administered face-to-face to get, as far as possible, spontaneous answers. They were not handed out to respondents ahead of time or left with them to be completed on their own. This was mainly to avoid the situation whereby someone other than the designated person completed the schedule or influenced the responses. Where possible, interviews were not held in more than one session, but this could not always be ensured. Answering the questionnaire took from 40 to 135 minutes.

The third phase of the fieldwork was devoted to another series of in-depth interviews with migrants who were still living abroad. Altogether 11 Ghanaians living in London and eight Ivorians residing in Paris were interviewed. These interviews were conducted with the help of another guide which was adapted from the one that had been used during the pilot phase (see Annex Three). It therefore included several questions that were also formulated for returned migrants as well as a more specific set

3 There is no particular reason why a few more questionnaires were administered in Accra than in Ghana; this was an initiative taken by one of the research assistants.

of questions that sought to explore return decision-making and future prospects in the host country. In addition to these interviews, a focus-group discussion involving a mixed group of six relatively young Ivorian immigrants was organised in Paris. This allowed the comparison of different experiences and views regarding migration and return.

Finally, it should be briefly mentioned that during all three field interviewing phases, complementary information was obtained from key informants. These included university professors or professionals from research institutions, high-level officials in government and international organisations, heads of non-governmental organisations, senior personnel in private companies and religious and political leaders. These interviewees responded to various queries during more or less formal interviews held in the different research sites.

Integrating Different Kinds of Data

The integration of qualitative and quantitative data operated at two levels, through the research design as well as data processing. In other words, the sequencing of different tasks and the way data were assembled and processed have greatly helped in integrating data obtained from a variety of sources. The qualitative data gathered during the pilot phase were utilised to inform the issues that needed to be raised during the quantitative survey. The preliminary analysis of quantitative data obtained in the course of the central phase was in turn used to refine some of the questions that were in the interviews conducted in the last phase of the fieldwork. Thus, in this study, knowledge was built up in a cumulative fashion.

Certain methods of data processing and analysis can help in strengthening the integration of different kinds of information. Data originally collected based on qualitative criteria may subsequently be transformed to fit quantitative standards and vice-versa. In this case the quantitative processing of qualitative materials has allowed the classification of persons by means of cluster analysis with reference to the degree of similarity and dissimilarity of individual migration experiences. Also, information obtained in response to the open-ended questions included in the questionnaire was elaborated and analysed using qualitative as well as quantitative methodologies.

Managing Information and Processing the Data

A coordinated process of collection, storage and retrieval of empirical materials was planned from the beginning of the study. First of all a decision was made that information obtained from preliminary and follow-up interviews would be tape-recorded, transcribed and analysed by means of a qualitative data analysis software. A suitable software package was identified in N5, a current version of NUD*IST. SPSS was selected for quantitative data analyses.

Information obtained from preliminary interviews was extracted by means of a content analysis based on an ex-post coding sheet. It was processed right after the end of the first phase in order to identify some patterns and initial hypotheses. A spreadsheet was developed for this particular purpose to help in presenting this information in a synthetic format. This significantly facilitated the task of questionnaire design because structured questions and alternative pre-coded response categories could be derived from this information.

Every in-depth interview was integrally transcribed, and sometimes slightly linguistically edited with careful attention to avoid loss of meaning, before it was entered into the data files. The interview notes that had concurrently been taken in the field were elaborated and edited on site. A synthesis was prepared and typed up for each interview and included in the database. Each one of the subsequent versions of the text files was kept on record and could be retrieved if the same study needed to be verified or repeated. The importance of building and consolidating an effective database cannot be overstated, to ensure that different information is readily available in a comparable format for each study site. The database that was put in place for this study contains different kinds of documents which are stored in numerical or textual computer files and information which is physically assembled such as raw field notes, photocopies, tapes and mini-disks.

Analysing Qualitative and Quantitative Information

Regarding data analysis, two major issues needed to be kept in mind: the lack of a representative sample and the fact that most of the data collected were of qualitative rather than quantitative nature. For the quantitative analyses of nominal- and ordinal-level data, a framework using non-parametric or distribution-free statistics was adopted. This seemed the most appropriate way to analyse the data from structured questions where no assumptions could be made about the shape of the distribution of responses in the population to which the sample of this study refers.

Therefore, descriptive statistics based on frequency counts and cross-tabulations seemed to be the most suitable techniques to analyse such data. In particular bi- and trivariate contingency tables were elaborated, chi-square statistics were calculated and levels of significance were established. This allowed identification of underlying relationships or whether distributions observed for one variable were independent from or depended on the distribution of another variable. Special attention was given to the country of residence among other independent variables such as sex, age, education and occupation which could be hypothesised to affect dependent variables as, for example, the degree of satisfaction with return. But in addition, odds ratios were determined. They also measure associations between nominal or ordinal variables but with the advantage of a more ready interpretability since in this case 1.0 indicates a complete absence of relationship, with deviations in either direction showing an increasing relation. Because of reasons of space most risk estimates are presented in a synthetic form in Annex Four.

A series of multiple regression analyses were performed on the combined data derived from the quantitative surveys in Côte d'Ivoire and in Ghana using SPSS. The purpose was to predict the variance in a dependent variable of a series of interval, dichotomous and dummy variables.[4] This kind of analysis can help to explain the proportion of the variance in a dependent variable at different levels of significance, and forecast the relative predictive importance of the independent variables. The latter was determined through the comparison of beta weights, and significance tested at the 0.1 per cent, 1 per cent and 5 per cent levels. The difference between different R-squared values was also calculated to see if adding one or a set of independent variables to a model helped significantly in explaining the phenomena under investigation.

In contrast, for the analysis of the qualitative information an interpretative framework was used. This was instrumental not only in the construction and refinement of working hypotheses but, in the search for patterns and relationships between conceptual categories and assumptions, also in the generation of evidence to support these hypotheses.

---

4 Dummy variables are the result of values of nominal or ordinal variables which are added to a regression equation.

CHAPTER FOUR

THE CONTEXT OF THE STUDY CONDUCTED IN CÔTE D'IVOIRE AND GHANA

This chapter traces the historical background and national profiles of Côte d'Ivoire and Ghana from their independence until the early 2000s when the data were collected. It shows that some trends in socio-economic development and in cultural and institutional change are common to these two countries. The growth of poverty, the degradation of basic services and the decline in the standards of living have affected both countries, though to a different degree. But there are also fundamental differences between the two countries. The most important one is that until the end of the 1990s Côte d'Ivoire has benefited from political stability, a condition which had helped this country to become a major economic growth pole in the region. That is why it has attracted more migrants than any other country in West Africa. In contrast, Ghana has long suffered from political instability and crisis, a situation from which it started to recover only in the late 1980s. Ghana had to face many important economic difficulties and therefore, in contrast with Côte d'Ivoire, has developed into a major country of emigration.

A Comparative Analysis of Two West African Country Cases

Because of their similarities in geographic, demographic and cultural terms, Côte d'Ivoire and Ghana have often been compared in the literature.[1] Yet their political and economic histories after independence are quite divergent. This has provided scope for some interesting debates regarding the causes and effects of the differing backgrounds and profiles. These contrasts are rooted not only in the pre-colonial and colonial periods under French or British rule, but do also reflect diverging post-colonial state formation plans:

1 See, for example, Tansel (1997).

> On 5 April 1957, Kwame Nkrumah, on his first official trip as Prime Minister of the newly independent Ghana to the Guinea of Sékou Touré, made a stop in Abidjan. His host, Félix Houphouët-Boigny, president of the Territorial Assembly of Côte d'Ivoire but also minister of the French Republic, had prepared him an official and a specially reserved reception. Everything contrasted these two men: their personal backgrounds, but also their political projects. The first had made himself the apostle of the African unity and had led his country to independence, whereas the second had chosen to collaborate with the métropole within the framework of the French Union. (Losch, 2000; translated from French)

Along with important differences in these two nations' critical processes of political élite and state formation (Crook, 1990), there are some crucial divergences in their post-independence developments and their social and economic transformations.

Côte d'Ivoire

The Republic of Côte d'Ivoire is situated between Ghana and Liberia on the West African coast and has a total population of approximately 16 million in 2003 and of 18 million in 2006 in 2007.[2] The 1998 census registered 15.4 million people, whereas the previous census conducted in 1988 had recorded 10.8 million. Thus, in this ten-year period the yearly population growth rate was 3.3 per cent, a rate at which the population was expected to double in 22 years. However, population growth projections were revised downwards due to the increasing burden of HIV/AIDS which is one of the highest in West Africa. In 2005, the population was estimated at about 18.2 million (UN Population Division, 2009).

In 1999, 55 per cent of the inhabitants were still living in rural areas. Nevertheless, during the following two decades, the proportion of people living in urban areas has very rapidly expanded. In the early 2000s Abidjan alone accommodated about 19 per cent of the total population and 44 per cent of the urban population. The population living in Côte d'Ivoire was relatively young: 43 per cent were less than 14 years old, 53 per cent were aged 15 to 59 years and only 4 per cent 60 or more. The average life

2 The sources of data included in this section are Institut National de la Statistique (INS, 2000), CERPOD (1995), World Bank (2001, 2009a) and United Nations (2009a).

expectancy at birth was 46 years for men and 47 years for women. The total fertility rate was 5.2 births per women. The crude birth rate was 37 and the crude death rate 17 per 1000 persons respectively.

French is the official language in Côte d'Ivoire and also used in school. However, there are a great variety of local languages that are spoken across the country.

Recent History and Contemporary Politics

The Republic of Côte d'Ivoire became independent from France on 7 August 1960.[3] The first president, Félix Houphouët-Boigny, led the country until his death in December 1993. Trained as a doctor at the famous *Ecole William Ponty* in Dakar, he quickly became involved with farming and with politics. Houphouët had been engaged in the anti-colonial battle since the 1930s and came into power with the help of the so-called "planter bourgeoisie". He also benefited from the support of a small consolidating élite including teachers and junior civil servants. Most of these had been to school with him in Dakar and shared his interest in large-scale commercial farming.

In 1944, Houphouët had helped to found the first agricultural trade union, the *Syndicat Agricole Africain*. Its main goal was to defend the interests of African planters who wanted to obtain labour supplies for their cocoa and coffee plantations. Two years later the trade union was converted into what became the sole political party of the country until the establishment of a plural political system at the beginning of the 1990s. Besides assuming its presidency Houphouët was elected a deputy to the French parliament in Paris where he successfully promoted the abolition of forced labour. Several laws proposed by African deputies were adopted by the French parliament in the course of the 1950s. One of them was the *Loi-cadre* in 1956 which introduced the principle of "Ivorianisation" of the economy and of the public administration. This aimed to bring Ivorian cadres into positions of responsibility and authority, replacing French expatriate officials.

An Ivorian bureaucracy did not exist at that time and started to emerge only after independence. Back in 1957 all executive positions in the civil service were occupied by French nationals (Crook, 1990).

3 The sources of the information included in this section include Crook (1990), David (2000), Fauré and Medard (1982), Kipré (1992) and Zolberg (1964).

Many white-collar positions were held by foreign African nationals such as Dahomeyans, Senegalese or Togolese. But the number of Ivorian managerial cadres in the private sector has long remained quite small. In 1984, for instance, Ivorian nationals still represented only 32 per cent of top management and 62 per cent of the *cadres supérieurs*.

Contrary to the heads of state of other newly independent West African nations such as Ghana and Guinea, Houphouët continued to rely heavily on the former colonial power after independence (Amondji, 1988). He significantly favoured French investment and technical cooperation. France has therefore remained very influential in Côte d'Ivoire's political and economic life for a long time. The flow of French financial capital along with membership in the CFA Franc zone, has influenced Ivorian economic development in a significant way. French firms have long dominated the manufacturing and agri-business sectors, whereas many small and medium enterprises were in the possession of Lebanese nationals. In the 1990s, the French community numbered about 20,000 members and the Lebanese more than 100,000.

From the beginning of his rule Houphouët did not encounter any major challenge, except for some alleged coup attempts and demonstrations and strikes in the 1980s. He remained the sole candidate at presidential elections and his party the only legal political party until the end of 1990. After Houphouët's death in late 1993 Henri Konan Bédié assumed power. The years of his rule were characterised by increasing dissatisfaction on the part of different opposition parties and groups of civil society (e.g., students) concerning the state of political affairs and by growing economic and social problems. In this climate of rising political tensions, a military coup occurred on 24 December 1999.[4]

General Gueï who had orchestrated the coup set up a transition government which remained in power for less than a year. Presidential and legislative elections were held as planned in late 2000, but many presidential candidates were eliminated from the race. Against many expectations, General Gueï himself ran for the presidency. His main opponent was Laurent Gbagbo, the leader of a long-established opposition party. The results of the poll indicated Gbagbo as the winner, but General Gueï and his military entourage did not want to give up power. Their claims of victory were roughly terminated by hundreds of thousands of people demonstrating in the street.

4 See, for example, Decraene (2000) for a full account.

The presidency of Laurent Gbagbo was officially acknowledged by foreign governments at the end of 2000, but development aid and credit agreements were only resumed in early 2002. Since then the political situation remains unstable with the country being divided in two parts and some scattered armed conflict in certain parts of the interior.

Social Organisation and Change

During the years of colonial government the power of the traditional élite was gradually undermined with local rulers being reduced to junior civil servants and persons with no legitimate power claims appointed to become local rulers.[5] In those areas where traditional leaders succeeded in keeping their position, this was often claimed and sometimes usurped by educated Ivorians who felt that, with their education and modern outlook, they were better suited for local leadership roles. The role of this emerging non-traditional African élite was strengthened by the institution and expansion of plantation agriculture. It was also supported by the French, who considered those who had gained wealth and prestige by exploiting new opportunities in the changing environment the most qualified for political decision-making on behalf of the colony.

The French also introduced some new social institutions which brought about fundamental changes in Ivorian society and culture. The network of churches and primary schools that was established by the missionaries provided an initial access to basic education. Some of the wealthier Ivorians could then pursue their education at the few secondary schools and go to university abroad. This made them adopt a certain number of European cultural traits and values and helped them to enter into the circles of the new African élite. Its members were far more respected by the French and usually exempted from military and labour services.

The years of Houphouët's rule were characterised by a rapid urbanisation, a relative unimportance attributed to ethnic differences and a patrimonial style of governing. These three factors produced important changes in social organisation and contributed to the strengthening of a self-perpetuating élite. As Handloff (1988) stresses, "social relations were ordered more by access to status, prestige and wealth than by

5 Information in this section was derived from Handloff (1988).

ethnic differences, and for most people the locus of this access was the government. Wealth and government service became so closely linked that one was taken as a symbol of the other".

Access to government service was mainly granted by higher-level education. Secondary and tertiary education represented a relatively scarce resource and an effective vehicle of social mobility. In fact, most children who entered primary school dropped out or were eliminated before reaching the end of the secondary cycle. The pupils' educational attainments commonly reflected their parents' level of education and wealth. Attending secondary school meant going to town, an activity which required important resources and extended social networks. It also contributed to draining the rural areas of their arms and brains, as successful students would be channelled into urban occupations and not return home.

By the 1980s, formal employment had become the most important indicator of social status. Government officers were guaranteed life-long employment and had all kinds of benefits. Many were granted free or subsidised housing and lived in relatively luxurious conditions. Some also received urban land concessions, a practice that often accompanied political appointments. Urban social services were accessible mainly to those working in the public service. Senior civil servants also earned highly attractive salaries which have long exceeded those in the private sector. This situation, however, turned around irreversibly when government started to freeze civil service pay scales in the late 1980s.

Access to higher education, employment, land, housing and urban social services has determined restricted paths of opportunities and social mobility in the Ivorian society. This has helped to perpetuate the privileged position of the wealthy and educated minority. The gap between this small ruling élite and the great majority of people who lacked privileged access to resources has continually widened.

Economic Profile

Four distinct phases can be identified in the evolution of the Ivorian economy since independence.[6] The first phase lasted from 1960 to 1980 and was characterised by the so-called "Ivorian miracle". These two

6 This section is based on the following sources: Cabrillac (2000), Sindzingre (2001) and World Bank (2001). General data refer to the most recent data available.

decades saw a dramatic growth in the gross domestic product (GDP) which averaged 11 per cent in 1960–1970 and 6–7 per cent in 1970–1980. But the economic boom had already started before independence with the opening of the canal of Vridi and the port of Abidjan in 1950.

Amin (1967) has examined the main factors that determined the extraordinary economic expansion that the country experienced in the early 1960s. First, economic growth concerned multiple sectors ranging from agriculture and forestry to manufacturing and building; and from public administration to transport, trade and services. The role of agricultural output in the generation of GNP decreased considerably. Second, public investment steadily increased over the entire period. At the beginning, most public investments were undertaken to develop infrastructure, whereas later they were increasingly devoted to industry. This key sector also increasingly profited from private investments. Third, despite its rapid growth, the country did not have any major problem with its balance of payments. This is primarily due to the priority that was given to the production of export commodities such as coffee and cocoa.

The development of large-scale plantations and cash crop farming was the basis for sustained economic growth in this initial highly prosperous phase. But it also made the Ivorian economy particularly vulnerable to fluctuations in world prices for its main export commodities. In fact, if the GDP continued at high rates until the beginning of the 1980s, during the second phase it started to decrease when international prices for coffee and cocoa began to weaken. This economic stagnation lasted until the end of 1993 and produced tensions in the labour force where underemployment and unemployment had become acute. Although it previously ranked among middle-income countries, Côte d'Ivoire started to be counted as a low-income country in the 1990s. And the economic situation continued to worsen in spite of the structural adjustment programmes introduced in 1991.

The devaluation of the Franc CFA in early 1994 marked the beginning of a third phase for the Ivorian economy. It benefited the country by bringing about renewed economic growth. Macro-economic indicators started to improve again and GDP per capita has since then progressed. In spite of these positive trends, the country has remained heavily dependent not only on fluctuations of world prices for commodities but also on flows of foreign aid. Cocoa alone represents 14 per cent of the GDP, 20 per cent of the country's revenue and 35–40 per cent of all exports. In 1999, international prices of coffee and cocoa dropped by about 40 per cent, along with those of non-traditional exports such as cotton, palm oil and sugar. These severe structural weaknesses, together with a questionable administration of public finance, helped to prepare the ground for the military coup of 1999.

The fourth and last phase characterising Ivorian economic development started after the coup which brought about a period of severe political crisis and of civil war. The uncertainty of the situation and lack of confidence of investors, along with the suspension of foreign aid and institutional resource flows, produced dramatic impacts in the economy and especially on employment. The Ivorian GDP dropped to US$9.3 billion in the year 2000, from US$11.2 billion the year before and US$10.7 billion in 1996. In the meantime, it rose again to reach US$19.6 billion in 2007 (World Bank, 2009). The gross national income (GNI) per capita in current US$ was 591 in 2000 and 902 in 2003 (United Nations, 2009a).

The Ivorian economy continues to rely to a great extent on agriculture even though the government has tried to reduce its dependency on international commodity prices. In the early 2000s, agriculture represented between a quarter and one third of the GDP and provided three quarters of all export earnings. Industry and services produced respectively 29 per cent and 43 per cent of the GDP, with agriculture still contributing 26 per cent of the total. Since the late 1980s, the government has shifted emphasis from import substitution to export promotion. In the course of the 1990s, exports started to exceed imports of goods and services. However, although the balance of payments was positive, the account balance for GDP remained negative. It is also worth mentioning that, after having benefited many years from credits from international financial institutions, the country at the time of writing is severely indebted and faces some major difficulties in servicing its debt.

Education, Health and Gender

The two last decades have been characterised by growing poverty and increasing inequalities.[7] The GNI has significantly declined over the past three decades, decreasing from 1,140 in 1980 to 640 in 1985, 780 in 1990 and 690 in 1999. But in spite of this deteriorating situation, the Ivorian GNI per capita has remained above the average registered in sub-Saharan

7 Information included in the section was obtained from UNICEF (2001). Data in this paragraph refer to the most recent data available in the 1995–1999 period.

Africa in the 1990s. It was and remains higher than that of neighbouring countries, including Ghana.

Children, rural women and farmers are among those who have been the most affected by poverty (Ouattara, 1997, 1999). Most of the poor live in rural areas, but poverty is expanding faster in urban areas. The Ivorian education system contributed to the perpetuation of these social inequalities (Sindzinger, 2000). In 1995, government was spending 60 times more per university student, and 30 times more for a student in technical high school than for a child enrolled in primary school. Children from poorer households were particularly disadvantaged by this uneven policy. Data from 1994 show that half of the children belonging to the poorest 40 per cent of households would drop out before having terminated the first year of primary school. On the other side, 80 per cent of the children belonging to the richest 20 per cent of households would pursue their studies until the end of primary school. In this respect, it should be noticed that the average level of education reached by poor Ivorian children is far below that of children in other countries such as, for example, Ghana, Kenya or Zimbabwe.

Important inequalities in access to education also exist based on gender. Data published by UNICEF (2001) show that 63 per cent of the boys compared to only 47 per cent of the girls were enrolled in school. The gender gap was even more striking when one looks at adult literacy rates at that time: 63 per cent of men aged 15 or more but only 37 per cent of women were literate. In spite of these very poor social development indicators registered at the turn of century, public expenditure for education has decreased from 7 to 5 per cent of the GNP between 1980 and 1999.

The Ivorian education system is adapted from the French. It includes a five-year primary-school system which in principle is compulsory. After an additional four years of school children have to pass an examination to obtain the certificate of lower cycle of secondary study, the *brevet d'étude du premier cycle* (BEPC). Three more years lead to the *baccalauréat* which is necessary to enter university. At all three levels the quality of education has much deteriorated in the last two decades. University establishments have moreover been shut down on several occasions following protests and demonstrations staged by students and academic staff. This has resulted in a situation where certain academic years were declared invalid.

The main health indicators in were also far from satisfactory in the early 2000s and remain so today. The mortality rate of infants aged less than one year is 102 per 1,000 live births, whereas the death rate of children under 5 years is 92 per 1,000 live births.

Migratory Movements

Having experienced a relatively long period of political stability and having generated and retained higher revenues than its neighbouring countries in spite of economic difficulties, Côte d'Ivoire has attracted a massive number of immigrants to the point that in 1998 one out of every four residents was a foreign resident (Table 4-1). Immigration had already started in the 1930s, when the country was still under colonial rule and additional labour was needed to increase agricultural production and natural resource extraction. Compulsory transfer of manpower mainly from Upper Volta (present-day Burkina Faso) was replaced in 1944 by recruitment of voluntary labourers, a practice which was further pursued after independence (Ammassari, 2003a; Makinwa-Adebusoye, 1992). This represented a cornerstone of Houphouët's liberal economic policy favouring the attraction of foreign labour, capital and investment.

Table 4-1 Number and percentage of Ivorian and foreign residents

Residents	1965	1975	1988	1993	1998
Ivorians	3,473,250	5,233,488	7,787,300	9,480,497	11,366,625
per cent	83	78	72	75	74
Foreigners	736,750	1,476,112	3,028,394	3,227,943	4,000,047
per cent	17	22	28	25	26
TOTAL	4,210,000	6,709,600	10,815,694	12,708,817	15,366,672

Source: Touré (2000)

Most immigrants come from neighbouring countries, particularly Burkina Faso and Mali. In the past an important proportion of foreign population was also constituted by non-Africans, chiefly Lebanese and

French citizens. More recently, however, the percentage of non-African foreigners has decreased considerably (Traoré and Bocquier, 1998).

Even though Côte d'Ivoire remains predominantly an immigration country, the number of Ivorian nationals who embark on intercontinental migration has grown in recent years. In post-independence years the government sponsored a large number of scholarships, with the help of foreign aid.[8] This was one of the strategies adopted within the framework of the "Ivorianisation" initiative of public administration. Later on, in the light of the deteriorating educational system, an increasing number of Ivorians have also gone abroad at their own expense (Blaud, 2001).

Ghana

The Republic of Ghana is one of the most densely populated countries in West Africa. Its population, which is larger than that of Côte d'Ivoire, was estimated at about 19.2 million in the early 2000s and today counts approximately 23.5 million.[9] In 1960 the population was only 6.7 million and it was 10.7 million in 1980, which means that in those two decades it has almost doubled. The average yearly population growth rate has decreased in recent years, and was 2.4 per cent during the 1994–2000 period. The share of population living in urban areas has continually increased, from 31 per cent of the total population in 1980 to 38 per cent in 2000.

Côte d'Ivoire and Ghana share an almost identical, youthful population structure. Those below 14 years of age represented 42 per cent of the population at the beginning of this century, while those 60 or more years old did only constitute 5 per cent. The total fertility rate was 4.5 births per woman compared to 5.7 in Côte d'Ivoire. Life expectancy at birth in Ghana was somewhat more than ten years higher than in Côte d'Ivoire (57 years for men and 59 years for women). The crude birth rate and death rate were more favourable (30 and 10 per 1000 people respectively) in the former country compared to latter.

---

8 Côte d'Ivoire and Nigeria are the only two West African countries that have been able to bear some of the costs of training their nationals abroad (Makinwa-Adebusoye, 1992).

9 The sources of the data included in this section are La Verle (1994), World Bank (2001; 2002a,b,c; 2009b) and United Nations (2009b).

Although English is the official language used in the public administration, schools, businesses and the media, many Ghanaians speak Twi (a dialect of Akan).

Recent History and Contemporary Politics

On 5 March 1957 the Gold Coast gained independence from the British Crown and assumed the name of Ghana.[10] The country's Legislative Assembly became the National Assembly, and Kwame Nkrumah, who had led the country to independence, continued in his role as prime minister. He had returned to Ghana in 1947 after having spent 12 years in the United States, where he went to study, and had been appointed Secretary General of the United Gold Coast Convention (UGCC). This nationalist movement was founded by the educated new urban élite with the aim of promoting the country's independence.

Under Nkrumah a series of clauses of the Constitution were amended or removed to effect changes that he and his party deemed necessary. The Deportation Act of 1957 and the first Preventive Detention Act of 1958 also empowered him significantly. The first was to be used only with foreigners, but several people to whom it was applied claimed to be Ghanaian nationals. The second Act enabled the authorities to detain certain persons without trial for up to five years. During those years several opponents were forced into exile to escape detention or alternatively joined the ruling party.

Three years after independence Ghana became a republic. Nkrumah won the presidential elections and, soon after coming into power, he proclaimed himself president for life and declared his party the only one admitted in the country. The years spent abroad and particularly the Pan-Africanist movement which was inspired by socialist ideologies had influenced his thinking and political views. He believed that Ghana, which was the first African country to gain independence, had to assume a leadership role in the battle against colonial and neocolonial oppression and more generally against capitalist interests on the continent.

The years of Nkrumah's rule were characterised by vigorous public spending to develop infrastructure and improve basic social services. Free compulsory education for children aged between six and 12 years

10 The sources of this and the following sections are Boahen (2000), Davidson (1977) and La Verle (1994).

was introduced and the post-primary system was reorganised to promote secondary and university education. A modernisation of the industrial and communication sectors was undertaken based, among other things, on the "Africanisation" of the civil service. While the number of Africans holding senior positions (also popularly called "European" posts) was only 171 in 1949, their number increased to 916 in 1954 and to 3,000 in 1957 (Boahen, 2000: 178).

In 1966, however, Nkrumah's government was overthrown by the military forces and the police. This military coup was in part determined by the worsening economic, social and political situation and the increasing resentment regarding the growing centralisation of power and Nkrumah's dictatorial tendencies. The military remained in power until 1969, the year of the first competitive nationwide political contest since the coup. Kofi A. Busia became prime minister of the Second Republic of Ghana and had to deal with many socio-economic and political problems which had lasted since the overthrow of Nkrumah's government. A revival of regionalist and ethnic feelings was also recorded. The situation of crisis provided suitable ground for a second military coup in 1972. This was led by Colonel Ignatius Acheampong who established a military regime which significantly limited inputs from the civilian sector. The assembly was quickly dissolved and all parties prohibited. The National Redemption Council was introduced and later replaced by the Supreme Military Council. But a third military coup took place in 1978 and General Frederik Akuffo replaced Acheampong. One year later elections were organised and power was handed over to a civilian administration headed by Dr Hilla Limann who had won the elections. This represented the beginning of the Third Republic.

But the Third Republic was also ended abruptly by a military coup, which took place on 31 December 1981 and was led by Flight Lieutenant Jerry John Rawlings. He had already attempted a failed coup in 1979 and had been imprisoned with other coup leaders. Rawlings remained in power for almost 20 years. His government was the eighth in the 15 years that had passed since the fall of that of Kwame Nkrumah. The country's situation had significantly worsened during those years so that, by the early 1980s, the economy was in an advanced state of collapse. When Rawlings came to power, the GDP had become very weak and the inflation rate had reached some highly critical peaks. Agricultural production had greatly declined and exports had also dropped considerably. The new government introduced a programme of economic austerity and reform to promote economic stability and growth. This programme started to show some results only after 1987. But even though Ghana benefited from much development assistance, unemployment remained at very high levels and the purchasing power of the population was extremely limited.

At the beginning of the 1990s there was great hope that a transition back to constitutional rule would take place. It is claimed that at that time more than half of the Ghanaian élite was living outside of the country (Puy-Denis, 1994). If the economy had improved due to the structural adjustment programmes implemented with the support of the IMF, not much had changed since 1981 in the socio-economic situation of the people. In 1990 the minimum monthly salary was about 218 Cedis, which represented approximately the price of a bottle of beer.

Constitutional rule was finally re-established in 1992. In early 1993, after the approval of a new Constitution voted by referendum, democratic elections were organised and Rawlings was elected for a four-year term. The Fourth Republic was inaugurated on 7 January 1993. Rawlings finally withdrew from power in 2000, because the 1992 constitution determined that a president can serve only for two four-year terms. The last presidential election of 2001 was won by John Agyekum Kufuor. Born in 1938, Kufour has studied abroad in London and also obtained a Master's degree from Oxford University.

Social Organisation and Change

Social and cultural changes have clearly been influenced by colonialism and urbanisation.[11] The first gave support to several key agents of change, specifically Christianity, formal classroom education and a money-using economy. Foreign-inspired cultural value systems and lifestyles were introduced with a striking social impact on Ghanaian society. Meanwhile, rural to urban migration started in the post-colonial period and was accelerated by, among other things, formal education and the money economy. The creation of public administration, industries, commerce and services and their centralisation in urban areas also enhanced this process.

The contemporary fabric of Ghanaian society is characterised by its dual but interrelated nature. While most of the population still lives in rural areas and observes ancestral customs and practices, the process

11 This section is based on Assimeng (1999), La Verle (1994) and Nukunya (1992).

of modernisation associated with urban life has affected the social behaviour and values of an important share of the population. The flows of people, goods, services and ideas between the urban and rural areas have helped to blur the distinctions between so-called traditional and modern life.[12] In the former, social relations are determined by family and kinship relationships, inherited status and ancestral beliefs. In the latter, relationships are, rather, based on achieved status, formalised education, membership in professional associations and ethnic affiliations. Although social relations and institutions have considerably changed in the past few decades, the traditional and modern value systems and behaviour patterns continue to co-exist at both the community and individual levels. Contemporary times are indeed characterised by a complex interplay between cultural conservatism and innovative change.

Important changes have, for example, occurred in the kinship system as the centrality of kinship as a means of articulating social relations has progressively diminished (Assimeng, 1999; Nukunya, 1992). There is a tendency to disregard traditional reciprocal obligations and responsibilities to relatives outside the nuclear family except perhaps the closest ones. The marital bond has assumed importance at the expense of that of kinship. Rather than remaining descendent-oriented, urban kinship is increasingly multi-directional. In sum, traditional kinship practices are less and less respected.

Once, the chiefs were among those with the highest status in society. But their powers were curtailed and gradually assumed by those who were able to take timely advantage of the above-described social changes. Literate people and traders were those who benefited most from the opportunities created by the money economy. Formal education opened most of the doors, in public administration as well as in commerce and trade, and became the key to acquire power, wealth and prestige. Initially only a few had the chance to pursue education to the higher levels and thus society readily attributed them important leadership roles and widespread recognition. They became not only politicians or senior government officials, but also university lecturers, doctors, lawyers, engineers, architects, accountants, businessmen or industrialists. Achievement orientation was usually transmitted in their family and social circles as they were considered highly successful role models. These pioneers and

12 The pre-colonial society was generally labelled "traditional" (Nukunya, 1992).

early leaders were also called the "big men" or *ebi te yie* – meaning "those who live well" (Nunkunya, 1992: 192).

Hence, combined factors of social change have introduced the conditions for a few to rise above the rest of the population in terms of wealth, power, prestige and privileges. The members of this new élite have generally achieved rather than inherited their status. They have usually encouraged the younger generation to follow their example and in this way they have transmitted their acquired social positions, along with the connected resources of power and prestige to their descendants.

Formal education has long been the most effective vehicle for self-improvement and access into the élite, but the development of cash crops has also played an important role. In recent times, however, access into this small higher segment of society has become much more difficult. Also it has become much harder to keep a high status position for oneself and one's family members as the élite is more and more an open system from which it is also possible to drop out.[13]

In the early years after independence it was possible for the child of a farmer to become a university graduate and to work as a doctor or banker. Despite the high fees usually demanded by secondary and tertiary education, quite a lot of the university students had fathers who were farmers or manual workers. Since then the situation has changed greatly. Financing higher education has become difficult and its quality has dramatically deteriorated. Ambitious students who can afford it nowadays go abroad to study. But even these privileged few encounter growing obstacles to finding good employment on return. In their fathers' generation, almost all graduates were absorbed by the civil service. Although élite parents have more means to ensure that their children will enjoy the same status as themselves, this inheritance is today far from guaranteed.

Economic Profile

In the early days of independence Ghana's economy was relatively stable and appeared promising.[14] The world's leading cocoa producer then

13 This information emerged from interviews with two returned university professors and the leader of a political party.

14 The source of the information included in this section is La Verle (1994), Boahen (2000) and World Bank (2001, 2002a, b, c).

had the necessary means to invest in road building projects, large-scale education of children and adults, improvement of health services and of other basic amenities as well as the construction of the Akosombo Dam to provide electricity and to promote industrialisation. The important government expenditures of those years, however, created heavy financial burdens.

Some important progress had already been made in the field of social services and especially in the educational system in colonial times. The pioneers in the development of educational institutions and spreading Western education were the missionaries. They contributed significantly to the promotion of primary and secondary schooling as well as technical and teacher training. These early activities created the foundation of an educational system that for long was more advanced than any other in West Africa. It is through this Western-style education that a new local élite was equipped with the means and the desire to strive for independence.

The first austerity budget was presented in July 1961. It involved greater taxes and created resentment in workers as well as farmers, who also disagreed with the drop in price paid to them for cocoa. This discontent characterised the Ghanaian political crises in the 30 years that followed. The weakening of the international price of cocoa in the mid-1960s further affected the Ghanaian economy and severely compromised the government's development policies. At the time of the first coup d'état in 1966, the country was already highly indebted. The weak commodity demand and overvalued domestic currency had also created a situation where cocoa would be smuggled to neighbouring countries to obtain payments in CFA Francs rather than in Ghanaian Cedis. As a result, the production and official exports dropped and made it hard for the government to obtain the foreign currency needed to import foreign goods and services and to repay loans. If the external debt was £20 million sterling at independence, it increased to about £400 million sterling by February 1966 (Boahen, 2000: 216).

Between the mid-1960s and the end of the 1970s, cocoa production continued to decline, as did the production of timber and the extraction of minerals. Moreover, the 1973 oil crisis hit the industry and transportation sectors severely. Inflation rates rose dramatically from 1976 to the beginning of the 1980s, reaching 200 per cent in 1981. Concurrently the Ghanaian GNP continued to decrease. Real minimum wages diminished from an index of 75 in 1975 to one of 15 in 1981. Not only economic productivity but also the standard of living of the people reached very critical levels in those years.

Concrete improvements in the economy started to be registered only towards the end of the 1980s. Nevertheless, the debt continued to rise until 1992, when it was equivalent to about 63 per cent of GNP. That same year the debt service ratio (debt service as a proportion of exports) was 27 per cent. It had reached as high as 63 per cent in the late 1980s. In the early 2000s the inflation rate remained very high and the resource balance was negative, which means that imports continued to exceed exports. In 2000, the Ghanaian GDP was US$5.4 billion, which means that, although Ghana's population was larger than that of Côte d'Ivoire, its economy was and remains considerably smaller (US$9.3 billion in 2001 and US$19.6 billion in 2007) (World Bank, 2001, 2009b). In 1999 it was US$7.8 billion and US$6.9 billion in 1996.

The Ghanaian economy also continues to rely heavily on agriculture, which in 2001 produced 35 per cent of the GDP. Industry represented only 8 per cent and services as much as 56 per cent of the total. A comparison of these numbers with those already cited for Côte d'Ivoire (respectively 26 per cent, 29 per cent and 43 per cent) reveals a very significant difference between the two countries. Whereas Côte d'Ivoire can count on a relatively balanced economy with a strong industrial sector, Ghana has produced only scarce industrial development. Evidently, in the latter case the rural exodus, not finding industrial job opportunities, has contributed to an over-extension of the mostly urban tertiary sector.

In the 1990s Ghana's GDP grew by 4.1 per year on average. Inflation reached quite high levels in 1995, but in subsequent years it returned to more reasonable levels. Although exports doubled in the 1990s, the budget deficit remained important. The GNI per capita in current US$ decreased from 430 to 390 between 1980 and 1999, and to 340 in 2001. In 2006, the GNI per capita was 522 in current US$ (United Nations, 2009b).

Education, Health and Gender

Education was vigorously promoted in the period after independence, particularly free and universal primary education. Important resources were also invested in the training of teachers and in the promotion of secondary and university education. Significant funding was devolved to the University College of the Gold Coast in Cape Coast and to the College of Art, Science and Technology, now the University of Science and

Technology, established in Kumasi in 1952. In those years the government used to award some scholarships to students to pursue studies abroad in fields and courses not available locally.

As a result Ghana ranked first in sub-Saharan Africa in terms of educational indicators. But this policy also had some negative side-effects because not enough attention was paid to the quality of education, which weakened considerably over the years (Tansel, 1997). Even so, the current education indicators remain significantly better than those registered in other countries in the region.[15] In 2001, the adult illiteracy rate was 25 per cent for men and 47 per cent for women, whereas the primary gross enrolment rate was 82 per cent for boys and 72 per cent for girls. The latter numbers, compared to the ones cited earlier cited regarding Côte d'Ivoire (63 per cent for boys and 47 per cent for girls), shed light on another distinction between the two countries. In fact, the general level of education in Ghana is significantly higher and in addition inequalities in school access opportunities by gender appear to be smaller.

In the early years after independence many resources in Ghana were also invested in the fields of health and other basic amenities. This contributed to raising the main health status indicators in Ghana above the average registered for sub-Saharan Africa. In 2001, the mortality rate of children below the age of 1 was 63 per 1000 live births (63 per cent for Côte d'Ivoire) and the child death rate for children below the age of 5 was only 73 per 1000 live births (73 per cent for Côte d'Ivoire).

Migratory Movements

Ghana is among those countries in sub-Saharan Africa that experienced the greatest out-migration flows after independence. Population movement from Ghana across national borders was mainly directed to other West African countries and overseas to Europe and North America. The emigration of the Ghanaian élite was amplified in the late 1970s and early 1980s when the economic situation had become particularly critical. However, in the preceding decade, Ghana rather constituted an immigration country. In 1960, 828,000 foreigners resided in Ghana, which represented 12 per cent of the total population. The number of immigrants decreased to 7 per cent in 1970 and to 3 per cent in 1984

15 The source of the data included in this and the following paragraphs is UNICEF (2001). Data refer to the most recently available in the period 1995–1999.

due to increasing economic problems and probably also to the Alien Compliance Order of 1969 (Zachariah and Condé, 1980).

Data from the 1984 census shows that most of Ghanaian cross-border emigrants had chosen a West African destination (Adeku, 1992). Those who picked a destination in this region principally migrated to Nigeria, Côte d'Ivoire and Togo. When choosing a East, Central or Southern African destination, they primarily opted for Kenya and Gabon. Out of those who moved to North Africa and the Middle East, the highest proportion went to Libya and to Lebanon. Out of the Ghanaians who left to go to Europe, 44 per cent went to the United Kingdom, 8 per cent to Germany and 5 per cent to the USSR. Of those who instead decided to move to North and South America, 72 per cent went to the United States and 16 per cent to Canada.

Information regarding the scale of the Ghanaian brain drain is rather limited as no clear distinction is generally made between highly-skilled and unskilled migrants. However, a study by Carrington and Detragiache (1999) for the IMF tried to estimate the extent of migration by level of education from Ghana and other developing countries to the United States and OECD countries.[16] The analysis is based on 1990 US census data and information drawn from the Continuous Reporting System on Migration of the OECD. A major finding of this study is that there is an "overall tendency for migration rates to be higher for highly educated individuals". This seems to apply particularly to Africans as 95,000 out of the 128,000 African migrants who were living in the US were highly educated. Most of these were from Egypt, South Africa and Ghana.

Among the migrants from these three countries more than 60 per cent had a tertiary education. The number of African migrants with only primary education was found to be almost nil. The authors then related the number of migrants to the estimated stock of highly-skilled people existing in the home country in order to evaluate the brain drain. Their conclusion is that, in general, "migrants to the United States tend to be better educated than the average person in their home (that is, the sending) country, and the proportion of very highly educated people who migrate is particularly high for Ghana, the migration rate of highly educated individuals [to OECD countries alone] is a dramatic 26 per cent".

Return migration in Ghana, especially of the highly skilled élite, has been even less documented. Whereas a few studies have dealt with the

16 Carrington and Detragiache (1999) acknowledge the limits of the data sources that they have used.

return of expelled Ghanaians from Nigeria, little research has focused on the return of Ghanaians from overseas.[17] A Migration Research Study conducted in the early 1990s is the only broader study having focused on the return of Ghanaians (Ghana Statistical Service, 1995), but it did not distinguish between migrants based on their education or qualifications. Return migrants were relatively young (under 30 years old) and had spent an average of ten years abroad. Many had combined studies and work to acquire some personal belongings which Ghanaian society expects a "been to" to possess, such as a television set, sound system, vehicle and other durable goods. Most had been able to upgrade their skills and capabilities abroad and had also sent back remittances and capital goods on a regular basis.

Colonial Heritage and Post-Colonial Development Policies

The differences in the socio-political development and economic transformations that have occurred in Côte d'Ivoire and in Ghana after their independence are rooted in their divergent colonial backgrounds.[18] It is therefore useful to recall briefly their respective colonial heritage and their post-colonial development policies.

In Côte d'Ivoire the Portuguese were the first Europeans who set foot on the South-Eastern coast during the fifteenth century with the aim of trading in spices and natural resources. The first French missionaries arrived in 1687, but a formal occupation took place only during the last quarter of the nineteenth century. The country was officially declared a French colony by a decree issued in 1893. After that date, the French organised their colony administratively and defined its territorial borders. A governor was appointed and the national territory was divided into different administrative units. The French promoted the production of export crops such as cocoa, coffee and palm oil. This demanded important commitments to labour supply and thus a forced labour system was put in place. This, as has already been seen, was later replaced by a vigorous immigration policy to recruit workers in neighbouring countries to work in Côte d'Ivoire.

17 See sources cited in Awusabo-Asare (1992: 156).

18 The principal sources of this section include the following texts: Boahen (2000), David (2000), Davidson (1977), Handloff (1988) and La Verle (1994).

After Côte d'Ivoire achieved independence from France in 1960, one of its major objectives became economic growth. This, according to the policy makers, was a necessary first step to improve income distribution and "Ivorianisation". During the 1960s growth was promoted mainly by developing import substitution industries, expanding and diversifying agricultural production and improving infrastructure. To finance these development strategies the government relied on foreign investment and imported technology, as well as unskilled and skilled foreign labour.

The maintenance of strong political and economic linkages with France, which were almost as great as the pre-independence ties, was critical in the years after independence. French public and private capital continued to help support the government, guaranteeing the external convertibility of the currency, financing many of the main commercial enterprises, strengthening the country's banking and credit structure and providing aid for development programmes. The total French population in Côte d'Ivoire almost doubled between 1960 and 1980, from 30,000 to nearly 60,000. French citizens filled technical and advisory positions in the government[19] and also occupied key positions in the private sector, whereas French enterprises continued to be an important employer of Ivorian labour. Until the mid-1980s Côte d'Ivoire had the greatest number of French-controlled multinational companies in all of Africa. In general, according to Handloff (1988), the larger the capital of an enterprise, the smaller was the proportion that was owned by Ivorians. Despite the establishment in 1973 of a National Commission on Ivorianisation, in 1982 the percentage of Ivorians in senior management position was only 21 per cent. For junior-level management posts, however, it had risen to 52 per cent in all private, public and parastatal enterprises.

The colonial and post-colonial experiences of Ghana differ in many respects. As in Côte d'Ivoire, the first Europeans who arrived in present-day Ghana, which at that time was called the Gold Coast, were the

19 These are known as *coopérants* and were hired by the French Ministry of Cooperation or directly recruited by the Ivorian government through private, generally French, companies on a contract basis. The Ivorian government was responsible for 80 per cent of the total cost of those hired under official cooperation agreements and 100 per cent of the total cost of those hired under private contracts. The economic difficulties of the early 1980s made the Ivorian government operate a gradual reduction in the number of *coopérants* in the country, but some of them were kept on in highly specialised fields such as the petroleum sector and computer technology.

Portuguese. They arrived in the late fifteenth century and during the next century remained the only Europeans present. The seventeenth and eighteenth centuries, instead, were characterised by power struggles involving the Dutch, the British, the Danish, the Swedes and the Prussians. These Europeans were not only interested in obtaining gold and ivory, but also in trading slaves. The slave trade began around 1500 and reached its peak in the eighteenth century. Although the size and volume of the slave trade are not known exactly, it is estimated that about 10,000 people were exported each year (Boahen, 2000). Britain and the United States abolished the trade in slaves in 1807, but it was completely suppressed on the West African coast only in the 1860s.

The British had established various forts and settlements which they converted into a Crown Colony in July 1874. Like the French in Côte d'Ivoire, they introduced new cash crops such as rubber, coffee and cotton, and the production of cocoa was particularly encouraged. The British continued to administer the country until its independence in 1957. The leadership of the newly independent Ghana saw the need to "extricate Ghana's economy from peripherialism" (Asamoa, 1996: 8). The post-colonial policies characterising the First Republic therefore followed the principle of taking stock of national resources, both (actual and potential) human as well as material resources, to address the problems created by the agricultural monoculture inherited from colonialism and to lay the foundation for an industrialisation which however, as pointed out before, continued to show a poor take-off.

Ghana maintained bonds with Britain and the Commonwealth and received aid for economic reforms. However, whereas these foreign relations provided a vehicle for transfers of technology and for economic and cultural cooperation, their influence on Ghana's domestic affairs was far less marked than that produced by the Franco-Ivorian relationship in Côte d'Ivoire. Efforts to "de-neocolonialise" the Ghanaian economy by gaining greater economic and political autonomy were accompanied by the "Africanisation" of all state organs, including the civil service. Yet some national institutions continued to be influenced by colonial traditions. For some authors – for example, Asamoa (1996) – the persistence of these fundamental contradictions in Ghana constituted fertile ground for the repeated coups and ongoing political instability in the country.

It is difficult to determine the extent to which post-colonial development policies have influenced migration and return patterns. Clearly, political instability, unfavourable characteristics of the labour market and socio-economic hardships experienced by the population in Ghana pushed many people out of the country and discouraged many others from returning home. Structural adjustment programmes advocated by international banking institutions in Ghana have provoked the progressive deregulation and liberalisation of the economy. Yet in the 1980s, despite efforts to stimulate private production, public sector jobs still accounted for more than 80 per cent of the labour force in the formal sector. The implementation of the Economic Recovery Programme (1983–1987) under the auspices of the World Bank and the International Monetary Fund contributed to the reduction of public expenditures and created incentives for private production. This was also enhanced through a privatisation policy and foreign exchange reforms to devalue the national currency, interventions which where followed by other measures aimed at boosting private sector growth (e.g., monetary reforms and reduction of private corporate taxes). During the 1990s the government remained committed to enhance private investment and economic liberalisation. This has had some positive outcomes which, in addition to the greater political stability that came about in the 1990s, have triggered return migration to Ghana and created new opportunities for self-employment initiatives.

Summarising the differential development profiles of Ghana and Côte d'Ivoire the following emerges:

1) Both countries have suffered the consequences of fluctuations in world prices for their main export commodities. Economic crisis has affected both of them, but at different times and to different degrees. In Ghana the crisis started soon after independence and became very serious in the second part of the 1970s. The continuous, sudden changes in leadership through repeated coups d'état have brought about much political instability and amplified socio-economic problems in Ghana. Yet, before and after independence, important infrastructural and social investments were made in Ghana, particularly in education and health. That is why Ghana has always had a better record concerning the main social but also human development indicators than Côte d'Ivoire. For Côte d'Ivoire, instead, major economic difficulties began at the beginning of the 1980s, and then rapidly grew at the end of the 1990s due to unexpected political turbulences and ensuing socio-economic difficulties.
2) Common to both countries is also their roughly comparable very high population growth rate. In both countries there is a preponderantly

young population and a strong propensity towards urbanisation, although a greater share of the population still lived in rural areas at the end of the 1990s and up to the time of writing. The urban areas are the home of a new élite born after independence. The conditions for its emergence were similar in each country setting. These conditions include the introduction, through colonialism, of Western-inspired formal education and of a money economy which in turn have accelerated migration and urbanisation processes. In addition, Ghana and Côte d'Ivoire are fairly similar in ethnic, cultural and social terms and there are many shared values and practices.

3) In Côte d'Ivoire as well as in Ghana the interaction of demographic growth and of economic crisis phenomena has fostered an increase in un- and underemployment. This has contributed to rising poverty and inequalities, among other things. The standard of living of the people had reached disappointingly low levels at different times after independence. Development policies were compromised and social services, including the systems of higher education, continued to deteriorate. The worsening quality of higher education pushed and is still pushing younger people out of their country in search of better education and training opportunities abroad. But over many years a growing number of people have started to emigrate in search of better employment and business opportunities. However, this downward trend turned around for Ghana at the beginning of 2000, in line with its improving stability and scocio-economic improvements.

Along with these similar background characteristics, however, the following differences have been identified which surely are relevant with regard to the objectives and hypotheses of this study. First of all, the colonial heritage and post-independence policies of Ghana and Côte d'Ivoire are quite different. Generalising, one could say that in Ghana the movement for independence has fostered more nationalistic attitudes. This has resulted in a marked sense of autonomy on the part of the local ruling class and of private initiative by members of civil society. On the other hand, in Côte d'Ivoire strong post-colonial linkages with the *métropole* have affected many aspects of life, influencing social attitudes as well as economic initiative.

Secondly, Ghana has experienced far larger migration out-flows than Côte d'Ivoire because of the critical labour market consequences of its peculiar economic structure (characterised, as pointed out, by the scarcity of industrial and manufacturing activities) and its much more conflict ridden political situation up to the time when this research study was conducted.

Finally, there always has been a very significant gap in per capita income between these two countries with Ghana's GNI per capita representing less than half that of Côte d'Ivoire in 2000 and a little more than half in 2006. For this and the other reasons, emigration of the highly skilled assumed considerable proportions in Ghana early on, whereas it has not been a real issue in Côte d'Ivoire. But in this latter country the brain drain also became a concern in the aftermath of the military coup of 1999 and the political and economic upheaval that has followed.

CHAPTER FIVE

BACKGROUND INFORMATION ON MIGRANTS INTERVIEWED ABROAD AND BACK HOME

The fieldwork allowed the acquisition of a wealth of empirical material regarding the migration experiences of Ivorians and Ghanaians, both those who returned home and those who remained abroad. The main findings are presented in the next sequence of chapters. But before turning our attention to the main body of research results, some background information is provided in this chapter as to who participated in this study in the four research sites. First a short profile is drawn of the returned migrants who took part in the preliminary interviews in Abidjan and Accra, as well as the emigrants who participated in follow-up interviews in London and Paris. Then, the main characteristics of the two main samples of returned migrants who responded to the questionnaire in Abidjan and Accra are reviewed. Since it was impossible to obtain random samples, this description aims to provide a better understanding of their attributes. Some biases which may have occurred in selecting the respondents are discussed and their possible implications for the reliability of the information and accuracy of the findings evaluated.

A Brief Profile of Participants in In-depth Interviews

In the preliminary interview round in Abidjan and Accra a total of 35 returned migrants participated in an interview; six were females (Table 5-1). A higher proportion of female emigrants were interviewed in London and Paris, in the European round of in-depth interviews. The age of the interviewees varied from 26 to 61 years; half were in their 40s. Most were married.

Those interviewed had various levels of education before going abroad, but most migrants had obtained a Masters or equivalent degree. Almost all had studied abroad and the great majority had also worked. Often they had done so in a job that was not related to their training. At the time of the interview most migrants worked for a private company, but a significant share was also employed as civil servants. The professions attracted fewer, but a fair number owned or managed a private company.

Table 5-1 Characteristics of migrants who participated in focused interviews by capital city

Characteristics	Returned migrants		Emigrants	
	Abidjan	Accra	London	Paris
Sex				
Male	15	14	6	7
Female	3	3	5	1
Age				
20–29	–	–	–	1
30–39	5	2	1	3
40–49	8	10	6	3
50–59	4	5	4	1
60–69	1	–	–	–
Marital status				
Married	7	16	7	5
Never married/divorced/ separated	11	1	4	3
Highest education back home				
High school or below	6	8	5	3
Vocational school	–	–	1	1
Bachelor	10	7	1	4
Masters or equivalent	2	2	4	–
Highest education abroad				
High school or below	1	1	1	–
Vocational school	–	1	1	–
Bachelors	1	2	1	–
Masters or equivalent	11	7	7	8
Doctorate or equivalent	5	3	1	–
No degree	–	3	–	–

Table 5-1 cont'd

Characteristics	Returned migrants		Emigrants	
	Abidjan	Accra	London	Paris
Current occupation				
Business owner	3	1	–	2
CEO/manager	–	7	2	–
Civil servant	5	5	–	3
Professional status	1	4	3	–
Employee in private company	7	–	4	1
Other	2	–	2	2
Valid cases	(18)	(17)	(11)	(8)

The great majority of the migrants had gone abroad to study or to receive some training. Work or business constituted the main migration motive for only a few as did the need to follow their spouse or another family member. Most originally emigrated by themselves because they were not yet married. One migrant declared that he had to migrate for political reasons. About half of all the respondents migrated at least twice and more than one in ten had moved three times.

Generally the initial migration plan of the migrants who participated in the in-depth interviews in London and in Paris was to migrate only temporarily. Yet, by the time of the interview, one third of them had decided not to return home. Half of the remainder were planning to go back and the rest were undecided about what to do. Most of those who were married were making these decisions together with their spouses, who mostly nurtured a positive attitude regarding return. Amongst those who had already made a return migration, most had expected to find good employment or business opportunities at home, an expectation which was met by only half of them.

Socio-demographic Characteristics of the Two Samples

Analysis of the main survey data allows a general profile of the returnees to Ghana and Côte d'Ivoire to be discerned. However, because both are non-probability samples, generalising by inferential means to the overall population of employed returned migrants in each country is not possible.

Residence, Gender and Age

First, although an effort was made to include female respondents, both samples comprised a much greater number of men than of women (19 per cent female respondents in Ghana and 15 per cent in Côte d'Ivoire). This partly reflects the situation that women less often belong to the élite as defined by this study. Their access to top positions of responsibility is limited in both the public and private sector compared to that of men, whilst they migrate less often than men, especially over longer distances (Chant and Radcliffe, 1992). The reasons why a smaller number of highly-skilled Ghanaian and Ivorian women migrate to Europe or North America are multiple. The most important is the greater involvement of men in higher education, especially in science. For instance, women are half as likely as men to have secondary or higher qualifications in Ghana (Ghana Statistical Service, 2000), and so have a smaller chance to obtain scholarships which are often an indispensable requirement to go abroad to study. Another important reason why men outnumber women in intercontinental migration flows is that the average age at first departure for women corresponds to that of starting a family. Women tend to engage in family commitments earlier than men. There usually is a greater social pressure on them, even though marriage and the family are considered important for both sexes, because a person is taken seriously in society only when married (Assimeng, 1999; Nunkunya, 1992). A 31-year-old Ivorian who worked in an international agency described her situation as a single woman:

> … each time that I'm introduced to someone … the person sees you a bit as someone who is not married. And sometimes the person may even dare to say – but at your age, you are still not married? What is going on? How come? People always think that at a certain age one has to be married, and there you become the wife of someone. And nobody will ever say, nobody will ever talk to you about your career or only rarely. In other words, it's good that you are brilliant; it's true, you are an executive woman, you are a young woman who has succeeded in her career, but that's not the most important.

Marriage assumes a primary role in life planning. It thus also significantly affects the decision to migrate or to return. A 38-year-old Ghanaian woman who settled back in Accra after she got a Masters degree abroad explained that marriage significantly influenced her decision to return:

> I met my husband about two months before I left for Nottingham, Britain. When I left we were corresponding with each other and I really came back because of him. Because I had an offer to do a PhD … but I didn't pick it up because I thought I was getting old and I needed to get married and have children. So I said look a PhD can come any time … but marriage can change. You may not get it when you want it. So let me just go for it and come back.

Intercontinental migration of women from these countries is also limited by what Chant and Radcliffe call the "social and cultural constructions of gender" (1992: 7). Particular gender roles and relationships can act as a deterrent to female migration which is expected to be the result of a decision made within the household. It is assumed that, if only one family member can be sponsored to go abroad, the male member has more chances. The reasons are the same as those explaining the lower school enrolment and higher drop-out rates of girls in the West African context.[1] A greater investment is generally made in male family members because of the long-standing belief that there will be better returns.

It is also held that whilst abroad women may adopt new attitudes and behaviours which are not necessarily praised back home. A Ghanaian woman who had worked in the United States illustrated this delicate issue:

> … they [men] call you a strong woman and all that, but it's not because they admire it but … because they are intimidated by it … The fact that they refer to you as a strong woman means they didn't expect a woman to be strong… You know, there's a stigma on women who are successful which I didn't think existed here … It's something they resent so they must single you out – this tough woman – and what they really mean is that that tough woman, she isn't really going to get far with this attitude. No wonder she's not married; a man is not going to be able to stand this.

---

1 See, for example, Ammassari (2001).

That migration can change the behaviour of women and men was shown by a study in Greece which compares return migrants and non-migrants and their gender role attitudes (Sakka et al., 1999). But the findings of the present study also suggest that women are more reluctant to return because of the traditional role and restrictions placed on them in their home communities. This seems to confirm evidence gathered in other parts of the world (Guarnizo, 1997; Perez-Itriago and Guendelman, 1989). Although the quantitative data do not allow us to draw any specific conclusions, this assumption is confirmed by some of the qualitative information gathered in the field.

The age structure of the sample interviewed in Abidjan is somewhat younger than that of the sample interviewed in Accra. The age of respondents ranged from 26 to 69 years in Ghana and from 26 to 60 years in Côte d'Ivoire. The age of female respondents in both countries reflected a younger and smaller age range than that of male respondents. The median age of female Ivorian respondents was 37.5 years and that of female Ghanaian respondents was 39 years, whereas that of male respondents in Côte d'Ivoire was 41 years and in Ghana 44.5 years. Overall, the great majority of all returnees had an age between 30 and 49 years (Table 5-2).

That only a few young returnees are present in the two samples is perhaps due to the fact that many of these migrants still remain abroad. It was also more difficult to find older returned migrants to interview. This may be related to the fact that a smaller number of people used to migrate over long distances before and right after independence. Unfortunately, there are no aggregate longitudinal data corroborating these trends. But, as we shall see, the accounts of some of the early migrants provide some valuable information regarding the evolution of intercontinental migratory movements over time.

In any case, two things need to be borne in mind when the age structures of the two samples are considered. First, this study was targeted exclusively at people who are economically active and employed. All those who were retired or unemployed at the time of interviewing were purposely left out. This, of course, has meant that people aged 30–49 years had more chance of being interviewed. Among older people there probably were more who had already retired, whereas among the younger ones there may have been a greater number of unemployed. Second, this research was targeted exclusively at return migrants who work in high-level positions. Such high-level positions are generally held by mature people who already have advanced in their professional careers. But it also needs

Table 5-2 Age of respondents, by country and sex (%)

Age groups	Côte d'Ivoire			Ghana		
	Male	Female	Total	Male	Female	Total
20–29	4.7	4.8	4.7	3.2	6.7	3.9
30–39	34.1	52.4	36.7	18.5	46.7	24.0
40–49	47.3	28.6	44.7	58.1	40.0	54.5
50–59	11.6	9.5	11.3	16.9	6.7	14.9
> 60	0.8	–	0.7	1.6	–	1.3
No response	1.6	4.8	2.0	1.6	–	1.3
TOTAL	100.0	100.0	100.0	100.0	100.0	100.0
Valid cases	(129)	(21)	(150)	(124)	(30)	(154)

Note: Percentages presented in this and subsequent tables and text may not always add exactly to 100 because of the effects of rounding.

to be kept in mind that the higher the position of potential respondents, the more reluctant they tend to become to participate in an interview.

Marital Status and Offspring

Among the Ghanaian respondents only 9 per cent were single at the time of interview (Table 5-3). This group is almost three times larger in the Ivoirian sample, in part explained by its younger age structure. There is a clear correlation between age and marital status: the older the respondents the more likely that they have been married. It is interesting to notice, however, that in both samples a more significant proportion of women were single. Among the Ivorian respondents there were 24 per cent male and 36 per cent female respondents who were not married. Among the Ghanaians the proportion of single women (20 per cent) is nearly three times that of single men (7 per cent). These figures suggest two major hypotheses: women who migrate encounter more difficulties in getting married and/or they tend to postpone this critical event in their

Table 5-3 Marital status of respondents, by country and sex (%)

Marital status	Côte d'Ivoire			Ghana		
	Male	Female	Total	Male	Female	Total
Single	24.2	36.4	26.0	6.5	20.0	9.1
Married/ cohabiting	66.4	54.5	64.7	87.1	60.0	81.8
Separated	0.8	–	0.7	0.8	–	0.6
Divorced	7.0	4.5	6.7	2.4	20.0	5.8
Widowed	1.6	4.5	2.0	2.4	–	1.9
No response	–	–	–	0.8	–	0.6
TOTAL	100.0	100.0	100.0	100.0	100.0	100.0
Valid cases	(128)	(22)	(150)	(124)	(30)	(154)

lives. Both assumptions could be explained by differences in gender roles and relationships existing abroad and back home. It is also possible that the line of causation is the reverse: namely that women who are more "independent" and who place less importance on marriage are more likely to emigrate. However, these data and interpretations need to be handled with some caution due to the limited number of females included in each sample.

A Ghanaian executive woman who was 46 years old when she was interviewed in Accra explained why she was still unmarried:

> I'm not even married. That's one of the things it [going abroad] did to me. I don't know whether it's the going and coming, but I think I lost some chances by moving. Maybe if I had stayed in Ghana for the six years I may have met somebody and married him. But being abroad and having to adjust and start and everything, I never got married, and I think coming back and having to adjust again – you're moving on, you're not sure if this person is the right one.

Most the respondents were married or living in a situation of cohabitation. It is not surprising that this group was more significant in Ghana than in Côte d'Ivoire given the older age structure of the Ghanaian sample. But other factors related to the life-course of the migrants also need to be taken into consideration.

The analysis of the data shows that there is no direct association between the marital status of the respondents and the length of time spent abroad. However, the fact that Ivorians tend to return right after they finished their studies abroad may adversely affect their ability to get married. Not having worked for substantial periods abroad, they may lack the necessary financial means to establish their own household on return. However, no significant association was found between those who were married and those who had accumulated savings abroad.

Most of the respondents were married to a compatriot at the time of the survey: 89 per cent of the Ivorians and 85 per cent of the Ghanaians. One of the main reasons why migrants prefer to marry a person who has the same origins is that, if they decided to return home, their foreign spouse may not agree with such a move or encounter too many difficulties in adjusting to the local living circumstances. By the same token, it is highly likely that migrants who had married exogenously whilst abroad would be less likely to have returned and be picked up by the returnee survey.

A 43-year-old Ghanaian who met and married a compatriot in London and returned with her to Accra illustrated this type of concern:

> … it was one of the things I had decided that I was not going to do, to marry an English woman … for the simple reason that beyond love there must be the living together, and having in the back of my mind that at some point I'd actually come back to Ghana, I had to ask myself if the person I'm with can adapt to a different environment. And if she can't and things are a bit harder? Then what do you do? So you got to make those considerations. So this does not mean I did not have white girlfriends or stuff like that. But to marry, if I had made up my mind that I was living in England for the rest of my life then fine, no problem. But not having made that decision and wanting it, it would have been unfair.

That a mixed marriage can become a factor hampering return migration was explained by a 46-year-old Ghanaian who himself tried not to become too involved with local girls while he studied in Germany:

> If you take a 25-year-old man who went to Germany and he married a German woman at age 27, you should not expect him to come back here. By the time he is 35, he has three kids who are speaking German, don't speak any Ghanaian language. It's natural that he wants to stay there. He may not necessarily like Germany better than Ghana, but his family

> situation makes it convenient to stay. That is why it takes a strong character to say that look I am not going to marry anybody here and I am going back and you need to be honest to tell your partner.

Spouses who were born abroad or lived most of their lives abroad also seem to be more reluctant to return, regardless of the nature of their origins and citizenship. This was for example the case of the first wife of a 40-year-old Ghanaian whom he married in the United States. About four years after their return they divorced and she went back abroad, taking their young daughter with her:

> Initially she wasn't inclined to move to Africa because she was born and bred in America, and everything she saw on TV about Africa was negative. So definitely she was not inclined to move to Africa just like many million Africans who don't want to be called even African-Americans. People say – man, I'm an American, I'm not African. Because this is what they know about Africa and when they come to Ghana it's just a total shock.

Diverging plans and views regarding return can lead to a divorce, as in this case, or just to a physical separation from the spouse and possibly the children. This happened, for example, to a 48-year-old Ghanaian who came back from the United States and whose wife decided to stay there with the children:

> She never liked Ghana. She was born in England and spent her primary years over there before they came back, so I guess she has always craved to be out. Things are very difficult over here and early, late 70s and early 80s, it was almost impossible for women to really keep a house without struggling it through. So getting a chance to be out, one feels that they must make their lives out there. I'm looking beyond that … and no matter how bad things get, I must do what I can for the children. But it's now impossible to get change, or send money from here to America. You can't do it that way, it's like throwing water uphill.

One out of ten Ghanaians interviewed, but only 5 per cent of the Ivorians, had a spouse who was living abroad at the time of the interview. The spouses of 13 per cent of the Ivorians and 9 per cent of the Ghanaians were in possession of two nationalities. Conversely, 6 per cent of the former and 13 per cent of the latter possessed exclusively European or North American citizenship. This last figure is quite high and may be explained in two ways. Ghanaians, having a more consolidated migration history and generally staying abroad longer, seem more likely to become involved with someone who belongs to the second generation of immigrants or has become naturalised in the host country. But it can also reasonably be assumed that there is a correlation between the length of stay abroad and mixed marriages. In other words, the longer migrants remain abroad, the greater are the chances that they will marry someone who has a different nationality. The results of this study seem to confirm these assumptions. It should also be noted that the spouse of one respondent out of ten was born abroad.

The respondents who had at least one child living abroad at the time of interview represented a quite important share: 39 per cent in Côte d'Ivoire and 27 per cent in Ghana. Among Ivorian respondents, 21 per cent had no children at the time of interview, compared to only 15 per cent of the Ghanaians. On average the former had fewer children than the latter and more children of younger age. All this makes sense if the younger age structure of the Ivorian sample is considered. Finally, it is of interest that in both samples there are very few respondents with more than four children, although again the relatively young age of some respondents means that they may have not yet attained their completed family size.

Education and Occupation

The Ghanaians and Ivorians who participated in this study were all highly skilled and qualified. In fact, at the time of the survey all of the respondents had an occupation falling into one of the three highest out of ten occupational categories as defined by the International Standard Classification of Occupations (ISCO).[2] The great majority of the

2 The ISCO classification has a hierarchical structure to classify different occupations. Major group 1, "Legislators, senior officials and managers" ranks at the highest level of the occupational hierarchy. This is followed by Major group 2, "Professionals", which is restricted to ISCO skill level 4 involving an education commensurate with a university degree or equivalent. Major group 3, "Technicians and associate professionals" is restricted to ISCO skill level 3 meaning an education beginning at the age of 17 or 18 years and leading to an award not equivalent to a first university degree. In the previous section it has been seen that by definition all returned migrants who participated in the questionnaire survey had an occupation that is included in one of these three major groups.

Ghanaians worked as legislators, senior officials and managers, and this was the case of less than half of the Ivorians (Table 5-4).

Table 5-4 Occupation level of respondents by country (%)

Occupation level (ISCO categories)	Côte d'Ivoire	Ghana
1 Legislators, senior officials and managers	43.3	78.6
Legislators and senior officials	1.3	4.5
Corporate managers	40.0	72.7
General managers	2.0	1.4
2 Professionals	47.3	20.1
Physical, mathematical and engineering science professionals	10.0	1.3
Life science and health professionals	0.8	0.6
Teaching professionals	12.7	1.9
Other professionals	24.0	16.2
3 Technicians and associate professionals	9.3	1.3
Physical and engineering science associate professionals	2.7	0.7
Teaching associate professionals	1.3	-
Other associate professionals	5.3	0.6
TOTAL	100.0	100.0
Valid cases	(150)	(154)

The occupations in major groups 4 to 9 require skills at the second ISCO level (education level which begins at the age of 14 or 15 and lasts about three years) or lower. These major groups include clerks (4), service workers and shop and market sales workers (5), skilled agricultural and fishery workers (6), craft and related trades workers (7), plant and machine operators and assemblers (8) and elementary occupations (9). Major group 10 includes the armed forces. The definitions of the International Standard Classification of Occupations (ISCO-88) were used in combination with those included in the variant developed for the European Union (ISCO-88 COM). See http://www.ilo.org/public/english/bureau/stat/class/isco.html and http://www.csv.warwick.ac.uk/ier/isco/brit/btext3.html.

An even more important difference between the two samples emerges in terms of education because the Ivorians more often had achieved a higher educational level than the Ghanaians. In particular, a much larger percentage of the former group held a Doctorate (Table 5-5). Among the latter a much more important proportion had instead stopped studying after having achieved a Masters or equivalent degree. Moreover, almost twice as many Ghanaians than Ivorians had only obtained an undergraduate degree.

Table 5-5 Educational level of respondents, by country and sex (%)

Highest education degree achieved	Côte d'Ivoire			Ghana		
	Male	Female	Total	Male	Female	Total
High school	0.8	4.8	1.3	–	–	–
Undergraduate	8.5	9.5	8.7	14.5	36.7	18.8
Masters or equivalent	41.1	42.9	41.3	70.2	56.7	67.5
Doctorate or equivalent	48.8	28.6	46.0	12.9	6.7	11.7
Other	0.8	14.3	2.7	2.4	–	1.9
TOTAL	100.0	100.0	100.0	100.0	100.0	100.0
Valid cases	(129)	(21)	(150)	(124)	(30)	(154)

Female returnees in the survey were overall less educated than their male counterparts. However, the difference in educational levels based on gender is more striking among respondents in Ghana. In Côte d'Ivoire an almost equal proportion of males and females had a Masters degree, but the number of females who held a Doctorate remained far below that of males. In Ghana, instead, far more males had either a Masters degree or a Doctorate while the proportion of females with just an undergraduate degree was almost twice that of males. This suggests that among Ivorian women an upward mobility process is taking place – at least as regards education – which is not yet to be found in Ghana.

The research was targeted at élite return migrants working in both the public and the private sector. Unable to establish quotas beforehand, an effort was made to include an equal number of both types of respondents. Nevertheless, the composition of the samples differs widely with regard to the sector of economic activity of their members. At the time of interviewing, 55 per cent of the Ivorians were employed in the public sector against only 16 per cent of their Ghanaian counterparts. Instead, whereas only 33 per cent of the Ivorian respondents were working in the private sector, 82 per cent of the Ghanaians who responded to the questionnaire were working there. The remaining participants in the study said they were working for a mixed institution.

These uneven proportions raise the important question of sampling bias. By using a snowball procedure interviewers may select cases who are easiest to reach and with whom they are most at ease without paying too much attention to a proper diversification of the sample. This could have been the case in Côte d'Ivoire, where the research assistants were young persons working in a public research institution who might have found it easier to interview returnees working in the university or in research institutions rather than seeking out entrepreneurs or private sector professionals. The Ghanaian research assistants were older and working as independent consultants, so they may have had an easier access to élite respondents in the private sector. This would also help explain why the occupational level of the Ghanaian respondents is somewhat higher than that of Ivorian respondents. But unfortunately it is not possible to determine the exact nature of a possible sampling bias[3] and thus it is hard to appreciate the "real" difference between the two countries.

While acknowledging again that in statistical terms we are dealing with non-representative samples, some conclusions can still be drawn when the difference in the composition of the samples regarding the sector of economic activity is compared with other information derived from in-depth interviews or secondary sources. In fact, the difference in sector preferences as between the public and the private seems to reflect well the different socio-economic development paths that the two countries have experienced over recent decades.

As was already pointed out in Chapter 4, Côte d'Ivoire has never been an emigration country. It has long been an immigration country due to the stable and prosperous situation it has known until recently. The few Ivorians who went overseas did so almost exclusively for educational purposes; they were generally sent by the government or institutions of

3 It is also possible that sampling biases (and also interviewer biases) have occurred related, for example, to the fact that some questionnaire interviews were conducted by local black male researchers and some others by myself, a white female European, and by another white female North American researcher.

higher education and usually equipped with a scholarship. It is therefore not surprising that most returnees are to be found working in the public institutions which sponsored their studies abroad.

The stable political and economic environment in Côte d'Ivoire (that is, until recently) has, moreover, determined a steady expansion and progressive diversification of the private sector. These developments have created concrete opportunities for return migrants who sought employment in already existing firms and industries. In Ghana, in contrast, the repeated coups and ongoing political crisis have hampered the creation of such opportunities and forced many migrants to find alternative solutions on return. Thus, Ghanaians more often than Ivorians – 33 per cent versus 10 per cent – had to set up their own firm if they wanted to return and work in the private sector. This type of endeavour was facilitated by the fact that Ghanaian migrants remained abroad longer and were more likely to have worked overseas. They therefore brought home more significant amounts of savings and professional experience. But since they remained abroad longer, on return they also found fewer, and probably in their eyes less suitable, work opportunities in the public sector. In fact, even the Ivorians who stayed and worked longer abroad had a significantly greater likelihood of seeking work in the private sector. More detailed analysis of these relationships and hypotheses follows in the next set of chapters.

The analysis of both countries' data shows that older respondents were more likely to work in the public sector. There are two main reasons that can explain why younger respondents have instead more often gone back to work in the private sector. Firstly, new recruitment into public administration was stopped following the adoption of structural adjustment programmes. Secondly, the salaries of public servants were frozen and quickly overtaken by those paid in the private sector. Prior to the economic crisis more money could be earned in the public sector, but since then remunerative professional opportunities can be found primarily in the private sector. The public sector is today praised almost solely for the job security it offers. Another principle also usually applies: the greater the foreign professional experience, the easier it is to find employment in the private sector.

In the light of all this it is not surprising that the Ghanaian sample includes many more returnees who were self-employed and had employees whereas the Côte d'Ivoire sample comprises a greater number of respondents who were working as employees. More than half of the Ghanaians worked in the business sector (e.g., banking and insurance), a field of activity which attracted only 14 per cent of the Ivorians, whereas 34 per cent of the latter group worked in a government department and 19 per cent in a university or research institution. These represented respectively only 11 per cent and 4 per cent among the Ghanaians. In both countries, a relatively small number of respondents were employed in the services sector: 14 per cent of the Ivorians and 11 per cent of the Ghanaians.

These contrasts reflect the differences in educational backgrounds and sectors of economic activity described above. A very significant number of corporate managers responded to the questionnaire in both countries but, as Table 5-4 shows, this was far higher in Ghana (73 per cent) than in Côte d'Ivoire (40 per cent). The Ivorian sample includes a greater number of teaching professionals and physical, mathematical and engineering science professionals. There are also more respondents belonging to the category of teaching and other professionals. This last category includes business and legal professionals, social science and related professionals such as economists, psychologists, communications specialists, writers and creative or performing artists. The proportion of associate professionals is also more significant in the Ivorian sample, one more reason why the occupational level of its members is somewhat below that of those belonging to the Ghanaian sample. There are no significant variations with regard to gender.

Family Well-being: Housing and Commodities

Family well-being, a driving force of mobility, is difficult to measure. But the questionnaire included one question regarding the number of rooms that returned migrants had in their homes. The analysis of this variable, which was used as a proxy or indicator of wealth, shows that the Ghanaians tended to be better-off compared to the Ivorians. Ghanaians had a median number of four rooms in their homes, whereas Ivorians had only three. Also, more Ghanaian respondents owned a house or an apartment, car or computer at the time of interviewing (Table 5-6).[4]

4 The question asked whether respondents themselves or their immediate families owned any of these three basic commodities. It was clearly specified that the "immediate family" included only the spouse or partner and their own or adopted children.

Table 5-6 Material ownership, by country (%)

Ownership	Côte d'Ivoire N (%)	Ghana N (%)
House/apartment	90 (60.0)	127 (82.5)
Car	111 (74.0)	144 (93.5)
Computer	93 (62.0)	131 (85.1)

These differences are probably due to the fact that most of the Ivorian respondents were employed in the public sector, whereas most of their Ghanaian counterparts were working in the private sector where nowadays better incomes can be earned. It was also seen that the latter were more advanced in their careers because of their older age and thus had reached higher occupational levels which generally involve a better remuneration. But these differences also need to be seen in relation to other variables such as the length of time that returnees worked abroad and the transfer and use of financial resources. Ghanaians usually spent a longer time abroad and worked for more extended periods. Hence, they were able to earn more to send back or to accumulate in savings. In fact, the amounts that Ghanaians transferred considerably exceeded those of their Ivorian counterparts.

Furthermore, such differences in the well-being of the respondents' families need also to be considered in the light of specific macro-economic factors. In Ghana, where the national currency has continued weakening, the hard currency brought back by migrants equipped them with a substantial local purchasing power. A 52-year-old Ghanaian who was interviewed in London put it this way:

> The economy in Ghana has deteriorated so much that if you have some money in Europe that you want to transfer you can actually set up a base, a respectable base in Ghana. I mean for example the house I have here, if I sold that house and transferred the money to Ghana I could get a much better appointed house, you know, than here and have some money left over ... So it's the opportunity provided by the collapse – not the collapse, but the deterioration. The rate of exchange is the key factor. Assets in Ghana are much cheaper than they have been. The prices of assets have fallen considerably, land, buildings and so on.

This same principle cannot so easily be applied in the Ivorian context where, since independence, the CFA Franc remained stable and relatively strong. But, more importantly, this Ghanaian returnee suggested that costs of assets have dropped in Ghana and he expected them to rise in the future.

Socio-cultural Origins and Intergenerational Mobility

The geographical origins of the returnees who participated in the study are fairly disparate. The great majority come from urban areas and a relatively high proportion was born in or very close to the capital city: 39 per cent of the Ghanaian respondents were born in the Greater Accra region and 37 per cent of the Ivorians in the region of the *Lagunes* where the economic capital Abidjan is situated. In Ghana, an important proportion of respondents also came from the Ashanti region whose people are well-known for their *Wanderlust* (Adeku, 1995: 4). A few Ghanaians were also born in Europe or in another African country. These persons were interviewed because they had returned to their original home countries when they were very young and had grown up there before going abroad again.

Most of the Ivorian respondents were Catholic (59 per cent), but only one out of five of the Ghanaian respondents. Most of these latter were Protestant (51 per cent), whereas the number of Protestants in the Ivorian sample was very small. Those who were Islamic made up 18 per cent of the Ivorian and 2 per cent of the Ghanaian sample. A relatively high number of returned migrants professing other Christian denominations were also interviewed in each country.

When searching for signs of intergenerational mobility it becomes apparent that the majority of the participants in this study already belonged to the local élite before migration. Judging from their fathers' occupation, the Ghanaians had a more élite family background than the Ivorians. In fact, the fathers of 76 per cent of the Ghanaians interviewed but also of 59 per cent of Ivorians already had an occupation fitting in one of the three top major occupational groupings.

However, Table 5-7 shows that a considerable intergenerational mobility took place. The percentage of those who had been upwardly mobile is almost equivalent in the two cases. Although their fathers had a lower-level occupation, they themselves had achieved the highest occupational level and were working as legislators, senior officials or managers. In Ghana the most frequent case is that of returnees who had attained the highest occupational level and whose father had an occupation of lower level. In Côte d'Ivoire it is that of returnees who had a lower-level occupation and whose father already had attained only that level. The share of returnees who had been downwardly mobile is identical in the two samples, and similar is also the percentage of those who had managed to maintain the top occupational level of their fathers.

Table 5-7 Occupation level of respondents by their father's occupational level and country

Occupation (ISCO) level of respondents	Côte d'Ivoire				Ghana			
	Father's level 1	Father's level 2–3	Father's level 4–9	Total	Father's level 1	Father's level 2–3	Father's level 4–9	Total
Level 1	22	19	25	66	17	73	28	118
%	15.5	13.4	17.6	46.5	11.6	49.7	19.0	80.3
Level 2–3	6	37	33	76	6	16	7	29
%	4.2	26.1	23.2	53.5	4.1	10.9	4.8	19.7
TOTAL	28	56	58	142	23	89	35	147
%	19.7	39.4	40.8	100.0	15.6	60.5	23.8	100.0

Note For this analysis ISCO Major group 10 was merged with major groups 2–3.

In general the fathers of Ghanaian respondents had higher occupational levels than the fathers of Ivorian respondents. Furthermore, the intergenerational mobility appears more striking in the Ghanaian than in the Ivorian case. Once again, we find that these differences can in part be explained by the younger age structure of the Ivorian sample. It needs to be kept in mind that, at the time of interviewing, many Ivorians still had most of their career in front of them. Whether these differences are also linked to the fact that Ghanaian returned migrants lived and worked abroad longer is another question. An analysis of the data shows that the association between the respondents' current level of occupation and the time they remained and worked abroad is not significant.

In order to better understand the family background of the returnees, these were asked if their father had already lived abroad for a period exceeding one year. The results of the survey show that 53 per cent of the Ghanaian fathers, but only of 27 per cent of the Ivorian fathers, had done so. This reflects the longer history of Ghanaian emigration, and strengthens the assumption that there is a linkage between migration experiences across generations. Although this hypothesis could not be tested in the absence of an experimental study design, some elements emerging from the in-depth interviews seem to confirm it. Parents usually nurture the ambition to offer their offspring the same opportunities, if not more opportunities, as they had themselves.

When asked what he would like his two daughters, aged 11 and 12 – who he wished could come and join him in London – to do to succeed in life, a 47-year-old Ghanaian emigrant replied:

> I can't say and that's [laughter] entirely for them to decide. But I certainly would like them to be able to have the opportunity, the best opportunity to do the things that they want to do. But not just opportunities, but also to be exposed to the best that is available in order for them to be able to make an informed choice, okay? So that it's not simply a choice that's based on a limited range or a choice that's based on the fact that they are not being able to develop other skills that they might have been able to develop.

Some parents, however, were against sending their children abroad when they are too young and immature. This was the viewpoint of a 48-year-old Ivorian:

> Our children have no longer our same cultural foundations. I think that before my children go abroad to study, they will have to finish at least high school here so that they acquire the basic African culture. Otherwise I make monsters of them who will never be real Westerners, nor will they ever be real Africans. Among all those who have studied in France, many send their children to attend high school in France because they think they will acquire a better education. But personally I believe that one kills the soul of these children, because they will never be Europeans and they also will not be Africans anymore.

The ambitions that parents nurture for their offspring have to be considered against the increasing degradation of the national education systems in Ghana and Côte d'Ivoire. As will be seen in the next chapter, this is one of the major reasons why parents encourage their children to go and study abroad.

Summary of Findings

The key characteristics of the returned migrants and emigrants who participated in this study in the two West African countries and the two European cities were presented in this chapter. The samples were dominated by young men. Ivorians were younger and less likely to be married. The Ghanaians had generally achieved a higher occupational level, whereas the Ivorians had achieved a higher educational level. Most Ivorians were employed in the public sector; most Ghanaians were working in the private sector. Ghanaians were also more likely to be self-employed and have employees.

The family well-being of the Ghanaian respondents was higher than that of their Ivorian counterparts, based on their housing and basic commodities. This is due to three main characteristics of the Ghanaians: (1) they had advanced more in their careers; (2) they had lived and worked longer abroad and taken back greater financial resources; and (3) their local purchasing power was greater due to a particularly weak national currency.

More Ghanaians than Ivorians already belonged to the élite before migration. The former also experienced greater intergenerational mobility measured with respect to the level of occupation of their fathers. Despite quite striking upward mobility, no significant association was found between the occupation of returnees and the duration of their absence or time spent working abroad.

CHAPTER SIX

THE ROLE OF RETURN MIGRANTS IN THE DEVELOPMENT OF THEIR HOME COUNTRY

The central hypothesis of this study is that migrants acquire different forms of capital abroad which are of use back home; and furthermore that the transfer of these resources has positive development implications in their country of origin. Before assessing the practical implications of return migration, the role that returned migrants are prepared to play in the development of their home country needs to be examined. This is the purpose of this chapter. A fundamental transformation in the ideology of return regarding the earlier and the more recent generations of migrants is illustrated. However, the potential of Ivorian and Ghanaian returnees to promote development is found to vary significantly and this variation is related to a number of factors, as this chapter demonstrates.

From Nation-building to Entrepreneurship: The Ideology of Return

As we saw in Chapter Four, one shared characteristic of Ghana and Côte d'Ivoire is the emergence of a new élite after independence. Another common feature is that both countries have, over time, experienced declining standards in the quality of education, due to the expanding economic crisis. This negative trend has also affected tertiary institutions and thus all those who had the means – notably the élite – did whatever they could to send their children abroad to pursue their studies. Hence, if the older generation went abroad soon after independence mainly to enrol in advanced courses that were not taught locally, the younger generation left primarily to study overseas because the general quality of education had seriously declined in their home country.[1]

1 Blaud (2001) describes how in many sub-Saharan Africa countries a person who has a foreign degree is perceived as someone who has succeeded. In his study on student migration he found that those who had such a degree had an

This has implied that over time the age at first emigration has decreased, with more recent migrants being more and more eager to get most of their higher education abroad and avoid a poor quality local education system.

Evidence gathered from the preliminary in-depth interviews suggests that the attitudes and main motivations towards return also differ across generations. The immediate post-independence period represented a unique historical moment which provided older-generation migrants with what they saw as ample opportunities to promote public-spirited values and translate them into practice for the benefit of the newly-independent states. This made many migrants anxious to return and to assume a special leadership role in their home context. In fact, many migrants did not even consider remaining abroad any longer than the time needed to complete their studies as, for example, this 60-year-old Ivorian explained:

> For us it was clear, we had to acquire some knowledge abroad, and return to work and make this knowledge available to our home country. We had done primary and secondary school under colonisation and the country had just acquired its independence, and so we had this nationalistic attitude which meant that we wanted to come back as soon as possible. There was no question of remaining abroad.

Older migrants expressed a particularly strong sense of indebtedness and obligation not only because at home they had received free education from the taxpayers' money, but many had also received a government-sponsored scholarship to study abroad. They said they considered it their duty to contribute to the development of their country of origin. How to do this once back home was left to them: some chose to teach in the university, some preferred to work in the government, others went into politics.

Often, the older migrants who had left with a scholarship had a job waiting for them on return because they were expected to replace the foreign officials who had been working in public administration since colonial times. Others, too, did not experience great difficulties on return. According to them there was relatively little competition in the labour market, as there were still many professional opportunities which appropriately matched their skills. Overseas, some felt frustrated since

---

advantage in the local labour market and were more likely to get jobs with more responsibility than people holding a national degree.

there were many others with the same skills and hence they thought that their efforts would not make any difference. At home it would certainly be harder to get things done, but to achieve success would make them feel "much better, much richer simply because there are so few people to do the kinds of things that you've been trained to do" (58-year-old Ghanaian returnee).

Although this feeling was shared by some migrants of the younger generation, the timing and scope of their return home were not the same. Many younger migrants left the home country at a time when public administration had begun to become saturated and new recruitment in the civil service had ceased. Few chances of finding a white-collar job in the public sector on return were left and salaries had generally been frozen. After the economic crisis, more remunerative professional opportunities were to be found in the private sector. In synthesis, whereas the older-generation migrants had a significantly greater likelihood to have gone back to work in the public sector, younger-generation migrants were more likely to have sought work in the private sector after return. This was also demonstrated by cross-tabulations in the two samples.[2]

With increasing numbers of young graduates offering their services, competitiveness in the job market grew in both countries. Younger returning migrants therefore encountered particular difficulties in finding employment, as did younger people in general, as was seen earlier. For the same reason the role of the young in nation-building appeared weakened. For the older generation of migrants who had helped in the drive for freedom and who represented the nation's intelligentsia, it was clear that nobody else could have taken on such an important role and responsibility. But times were changing and the national context was no longer the same. From the in-depth interviews one can gather that today migrants more easily trust that their country will develop anyway, with or without them. Since a growing number of young people go abroad to study and gain foreign work and life experience, their role and contribution are no longer considered to be particularly exclusive.

---

2 Because of reasons of space only a few cross-tabulations were included as tables in the text. The others can be consulted in Annex Four. Cross-tabulations included the use of Fisher's exact test for the calculation of odds ratios. In general, consideration was given only to relationships with a level of significance below 5 per cent, but in a few cases reference was also made to relationships with a level of significance below 10 per cent.

Moreover nowadays younger élite migrants sometimes have a very different conception of life, based among other things on a broader-minded worldview, as was stressed by a 37-year-old female Ghanaian returnee:

> Something I find not only in the younger generation but also in our generation, we are no longer nationalistic. Ghanaians can find their home everywhere now. We are not nationalistic at all any more. People are no longer proud to say – hey I'm a Ghanaian, so I've got to do this for my country … The older generation always had this really strong nationalistic feeling that Ghana is our home, we are proud to be Ghanaians, we've got to come back home to build.

If building the nation was a strong imperative for migrants belonging to the older generation, this does not mean that migrants belonging to the newer generations believe that there is no role left for them to play of this kind. Some claim to have dealt with such questions of conscience and principle as did, for example, this 45-year-old Ghanaian who returned to set up his own NGO promoting good governance and democracy:

> My mind has always been focused on going back home to work for two reasons. I felt that the education I have received and the opportunities given me could take me only so far. I mean, materially I could do better abroad than in Ghana. I could dress well, live well, have the best of everything if I wanted to, but I'm not sure if life really has a lot of meaning in those material terms, like driving the latest car, living in a nice house … because if you are an African, you always know that the media in the West have this penchant for negative reporting. So no matter how high you stand, there is always this picture brought to you into your bedroom, or wherever, reminding you that there it is not alright. You come from that place, I mean it's your responsibility. You wouldn't leave everything to wealthy Europeans and Americans to always give aid and try to fix all the problems for us. I mean you can't do that when you have also been trained in these societies and you have acquired that knowledge and skills.

During the last decade the process of privatisation and the development of small and medium-sized enterprises have created many new work and business opportunities. The younger generation of migrants has drawn particular benefits from these more recent developments, above all because they have been willing to take greater risks. For many of the younger migrants who have returned in recent years, the private sector represents not just a place where they can find the most profitable professional opportunities. As a 40-year-old Ghanaian migrant who launched his own private firm after return stressed:

> The private sector is the engine and the catalyst of growth in Ghana. Where there is competitiveness, you find more opportunities, where there is a monopoly, you find less opportunities and more hardships. And you find that Ghana has decentralised and diversified most of the monopolies … they are now giving the opportunity to own enterprises, create more jobs, create more transparency in the system. So you see the economy has dramatically turned around as opposed to some other countries which have most of their industries monopolised by government. So I see that the private sector has a lot to contribute to the socio-economic development of its own people.

In their eyes the private sector is where more creative innovations can be introduced. However, as was emphasised by this above-quoted Ghanaian entrepreneur, the public sector also has an important role to play, not least, he thought, to ensure that people did not abuse their new wealth and use it for equivocal political purposes.

Financial, Human and Social Capital Transfers and their Development Potential

In general, international migration has allowed Ivorian and Ghanaian élite migrants to have a valuable experience and to acquire various kinds of capital. Migrants gained money which they sent back in the form of remittances and also repatriated in the form of savings. They also returned with many new ideas, skills and knowledge and, more generally speaking, with a broader perspective. Their foreign experience moreover helped them to make fruitful contacts, to broaden their personal and professional networks and strengthened their ability to deal with different people and situations. All three forms of capital are important for the development of their country of origin.

Remittances and Savings, their Transfer and Utilisation

Three factors are important in order to assess the development potential of remittances. Irrespective of the amounts that migrants transfer, critical factors include the frequency of these transfers and the deployment of these funds[3]. In practice about two thirds of Ghanaians and about half of the Ivorians interviewed sent home remittances (Table 6-1).

Ghanaians reported sending money more regularly than Ivorians did, reflecting the fact that more of the latter went abroad primarily to study. Ivorians usually worked for very limited periods or on a part-time basis; their focus was to complete their studies and quickly return home. Families may place more limited demands on this type of migrant, as research in Vietnam has also found (Iredale et al., 2002). Cross-tabulations in the Ghanaian sample showed that returnees who worked abroad were more likely to have sent remittances regularly, especially those who had worked longer than the average.

That Ghanaians remitted part of their earnings more regularly than Ivorians is not surprising because they worked abroad for more extensive periods. But remittances can be considered both as an independent and as a dependent variable. Thus, their transmission depends not only on whether migrants worked abroad and if so for how long, how much they earn, save etc., it also rests on the needs and demands that their families place on them. This in turn depends to a large extent on the socio-economic situation of the migrants' home country. Since, as was seen in Chapter Four, Ghana went through greater difficulties than did Côte d'Ivoire, Ghanaian migrants presumably had to deal with more urgent needs at home. This, at least, is what was reflected in in-depth interviews. Some Ghanaians, as for example a 45-year-old female returnee, explained how bad the situation had become in the critical years following the fourth military coup. Conditions had degenerated so much that shops were empty and it was difficult to buy even very basic things:

---

3 The question about the amount that the migrant transferred was not raised in the questionnaire mainly because it appeared difficult to find an appropriate measure. Preliminary in-depth interviews had revealed a considerable irregularity in these transfers, and difficulties were related also to the different currencies used by migrants and their variations over time, as well as to major fluctuations in the Ghanaian Cedi. Another problem was linked to the need to limit the number of questions included into the questionnaire as much as possible.

Table 6-1 Remittances and related expenditures, by country (%)

Remittances and related expenditures	Côte d'Ivoire	Ghana
Did you send any remittances?		
Regularly	10.7	42.2
Occasionally	36.2	31.2
No	53.1	26.6
TOTAL	100.0	100.0
Valid cases	(149)	(154)
*How did you transmit the remittances?**		
Individual bearers	14.3	79.8
Banks	34.3	31.6
Post/courier	47.1	6.1
Personally	18.9	18.4
Other	11.4	0.9
*How were the remittances used?**		
Upkeep of spouse/children	14.3	7.9
Upkeep of parents and siblings	84.3	75.2
Financing of projects	2.9	25.7
Savings	1.4	4.4
Gifts/donations	1.4	21.2
Other	4.3	1.8

* More than one pre-coded response was possible.

> In 1982–1983 we didn't even have toilet paper ... and any time I came to visit I'd carry a suitcase or so full of toilet paper, sardines, soap, you name it, toothpaste everything. You cannot believe what we had to carry to bring back here!.

Yet, more than one quarter of Ghanaians and more than half the Ivorians said they never sent remittances during the time of their absence. These figures seem rather high compared to other findings in the

Table 6-2 Cross-tabulation: worked abroad longer than average by sent remittances regularly (Ghana)

Ghana	Sent remittances regularly		Total
Worked abroad longer than average	Yes	No	
Yes	39	30	69
No	26	59	85
Total	65	89	154

Notes: Risk estimate 2.95; Significance: 1%.

region regarding low- or unskilled migrants.[4] They suggest that highly-skilled élite migrants may remit less than low- or unskilled migrants. A comparison between this data regarding élite migrants and very similar data collected for "less skilled" migrants confirms that former remit less frequently than the latter.[5] But this does not allow us to conclude that élite migrants remit generally less, because the amounts of their transfers are unknown. They may have sent money home less often but transferred greater amounts. Still, the argument that highly-skilled migrants tend to remit more because they have more earning potential abroad, did not find much confirmation in in-depth interviews either. Several returnees specified that for them there was no need to remit because their families could easily cater for themselves. This was the case of this 45-year-old Ghanaian who spent 17 years in the United Kingdom:

> Fortunately my family did not need money from me. I just sent something as a token to my mother when she was alive and to my father just alike. It was like my son had sent me something … it wasn't the sort of money I needed to send because my family was waiting and they were depending on it. So it was an occasional thing, a symbolic thing.

"Symbolic transfers" of this kind need to be seen in the light of certain traditional values where gift exchange is based on the principle of

---

4 See, for example, Blion (2001).

5 Data concerning "less skilled" migrants were collected within the framework of the Transrede project. For comparisons of remittances see Black et al. (2003a) and Tiemoko (2003).

reciprocity and reaffirms certain social ties and mutual obligations (Nukunya, 1992). It is also worth noting that élite migrants seem more likely to have received money from their families while they were away to finance their stay abroad: a kind of "reverse remittance flow". This applied mainly to those who left home without a scholarship, even though some of them worked and earned money to pay for their studies and subsistence in the host country. Blaud (2001) has also indicated that some African student migrants receive financial support from their families, but he suggests that this kind of support was usually temporary. Once abroad, these migrants were generally expected to find alternative sources of income.

However, there are also other reasons for the occurrence of a reverse financial capital transfer. A 41-year-old Ghanaian returnee who had never remitted any money while he was abroad because his parents had their own resources and never asked for money, admitted that soon after return he had started sending money from Ghana to the United States to his former wife and child, who had re-emigrated. He was not the only one who recognised that he was transferring money abroad rather than repatriating funds.

The way remittances were transmitted is also important to determine because, as Ghosh (1992) has pointed out, the use of formal channels enables governments to control the use of much needed hard currency and to encourage a productive utilisation of remittances. In this survey only one third of the respondents in each sample said that they had sent remittances through regular banking channels (Table 6-1). Remittances were sent mainly through post/courier by Ivorians, whereas they were predominantly transmitted through individual bearers by Ghanaians. The widespread use by Ghanaians of this informal channel of transmission raises some concerns as to how the real volume of these flows can properly be evaluated and assessed.

Returned migrants were also asked how the money they had remitted was used. Their responses, displayed in Table 6-1, show that remittances were used primarily for the upkeep of parents and siblings (84 per cent of Ivorians and 75 per cent of Ghanaians). Kabki et al. (2003) found the same in their study on the impact of the remittances of Ghanaian migrants based in the Netherlands. Indeed, several studies focusing on West Africa corroborate this finding and emphasise the critical importance of these resources for migrants' households in moments of crisis as well as in ordinary times.[6]

A Ghanaian migrant in London explained that the £100 he used to send each month to his parents was used by them to maintain themselves, to pay electricity and water bills and also for transportation and other day-to-day expenditures. From the migrants' accounts it also emerged that a significant part of remittances was invested in the education of younger siblings and other relatives (and even for the children of friends or people originating from the same village), to cover school fees and purchase items and books.

A relatively high percentage of Ghanaians said that some or all of their remittances were used to finance projects (26 per cent) or were sent as a gift or donation (21 per cent), but hardly any Ivorians referred to these categories of remittance utilisation.[7] Yet, during the in-depth interviews some Ivorians claimed that they had provided financial aid not only to relatives but also to some of their friends. This was the case of this Ivorian migrant interviewed in Paris:

> There were a few friends to whom I have sent money in the last ten years to help one to get a driving license and another to pay her studies. I sent about 300,000 CFA Francs because I said to myself that I have had the chance to study and everybody should have that chance. Unfortunately even in my family there were certain problems which have meant that some of us have not been to school. These relatives now have problems to survive and need to be helped.

Another Ivorian, aged 43 years at the time of his interview in Paris, explained that most of the money he had sent or brought home was invested in income-generating activities for his own and his spouse's family:

> For my brothers I already bought a house so that they have a place to stay. For our mother I set-up a *maquis* [small informal restaurant] so that she can generate some income and feed the others… I did the same for

---

6 See for example Blion and Verrière (1998), Daum (1994) and Tall (2003).

7 "Financing of projects" was found to be a too generic formulation and thus by picking this response category reference was not necessarily made only to development or business projects, but also to personal projects such as building a house.

Table 6-3 Savings brought back from abroad and related expenditures and investments, by country (%)

Savings brought back from abroad and related expenditures and investments	Côte d'Ivoire	Ghana
Did you accumulate any savings abroad?		
Yes	56.7	89.0
No	43.3	11.0
TOTAL	100.0	100.0
Valid cases	(150)	(154)
How much savings did you bring back on your last return?		
No savings	10.5	8.8
< US$10,000	70.9	54.0
US$10,000–50,000	11.6	24.8
> US$50,000	4.7	10.9
No response	2.3	1.5
TOTAL	100.0	100.0
Valid cases	(86)	(137)
*Which of the following best describes your major expenditures/investments on your last return?**		
Housing related expenditure	51.7	69.6
Durable consumption goods	59.8	49.3
Electronic appliances	57.5	31.9
Providing support to other family members	35.6	38.4
Investment in business	24.1	44.9
Investment in stock market	10.3	17.4
Other	26.4	26.1

* More than one pre-coded response was possible.

> my wife's family so that she can also generate some income and care for the five children who live with her. I also bought a house for them and all the furniture so that they can live properly.

The number of respondents who claimed to have sent some remittances with the aim of saving the money back home was also very limited in both cases. Savings were generally accumulated by migrants abroad and brought back only on return. Table 6-3 reveals that far more Ghanaians than Ivorians accumulated savings while they were living overseas. The amount of savings that Ghanaians brought back was much higher than that transferred by Ivorians; and few left all their savings abroad. This last strategy was often the case of those migrants who were concerned about a possible devaluation of the local currency back home. A 39-year-old Ivorian returnee explained for example:

> You always have this little reflex that you need to keep something abroad, so if there is another devaluation you will be glad to have kept some savings in hard currency. That's why I continue to keep some of my savings in France, notably for my retirement.

Cross-tabulations revealed that the amount of savings that migrants transfer back home depends significantly on the length of time that they stayed and worked abroad (Tables 6-4 and 6-5). Interestingly, Ghanaians who lived overseas longer seemed more likely to have left all their savings abroad. The same applies to returnees who were in possession of a foreign citizenship. This can be explained by easier access to their foreign savings compared to those who would have had to apply for a visa.

Table 6-3 shows that Ghanaians invested their savings mainly in housing, business and the stock market, whereas Ivorians spent more on consumption goods (e.g. vehicles, furniture, clothing) and electronic appliances (e.g. computers, household equipment). This is largely because Ivorians brought home smaller amounts of money which did not allow them to make any major investments. Ghanaians, who transferred more significant amounts of financial capital from abroad, could undertake more ambitious projects such as the construction of a house or the start-up of a business. Or, conversely, Ghanaians may have transferred larger amounts because they wished to make more important investments. It also needs to be kept in mind that people disposing of foreign currency in Ghana have a greater local purchasing power, because the Ghanaian Cedi has been particularly weak compared to the CFA in Côte d'Ivoire.

Table 6-4 Cross-tabulation: worked abroad longer than average by returned with more than US$50,000 savings (Ghana)

Ghana	Returned with more than US$50,000 savings		Total
Worked abroad longer than average	Yes	No	
Yes	13	56	69
No	2	83	85
Total	15	139	154

Notes: Risk estimate 9.63; significance: 1%.

Table 6-5 Cross-tabulation: worked abroad longer than average by returned with more than US$50,000 savings (Côte d'Ivoire)

Côte d'Ivoire	Returned with more than US$50,000 savings		Total
Worked abroad longer than average	Yes	No	
Yes	4	0	4
No	63	83	146
Total	67	83	150

Notes: Risk estimate 2.32; significance: 5%.

The patterns of expenditure outlined above, especially those related to housing and the acquisition of land to build a new home, along with the purchase of durable consumption goods, are very much in line with empirical findings from other regions of the world.[8] Real estate usually represents a profitable investment from many points of view. Migrants need a place to stay relatively comfortably and independently after return. But for many of them land purchase and house construction also

8 See, for example, Gmelch (1980, 1987) and King (1986, 2000) for Southern Europe, Nada (1991) for North Africa and Stinner et al. (1982) for the Caribbean.

represent a profitable financial investment. In countries where other forms of financial investment (e.g. securities, mutual funds, pension plans), and even ordinary banking services, are still to be fully developed, many of those who can afford it invest in real estate. In fact, only 10 per cent of the Ivorian and 17 per cent of the Ghanaian respondents said they had invested some or all their savings in the local stock market. A 35-year-old Ghanaian banker in London pointed out why investment in real estate represented a better option:

> I have significant investments in property [back home] ... It starts off with the emotional tie of having to build a place for yourself and the rest becomes an investment because the return is better there ... I don't invest there because I'm Ghanaian, I invest there because the return is better.

The return on such an investment must be quite considerable if one considers that at the time of the survey, at least in Accra, it was becoming a common practice to rent houses of a certain standing only to people who could afford to pay up to three years rent in advance and in foreign currency. A 42-year-old Ghanaian business person mentioned this as one of the difficulties that migrants encounter after return:

> It's their entry on an economic level which is difficult. It's a cash economy [here] and for most of us living there [overseas], we lived on credit, you can get a mortgage, a loan for your car, you can get a credit card ... Ghana requires you to put cash down, you buy a car with cash, if you are buying a house, until recently there was no mortgage, even if you were renting you had to put one, two, three years rental down. If you are setting up an office, you know, the re-entry can be difficult in that economic sense.

All this suggests that building-related expenditures may have a positive multiplier effect since returnees may use their property themselves and save the money they would have to pay for rent for other more productive purposes. Or otherwise they may rent it out and generate some additional revenue or capital to invest in a productive venture. Anyway, like return migrants who have been studied in other countries, Ivorians and Ghanaians, through the size and quality of their accommodation back home, usually try to demonstrate that their migration experience was successful and that now they enjoy an improved social standing. A 49-year-old Ivorian university professor explained that he was planning such a "social" investment in his little home village:

> I'm obliged to build a house there which for me is an economic nonsense. But I'm obliged to do it because it's almost like a social investment, because in our rural areas you are not respected if you cannot be located territorially. You need to have a place where you can invite people, they come and you can provide directions, and they will listen to you. And then we have certain traditions. If for example you have difficulties in conveying your message, you will have people coming at 3 or 4 a.m. to tell you the source of the problem, how to speak to the right people. But they will say – don't tell anybody that we met ... So it's an aberrant investment because I spend a lot of money in a place where I will live perhaps maximum five to six years. But it's important because it will enable me to do many things that can make society progress.

Building-related expenses can therefore represent an advantageous personal investment to reach specific long-term financial goals and to balance financial and social risks (Smith and Mazzucato, 2003). They are also usually an effective way to reaffirm the returned migrant's improved social status which confers the authority and power that are generally needed to assume a meaningful development role after return and to promote some lasting changes in the home society and economy.

From Table 6-3 we see that savings were spent more on durable consumption goods and electronic appliances, and less on providing support to other family members, in comparison to the use of remittances. The greater propensity of Ghanaians to invest in business reflects the fact that they remained abroad longer, accumulating more financial, human and social capita. As was seen in Chapter Two, various empirical studies have shown that returning migrants prefer to go back to self-employment.[9]

Since the respondents who were self-employed and who had employees are almost three times as many in the Ghanaian as in the Ivorian sample, it is not surprising that, when asked about the importance of the financial capital they had transferred, 66 per cent of Ghanaians and only 28 per cent of the Ivorians replied it was "important" or "very important" in their current work.

Before turning our attention to the question of whether, when they were abroad, returned migrants acquired any new knowledge, ideas, work skills and experience and, if so, what kinds, it should be pointed out that Ivorians as well as Ghanaians considered financial capital the least

---

9 See, for example, Arif and Irfan (1997), Murphy (1999), Nambiar (1998) and Zacariah et al. (2000).

important element of their work. According to them, the accumulation and transfer of human and social capital were more important.

Acquisition of New Knowledge, Ideas, Work Skills and Experience

In the migration literature it is stressed that, with specific regard to human capital transfers, the role of return migrants in the development of their home country depends on three main conditions:

1) that migrants have learned something abroad and/or acquired experience;
2) that what they have learned is useful in their home context; and
3) that migrants are willing and able to apply what they have gained abroad (Athukorala, 1990: 332).

In this particular case all three conditions were confirmed. In fact, almost all return migrants who took part in the survey affirmed that they had gained some specific knowledge, ideas, work skills and experience overseas which were potentially useful and which they had tried to apply in their current work. Evidence concerning the relevance and application of skills and experience was also gathered through in-depth interviews; this too reveals that they made some meaningful contributions to development. However, we must acknowledge that these achievements and contributions are as stated by the migrants themselves, and the possibility of exaggeration or distortion cannot be discounted.

Since the concept of "human capital gain" refers to a complex phenomenon which cannot be directly assessed, three kinds of indicators were used: increases of educational level while abroad; increases in occupational experience while abroad; and amount as well as kind of learning while abroad. That Ivorian and Ghanaian returned migrants had expanded their human capital while abroad is mainly confirmed by the higher education level with which they returned from abroad. However, many also reported gaining occupational experience abroad.

For the returned migrants who left when relatively young, the timing of their first emigration was determinant in making it a decisive life experience. Such was the case with this 51-year-old Ivorian returnee who was asked what he had learned abroad:

Table 6-6 Foreign financial capital gain and its importance in current work, by country (%)*

Importance of foreign financial capital gained abroad	Côte d'Ivoire	Ghana
Very important	12.3	43.6
Important	15.4	22.2
Fairly important	12.3	12.8
Not important	60.0	21.4
TOTAL	100.0	100.0
Valid cases	(85)	(117)

* A number of Ghanaians (20 respondents) who said they had accumulated savings abroad did not reaffirm here that they acquired some financial capital abroad. It is possible that their savings were too small for them to consider them as "financial capital" or simply that the question was not administered thoroughly enough.

> I would say that it has taught me almost everything, in part due to my age because before I left I was an adolescent. The period between adolescence and adulthood is the richest where generally you acquire all the behaviours that you will have as an adult ... I gained not only what I learned in school, but much also from a relational, behavioural point of view, including how to live in society, how to live by yourself.

It needs to be stressed that migrants who, in addition to higher education, also gained some relevant occupational experience (and related life experience) were much more likely to have acquired different kinds of human capital abroad and therefore to assume a meaningful role after return. Some migrants emphasised that working abroad was probably what had enriched them most. A 46-year-old Ivorian who come back from Canada stressed the importance of the migrants' duration of absence and the activity(ies) they engaged in abroad:

> The mentality of our brothers who stayed here and that of us who went abroad is not the same. There really is a difference. The way we approach things, the way we do business, manage business ... it's totally different ... Even those who went to France or to the Unites States for holidays or for a business trip, those who stayed for only 5–6 months or even those

> who only studied and came back, it's not the same. You need to have *lived* in the host country, with the local people, and then without realising it you acquire certain habits, you absorb the culture and you get to know the people, you bear the fruits of the environment, and without realising it you are being transformed. That means that when you return – I don't know whether it is positive or negative – you see things differently than before you went abroad.

When asked in the questionnaire survey what kind of human capital they acquired, returned migrants often provided several answers which offered a vast array of examples. In Table 6-7 these examples are grouped into five categories which distinguish between different kinds of human capital ranging from practical know-how, across interpersonal skills to professional and ethical awareness.

The first major difference to be noted between the two samples is that a far greater number of concrete examples were provided by Ghanaians. This may be explained by the fact that they worked abroad longer and had more varied professional activities. But another explanation could be that "brain drain" and "brain re-gain" were highly debated issues at the time of the survey.[10] This may have made some returnees more aware of their role and possible contributions. Whereas three quarters of them were able to provide two examples and one third three examples, respectively less than half and slightly more than one of ten Ivorians could do this.

Ivorians referred much more often than Ghanaians to forms of human capital that could be classified as "specialised technical expertise". For Ghanaians, instead, "organisational and managerial competence" as well as "communication skills" (i.e. interpersonal skills) were of much greater importance. Communication skills ranged from broadmindedness and adaptability to cultural sensitivity, from language and interpersonal skills to training and presentation capacities, from computer proficiency to information technology competence. "Organisational and managerial skills" included a vast array of professional qualifications such as leadership, entrepreneurial, management, organisation and administration, negotiation, networking and leverage skills. It also encompassed special competencies in the field of human resources and customer relationships.

10 A major Homecoming Summit was organised by the Ghanaian government in Accra the same period.

Table 6-7 Kinds of foreign human capital gains, by country (%)

Kinds of foreign human capital gains*	Côte d'Ivoire	Ghana
	N (%)	N (%)
Specialised technical expertise	110 (69.3)	81 (51.3)
Organisational and managerial competence	32 (21.3)	85 (53.9)
Communication skills	60 (39.3)	98 (64.3)
Sense of professional responsibility	27 (32.0)	(40) 31.8
Other	32 (4.7)	(26) 5.8

* Responses given to an open-ended question.

A final important category of examples was related to an enhanced "sense of professional responsibility". Concrete examples of work skills as well as life experience gained overseas ranged from greater self-confidence, responsibility, autonomy, initiative, commitment and drive for efficiency and effectiveness to increased "work ethics" or "professionalism" including punctuality, discipline, rigour and attention to detail for quality results.

A 45-year-old Ivorian professor who taught Economics, for instance, stressed that he got rid of the inferiority complex that afflicts so many of the people he knows who had never lived overseas:

> I can now discuss with everybody. If I talk about Washington, for example, I know what I am talking about. It's not only because I read about it in books but also because I went there personally, I lived there. If the President of the World Bank comes here and I talk to him, I have no inferiority complex. When I talk to someone from the World Bank who visits I speak to him equal to equal, because I know what I am talking about and he understands what I am speaking about. So it's very useful to have been abroad since I have lost my inferiority complex… and that helps me to better represent my community because I can do that with all the self-confidence and reassurance that is required.

A 42-year-old Ghanaian manager made a similar point when he referred to the greater awareness he had acquired abroad regarding his competencies and also his civil duties and rights. He said that he was more confident that his skills were comparable to those of other people in similar positions in the North. He also stressed that he had gained a real sense of citizenship and that he had become more rights-conscious as opposed to most of the local people who "feel that they are subjects and they don't exercise their rights ... they can't exercise their rights as much as they should".

Table 6-8 illustrates that a very high proportion of respondents considered that the "knowledge and skills" they had gained were "very important" or "important" in their working activities. Foreign "work experience" was gained by more than 80 per cent of the respondents and was again seen as an "important" or "very important" professional asset by the vast majority. Work experience was seen as important by slightly fewer Ivorians, again probably due to the fact that they not only worked abroad much less than the Ghanaians but also more often in training-unrelated jobs.

That many migrants are not only willing but even eager to apply what they learn abroad has already emerged from some of the accounts quoted above. The survey addressed this fundamental issue first of all by asking return migrants if they had tried to apply any new procedures, methods or ideas in their workplace. The vast majority said they had (Table 6-9).

But another indicator also assumes importance in this respect: more than one half of all the respondents considered the way they worked to be very different from that of their colleagues who had not lived abroad. According to both groups of returnees, the main differences consisted in the way work was planned, organised and managed, and the type of attitude and approach adopted in the workplace. Not only did they think that their organisational and management skills exceeded those of colleagues who had not been abroad, but they also felt they had attained greater "professionalism" as well as better "work ethics" including more ambition, commitment, initiative, creativity and broadmindedness. Interestingly, cross-tabulations in the Ghanaian sample reveal that return migrants who initially moved to Europe were more likely to consider their work somewhat different, but not very different, from that of their colleagues who never moved, than returnees who first migrated to North America or other parts of the world.

The evidence which has so far emerged, based on objective and subjective indicators, suggests that migration leads to human capital accumulation which in turn motivates return migrants to attempt to introduce changes in their workplace. In terms of the working hypothesis, this means that élite return migration certainly has the potential to produce socio-cultural, political as well as economic change potential at

Table 6-8 Foreign human capital gains and their importance in current work, by country (%)

Importance of foreign human capital gains	Côte d'Ivoire		Ghana	
	Knowledge and skills	Work experience	Knowledge and skills	Work experience
Very important	73.3	56.2	82.4	77.1
Important	20.7	21.5	14.4	17.6
Fairly important	4.7	5.0	2.6	4.6
Not important	1.3	17.4	0.7	0.8
TOTAL	100.0	100.0	100.0	100.0
Valid cases	(150)	(121)	(153)	(131)

Table 6-9 Application of foreign human capital gains, by country (%)

Application of foreign human capital gains	Côte d'Ivoire	Ghana
Have you tried to introduce and apply any new procedures/methods/ideas in your workplace?		
Yes	89.3	95.4
No	10.7	4.6
TOTAL	100.0	100.0
Valid cases	(149)	(153)
Do you consider the way you work particularly different as compared to the one of colleagues who have not lived abroad?		
No, not really	15.3	7.8
Yes, very much	50.7	55.2
Yes, to some extent	34.0	37.0
TOTAL	100.0	100.0
Valid cases	(150)	(154)

home. But it needs to be mentioned again that return migrants' accounts may be subjectively biased.

In the survey respondents were asked how frequently the application of new procedures, methods and ideas caused difficulties or tensions, for instance with colleagues. This type of problem was not infrequently encountered (Table 6-10), with only slightly less than one third of all respondents affirming that they were "never" or "only rarely" confronted with these difficulties.

Table 6-10 Frequency of difficulties or tensions with colleagues, by country (%)

Frequency of difficulties and tensions	Côte d'Ivoire	Ghana
Very often	16.4	11.6
Often	26.9	13.7
Occasionally	25.4	40.4
Rarely	8.2	15.1
Never	23.1	17.8
No response	–	1.4
TOTAL	100.0	100.0
Valid cases	(134)	(146)

When asked how the tensions or difficulties manifest themselves, most returnees put emphasis on their colleagues' resistance to change, ranging from lack of participation and initiative to minor sabotage, from discussions to arguments, from the disregard of instructions to carelessness in the execution of tasks. That these difficulties and tensions were encountered more often by Ivorians than by Ghanaians is probably due to the fact that, as the survey shows, they were working in larger workplaces. In these wider workplaces Ivorians were confronted with more interpersonal relationships and they also held lower management positions compared to Ghanaians. A far greater proportion of the Ghanaians were their own boss and at the top of the organisational structure, a position which conferred on them more authority and power and also a greater margin of manoeuvre.

In general it seems that Ivorians who have acquired less job-related experience abroad and who have tended to return as civil servants to bureaucratic structures have encountered more resistance to their efforts for change than the more practically trained Ghanaians, who have mostly promoted entrepreneurial activities on return. But more significantly, in theoretical terms, is the evidence that the development impacts of return migration depend on the attitudes of the receivers almost as much as on the efforts of the proponents.

The way return migrants are perceived back home by those who have never emigrated is fairly contradictory. On the one hand, return migrants are valued because they are seen as those who bring back innovations from abroad and what comes from abroad is often considered to be better than what exists locally. According to this 51-year-old Ivorian migrant who returned from France:

> You are admired because you are seen as someone who has ideas, someone who can help, contribute to change and improve the situation. Perhaps sometimes people even expect too much from you, both resources and ideas.

On the other hand, returned migrants are seen as a threat to the existing order and values, as revealed, for example, by the statement of this 37-year-old Ivorian migrant who returned from the United States:

> When you get here people point at you with their finger, meaning there he is the newcomer who has new ideas, who wants to change everything. Perhaps it's a bit caricatural, but essentially it's like that especially in the workplace.

Also, the migrants' accounts confirmed the existence of an ambiguous and sometimes contrasting relationship between return migrants and non-migrants, a problem that has been addressed quite extensively in the return migration literature (Gmelch, 1980; King, 2000). A 43-year-old Ghanaian explained how he and others who returned from abroad are seen by those who never emigrated and described the resistance the former encounter when they try to promote any change:

> What we normally say in this country is that he's a person that is "too known" [i.e. a "know-all"] – you think you know everything, you think you are cleverer than anybody else. But there's a habit in this country of people saying that this is how we used to do things, this is how we've been

> doing things for the past ten years and it's good, when it's obvious to the most basic mentality that this is no good, it's not getting us anywhere.

Another expression that is widely used in Ghana to denote return migrants is "have been to", a term which also reflects their "know it all" and often arrogant and condescending attitude towards those who have never moved. From the interviews it emerged, however, that an increasing number of returnees were starting to realise that they did not know it all; they could not change the system overnight; they first had to regain a thorough understanding of how the local system worked. In fact it was commonly claimed that, having been abroad for prolonged time periods, returned migrants had lost contact and thus realistic insight into their home context; non-migrants were frequently considered more knowledgeable in this respect. Concurrently returnees felt that non-migrants were warming to the idea that returnees had something special to offer, in particular a wider and more detached perspective and broader frame of reference to examine and act on certain development issues. In brief, those who have been away are usually in a better position to compare and to contrast.

When asked if he would have been the same person today if he had never left his home country, this 57-year-old Ghanaian lecturer replied:

> Definitely it would not have been the same. I mean there is always education and exposure, I think even a British student who comes here for a year will not be the same as the English boy who studied all, everything in England. There is always the comparative advantage of having seen how others do things and of course in a very advanced society as the UK – not that everything is perfect, oh no! – but it helps you to make a comparative analysis and it helps you to have something to use as a standard of measure. And if in this world you don't have something to compare a situation with, I think it is very difficult for you to be global in your perspective.

Similarly, when asked what role migrants can assume when they come back from abroad, another Ghanaian (45 years old) who set up an NGO in Accra replied:

> Big one! Development really calls for a vision that must be rooted in knowing what has worked elsewhere. You can't sit here and imagine all the nice things and say – oh I want Ghana to become an upper, middle-

> income country and in ten years people should be earning US$3,500. I mean you need to know how others did get there and ask yourself what kind of institutions, what kind of working ethic, culture is needed, what kind of linkage should exist between the various sectors so that you have an integrated approach to these things. You can read this in a book as a scholar, but doing it is something else. And what strikes me about my colleagues who haven't travelled or studied, or lived and worked abroad and gained exposure, they know the system so well, but they know how to maintain it.

The return migrants' capacity to apply foreign human capital gains in their workplace or elsewhere is not only hampered by the ambivalent relationships they have with non-migrants and the latter's resistance to change and reluctance to participate in new initiatives. It is also influenced by the difficulty that return migrants have in readapting to the local work culture and conventional ways of doing things, the poor local physical working conditions, the lack of basic facilities and effective equipment and the slow bureaucracy, including red tape and corruption. As we have seen, this results in a situation where a high proportion of returnees had to admit that "often" or "very often" they felt frustrated at being unable to apply some of their expertise and skills.

Many more Ivorians than Ghanaians felt frustrated, probably because a greater share of the former was employed in the public sector and in large institutions. Those who were working in the public sector were not only more likely to feel frustrated, but were also more generally less satisfied with their current work conditions (e.g., income, career opportunities, responsibility, management, relationships with colleagues, organisational culture). Moreover, some other problems, such as the lack of adequate infrastructure, equipment and facilities, or oppressive bureaucracy, tend to be amplified in the public sector.

Links Established Abroad and Kept After Return

As we saw in Chapter Two, an important element of the development potential of return migration is related to the acquisition abroad and transfer back home of social capital. The empirical measurement of social capital is not an easy task (Stone and Hughes, 2002), but in this study an effort was made to capture at least one of its main dimensions. Thus, in the questionnaire returnees were asked if they had established and kept any personal and/or professional contacts abroad. It was expected that participation in networks and collectives abroad through social and institutional relationships would help in leading to successful initiatives back home, a hypothesis which is largely based on the assumption that social capital is often a prerequisite for the acquisition of financial and human capital (Faist, 1997; 2001). In fact, one of the key aspects of social capital is its ability to "operationalise" and "transfer itself" into other forms of capital.

Table 6-11 shows that at the time of interview almost three quarters of the Ghanaians and half of the Ivorians had maintained both personal and professional contacts abroad; the lower proportion of Ivorians is probably due to the fact that they remained and worked abroad for generally shorter periods.

Of course, it was important to ask returnees how they were using these contacts; this was done mainly through in-depth interviews. In one of these a 46-year-old Ghanaian who headed a major national research institution indicated that he derived several concrete advantages from the links and relationships he established abroad:

> I have developed in my career much, much faster than one could have anticipated, and it's largely as a result of opportunities that I have either created myself or have been created for me together with my colleagues outside ... [These] have allowed me to spend a lot of time ... in some of the best universities in the world, with some of the best-known people. I have had time to work at the World Bank, I have had time to do things with the UN University in Tokyo, I've done seminars in many European countries ... I have been very, very lucky in that sense [laughter]. So when you live here and you have the chance to go to the World Bank twice a year to do seminars and then they ask you – why don't you come and do this for us, why don't you write this report for us, why don't you do this, and you spend six months in Washington, you don't have any incentive to want to have a long term job in London, for example ... So that's why I said I live in Ghana, but I do work in several spots of the world, which means I can do here everything I would have done while let's say working in London. It's been made much, much easier now also by the internet. It probably was a bit more difficult before the internet came, but having access to the internet means that almost every other month I can do a journal article with a colleague at SOAS or with a colleague at the World Bank or with a colleague at Yale, so many of the things that I get to write I'm only contributing about half of the actual piece whilst my

Table 6-11 Contacts established and kept after return, by country (%)

Contacts kept abroad	Côte d'Ivoire	Ghana
What type of contacts have you kept abroad since you returned?		
Personal	42.0	19.5
Professional	2.7	4.5
Both	51.3	74.0
None	4.0	1.9
TOTAL	100.0	100.0
Valid cases	(150)	(154)
In what way do you keep these contacts?		
By postal mail	54.9	32.5
By telephone/fax	64.6	72.7
By email	58.3	87.7
Through visits	34.0	50.0
Other	–	–

> colleagues here, who don't have that opportunity, are spending a whole year doing that piece of work by themselves. So I produce six articles and they produce one. This doesn't mean that I'm smarter than they are, but I have more opportunities than they have and it's largely so because I've invested time in building a network.

This and other accounts confirmed that migrants utilised their foreign links and relationships not only for themselves. They also employed them in their work and thus often to promote changes affecting the home society and economy. Emphasis was placed by several returned migrants on how they had facilitated international collaboration and exchanges in their workplace and gained some external support and assistance for community development initiatives. A 49-year-old Ivorian professor, for example, specified that, based on his contacts, his department had developed a fruitful collaboration with some French universities. Among other things this involved regular student exchanges and joint research projects. So migrants put in place networks which stimulate transfers of knowledge from abroad and collaborative ventures, a finding also confirmed by Kaplan (1997) in a study focusing on South Africa.

Table 6-12 confirms that migrant networks of social relations and ties abroad are also beneficial to others. In fact, among all those who said that they had mobilised a network abroad – 92 per cent of the Ivorians and 94 per cent of the Ghanaians – more than two thirds of the Ivorians and almost three quarters of the Ghanaians believed that this constituted an "important" or "very important" advantage in their current work.

Table 6-12 Foreign social capital gain and its importance in current work, by country (%)

Importance of foreign social capital gain	Côte d'Ivoire	Ghana
Very important	38.4	47.6
Important	30.4	26.2
Fairly important	15.9	21.4
Not important	15.2	4.8
TOTAL	100.0	100.0
Valid cases	(138)	(145)

From these networks some returnees were also able to derive some benefits for their community. For example, a 60-year-old Ivorian architect said that the contacts he had kept overseas, and also those he had established later, had helped him to put in place some development initiatives in his home town:

> I try to use these relationships to obtain benefits for our people who have various needs. As a parliamentarian and a member of the Rotary Club I have contacts with some NGOs, some organisations such as *Pharmaciens Sans Frontières*, so I was able to get drugs to give to the people, and those are things that I do through my contacts abroad.

It was seen earlier that the greater broadmindedness and language skills which migrants acquire abroad represent valuable assets to build and nurture interpersonal relationships and social ties overseas. The "cultural knowledge" that they gain about foreign norms, customs and values, which often differ remarkably from the ones that prevail at home, is particularly useful to promote fruitful international exchanges. In total about 41 per cent of the Ivorians and 31 per cent of the Ghanaians said that while away they had learned at least one foreign language. For Ivorians, this was usually English, whilst Ghanaians learned French.

Language skills are of course an important means to establish and maintain productive links and relationships abroad. This was highlighted by a 45-year-old Ghanaian returnee who explained why she envisaged that she would remain permanently in Accra:

> I really want this place to be a sort of regional centre, that's too pompous though [laughter]. But I keep my links with the Francophone countries, because I've been in Francophone countries for such a long time … because of my background with the Francophone countries I'm now the chairman of the Board of the *Alliance Française* in Accra, and I'm also the Legal Counsel for the French Embassy and the UNESCO. I'm also keeping the accounts of the French school, so little by little I am getting the French connection, and I've been getting queries and expressions of interest in jobs from Ivory Coast, Gabon, Benin, Togo and Nigeria.

From the survey it emerged that, in addition to contacts, returned migrants had also kept other linkages abroad. A number of them were still the owners of foreign property or remained in possession of a foreign nationality. Here is the case of a 43-year-old Ghanaian, for example, who returned to Accra in 1997 and illustrated the ties he was keeping abroad:

> We have a family house in England. In fact we have two houses, we have my house which my wife goes to visit once a year and my parents' house … [and then] everybody that I worked with in my last job, I talk to them on the internet all the time, everybody, and a group of them from my last job are coming here to visit with me. My wife has had friends from her last job over here, we've had about three or four or them here staying with us for about three weeks or so, which is encouraging, to use this as a holiday destination … and of course I have to run my father's affairs to a certain extent for him, so I have to maintain some involvement in the house in England. So I'm corresponding weekly with our lawyers in England about that. Those kind of ties, and of course we've a lot of relatives there as well.

The question of whether returnees had owned some property and were still keeping that abroad was also raised in the questionnaire. From the responses it appeared that 46 per cent of the Ghanaians and 10 per cent of the Ivorians had owned a house or an apartment overseas, and

40 per cent of them said they still owned this property. This difference is again mostly due to the fact that Ghanaians stayed and worked abroad and thus had a greater ability to earn and invest money overseas.

Main Factors Influencing the Acquisition of Capital

From what has been presented so far it appears that the migrants' duration of absence is one of the most critical factors influencing migration outcomes. The longer migrants remain abroad, the more they seem to acquire all three forms of capital – financial, human and social – which they can productively employ back home. However, when analysing the survey data more closely by means of multivariate analyses, some quite interesting findings can be derived.

Three models were developed with this aim: model 1 assesses the factors influencing the acquisition of financial capital, model 2 the factors influencing the acquisition of human capital and model 3 the factors influencing the acquisition of social capital. These three dependent variables were constructed based on several indicators. Financial capital is a combination of "sent remittances regularly" and "returned with >US$10,000 of savings". It can take values from 0 to 2. Human capital is a combination of "works very differently from colleagues who never migrated" and acquired any of the following skills: "specialised technical expertise", "organisational and managerial competence", "communication skills" and "sense of professional responsibility". This variable therefore takes values from 0 to 5. Social capital is a combination of "participated in association/movements/clubs abroad", "established a network" and "established/kept professional contacts abroad". This last variable has values from 0 to 3.

The same set of explanatory variables was introduced into each of the three models. The "total duration of absence" assumes increasing logarithmic values. The length of time worked abroad is reflected in three variables "worked 0–12 months", "worked 13–60 months" and "worked 61–120 months"; each one takes the value of 1 if the respondents' length of work falls into the defined categories and 0 if they have worked fewer/more months. The "country of interview" takes the value of 1 if migrants are Ivorians and the value 0 if they are Ghanaians. The values of the variable "age group" is 1 if respondents are aged more than 44 years and 0 if they are younger. "Sex" takes 1 for male and 0 for female respondents. The variable "destination" assumes the value 1 if respondents have first moved to Europe and 0 if they originally migrated to North America or to another part of the world. "Worked abroad" is a variable that is 1 if respondents have replied yes and 0 if they answered no.

As the dependent variables took more than two values, three multivariate linear regression analyses were used. The results (beta coefficients) are presented in Table 6-13. Significance of the beta coefficients was tested at the 0.1 per cent, 1 per cent and 5 per cent levels.

Among the explanatory variables which were introduced into the three models, not all have the same significance. The most significant variable was whether return migrants had worked abroad or not. Migrants who had worked abroad were much more likely to have acquired all three forms of capital during the period of their absence. The models also reinforce this point by showing that the likelihood of acquiring financial and human capital in the host country(ies) increases with increases in the migrants' length of work. Migrants who only worked one year are significantly less likely to have acquired these two forms of capital compared to those who have worked for longer periods.

The same applies to migrants who have worked from one to five years, but for this group additions in the length of work produce less prominent increases in the likelihood of acquiring financial and human capital. Beyond five years, additional increases in the length of work abroad do not produce any significant changes in the migrants' likelihood of accruing either of these two forms of capital. This suggests that, as far as the acquisition of financial and human capital is concerned, there may be an optimal duration of work abroad.

Against initial expectations, the duration of absence turns out to have relatively little independent positive influence on the acquisition abroad of different forms of capital, with the exception of financial capital. The longer migrants remain overseas, the more they are likely to accumulate financial resources, which is an entirely logical outcome. Age had no significant explanatory value. By contrast, sex influenced the likelihood to have acquired social capital whilst away, with men being more likely to gain social capital than women. Also, the destination appears to influence only the acquisition of human capital. Migrants who moved directly to Europe were less likely to have acquired this kind of capital compared to migrants who initially migrated to other destinations.

Another factor which has a very significant influence is the country of origin of the respondents. This confirms what has emerged so far, namely that the Ivorians who participated in this study had a lower propensity than their Ghanaian counterparts to acquire financial and human capital

Table 6-13 Linear regression of acquisition of different forms of capital (standardised coefficients)

Variables	Model 1 Financial capital	Model 2 Human capital	Model 3 Social capital
	Beta	Beta	Beta
Total duration of absence	.168*	.148	.031
Worked 1–12 months	-.262***	-.244**	-.123
Worked 13–60 months	-.162*	-.155*	-.141
Worked 61–120 months	-.052	-.009	.068
Côte d'Ivoire	-.390***	-.237**	-.118
Age >44 years	-.009	-.020	-.095
Male	.060	.070	.129*
Europe	-.026	-.103*	-.026
Worked abroad	.308***	.400***	.222**

Notes: Coefficient significant at ***0.1% **1% *5%.
Adjusted R^2: model 1 27.6%; model 2 25.5%; model 3 8.6%.

abroad. This is mainly due to the shorter time they spent abroad and the correspondingly shorter time they worked in the host country(ies).

However, it needs to be noted that the variables entered into the three models explain only about 25 per cent of the variation in the dependent variables which were developed to assess the acquisition of financial and human capital and only 8 per cent of the dependent variable constructed to appraise the acquisition of social capital. This is not altogether surprising as there are generally admitted to be some problems associated with this kind of multivariate analysis. Firstly, concepts such as financial, human and social capital are highly complex and very difficult to measure. Even a good proxy indicator can capture only so much of their intrinsic nature and variations. Secondly, due to the complexity of the issue under investigation, very many different variables could be taken into consideration. Their interrelations are highly complicated, but a multivariate regression model allows us to test only a limited number of variables. Thirdly, the indicators used for these multivariate analyses were constructed in part from data obtained through open-ended questions formulated in the survey. This may have also affected the explanatory value of the models tested. To overcome these limitations, particular attention was focused in this study on the cross-validation of findings derived from the analysis of information obtained from different sources, such as simple descriptive statistics and cross-tabulations of selected variables from the main questionnaire survey, narrative quotes from the qualitative interviews, and secondary sources.

Summary of Findings

This chapter first examined the changes that have occurred in the reasons for migration and return. The role that returning migrants are prepared to play in the development of their home country has evolved over time and with changing macro conditions. Old-generation migrants, who emigrated mainly to enrol in courses that were not taught locally, mostly went back to the public sector and played a key role in nation-building. Young-generation migrants, who left principally because the quality of education had significantly worsened, are more entrepreneurial and contribute in a more marked way to private-sector development.

However, some interesting differences have emerged between the two countries, because Ghanaians appear more willing and better equipped than Ivorians to take on a meaningful developmental role. The multivariate analyses have shown that their role is strengthened by their longer duration of absence and length of work abroad. Whether élite migrants have worked whilst away and whether this was for significant periods are the most critical factors influencing their acquisition of different kinds of capital. The duration of absence is less important than the kind of activities that migrants undertook abroad, because these latter really determine their lifestyle in the host country. This strengthens the expectation that capital acquisitions depend not only on the migrants' education and work experience, but also on their broader life experience.

The results of the linear regression analysis of the acquisition of different forms of capital suggests that there is an optimum length of work abroad – approximately five years. After that time the likelihood of élite migrants gaining additional financial and human capital decreases and is no longer significant. This means that these benefits tend to stabilise after a certain time period and no spin-off effects could be detected.

It seems that more or less all élite migrants had chances to gain capital abroad as long as they worked as well as studied whilst abroad – either at the same time, to pay their way through university, or with work following a period of study. This enabled them to send some money home or repatriate it on return. That a relatively important share of élite returnees never sent any remittances, or made only symbolic transfers, suggests that this group may not only remit less frequently, but may also transfer overall smaller amounts. Some reverse flows of remittances were moreover detected. The findings suggest that financial capital transfers are influenced not only by the migrants' situation in the host country, but also by the macro conditions affecting migrants' families back home. This explains why Ghanaians transmitted remittances, which were mainly used for the upkeep of parents and siblings, more regularly than Ivorians, although the use by the former of informal transmission channels raises some concern. But it also explains why Ghanaians transferred more savings on return and were able to invest them in more productive initiatives, such as the development of private businesses. However, these types of initiatives are not only influenced by migrants' experiences in the host country(ies), enabling them to acquire and bring back different forms of capital which are of use back home, but also by the opportunities and constraints that they encounter after return in their country of origin.

The human capital gains of élite return migrants embraced a wide spectrum of different knowledge and skills and a great deal of practical expertise. Most migrants considered this acquisition of human capital critical for their work, and claimed they had tried to introduce some new ideas, methods or procedures in their workplace. This kind of initiative turned out to be not always an easy task, because of the difficulties and tensions with colleagues and other problems of re-adaptation that return migrants faced in their home context. In addition to human and financial capital, returnees acquired social capital abroad. They established both personal and professional contacts which they kept alive after return. They also gained useful language skills and an overall broader outlook, which helped them to maintain old and to establish new productive relationships abroad.

In general return migrants considered social and financial capital of somewhat less importance for their work than human capital. But before attention can be turned to how these different forms of capital were employed by élite return migrants back home, and how this has affected the development of their home societies and economies, the conditions under which these migrants acquire different kinds of capital deserve closer attention. The next chapter therefore deals in more detail with the migrants' study, work and life experiences abroad.

Chapter Seven

Ghanaian and Ivorian Élites in Europe and North America

In the previous chapter it was seen that the development potential of Ghanaian and Ivorian highly-skilled migrants who return home is significantly influenced by their migration experience. To better understand exactly what comprises the "added value" of return migrants we need to look in more detail at the life and activities they led in the host country(ies). These are important determinants of the resources they take home upon return and which consequently shape their development potential after return. The education and training that migrants received abroad are important, but also their working and everyday life experiences. The experience of working abroad crucially affects their development potential, as this enables migrants to earn money, gain practical knowledge and skills and establish fruitful contacts, all of which are valuable back home. Thus, a better grasp of the migrants' experiences abroad, and of the circumstances under which they returned, is necessary before the impact of their return can be assessed.

Migration Motives and Dynamics

This section explores the reasons why Ghanaians and Ivorians have emigrated, and possibly moved back or forth to another country. It provides an account of the general dynamics of their migratory movements. Special emphasis is focused on what these two groups of migrants have in common as well as on their main differences.

Frequency, Reasons and Timing of Migration in the Life Course

First of all there is an important difference between the two countries in the propensity to move: 43 per cent of the Ghanaians compared to only 29 per cent of the Ivorians had migrated at least twice, and 18 per cent of the former and 8 per cent of the latter had moved at least three times. About one half of the multiple-mobile returnees had moved directly from one destination country to another without returning home. The proportion of those who undertook such a "transilient" migration increased with subsequent moves.

Study and training constituted by far the most important motive for the initial emigration of the great majority of the respondents (Table 7-1). Highly-skilled migration occurring for educational purposes was also found in Asia (Iredale et al., 2002).

Table 7-1 Migration motives for subsequent migrations, by country (%)

Main migration motive	Côte d'Ivoire			Ghana		
	Mig1	Mig2	Mig3	Mig1	Mig2	Mig3
Study/training	96.7	74.4	41.7	81.2	53.0	46.4
Work/business	2.0	23.3	41.7	7.1	31.8	42.9
Join/follow family member(s)	0.7	2.3	–	8.4	12.1	10.7
Seek asylum	–	–		0.6	1.5	–
Other	0.7	–	16.7	2.6	–	–
No response	–	–	–	–	1.5	–
TOTAL	100.0	100.0	100.0	100.0	100.0	100.0
Valid cases	(150)	(43)	(12)	(154)	(66)	(28)

However, as mentioned in the previous chapter, the specific contextual reasons for which different "generations" of Ghanaians and Ivorians decided, or were encouraged, to move abroad. A 48-year-old professor who had studied with a scholarship in France illustrated these differences in the Ivorian context:

> At the level of students, the cycle here started in 1946. Because when President Houphouët-Boigny became a member of parliament in this country there were no intellectuals, there were no technicians and it was necessary to train all those people. Hence a group of about 180 students was sent to high school in France so that they could achieve the Baccalauréat, because since colonisation until that moment there was no Baccalauréat here. When they returned with their degree they were called the *aventuriers*

> (adventurers) since they had left on a ship called *L'Aventure*. And it was a real adventure for them because they were young people of 12 to 15 years who sometimes even knew little about a town, who came from their little village and who found themselves in France, it was – I really don't know! This was at the beginning of the sixties, at the beginning of independence. After that, every parent who had the means wanted to send his son to Europe with the hope that he would come back with the knowledge of the whites. He had to go and come back with the secret of the whites. There has been a wave of those people who left either with a scholarship or were sponsored by their family until '65. From that date onwards government preferred that people remained on site to study because they could be better controlled. When they went to Europe they came back with some Western ideas, they wanted democracy, they wanted that and things which the administration did not want because they came back as protesters. That wave has passed and progressively new courses were introduced here. But when starting in the nineties the school system has known its first big crisis, and every time the school has problems there is a great mass of people who are sent to France or to the United States.[1]

The Ghanaian education system suffered from similar difficulties but these started earlier. A description was provided by this 45-year-old returnee who did a Masters and a Doctorate in Sweden:

> [I did] my first degree at the University of Ghana. You know the '80s was quite a turbulent period here with the revolution and it affected the university. We were out there doing task force collecting, helping farmers and so on and then the whole crisis started within the student movement and whether we could put our schooling on hold, while doing revolution, all this. But it affected the academic calendar quite considerably from the late seventies, '79 onwards, so I left the university eventually in '82.

Another Ivorian professor illustrated the current problems affecting the public university in his country:

> … today you cannot say to your children you remain here in Côte d'Ivoire as you know very well that the study environment is pretty bad. We are in

1 This account confirms what N'Diaye (1969) had found in his early study on West African students in France: going to study in the métropole is an important challenge for personal realisation since there is a strong myth of abroad.

> a university which works a little bit the other way around. Our academic years are completely truncated because there have been strikes and strikes that never ended and that has contributed to a complete drop in the quality of education. The government was also no longer able to mobilise the resources, those were also problems for which the quality of teaching has considerably deteriorated. And that is what today pushes the majority of the élite to send their children abroad, to Morocco, to France and a bit everywhere. And those who do not have the means are those who leave their children here.

Apparently, what has remained unchanged across time is the élite's basic demand for quality education.

Only a very small proportion of the returned migrants initially went abroad to work or to do business. That professional reasons prevailed in the migration decision-making of more Ghanaians than Ivorians is not surprising considering the greater hardship experienced by the former. A 45-year-old Ghanaian returnee who emigrated to work in a multinational petroleum company in Gabon recalled the difficult years:

> …'81–'82 was a very, very, very bad period for Ghana and … there were ten of us children in my family and six of them are after me, six boys. They were all in school-going age and it was very difficult. My father died … in 1982 and all these factors made me really want to leave and go do something else… I was very lucky with this company, after three months they decided to keep me much longer … [and it was] extremely helpful to my family.

There were many problems which have pushed the educated élite out to search for better opportunities. A 58-year-old Ghanaian architect who returned from Canada in 1977 explained why he left again in 1982 first to work briefly in Nigeria and then again in Canada before he resettled for good in Accra in 1993:

> It was a period when the political scene in Ghana was becoming very convoluted. We had the military regime at that time which had failed to live up to its promise … civilians were rising up in protest. I came in just at the beginning of those troubles and the economy was just about to go into a tailspin. I was well paid, I had a nice life, I was paid very well, but the country was incredibly unstable and within the next five years the economy and politics went from bad to worse. Even though as an

> architect I was getting a lot of commission, very, very few were getting jobs because inflation was just rampant, crazy, and … the brain drain had started. Huge numbers of workers were leaving, principally to go to Nigeria, but then to other countries as well. So even the buildings we were designing, there were fewer and fewer workmen to execute them. It got to a point after five years when I decided that this is not the way I want to live my life. Two or three coups d'état had occurred within that time and the situation looked totally bleak and helpless. So after five years I decided well, maybe I should go back to Canada. So I left and I went back … I already had been fortunate taking up citizenship papers so going back was no problem all.

Overall only two Ghanaians said they left their home country to seek asylum abroad. This suggests that political persecution was not an important issue in the two country contexts. Yet the data obtained from in-depth interviews shows that persecution and political exile have been a reality in Ghana.[2] An example is provided by this 52-year-old person who was adopted by an English family in Ghana and then followed his adoptive father into exile in the United Kingdom:

> He first worked as attorney general of Ghana for Nkrumah, and then he became the special advisor to him which was why in '66 when the coup happened he was deported and so I came here.

That 11 per cent of the Ghanaians who responded to the questionnaire declared that their fathers went abroad for political reasons shows that, if this problem no longer represented a major concern for the younger generation, it had been quite important for the older one.

A very limited number of respondents emigrated the first time to follow or join a family member. Ghanaian women were more likely to have left for this specific reason, as were those who migrated and returned more than once. Considering that most respondents originally left the home country for motives related to their education, it is not surprising that 90 per cent of them were less than 30 years old when they first moved. The median age at the time of first departure was 24

2 Another explanation consistent with this limited number of responses is that they knew they had to leave for political reasons but, rather than experiencing the trauma of flight and claiming asylum, they preferred to use their qualifications and contacts to obtain scholarships.

years, but this generally increased with subsequent migrations. Those who emigrated when they were younger (i.e. less than 25 years old) had a greater likelihood of having moved more than once compared to those who were older at that time. Respondents who left the first time when they were very young (i.e. less than 20 years) were also significantly more likely to have stayed away longer.

Date of Migration, Duration of Absence and Destination

Since the timing of the initial and subsequent migrations should be examined in an historical perspective, three specific time periods were identified in relation to the socio-economic and political developments that occurred in each country setting. In Ghana, the first period is constituted by the years before 1976 when the economic crisis became more acute due to rampant inflation rates. The second period stretches between 1976 and 1991 and distinguishes itself first by serious economic hardship and subsequently by a slow recovery which started after 1981, the year of the last military coup. The last period began in 1992 with the re-establishment of constitutional rule. From the survey it emerged that 26 per cent of the Ghanaians interviewed originally left before 1976, 55 per cent in the course of the second period and 20 per cent during the third period.

In Côte d'Ivoire the first period is, instead, represented by the years preceding 1980, when the economic crisis started. The second period (1980–1993) is characterised by a worsening economic situation; and the third period, which started in 1994 with the devaluation of the CFA Franc, by a slow recovery of the economy. The Ivorian respondents who initially emigrated during the first period represent 35 per cent and those who left during the second and third respectively 55 per cent and 9 per cent. The Ivorians who first emigrated before 1976 constitute only 5 per cent.

Therefore, Ghanaian respondents emigrated earlier compared to the Ivorians. But they also stayed abroad much longer. The median total time spent abroad by Ghanaians is 11 years and that of Ivorians only six years. The duration of absence of the Ghanaians significantly exceeds that of the Ivorians, no matter whether it was their first, second, third or fourth migration. One of the reasons why Ghanaians spent so much more time abroad is that they invested a considerable amount not only in studying but also in working. Cross-tabulations show that, on average, those who did not work stayed abroad for less time.

The findings confirm that spatial mobility patterns have changed over time. Whereas the respondents' fathers, following colonial traditions, migrated mainly to Europe, the returnees themselves moved increasingly to North America. The fathers of 85 per cent of the Ivorians went to France and those of 56 per cent of the Ghanaians left for the United Kingdom. A considerable number of the latter also moved to another African country (16 per cent). Overall, only 8 per cent of the Ghanaians' fathers and 1 per cent of the Ivorian fathers had migrated to the United States.

Table 7-2 shows, in contrast, that at their first migration 66 per cent of the Ivorian respondents went to France and 47 per cent of the Ghanaians to the United Kingdom. A considerable number of Ghanaians later moved on to the United States as another English-speaking country, while many Ivorians migrated onwards to the French-speaking part of Canada.

Table 7-2 Destinations for subsequent migrations, by country (%)

Destinations	Côte d'Ivoire			Ghana		
	Mig1	Mig2	Mig3	Mig1	Mig2	Mig3
France	66.0	41.9	25.0	–	3.0	7.1
UK	1.3	7.0	–	46.8	37.9	25.0
Other Europe	16.0	18.6	25.0	16.9	18.2	–
United States	8.0	14.0	8.3	22.7	25.8	28.6
Canada	7.3	16.3	25.0	7.8	3.0	3.6
Africa	1.3	2.3	16.7	5.2	10.6	25.0
Other	–	–	–	0.6	1.5	10.7
TOTAL	100.0	100.0	100.0	100.0	100.0	100.0
Valid cases	(150)	(43)	(12)	(154)	(66)	(28)

A 47-year-old Ghanaian lawyer who lived and worked in London at the time of the interview explains the difference between the mobility of his own generation and that of his father:

> Obviously we are more interested in seeing the world you know, whereas my father's generation is more conservative … that sort of changes, they find it disruptive … but you know my generation and the one that's coming

> after wouldn't think twice about going to live wherever. I mean, they say you'll find Ghanaians in Iceland which is probably true. I've got a younger brother in Finland, he is in university in Helsinki and I went there last summer. He is quite at home there, unlike my father's generation, they would have a problem with that.

There is no doubt that spatial mobility has increased over time also due to world-wide improvements in transportation and communication systems. A 59-year-old Ivorian returnee who studied architecture in Italy referred explicitly to these recent developments:

> I think that exchanges today have become much easier than they used to be 30 years ago when there were no newspapers. We actually didn't have access to all those newspapers, we didn't have access to all kinds of media in general. Today it's no longer the same, our children have an open-mindedness that we could not have, we could not even dream of having. Because I did all my primary school in a village and when you were living in the village there were those who passed the whole primary cycle without ever seeing a car for example.

The analysis confirms that migrants more frequently opt to go to a country which is more distant in spatial and cultural terms when they have already migrated at least once. It is generally assumed that at this stage a migrant has already acquired some experience abroad and possesses more information and knowledge, more extended and better consolidated networks and also the financial means. With less of all these things, at their first departure, prospective migrants prefer to move to a place where they will encounter fewer difficulties and incur a smaller risk. Early migration studies (Lee, 1966; Ravenstein, 1885) were already postulating that migrants proceed step-by-step. Nonetheless, as seen in Chapter Two, research on Sahelian migrants shows how even poorly educated and illiterate migrants nowadays move from their small villages directly to a big European or North American capital city.[3]

For both country samples, the choice of an initial destination was heavily influenced by considerations related to education.[4]

---

3 See for example Blion and Rigoni (2001) and Timera and Quiminal (2001).

4 Blaud (2001: 149–56) stresses that the decision of African migrants who go abroad to study is based on five main considerations: (1) conditions set within the framework of scholarships; (2) opportunities to enroll in higher education

Language obviously assumes primary importance in such a decision but consideration is also given to the educational and professional opportunities existing in the different emigration contexts. This 26-year-old Ivorian student who was interviewed in Paris explained why he did not go to an English-speaking country:

> … France seemed the best opportunity because I had family there and I also knew the language. So that is why we have immediately opted for France… in a francophone country… I better understand what happens … whereas in the US, in the UK, I would have needed a period of adaptation … and there's not necessarily enough time.

Cross-tabulations suggested that the Ivorians who while abroad had achieved a Doctorate were more likely to have moved directly to Europe, whereas those who obtained a Masters were more likely to have gone straight to North America. The opposite is the case for the Ghanaians as those with a Masters were more likely to have studied in Europe, whereas those with a Doctorate had a much higher probability to have earned it in North America. This reflects the fact that for Ivorians it is easier to get a scholarship to study in France and for Ghanaians to study in the United States. The account of a 46-year-old Ghanaian professor who explained why he wanted to send his son to the United States rather than to the United Kingdom confirms this trend:

> It's more expensive in the UK and there are more opportunities for getting scholarships in the US. So after paying for him for a first year my hope is that he will find some kind of scholarship for minorities in the US.

This respondent had himself decided to go to study Economics in Germany because, he said, there was ready funding available there. But the question of funding is only one of the issues that are considered by prospective migrants. Some also carefully take the characteristics of different education systems into account, as for example this 38-year-old Ivorian who regretted having received all his higher education in France:

> I preferred the Anglo-Saxon context compared to the French context on the human level as well as on the educational level. Because I think I

---

establishments abroad; (3) presence of family and friends; (4) language; and (5) type of education or training sought.

> would have preferred a system which left more choice than a system which was, I would say, more didactic. From my viewpoint the French system took a very didactic approach with some courses which were more or less imposed, with a mechanism to monitor marks which remained very scholastic. You had the impression of being still in school. Although constraining, the university in the United States offered a more important choice for personal development. It would teach you faster how to perform well in an enterprise for example, or in the human field.

Information regarding possibilities of finding a job or improving one's own professional situation is obviously more valuable for those who go abroad with the intention of working. A 45-year-old Ghanaian lawyer went to the United Kingdom for a few months and then moved on to the United States to seek some legal experience:

> ... I was sort of dithering: should I go to the US or should I stay in the UK? Then I decided to go to the US because everybody told me it would be easier to get work.

Cross-tabulations seem to confirm this statement because the Ghanaians who directly migrated to North America were significantly more likely to have worked abroad longer than average compared to those who moved to other parts of the world. Although international flows from Ghana and Côte d'Ivoire are becoming more diversified, spatial mobility patterns continue to be shaped by historical and cultural ties and by contemporary communication, commercial and political links. The majority of Ghanaian respondents migrated first to the United Kingdom and most of the Ivorians to France. But in general there is a growing interest in the United States – at least, this clearly emerged from in-depth interviews. According to this 48-year-old Ghanaian who had lived there it is because:

> Traditionally Ghanaians love America. They feel America is their dream ... that's their whole dream, to be out there in America.

Instead, a 59-year-old Ivorian who was interviewed in Paris emphasised another major factor that constrains the migrants' choice of destination:

> ... there's greater information on the United States. The radios, the television show only one culture, the culture which is in fashion is that of

> the United States. And then there's the fact that the consulates humiliate a little bit too much the people ... especially in French consulates when you want papers to come here. The United States, they give them to you when you are qualified ... That's what the French do not realise, that they are in the process of losing a lot of good people.

Cross-tabulations reveal that respondents who migrated initially to North America were less likely to engage in further migration or multiple returns. This finding is consistent with the United States and Canada being regarded as the "ultimate" or most "desirable" migration destination.

Migration Networks and Systems of Mutual Support

Moving to one place rather than to another is, of course, also a matter of financial resources. That is one of the reasons why migrant networks assume such a primary importance in the determination of the direction and volume of migration flows. The findings of this study demonstrate that the networks of Ghanaian migrants are far more extended than those of Ivorian migrants. Returnees were asked if they had any brothers or sisters and whether any of them was currently living abroad.[5] The analysis of the responses suggests that Ghanaians, both males and females, are more prone to migration because a far greater proportion of their siblings were living abroad.[6] Among all those who had only one brother, for example, 65 per cent of the Ghanaians and only 24 per cent of the Ivorians indicated that he had left the home country.

The findings show that the greater the number of brothers of a respondent, the greater the likelihood that some were living abroad. But this trend occurs only up to a certain stage. Starting from a certain number of brothers, four in Ghana and three in Côte d'Ivoire, the proportion of those who emigrated declines. This is presumably due to the costs of migration and the distribution of roles and responsibilities within the family or household. The analysis also corroborates the assumption that gender significantly influences the propensity to move, as a far smaller number of sisters were living abroad. This gender-determined inequality in

5 It was always specified that reference was made exclusively to brothers and sisters having the same mother and the same father.

6 The Ivorians have a slightly higher number of siblings than the Ghanaians – 5.2 as against 3.9.

opportunities is more marked in the Ivorian than in the Ghanaian sample, since only 14 per cent of the Ivorians but 38 per cent of the Ghanaians who only had one sister indicated that she had left. As in the case of the brothers, the more sisters the greater the chances that at least one of them had moved away, but here, too, the trend is reversed at a certain point with an increasing number of sisters.

As was noted earlier, migrants are more inclined to move to a place where some family or kin are already settled because these can provide valuable information and support. The assistance that is obtained upon arrival at destination can help in reducing significantly both the financial and psychic costs of migration. A 45-year-old Ghanaian who first moved to the United Kingdom and then to the United States illustrated the type of help she received:

> I went to the UK now and then … it was not easy to go to the UK, but it gave you a break from this place. So whatever money we had saved previously, we could always go on these charter flights, students flights to the UK and stay with an aunt or something and do a little work for two or three months and come back with a little money to pay back yourself for the airfare, and a little more … [then] a friend of mine … invited me over [to the US] so she arranged for me to have my papers and had me stay … [then] I found that I knew an old friend who lived in Boston and I went and lived with him.

In addition, migrants receive vital information regarding the situation in the prospective country of immigration. Many of the interview accounts describe how and from whom information regarding education, work or accommodation was obtained. Relatives, friends or just contacts provided by someone else play a pivotal role in this respect as they help in influencing the migrants' choice of destination. But material or financial support is also a recurrent element which is exchanged in these social networks.

A 43-year-old Ivorian returnee explained how, with the assistance of his brother, he made a successful move from France to Canada:

> When I was in Montpellier, my older brother asked me to send him my resumé so that I could be registered there … When I got to Montreal, the same day I found employment … I arrived in Montreal at 1.30 p.m., we took the subway and got home and then Siméon, my older brother … said – let's go and see a man whose name is Stefan. He's a Hungarian,

> it's through him that I used to send you money ... So we went to see him and he said ... but who's this guy? How much money did he swallow?! Let's put him straight to work and start with the dish washing. And it was as simple as that, I started working for Stefan and he used to give me US$6 an hour, and I did not have to pay for my food. Through that work I could give money to Siméon, so that he could start his research in African linguistics ...

This shows how not only solidarity but also reciprocity works in practice. Roles can be inverted, with the one who received help starting to help the one who previously provided help. Several other examples were found which illustrate that the older and more successful siblings who are already independent are generally expected to help the younger ones who are not yet able to cater for themselves. But migrants have strong obligations not only towards their siblings abroad and back home but, of course, also with regard to their parents. This explains why siblings and parents are among the main beneficiaries of the financial assistance that migrants channel home in the form of remittances. Additional direct help may sometimes be needed on site back home to manage the family firm or assist ageing or ill parents, for example. Who among the siblings has to remain at home or to return to assume such a specific responsibility is often the result of a more or less explicit negotiation involving various family members.

And yet, the quantitative analysis revealed that only 18 per cent in each sample consulted with other family members before they left the first time. For 23 per cent of the Ivorians and 14 per cent of the Ghanaians it was the parents who took this decision. That very few made this decision together with their spouse is due to the fact that most were not married at that time. At subsequent migrations, in fact, an increasing number involved their spouse in the migration decision-making, whereas the role of parents and other family members declined.

Migrants' Experiences Abroad

In the last chapter it was seen that what return migrants did abroad determines what kinds of capital they acquired and brought back home. This section assesses more in detail the education and training that migrants received while they were away. It also examines their foreign work experience which, as was seen before, is of particular relevance.

The migrants' residence status, their lifestyle and social relationships in the host communities are secondary factors which also deserve some consideration.

Education and Training

Almost all the returned migrants who participated in the survey studied abroad or received some form of education or training – 99 per cent of the Ivorians and 97 per cent of the Ghanaians. That education represented the main migration motive for only 81 per cent of the Ghanaians demonstrates that many of those who left mainly for work or another reason ended up also studying while abroad.

Tables 7.3 and 7.4 show that the Ivorian respondents achieved a higher education level while they were away. The data show that most Ghanaians left home with an undergraduate degree and achieved a Masters level abroad. In contrast, most Ivorians went abroad with a Masters or equivalent degree and completed a Doctorate abroad.

This 58-year-old Ghanaian returnee for instance did both a Bachelor and a Masters abroad:

> I left Ghana in 1964 to go to the US to study architecture in Washington DC. I stayed in Washington for five years at the end of which I got my Bachelor of Science in Architecture. Then I went on to New York City where I attended the Pratt Institute and in 1970-71 I got my Masters of Science in Architecture. After I worked in New York City for about a year, then I went to Montreal, Canada in 1971 and I worked there for about six years'.

Some returned migrants left with a scholarship whereas others either did not apply for or did not obtain one. The latter were either funded by others or had to fund themselves through working abroad, or both. A 36-year-old Ivorian explains how her and her siblings studies abroad were in great part funded by her parents:

> ... when the first of us left, that was in '82-'83 ... our parents had more resources because the economic situation was better ... and we were only two or three abroad. When we ended up being five or six in Europe it's been difficult and they have asked us to contribute to pay for the rent, the food and fees ... We have tried to find a scholarship, something that

Table 7-3 Highest education level achieved by Ghanaians back home and abroad

Highest degree achieved back home	Highest degree achieved abroad				
	Undergrad. Studies	Masters or equivalent	Doctorate or equivalent	Other	Total
High school or less	15	32	5	2	54
%	10.0	21.3	3.3	1.3	36.0
Undergraduate studies	7	62	11	3	83
%	4.7	41.3	7.3	2.0	55.3
Masters or equivalent	–	4	1	–	5
%	–	2.7	0.7	–	3.3
Other	2	4	–	2	7
%	1.3	2.7	–	1.3	4.7
TOTAL	24	102	17	7	150
%	16.0	68.0	11.3	4.7	100.0

> my oldest brother had never done … I worked in a night-club, it was a student job, I had to look after the cloakroom and I also worked on a part-time basis in a dental practice …

Only 17 per cent of the Ivorian and 12 per cent of the Ghanaian respondents did nothing but study whilst abroad. The majority in each sample both worked and studied, often taking jobs that were related to their training. The professional and work experience that migrants gained in the host countries enriched them from many points of view: indeed, this is one of the key findings of the study, especially as regards development impacts for the home countries.

Professional and Work Experience

Whereas the Ghanaians stayed abroad twice as long as the Ivorians, they worked on average for a period four times longer. The median length of time that Ghanaians worked abroad is nine years; for Ivorians it is only

Table 7-4 Highest education level achieved by Ivorians back home and abroad

Highest degree achieved back home	Highest degree achieved abroad					
	High school	Under-grad. studies	Masters or equivalent	Doctorate or equivalent	Other	Total
High school or less	2	13	24	18	1	58
%	1.3	8.7	16.1	12.1	0.7	38.9
Under-graduate studies	–	1	10	8	2	21
%	–	0.7	6.7	5.4	1.3	14.1
Masters or equivalent	–	1	22	37	3	63
%	–	0.7	14.8	24.8	2	42.3
Doctorate or equivalent	–	1	1	–	2	4
%	–	0.7	0.7	–	1.3	2.7
Other		–	2	1	–	8
%	–	–	1.3	0.7	–	5.4
TOTAL	2	16	59	64	8	149
%	1.3	10.7	39.6	43,0	5.4	100.0

two years. Furthermore, the Ghanaians who migrated to North America first had a greater likelihood of acquiring more extensive work experience than those who went straight to Europe. They also had a greater chance of having worked in training-related jobs for a period exceeding the average. In general, all the respondents who stayed in Europe first were less likely to have worked for very long in jobs related to their training.

An analysis of the types of jobs that respondents reported having had abroad reveals that the Ghanaians did much more varied work than the Ivorians. Among those who worked while they were away, 26 per cent of Ghanaians but only 3 per cent of Ivorians did at least four different kinds of work, 50 per cent against 18 per cent did three and 79 per cent compared to 42 per cent did two. Table 7-5 shows that the Ivorians held foreign occupations of a higher level than the Ghanaians.

Table 7-5 Kinds of work done abroad, by country (%)

Kinds of work*	Côte d'Ivoire			Ghana		
	Work1	Work2	Work3	Work1	Work2	Work3
1 Legislators, senior officials, managers	21.8	21.2	18.2	3.0	4.7	8.8
2 Professionals	40.3	23.1	31.8	29.6	21.5	27.9
3 Technicians and assistant professionals	21.0	11.5	22.7	16.3	22.4	11.8
4 Clerks	0.8	7.7	4.5	7.4	7.5	7.4
5 Service work and shop/ market sales work	6.5	19.2	13.6	21.5	26.2	23.5
6 Skilled agriculture and fishery workers	3.2	3.8	–	–	–	–
7 Crafts and related trades workers	1.6	3.8	4.5	–	2.8	1.5
8 Plant/machine operators and assemblers	–	1.9	–	2.2	–	5.9
9 Elementary occupations	4.8	7.7	4.4	20.0	15.0	13.2
TOTAL	100.0	100.0	100.0	100.0	100.0	100.0
Valid cases	(124)	(52)	(22)	(135)	(107)	(68)

* All categories are at ISCO levels 1–3 requiring at least an education beginning at age 17 or 18 and leading to an award not equivalent to a first university degree: http://www.ilo.org/public/english/bureau/stat/class/isco.html.

The largest share of the Ivorians worked as professionals, especially in teaching or scientific research. These activities are also relatively well represented in the Ghanaian sample. A considerable number in each sample worked as business, legal, social science or related professionals and in professions such as finance or sales, business services agents or trade brokers. These two accounts illustrate two successful examples which fall into the first category:

> … when I quit the Institut d'Assurance de Paris I did not have to search for long before I got my first job. I was employed that same year, three weeks after having left the IAP, in one of the most important insurance broker companies… and I was hired to work as a technical and commercial cadre … (38-year-old Ivorian returnee)

> I went into Columbia in 1980 and did Economics, which I wanted to do, finished that after four years, went on to work on Wall Street. It was the eighties and Wall Street was doing very well. I worked for three years with Morgan Stanley in New York City and then went on to graduate school at Yale School of Management and did the two years '86 to '88. And then I came back to Wall Street and worked with Solomon Brothers for a couple of years. (42-year-old Ghanaian returnee)

The number of returnees who said they worked as corporate managers abroad is quite high, particularly in the Ivorian sample. The accounts below are examples drawn from London, New York and Paris respectively:

> I worked in my own [dental] surgery… I was the principal. I had a partner and over the period we acquired two practices from different parts of London and we had people working with us as well, so we expanded the practice. (48-year-old Ghanaian returnee who spent several years in Italy, Zimbabwe and the United Kingdom)

> I actually started my company somewhere in 1993 I believe. That's a while back and it was a computer set-up, very much like a company called Kinkos … a public facility where people come and use computers, colour copiers and you pay for the time used on the machines … I set up a company like that in Manhatta. (40-year-old Ghanaian returnee who lived in the United States)

> … in 1989 I created the firm of chartered accountants … then in '99 I created the transport company … and in 2000 I created Net-express, an industrial cleaning company. (43-year-old Ivorian migrant who was residing in Paris at the time of the interview)

From cross-tabulations it was found that those who left home when they were younger and those who received most of their education abroad had a greater probability to have worked abroad longer and done so especially in training-related jobs (Tables 7-6 and 7-7).

That it is more difficult to find a good job abroad for migrants who bring a higher degree from home was confirmed by information obtained through in-depth interviews. This 35-year-old Ghanaian migrant, for example, who did a Masters in Economics and Statistics in Ghana, explained why he had to go back to college in the United Kingdom:

Table 7-6 Cross-tabulation: first emigrated when aged under 25 by worked abroad longer than average (Ghana)

Ghana	Worked abroad longer than average		Total
First emigrated when aged under 25	Yes	No	
Yes	43	41	84
No	20	50	70
Total	63	91	154

Notes: Risk estimate 2.62; significance: 1%.

Table 7-7 Cross-tabulation: first emigrated when aged under 25 by worked abroad longer than average (Côte d'Ivoire)

Côte d'Ivoire	Worked abroad longer than average		Total
First emigrated when aged under 25	Yes	No	
Yes	48	43	91
No	21	38	59
Total	69	81	150

Notes: Risk estimate 2.02; significance: 5%.

> It wasn't easy to come with a degree from Africa. People would ask you what did you study in? Checking out if you spoke English, even if you were communicating in English … it was not common in the City to see a black boy working here … and after just doing sort of odd clerical jobs I came into the area of accountancy. It came to me naturally as something I could build as a profession. I'd always wanted to be a trader in a bank but I realised I needed some sort of qualification to pull me up. So … I did the Chartered Institute of Management Accounting and … I passed the first time back to back in two years. Not that I'm clever, because I think I'm just average, but when you are looking after yourself, you cannot fail … It's not like your parents feeding you and you just have to pass. I had to excel so I passed in two years and became an accountant. After this I'd always wanted to fulfil my dream which was to go to London School of Economics. I, I'd always viewed London School of Economics as a

> place which prepared African leaders. Not that I wanted to be a leader, I thought well if Nkrumah and the rest met in LSE and did their political revolution maybe the finance revolution could be launched from LSE. I was also deeply attracted to the depth of economists, the fact that they'd won Nobels and I also wanted to be part of that. So I further punished myself by going to school and going to London School of Economics to do my Masters in finance.

Cross-tabulations confirmed that many of those who had most of their higher education abroad were obliged during their studies to do some little jobs to earn some money. However, the fact that they received most of their higher education in the host country helped them to find training-related jobs more easily in the long run. Many Ivorians who emigrated with a Masters did not work initially, but rather focused all their attention on studying with a view to obtaining a Doctorate. Whether they did not need to work because they had a scholarship and they did not have to send back any remittances, or if they did not want to work in a lower level job, remains an open question. It probably is a mixture of both reasons.

Doing lower-level menial work can be hard, especially for a highly qualified person like this 48-year-old Ghanaian returnee who obtained a Masters in Engineering in his home country and had difficulties finding a good job in the United States:

> Yes, I had to begin on a farm and you can imagine how that felt. From a top engineer to a farm hand, but I took it just to get my papers changed and it was a seasonal job … it was an old historic farm and things had to be kept at the historic level. So I was in charge of maintenance and everything on the farm was practically under my care. It was fun for me, it was close to being outdoors and just repairing things.

Table 7-5 confirms that more Ghanaians than Ivorians worked abroad in elementary occupations. Certain migrants had to do all kinds of work abroad not only to finance their studies and cover their living expenses abroad but also to send some money back home. When asked what type of work he did when he lived in the United States, this 40-year-old Ghanaian manager replied:

> Oh my goodness, if I told you what kind of work that I did there, it was incredible! I was a taxi driver, I was a bus boy, a dishwasher, a security guard, I was a messenger, I mean all the odd jobs. I worked in a store

> as a clerical person, and you know just saved that money to support me through school. So I did all the menial jobs that you can imagine and had just a rough life in college.

Among those who took lower-level occupations there is a high percentage who did service work and shop and sales work. The number of those who worked as personal and protective service workers is also relatively important. This is a particularly common occupation for West African immigrants in Paris, as suggested by this 33-year-old Ivorian migrant, who had to work because his family was unable to finance his studies beyond the second year of university:

> … when I was doing my undergraduate studies … it became more and more difficult in Côte d'Ivoire. It therefore became necessary to do some little jobs, you know. To study in the mornings and in the evenings to hurry to do some little jobs. Also because black students, I can tell you, it's not gleaming jobs that they reserve for us! There are two fields: either security services, or cleaning offices.

As will be seen in the next section, an important factor influencing the migrants' job search is the type of residence status they have in the host country.

Residence Status and Difference in Lifestyles

Finding employment, and particularly a good job, while away often remains the prerogative of those migrants who have an adequate work permit and that in turn depends on their residence status abroad. France has generally been very protective of its labour market (McLaughlan and Salt, 2002: 83). Foreign nationals with a student visa are not allowed to work, and once students have completed their course of studies they must return home. In the United Kingdom graduates can now switch into work permit employment if they meet certain criteria.

The residence status of migrants often influences the outcomes of their job search. This 33-year-old Ivorian student continued working in several precarious jobs before he found something related to his training:

> … there also is a problem of papers. This system is very complex, when you don't have papers … because I only had a student entry permit.

> When you only have that it's very difficult to work … But when … I had my daughter … I was able to obtain a residence permit. With this residence permit I became able to apply my knowledge, I have worked as an assistant teacher …

Cross-tabulations confirmed that the Ivorians who never had a permanent residence status were far less likely to have worked abroad compared to those who had obtained such a status or acquired the local citizenship.[7] The Ivorians who did not have permanent residence status had more limited chances of working in both training-unrelated and training-related jobs, but the likelihood of their working in this last type of job was even less. This was not necessarily the case for the Ghanaians but they too had a smaller probability of working abroad for extended periods if their residence status was problematic in some way.

The majority of Ghanaians and Ivorians never had a permanent residence status in the country where they moved first. When all migrations are considered, twice as many Ghanaians (40 per cent) as Ivorians (20 per cent) turn out to have either acquired a permanent residence status or obtained/kept a foreign citizenship. Cross-tabulations in the Ghanaian sample show that whether migrants had got a permanent residence status or not is very significantly linked to the length of their residence and work abroad (Tables 7-8 and 7-9). The longer time migrants stayed abroad, the more likely they were to have acquired a permanent residence status.

The returnees who remained abroad longer and left the home country when they were younger were more likely to have had a more permanent residence status abroad, including local citizenship. They were also more likely to have received most of their higher education abroad. In addition, those with a permanent residence status or local citizenship appeared to have a greater propensity to move. This seems to substantiate the argument of some authors who have stressed that tightening immigration policies may, in fact, produce the opposite effects to those desired (Blion, 2001). Migrants may be too concerned to return or move on to another place because they fear they will not be permitted to enter the country again. A significant relationship between returnees' residence status and destination was only detected in the Ghanaian sample. A greater proportion of those who moved to North America kept permanent residence status

7 These were done on the basis of the residence status that migrants had in the last country they lived before returning home.

Table 7-8 Cross-tabulation: never had permanent resident status by stayed abroad longer than average (Ghana)

Ghana	Stayed abroad longer than average		Total
Never had permanent resident status	Yes	No	
Yes	12	67	79
No	59	16	75
Total	71	83	154

Notes: Risk estimate 0.04; significance: 0.1%.

Table 7-9 Cross-tabulation: never had permanent resident status by stayed abroad longer than average (Côte d'Ivoire)

Côte d'Ivoire	Stayed abroad longer than average		Total
Never had permanent resident status	Yes	No	
Yes	34	66	100
No	39	11	50
Total	73	77	150

Notes: Risk estimate 0.15; Significance: 0.1%

or acquired local citizenship than those who moved to Europe or other parts of the world.

In order to discern the migrants' experiences abroad better, they were asked during in-depth interviews to describe the lifestyle they had abroad and to illustrate the differences between this and the one they used to lead back home. Very few of the respondents affirmed that life did not change much when they arrived in the host country. The migrants who had this perception were mainly those who were already familiar with the host country because they had visited it or lived there when they were young. The experience of this 31-year-old Ivorian who went to France to study illustrates one of these cases:

> … my lifestyle did not change as it's true I was very privileged because I was in The Hague. I had very good accommodation. I did not live on campus but had an apartment on a marina. Every week-end I went to Paris and stayed in a family house because my grandfather has a hotel in the 16th *arrondissement*. I really was not … disoriented because it's a city which I already knew and thus I had my landmarks.

Often the younger migrants – who at home were used to a more regimented lifestyle, in great part dictated by their parents – acquire sudden freedom when they go abroad. This applies particularly to young female migrants. This Ghanaian returnee was 18 years old when she started studying in London:

> I realised that even at that age in Ghana you are very sheltered. At that age you are not left on your own to take your own decisions, your parents are still guiding you, they are still feeding you. I never had to work before … so I was very much under the shelter and umbrella of my parents. Everything I had to consult with them. But when I went to England and it was like – fine we will find you a job, that's your money, you manage it yourself, you can go out as and when you want to, these are the keys to the house – and that was quite a shock for me.

Migrants' were struck by various aspects differentiating the lifestyle they had abroad and the one they used to have back home. The most obvious change involved with moving to the Northern hemisphere was related to the climate and food, as exemplified by these two stories:

> … my first day in Heathrow was not the best because I was not properly dressed … it was September, it wasn't too cold. But then somebody who had travelled from a hot country, who had never experienced this cold weather before, to be confronted so to say with this weather. I wept and I regretted ever taking that decision to go to England to study. (53-year-old Ghanaian returnee who did a Doctorate in the United Kingdom)

> … at my parents we used to eat European food but not every day, or a European dish along with an African dish … finding yourself in a context where you are obliged to eat nothing but that, from night to morning and morning to night, 24 hours out of 24 hours and 365 out of 365 days, I make a caricature in fact, but it's not the same thing! I ate at the university restaurant as everyone else but from time to time with the associations

etc. in those occasions there was African food to eat. (50-year-old Ivorian returnee who went to France to get a Doctorate)

Many migrants not only missed the warm climate they were used to back home but also the warmth and friendliness of their people. Some endured a strong feeling of loneliness, as for instance this Ivorian returned migrant who studied and worked in Paris:

> At the beginning ... it's was very hard, very very very hard, because you felt that the French are reserved people. Even if you lived on the same floor and you said Good morning to them they did not answer. And frankly that's very hard, because you didn't have someone to talk to, besides at school where you had friends. But afterwards everyone went home and you really were very lonely.

The 48-year-old Ghanaian engineer who lived in the United States emphasised what struck him positively in the local context:

> Everywhere, everybody seems to mind their own business. Unlike Ghanaians, Ghanaians will like to talk about you. Over there you can wear anything you want and feel at ease and nobody seems to bug you. The first thing a Ghanaian will talk about is your clothing, your look and whether you've got money or not, and things like that. It therefore can be quite irritating. In that respect I found myself pretty relaxed out there and I liked them because they are very carefree. And another good thing about them is that they never look down on what you are doing for a living, never. Down here in Africa, we would giggle if we saw a friend sweeping somebody's shop. It is considered demeaning. Over there it's a job and at the end of the day – hey let's meet, let's have a drink.

This returned migrant also drew attention to some of the differences that exist in the way people work in the United States and Ghana:

> ... there people work according to time. Okay, time is everything and you got to have a certain output of work. Here it's very different, I hadn't experienced this pace before leaving. I'd say that it's easy to get angry with somebody who doesn't work hard or you think he doesn't work hard for this, but it's the other side of it. If I wake up any of my workers on a Sunday, and I say look I need to do this so come and help me, they would come. In America they would bang the phone, they'll tell you – man, you

> don't call me over the weekend, you don't this, you don't that. So there's a difference in the way we do things here. So I think we work more with our hearts here than with the watch.

Time is perceived and managed differently in the two contexts. This was a common aspect to which returnees referred in the interviews. A 43-year-old Ghanaian media professional who studied and worked in the United Kingdom found that there is too much routine in Europe, an issue he visualised with humour in quite some detail:

> When you … work in England you have to take a train, you take a specific train every morning, you don't vary the train because if you do you will not get to work on time. Everything is a laid down pattern of events. The buses arrive at certain stops at certain times and you tune your life to those events. You tune your life to the TV, you tune your life to the lottery results at the weekend, you tune your life to everything, ordered life, even your holidays are ordered several months in advance, everything is an ordered existence. Your coffee break is at a set time, your lunch is at a set time, don't go before or after … Even the criminals, their decision to rob a house is based on the habits of the household, so their thievery is a habit, is based on society's dictates as to how and when it is a good time to rob, so they themselves are stealing at good times … Then we come to Ghana, I mean you have to be in this country like 20 minutes maximum and you'll know you are in a different world. 20 minutes from the time you land, you going through customs and it hits you. Forget about the heat, just look at the people who are supposed to be working at the airport, not one of them looks halfway efficient, they're slovenly in appearance, slovenly in the way they do things, the whole process of running an airport, and you think to yourself immediately so what if the plane lands in an emergency, will these people react in the same way they are reacting here? You come into the arrivals hall, its bedlam, and immediately you understand that the bedlam that is right there in front of you is just going to be extrapolated into a larger bedlam in the society into which you are going to. You can't find your suitcases, there's people milling there, who have no business being there, you don't know who they are. There's trolleys all over the place and also you find that the people who've just gotten off the plane from the society which we thought was so ordered, where they put their hands behind their back and did everything in a nice orderly fashion, they have changed. The same people who would act differently at Heathrow, they get here and it's like, get out of the way,

> move out of the way. They themselves have changed. It's like the journey down the Greenwich meridian has changed them.

The contrast existing between the individualistic values that characterise the Western context and the communal values on which emphasis is placed in African societies is an issue that was raised by this 36-year-old Ivorian migrant who did her Masters in Belgium:

> ... social relationships are not at all defined the same way. The big difference from my point of view is that in Europe one privileges the well-being of the individual, an individual has his importance. He is quickly conscious that he needs to do something with his life. Here you are always an element of a group or family, which means that personal ambitions and what you like to do is sometimes drowned in what you have to do to ensure correspondence between an idea or a social status at least and the family or social structure to which you belong. In Europe it's very different, the freedom is very great at the level of the individual because he can express things and even if they shock others they will anyway be tolerated.

The way communication occurs abroad was another aspect that impressed Ghanaian and Ivorian migrants, particularly the communication between children and their parents. On this, a 40-year-old Ghanaian returnee who spent two periods of her life in the United States to study said:

> I think we have a more formal relationship with our parents here ... [There] very sensitive issues can be discussed openly without any negative feelings towards anybody, whereas here the parent is always right ... generally people were a bit more open than here, I mean you learned to call a spade a spade. We have a very sort of roundabout way of dealing with issues that it's very difficult for us to call a spade a spade here in Ghana. But if you are not nice there's no way somebody will tell you in Ghana ... they will find some euphemisms that you know. In America a lot of people would not hesitate to tell you – you did XYZ wrong, let's move on, but here people bottle a lot inside and they are not very open.

The same issue was raised by a 45-year-old Ghanaian who also lived in the United States:

> ... it was a cultural shock for me, like I go to families on Thanksgiving and the way the kids talked to their parents – oh man don't be silly. That, you know, you can never say that to your mother or father. Don't be silly is like a major insult here [laughter] – mum, don't be silly ... So these kids can tell their parents everything?! I wouldn't dare tell, you know.

The migrants' perception of the differences existing in the lifestyles abroad and back home and their capacity to overcome problems of adaptation are two of the factors influencing the way they felt while they were living abroad.

Citizenship, Identity and Discrimination

The feelings that the survey participants nurtured regarding their presence in the host country were generally more positive than negative. More than half of them felt either like a "national" or as a "welcome guest" in the first host country, with more Ivorians feeling the first way and more Ghanaians feeling the second way. The percentage of those who had this type of feeling increases with subsequent migrations, which suggests that migrants tended to feel better the more times they went to live abroad. But obviously it can also reasonably be assumed that the better migrants felt abroad, the greater their migration propensity.

Cross-tabulations showed that those who worked a longer time abroad than average were more likely to feel like "nationals", as well as those who worked longer (Tables 7-10 and 7-11). But this was especially true for Ghanaians who had owned an apartment or house abroad. The Ivorians who possessed a foreign nationality at the time of the interview were rather obviously also more likely to feel like "nationals", whereas those who never had a permanent residence status abroad were less likely to have expressed this positive feeling. All this suggests that such feelings improve with the "integration" of migrants into the host context.

Furthermore, it appears that the sense of identity and belonging of migrants is very subjective and far from being based on their nationality alone.[8] The identity of migrants is shaped by multiple origins, experiences

---

8 In any case, several returned migrants had multiple citizenship – 16 per cent of the Ivorians and 23 per cent of the Ghanaians. It had already been mentioned that a few foreign nationals, including British, American and Canadian, were included in the sample because they were born abroad but were of Ghanaian

Table 7-10 Cross-tabulation: felt like a national abroad by worked abroad longer than average (Ghana)

Ghana		Worked abroad longer than average		Total
Felt like a national abroad		**Yes**	**No**	
	Yes	15	8	23
	No	54	77	131
	Total	69	85	154

Notes: Risk estimate 2.67; significance: 5%.

Table 7-11 Cross-tabulation: felt like a national abroad by worked abroad longer than average (Côte d'Ivoire)

Côte d'Ivoire		Worked abroad longer than average		Total
Felt like a national abroad		**Yes**	**No**	
	Yes	20	11	31
	No	47	72	119
	Total	67	83	150

Notes: Risk estimate 2.79; significance: 5%.

and interests, as one can gather from the migrants' personal accounts. Due to a lack of space only a few can be presented here. The first is a 43-year-old a Franco-Ivorian migrant who was interviewed in Paris.

> Ehm, culturally it's difficult, but in my soul I'm more French because I learned everything here. I've done everything, it's difficult to dissociate. There I will have to learn once again to be Ivorian.

The complexity of the issue was illustrated in more detail by this 50-year-old Ghanaian interviewed in London:

---

origin. They had come to Ghana when they were very young and grew up there before they returned abroad.

> I became less and less of an immigrant and more and more of a pseudo-British, a sort of Black-British, even though I know that that term is not a very helpful one, because I lived here longer than I lived in my own native land. There is a bit of a dichotomy because when you go back on holiday they say – oh you're so English and when you're here they say – oh you're so African or you're so Ghanaian. You can't seem to win.

This returnee went on to explain that to keep her original identity it has been important to have kept on speaking Twi, her mother language. Yet she felt she had a double attachment, one to the home country and one to the host country,[9] which sometimes produced conflicting feelings:

> I am happier when I'm in Africa than I am when I'm here, because I'm not constantly thinking this isn't my place, I'm not wanted here... even though I've got a British passport, even though I've lived here for so long, even though my children are here, I still don't feel like I want to claim it or I can claim it and that's, you know, that's a schizophrenic kind of [laughter] lifestyle.

About one third of the respondents felt that they were treated as a "tolerated guest" during their first stay abroad, but this proportion diminishes with subsequent moves. Only a very limited number of respondents experienced the feeling of being "rejected". One of them who lived in France specified in the questionnaire that the racism of some Europeans had pushed him to return to his own country, Côte d'Ivoire. So undoubtedly discrimination and racism are an integral part of West African migrants' experiences abroad. Ghanaian and Ivorian migrants felt discriminated against primarily because they represented a foreign minority, because they were black and of African origin. Several migrants who returned or remained abroad said that on arrival in the host country they were startled by the idea that they represented a minority. This 45-year-old Ghanaian who returned after having spent 17 years in the United Kingdom recalled his first impression:

> I did not know there was that many white people in the world ... that was the first shock. The first shock of being there was being a minority.

9 Rogers (1984: 287) found similar feelings among Yugoslav migrants in Austria and concluded that their attachment to the host country was "instrumental" and the attachment to the home country was primarily "sentimental".

Racial harassment was often evoked during in-depth interviews and also cited as one of the main reasons for returning home. A 48-year-old Ivorian returned migrant outlined the problem as follows:

> Abroad you always have the impression that you cannot mind other people's business, because you're always reminded that you are a foreigner. And I said to myself that eventually I needed to be in a place where I could get involved in what is of my concern. Because abroad I would always be told to shut up, you are not home, mind your own business. I therefore wanted to come back to get involved in what concerns me, to avoid feeling uncomfortable because whatever people say, abroad there always is a certain racism which can be unconscious, which implies that people see you as a foreigner. Because as a black person you are visible, you are a visible foreigner. If I went as a foreigner to an African country, I would get lost in the mass. But in Europe, even if I get the nationality, I will always be considered a foreigner because I'm visible. And I will always be asked to mind my own business.

The discrimination experienced by black people is particularly severe, especially when their origins are associated with the African continent. The 48-year-old Ghanaian engineer who had not been able to find training-related employment in the United States reported what an employer told him during an interview for a job:

> He said to me ... I want to be very frank with you because I like you. Over here, it's the white American first, then the African American before we think of you down the line ... unfortunately, this is the thinking of it and since you are not schooled in one of our universities out here, they won't look at you at all.

Black immigrants are particularly affected by racist stereotypes which associate them all too easily with poor education, poverty and misbehaviour (Fall, 1987). Some of the migrants' accounts show that the élite is not necessarily shielded from such racist prejudices and assaults:

> You see black people had a bad reputation as a group and I hated the idea of being tagged with the same brush as everybody else by virtue of the same colour. When you go into the Brondby shopping centre, you are wearing jeans and a T-shirt and because you're black the assumption is made that you are a pick pocket, you're a thief, and it's not even a conscious

> assessment made by a woman who is approaching you. There's just one reflex, she does this to her bag [simulates the gripping of a bag under his arm]. It's a wise precaution, but there's always the phrase that the person who feels it, is the one who knows it. So when you are approaching such a person and she does that, you're affected by it. You think by yourself, after this long time here, I am doing what I consider to be reasonably good work, I'm not breaking any laws, I'm just being another ordinary Joe.

Finding suitable accommodation or good employment can be difficult for Ivorians and Ghanaians regardless of their financial means or qualifications. The accounts of these two Ivorian young women who returned from France exemplify some of these difficulties:

> Even though I lived in privileged neighbourhoods, I have still experienced some racism. For example, I call to reserve an apartment and when I get there I'm told the apartment is no longer available. It's a friend of my father … who had to find me an apartment, take all the necessary steps with the agency and I arrived just to move in. It's to say even the privileged experience that in their daily lives. (31-year-old woman who returned to Abidjan)

> I had applied for a job which corresponded to my profile in a temporary employment agency and the head of the agency called me to tell me, I don't think there will be any problem, your profile corresponds and all that. And I wait for two, three days to get some news, then I called her and she tells me – I'm really sorry, I'm really very disappointed because I cannot hide that it did not work out for the simple fact that I mentioned to my client that you are of African origin. So this was a real shock for me because I knew that that existed but I never had experienced it. (36-year-old woman who returned to Abidjan)

That major obstacles can also be encountered by those who intend to develop a career abroad was explained by this 38-year-old Ivorian migrant who went back to Abidjan:

> One needs to be frank, in France there is a colour barrier. It's normal. Even if we are of French origin, we are mulatto because my spouse also had a white mother and an Ivorian father, there is a colour barrier in France. With equal qualifications, you will do worse than a French of pure origin. I don't want to pursue this, it's like that. You see the people

> from the French West Indies who also are French ... even if they have the qualifications at a certain point there is a barrier, there is the colour.

Another Franco-Ivorian migrant who was living in Paris stressed that in Côte d'Ivoire she used to encounter a more positive than negative form of discrimination:

> In Africa this is less of a problem. Even if as a mulatto you are sometimes considered a bit white you remain an African. Back home it's rather an advantage to have received a French education and culture, to have another perspective on things because that, in a context of former colonisation, is important and means that what comes from abroad always is perceived as better. What comes from the white is better experienced and perceived, it's more respected. It's good or bad, there is no need to justify it. It's just like that.

But the notion that Ivorian and Ghanaian migrants feel more at ease in another West African country where, as one of the respondents said above, they can be confounded with the mass, is not necessarily the case. This Ghanaian returnee explained why he felt less comfortable in Nigeria than in North America:

> I felt more excluded in Kaduna in Northern Nigeria, which was, which I suppose still is, fairly Islamic. I went there and for the first time in my life I was in a society which made no overture to me. They had a language, Hausa, which everybody spoke, which appeared on TV and on radio and in the newspapers, so if you don't speak it, too bad! And they had a religion which did not recognise infidels ... which is one of the reasons I left Kaduna, I left Nigeria. I just did not feel that I had any room there ... But in America I always felt that I could do whatever I wanted, go wherever I wanted and it was intellectually accessible to me and for me that's an important aspect of integration.

Much qualitative evidence indicates that many stereotypes are often the result of a lack of knowledge about the migrants' origins and culture. The account of this 40-year-old Ghanaian who lived in the United States is one example:

> ... my first host parents ... the only thing they knew about an African was that we liked bananas, and I had never eaten bananas in my life before.

In fact, I would probably throw up if I ate a banana. So they came to the airport with a basket full of bananas … So I got to the airport and they presented me with flowers and they thought I was hungry and gave me a basket of bananas and I just started crying because I said I'm going back home.

The social relationships that migrants had abroad and their affiliation to social institutions such as associations, clubs and movements were also investigated, to gain a better idea not only of their professional but also their personal experiences abroad.

Social Relationships and Affiliations Abroad and Links Kept Back Home

During in-depth interviews migrants were asked what type of social relationships, if any, they established and maintained in the destination country. From the responses it appears that these relationships usually involved persons who had a common origin, religion or activity. Although there were some migrants who interacted exclusively with compatriots, or with locals, or with other foreigners, most had a social life involving a mixture of people. As anywhere else, social relationships evolved over time and in the course of the migrants' life. A 45-year-old Ivorian returnee who had lived in New York for more than 15 years said that when he was a student he spent all his life on campus to study and to work. But later, when he started to work in factories, he met all kinds of people and dramatically diversified his social circle. In general those who not only studied abroad but also worked had more opportunities to interact with the locals because the work environment provided a particularly fertile ground. Instead, campus life offered more chances to meet compatriots or other foreign nationals. A 43-year-old Ivorian returned migrant described his social life in France as follows:

When I was a student I went around with a lot of Africans. But when I started to work, I completely separated from those African circles. I've lived with some French, Alsatians, some Americans because there, where I worked, they brought in people from everywhere, from Poland, from Australia … the last eight years that I spent in France, I have mixed very little with Africans. Let's say I've become an Alsatian.

Other migrants preferred to spend most of their time with people who had a similar background because they felt that they had more things in common. N'Diaye (1969) found that this is a very common attitude among African students in France, and was for example the case of these two Ivorians in their thirties:

> … [I had] a circle full of African friends, some Togolese, Senegalese, Cameroonians and Ivorians … not that I did not have any French friends at all. But maybe it was a question of culture. One probably feels better with people who have the same lifestyle and the same way of thinking.

> From Lyon to Mont d'Or I was bathing in an environment I would call Africano … it was as if one displaced my friends from here to there. We were in an environment where we had very little contact with Europeans for the simple reasons that we had recreated a sort of ghetto in which we felt secure, we did nothing else than reproducing in a different environment the reflexes and things we already knew and which we had brought with us.

To the question about social relationships, a 50-year-old Ghanaian who was interviewed in London replied:

> Oh God, it's probably one of the most difficult questions, I mean because of the work I do, it's mainly with Caribbean people. I tend to mix a lot more with Caribbeans during the week, in terms of forging a social framework amongst achieving black people, so in terms of my, my business associates and business friendships there are some Ghanaians, but very few Ghanaians. In terms of my own social affiliations during the weekend its entirely with Ghanaians and it revolves around the family and it also revolves around Ghanaian social units, like, I'm a member of, I've helped set up many Ghanaian organisations.

In the questionnaire, returnees were specifically asked whether they participated actively in an association, club or movement while they were living abroad. From this it emerged that 61 per cent of each sample took an active part in such an institution; 31 per cent of the Ghanaians and 24 per cent the Ivorians were participants in at least two associations, clubs or movements, and 18 per cent of the first and 7 per cent of the second participated in at least three. This shows that the Ghanaians were somewhat more involved in associational activities than the Ivorians, again consistent with their longer average residence abroad and their tendency to engage both in study and various types of work experience.

It is assumed that such participation favours social relationships and interaction and thus the respondents were asked to list the type of structure they had belonged to. The greatest proportion of them – 59 per cent of Ivorians and 41 per cent of Ghanaians – belonged to an African cultural or ethnic association.[10] Some got involved in this type of association for political reasons; witness this 48-year-old Ivorian returnee:

> I campaigned in a militant way in African students' associations in France … for us we had to fight so that Africa could have the place it deserved, and that it could truly be independent. And we believed that it was first of all the élites who had to do that and that studying was part of a certain mobilisation because we were going to acquire some knowledge to bring back to the attention and into the reach of our people … Well it's true that I was the head of the African students and so often on week-ends we would get together at my place, they called it the House of the People. So when we would meet at my place, I would receive food from here, we would cook as back home, we would eat together, play cards, tell our jokes, laugh, we would be a bit among ourselves.

A quarter of the Ghanaians also took part in a professional association. The Ivorians who listed this type of association in the first place represent only 8 per cent, but 22 per cent and 20 per cent mentioned it respectively in the second and third place. Finally, it can be mentioned that participation in religious associations and in sports clubs was also important, as was the affiliation of migrants to local students' movements and alumni associations.[11]

Another important issue that was raised in the questionnaire was the number of times that returned migrants had visited their home country while they were away. It is expected that visits are beneficial for migrants because they equip them with more realistic views regarding

10 Daum (2000b) has produced a report on the organisations of migrants in France and their activities. He found that West African migrants are particularly well organised and participate in the development of their home country through some of these organisations.

11 Any association, club or movement with a focus on Ghana, Côte d'Ivoire, Africa was listed under "cultural and ethnic" including student groups with that specific focus.

the opportunities and constraints that they may encounter after return. But, as Asiedu (2003) has stressed, visits also benefit the home country because of the migrants' donations, expenditures and investments. From the present analysis it emerges that the Ivorians visited their home country more frequently (i.e. once a year or more) than their Ghanaian counterparts. Almost twice as many Ghanaians than Ivorians said that they never visited home during their first stay abroad. But a smaller percentage of the former also never went back for a visit during subsequent periods of emigration. In both cases, however, the percentage of those who visited very frequently increases with subsequent moves, while that of those who never visited or visited less often diminishes. This may be due to the fact that migrants have grown older and have advanced in their careers and therefore they are able to afford more trips home. Cross-tabulations in the Ivorian sample confirm that those who worked abroad were more likely to have visited home frequently during the last period they spent abroad, whereas those who only studied overseas had a lower probability of making regular visits.

Summary of Findings

The experiences of Ghanaian and Ivorian migrants in Europe and North America who were the focus of this chapter have some things in common, but also differ significantly from many points of view. Both groups originally left their home country for educational reasons, but Ghanaians generally emigrated when they were younger and had a greater propensity to move on to subsequent destinations. They have also remained away much longer than Ivorians, which can partly be related to the problematic conditions in Ghana. These have probably had a considerable effect on the duration of absence of Ghanaians, making it eventually and overall a richer and more diversified migration experience.

Ghanaians not only stayed overseas much longer than Ivorians, but they also worked there much longer and at far more diversified jobs. Their longer and more varied work experience explains why they were able to gain more financial and human capital while they were living abroad. Ivorian migrants mainly concentrated on their studies and then relatively quickly returned home. They accumulated more in the form of academic qualifications, especially doctorates, but have gained little overseas working experience. This, in addition to the fact that they stayed away less time, has resulted in a situation whereby Ivorians have had fewer opportunities to acquire any of the three forms of capital abroad. Their development potential back home is therefore more limited than the Ghanaians.

From in-depth interviews it is possible to conclude that highly-skilled, élite migrants who have lived and worked abroad longer are usually more exposed to different ways of dealing with various issues and of solving problems. This has contributed to broadening their perspectives and enabled them to see things from more than one angle. Living and working abroad longer also tends to favour closer contacts with the local people and a greater "integration" into the local context.

In many foreign contexts this confers on migrants a greater ability to acquire a more permanent residence status or the local citizenship, which in turn influences many other things, such as their duration of absence and propensity to return. But the findings also show that the migrants' residence status in the host country(ies) influences some of their decisions, such as whether to invest some money abroad, in a house or an apartment, for example, or to leave part or all of their savings abroad rather than transferring these funds back home.

Chapter Eight
The Dynamics of Return Migration to Côte D'ivoire and Ghana

The reasons why migrants return home and the way this move occurs can be expected to influence their post-return impacts. At least this is what has been argued in some of the return migration literature, as was seen in Chapter Two even if it was not found to be significant in the models of factors affecting capital transfer developed in Chapter Six. It therefore seems useful to take a look at the dynamics of return migration of Ivorians and Ghanaians and to examine their implications on the development potential of the migrants. This is the purpose of the present chapter which focuses first on how migrants make the decision to return and then on how return is planned and organised. How resources were mobilised for return migration, and if migrants derived any benefits from return incentive programmes or policies are also dealt with in this chapter. Returnees surveyed drew very little benefit from such interventions and their awareness of the existence of such measures was generally limited.

Making the Decision to Go Back

Migrants returned home for different reasons, but mainly they returned either because they had accomplished what they had planned to do in the host country (i.e. termination of studies), or because they estimated that the macro conditions were right for them to achieve their professional goals in the country or origin. The first was the main rationale for the return of Ivorians and the second the main thrust for the return of Ghanaians. It seems that migrants who returned primarily for the first reason have a more limited development potential, because they usually spent no or only limited time working abroad. By contrast, those who returned because they expected to find better professional opportunities back home were found to be more enterprising.

Timing and Reasons for Return

The majority of migrants returned when the economic situation in their country of origin was improving. Yet, a certain proportion of Ivorians, often destined to become civil servants, moved back during a period of economic crisis. Ghanaians, who were keener on promoting their own enterprises, preferred to wait for better times. This needs again to be seen in the light of the specific background and profile of their countries and the differences in their migration experiences.

The analysis of the main survey data shows that, with regard to their last return, only 9 per cent of the Ivorians came back before 1980, 38 per cent returned between 1980 and 1993, the period characterised by economic recession, and 53 per cent returned from 1994 onwards. By comparison, almost no Ghanaian respondent returned before 1976, 21 per cent went home during the years between 1976 and 1991, the period of greatest economic hardship, and 78 per cent came back after 1992.

Migrants usually embark on return as a result of multiple reasons rather than a single overriding factor. This 48-year-old Ivorian classified his main return motives into four categories:

> There were cultural, ideological, political as well as family reasons. Cultural reasons, because consciously or unconsciously we have internalised our culture and in our culture we think that the tribal and ethnic community forms a sort of collective soul, and it's because you are part of this community that you have a certain vitality. When you exit this community you devitalise a bit. So generally when you leave you always tend to come back. Here we have a proverb which in French says "chicken is in the village, not in the bush" – which means that the chicken goes into the bush to search for food, but then it always returns to the village. So there was this cultural reason. Political reasons, because for a long time in France I campaigned as a militant in African students' associations … we were a bit like the protagonists of a local tale who live in a village where there is a drought. There is a drought and a few villagers are chosen to whom all the water that is left in the calabashes is given so that they have enough strength to go and search for water and bring it back to the community … it means that, contrary to an individualistic attitude, where you get to the water and you settle there, you are fine, you forget the others, you come back looking for your people and telling them that you have found the water. It's a more ideological, political attitude. Well, I said to myself that at the end my place was at home, I needed to help

> in developing my country, I needed to contribute to making my country progress, it would have been a betrayal to remain in Europe. I knew that it would not have been easy, but it was an option and I chose that option. Family reasons, because I had an elderly mother and I needed to be here to take care of her. The money that I would have sent home from abroad could never have replaced my presence.

The reasons for return were explored in the questionnaire through a multiple-response question (see Table 8-1). From this it was found that only a very small number of respondents felt they had no other choice but to go back. In both countries the great majority said they returned home on a voluntary basis. However, the greatest share of Ivorians said they went back because they had terminated their studies, and since the majority of these respondents studied in France, most were obliged to return after the completion of their study course.[1] In other words, many of the migrants who completed their studies in France had little choice but to go back home.

Also, many migrants who went overseas with a scholarship felt they had a special commitment to return home quickly, as this 53-year-old Ghanaian explains:

> I went to Reading as a student and ... my objective was to finish my course within the stipulated time. I knew that I was a University of Ghana scholar and therefore I always had it at the back of my mind that I should not let my University down and that I was fortunate to have been counted as one of the best, to have been given a scholarship to continue with my studies in England.

Most importantly, however, it emerged that migrants who returned because they finished studying were less likely to have transferred financial and social capital from abroad. Some cross-tabulations in the Ivorian sample show that these migrants were much more likely not to send any remittances whilst away, whereas others in the Ghanaian sample also show that they were less likely to have sent remittances regularly (Tables 8-2 and 8-3).

In both samples they were also found to be significantly less likely to have brought back substantial amounts of savings (i.e. more than

1 It was seen in Chapter Six that in France migrants holding a student visa must return after the completion of their study course. This means that only those students who had a permanent residence status or French citizenship, which cross-tabulations showed to be small in number, were allowed to stay on.

Table 8-1 Reasons for return, by country and sex

Return reasons*	Côte d'Ivoire			Ghana		
	Male	Female N (%)	Total	Male	Female N (%)	Total
Termination of studies	93 (72.1)	17 (81.0)	110 (73.3)	18 (14.2)	7 (25.9)	25(16.2)
Government policies or programmes favouring return	4 (3.1)	1 (4.8)	5 (3.3)	16 (12.6)	4 (14.8)	20(13.0)
Family reasons	39 (30.2)	5 (23.8)	44 (29.3)	44 (34.6)	16 (59.3)	60(39.0)
Expectations of better job opportunities	33 (25.6)	8 (38.1)	41 (27.3)	40 (31.5)	10 (37.0)	50(32.5)
Expectations of better business opportunities	18 (14.0)	1 (4.8)	19 (12.7)	40 (31.5)	6 (22.2)	46(29.9)
Difficulties in getting a good job abroad	8 (6.2)	2 (9.5)	10 (6.7)	12 (9.4)	3 (11.1)	15(9.7)
Had to return, no other choice	2 (1.6)	2 (9.5)	4 (2.7)	15 (11.8)	3 (11.1)	18(11.7)
To receive due recognition and respect	–	–	–	44 (34.6)	12 (44.4)	56(36.4)
Other reasons	48 (37.2)	10 (47.6)	58 (38.7)	66 (52.0)	77 (63.0)	83(53.9)

* More than one pre-coded response was possible.

Table 8-2 Cross-tabulation: sent remittances regularly by reasons for return: termination of studies (Ghana)

Ghana	Reasons for returning: termination of studies		Total
Sent remittances regularly	Yes	No	
Yes	3	62	65
No	20	69	89
Total	23	131	154

Notes: Risk estimate 0.17; significance: 1%.

Table 8-3 Cross-tabulation: sent remittances by reasons for return: termination of studies (Côte d'Ivoire)

Côte d'Ivoire	Reasons for returning: termination of studies		Total
Sent remittances	Yes	No	
Yes	47	26	73
No	63	14	77
Total	110	40	150

Notes: Risk estimate 0.40; significance: 5%.

US$10,000). Furthermore, cross-tabulations in the Ghanaian sample indicate that migrants who returned because they finished studying were far more unlikely to have established and kept professional and professional contacts abroad (Table 8-4).

A significant proportion of Ghanaians returned because they expected to find better job or business opportunities in the country of origin. This expectation was also shared by Ivorians who remained abroad longer and acquired some work experience. Migrants who returned for these reasons were not necessarily more likely to have acquired social capital abroad than those who returned for family reasons or because of policies or programmes favouring return. But cross-tabulations in the Ghanaian sample showed that all those who expected to find better business

Table 8-4 Cross-tabulation: kept professional and personal contacts by reasons for return: termination of studies (Ghana)

Ghana	Reasons for returning: termination of studies		Total
Kept professional and personal contacts	Yes	No	
Yes	12	104	116
No	11	27	38
Total	23	131	154

Notes: Risk estimate 0.28; significance: 1%.

opportunities were more likely than anybody else to have transferred large amounts of savings (i.e. more than US$50,000).

Fewer than one in ten migrants said they returned because they had difficulties in finding a good job abroad; it appears more likely that they were attracted by the better job or business opportunities existing back home. A 46-year-old Ivorian who returned after 15 years overseas explained the difference between the professional opportunities existing abroad and back home:

> Many people who go abroad to study realise at a certain moment that they have a much greater potential back home. They say to themselves that by going back they can achieve a better social status … because I take the example of the United States, it's fine you can make some good money and all that, but at a certain point you realise that you are not at home… and socially you will never be able to advance beyond a certain level, you're stuck, you see your limits. And when you have studied, there's a time where money no longer counts. The aim is to be socially recognised, achieve a certain status where you have some power in decision-making and are involved in making certain decisions. I think that is truly satisfactory and that is why I said to myself I should return to Africa. If I want to be a candidate for mayor, if I want to be a presidential candidate, I've got all the opportunities there, nothing can stop me.

If Ivorians who acquired some work experience abroad were more likely to expect better work opportunities back home, this was not necessarily the case for Ghanaians, since those who remained abroad longer and who worked longer than average in training-related jobs were less likely to have such positive home expectations. This contrasting evidence is probably due to the fact that, on average, Ghanaians' much wider work experience gave them far better job opportunities abroad which raised their standards. This explanation is confirmed by the fact that the more successful Ghanaians, who bought a house or an apartment abroad, were less likely to have returned home to seek better job opportunities. This hypothesis is also supported by the fact that Ghanaians who moved directly to North America rather than to Europe were less likely to have this kind of positive expectation, having acquired more work experience and higher employment qualifications abroad.

Better job and business opportunities at home do not necessarily involve better remuneration, but certainly involve more responsibilities and better career prospects. In fact, some migrants felt that overseas there was a sort of "glass-ceiling" which hindered them in their higher-level career. A 41-year-old Ivorian immigrant working in Paris described how this obstacle prevented her and other Africans, and more generally black people, from gaining access to top positions:

> For a company you get hired through an interview like anybody else, and then, while your colleagues move from one department to another with an increase in responsibilities and an increase in salary – well, you don't move. In the best of the cases you circulate in different departments in the middle of the hierarchy, but always at the same level. Starting from a certain level nothing works anymore for someone of foreign origin; the few posts at the highest level are almost inaccessible. So if after having studied here you have started working, or at least if you've been here for a long time you can make a good career, but at a certain level you get stuck ... it's not a matter of nationality, it's not a matter of being a foreigner or non-foreigner, it really is a matter of colour.

Discrimination and racism sometimes represent a significant push factor for return. But many migrants were simultaneously pulled home because they expected to draw benefits from an improved social status and to receive due recognition and respect. This latter aspect was an important return motive for migrants and was closely related to the expectation of finding a good job or better business opportunities in the country of origin. More than one third of the Ghanaians who responded to the questionnaire said they returned for exactly this reason.[2] When asked for the reason why he decided to leave France after having lived there for 24 years, a 39-year-old Ivorian replied:

> Social recognition: because in France you are assimilated to the mass. Here you are an African, a black who has succeeded and that gives you a certain social recognition. Here you are in a smaller context where there is a greater social recognition. Even if you don't seek any particular social recognition, when you succeed professionally it's always good that [your foreign experience] is recognised by others.

There is no doubt that, far from family and kin and detached from their original social networks and social and symbolic ties, many highly-skilled migrants felt quite isolated and forsaken when they were abroad. They lacked not only general consideration but also personal appreciation and gratification, as shown in the statement of this 44-year-old Ivorian engineer who returned from France to set up his own IT firm:

> Not only in Europe but in the West in general, you have the impression that everything has already been done, there's nothing left to contribute. You feel like a number, you don't feel "someone", like we Africans say.

At home, life proceeds in a smaller social context where everybody knows everybody else; thus returned migrants more easily get recognised for their personal successes and professional achievements. This is where they draw the benefits from social and cultural capital that is territorially bound and "location-specific" (Da Vanzo, 1981; Faist, 2000). When asked about his expectation before return, a 57-year-old Ghanaian lawyer and university lecturer answered:

> That I would be successful in Ghana, that I would have satisfaction, that I would contribute to my own nation's development, that I would matter the way I would not have mattered in Britain. I would gain recognition. No matter how well I did in Britain, I was still a black man, I was still an African, I was still not a British person but I was still an alien.

2 This pre-coded response category was inadvertently left out in the French version of the questionnaire. As a result data for this variable are not available for Côte d'Ivoire.

From Table 8-1 we see that one of the most important series of return motives was family reasons. About one third of the Ivorians, and even more Ghanaians, referred to this type of return motive, which ranged from homesickness to a specific event that occurred in the migrant's life-course. The death of a parent or a close family member, for example, can provoke or accelerate return, as shown in the account of this 43-year-old Ghanaian:

> I planned to come back, [but] then I came here on one of [my] missions and my mother died whilst I was here. When she died I went back to England, came back to Ghana for the funeral, went back to England and resigned. So I made the decision based on that event, when it happened.

As this case demonstrates, migrants may be obliged to return because they feel they are needed back home (King, 2000). A 43-year-old Ivorian suddenly left Canada because he and his older brother had to care and cater for the wives and children of their father:

> It's with that problem, the death of my father that we two … who are the first two sons of my father, were obliged to return, because the children were left by themselves and my father had four wives. We found ourselves with more than 25 children on our backs. Therefore I could not remain in North America, I was obliged to return.

More abstract feelings and ideas, such as homesickness and nostalgia or a pressing desire to "feel at home", figure as well among some of the migrants' main return motives. This was also found by other return migration studies (King, 2000).

Table 8-1 does not reveal great differences based on gender. Compared to men, women were more likely to have returned right after terminating their studies abroad and before coming back they nurtured somewhat more optimistic expectations concerning job opportunities back home. But, interestingly, Ghanaian female respondents were more than twice as likely as Ivorian females to have come back for family reasons.

Return Decision-making and Involvement of Spouses

The majority of the returned migrants who participated in the survey said they made the decision to return on their own: 81 per cent of the Ivorians and 57 per cent of the Ghanaians. The reason why many more Ghanaians than Ivorians involved other family members (e.g. spouse/partner and children) in the return decision-making may be simply that many more of them were married (or had a partner) at the time of return. Among all those who at that time had a spouse/partner, 41 per cent of Ghanaians and only 18 per cent of Ivorians said they had made the decision to return with this person, percentages which appear quite small. One possible hypothesis is that all those who assumed their spouse/partner agreed with them did not explicitly associate this person in the decision-making, particularly Ivorians who were more likely to have left their spouses back home when they emigrated.

This hypothesis seems to be strengthened by the fact that when those who were married or had a partner at the time of return were asked if this person had supported their decision to return, 77 per cent of the Ghanaians and 72 per cent of the Ivorians replied affirmatively. In both cases, only one out of every five indicated that their spouse or partner was against this decision, and the rest said the reaction was neutral. However, the fact that the great majority of respondents are male should also be taken into consideration. As heads of household, men do not always consider it necessary to involve their wives or partners in major decisions concerning the family.

The fact that it is not always easy for a couple to agree on an issue such as migration or return was already seen earlier. This 53-year-old Ghanaian who studied in the United Kingdom and then worked there for a short period at an experimental station explained that his decision to return soon after his studies was largely influenced by his wife:

> She has always been supportive. Even when Rothamstead wanted me to stay on, she was objecting saying that no, no, no, we are going back home because we would be more useful back home than in England … she kept on telling me, look … don't behave like the Ghanaians who are here, they've acquired all the qualifications, and they want to be here. You've worked hard, you have acquired your PhD, please go back home and let's contribute our little quota. You will be more respected there as a young man with a PhD than a young man with PhD in England, because there are millions, thousands of professors and doctors in England. You won't be recognised. Nobody will take care of you. Moreover you are black, you are not likely to get any good job, so let's go back.

Some migrants purposefully avoid consulting their spouse or partner, or other family members, because they want to reduce possible interference, like this 43-year-old Ivorian returnee:

> My parents did not know much about what I was doing, and I did not want that my parents knew too much to avoid pressures, so really I've had no pressures. However, it's a decision that I have made with my wife because she was never opposed to it, because when I told her that I was going to set up a business in Côte d'Ivoire she was the first to put money in the pot. She agreed, and that was a surprise to me because my wife grew up in Algeria and then moved to France. And so when I decided to take her to Côte d'Ivoire I was not sure how she would have reacted.

We saw earlier that those who are born or have spent most of their life abroad are more hesitant about following their spouse back home. However, they are not the only ones, as is seen from the account of this 45-year-old Ivorian who returned from the United States with his spouse and children:

> African women who go abroad with their husbands are generally more reluctant to return … because socially when they get there their social status improves dramatically. In America women are protected, women are actually free and have their rights … whereas in Africa they are treated as "inferiors" which means they are subordinated to men. So when women get there and feel at ease socially, very often they find it hard to come back. Many friends of mine have that problem, they want to return, but their spouses categorically say – we are here, we're doing fine, living well; I don't want to go back to Africa where, as soon as we arrive, you will change and treat me as an "inferior" person, where your family will have all the influence on you and our life will be totally different.

Women tend therefore to be more reluctant to return, at least on a permanent basis. This was confirmed by cross-tabulations performed for the Ghanaian sample which revealed that female respondents were more likely to have returned only temporarily; the analysis also showed that those who had been abroad longer (and those who acquired foreign citizenship) had a significantly greater probability to have returned only on a temporary basis (Tables 8-5 and 8-6).

Table 8-5 Cross-tabulation: temporary return by stayed abroad longer than average (Ghana)

Ghana		Stayed abroad longer than average		Total
Temporary return		Yes	No	
	Yes	14	5	19
	No	57	78	135
	Total	71	83	154

Notes: Risk estimate 3.83; significance: 5%.

Table 8-6 Cross-tabulation: temporary return by stayed abroad longer than average (Côte d'Ivoire)

Côte d'Ivoire		Stayed abroad longer than average		Total
Temporary return		Yes	No	
	Yes	12	4	16
	No	61	73	134
	Total	73	77	150

Notes: Risk estimate 3.59; significance: 5%.

Overall, at the time of return 12 per cent of the Ivorians and 14 per cent of the Ghanaians returned intending to stay home only temporarily, and an even smaller percentage with the idea of coming and going on a repeated basis (respectively 5 per cent and 3 per cent). The great majority – some 83 per cent of all the respondents – intended to settle on a permanent basis. Married respondents were more than twice as likely to have envisaged a permanent return, than those who at the time of interview were single or separated, divorced or widowed. It seems worthwhile to notice that migrants who remained abroad longer were much more likely to have returned only temporarily. The same was the case for migrants who affirmed that their work is very different from the one of their colleagues who had never lived abroad.

From the in-depth interviews it has appeared that, to ensure the success of their return, some migrants felt it was important to consider their return as a definitive move. The Ivorian returnee who was just quoted above recalled for example:

> I resigned and came back. At work I was asked why I didn't take a leave of absence, leave my family there and go back to see if it would work out before I had them leave. I said no, if I did that, the first occasion, the first difficulty, I would pack my suitcase and return abroad, and that would not be good.

As another returnee points out, it is important to "realise that there was no turning back" because otherwise it is too easy to give up and to leave again when the reintegration proves more complicated than anticipated. Since migration involves a considerable degree of disruption, not only for the migrants themselves but also for their families, determination and perseverance become essential for a successful return. It is therefore interesting to see who participated in return and what reaction the migrants' return provoked among their friends abroad.

Participation in Return and Reaction of Friends in Host Country

The survey's findings reveal that the great majority of returned migrants – 87 per cent of Ivorians and 75 per cent of Ghanaians – went back alone. Only about one out of five Ghanaians and one out of ten Ivorians came back either with the whole immediate family or alone with their spouse or partner.[3] This means that 84 per cent of the Ivorians and 59 per cent of the Ghanaians who were married (or had a partner) at the time of return had left their spouse/partner back home when they originally emigrated, or abroad when they returned, or their return was preceded by that of their spouse/partner. Cross-tabulations show that female respondents had a greater likelihood to have returned with somebody else than only with their spouse/partner or their whole immediate family. Female respondents also had a smaller likelihood to have moved back alone; presumably that means they more often returned only with their children.

Male migrants who returned home before their spouse and/or children usually did so with the aim to plan and organise the return for the rest

3 In the questionnaire it was specified that "immediate" family included only spouse or partner and own or adopted children. "Extended" family included in addition parents, siblings, cousins, aunts and uncles, other relatives, close friends, etc.

of the family. They first wanted to get settled before they called upon the others to follow. This was for example the case of this 43-year-old Ghanaian who returned after almost 20 years of absence and initially left his wife working in the United Kingdom:

> I left my wife there with my eldest daughter and came with the boys and then a year and a half [later] … she came to join me. So basically I came to explore what I could do in the Ghanaian environment. Now, basically I had no idea. I knew what I wanted to do but I didn't know whether it would work in this country … To her I said – well you don't have to come down with me, I'll go and see what the situation is like, how we can live, if we can live, if you can find the work you're used to do here, whether I can find the kind of work I'm used to do here, whether we can live a decent life, the kind of life you are used to … If I had come and things did not work out, I didn't want to be starving here in Ghana. So she was working, okay? I was not going to ask her for money, but if my savings would have run out, there would have been some safety for at least the children, their school fees and that sort of thing.

As far as the reaction of the migrants' friends in the host country is concerned, the analysis shows that a little less than one third of all the returnees did not receive any moral support from them. Much to the contrary, all of the friends abroad tried to dissuade them from returning home. Full support was received by only 8 per cent of the Ghanaians and 17 per cent of the Ivorians. Instead, the remainder was supported by at least some of their friends abroad or they said that their friends' reaction was neutral. Cross-tabulations demonstrate that those who only studied overseas were much more likely to have received the support of all their friends than those who also worked abroad. Among the Ghanaians, this was also the case of those who had returned more than once which suggests that in their social sphere they were seen as already more experienced migrants who knew what they were doing.

The majority of the respondents who knew someone who returned before they did said they considered these as an example to follow. During in-depth interviews returnees were also asked if they thought their return had influenced others. To this query a 45-year-old Ghanaian who had lived in the United States for about five years replied:

> Following my return and what you could refer to as a "successful return", because I have my own problems as well, so I don't know how successful,

> what the measure of success is – a number of people have also come home trusting that if I was able to do it, they could as well. So I've set an example for a few other people, I know. Oh, because people thought I was crazy!

Similarly, when questioned if his three younger siblings would have returned if he had not come back in the first instance, a 42-year-old Ghanaian who stayed abroad for more than 11 years responded:

> I guess maybe not, because I think it really broke either a cycle of the unknown or a cycle of fear, or also it shocked them thinking how could ... [I] leave Wall Street to come to Accra? And I guess that created excitement in itself.

Family members often influence migrants' return decision-making. A 58-year-old Ghanaian admitted that his sister persuaded him to go back:

> When I left the situation in this country was so bad that I could not imagine returning to it... But then I started hearing, I mean, I had my sister who at that time was also living in Canada, but who made it a point to come home every Christmas, and she started telling me – look things are changing, it's not perfect but at least there's a forward movement, so why don't you, if you are not so happy in Canada, why don't you reconsider going back?

This account shows how information gathered from different sources such as family and friends or the media helps in shaping the migrant's perception about the situation back home. In general, the analysis of the qualitative data confirmed that successful examples tend to encourage return. Conversely, unsuccessful examples tend to discourage return. However first we must see how migrants who made the decision to return organised this sometimes complicated move.

Planning and Organising Return

Assessment of the time it took migrants to organise return is relevant because it is often presumed that the most information migrants acquire beforehand and the better they plan return, the smoother will be their readjustment and reintegration after return. This, in turn, is likely to affect the ability (and willingness) of migrants to live up to their expectations and make some meaningful contributions to development and to their home society. But a great deal also depends on the expectations with which migrants return home, and whether these are sufficiently realistic.

Expectations before Return and Information Sources

Migrants had many expectations before they returned, which on the whole were more positive in the case of Ghana. Table 8-7 displays the answers of returnees to a multiple-response question and shows that a very high percentage of both groups thought they could utilise at home what they had learned abroad. Interestingly, Ghanaians who remained abroad longer than average were half as likely to have this expectation. Whether they felt that what they had learned was not adaptable to the local context remains an open question.

Table 8-7 Expectations before return, by country

Expectations before return*	Côte d'Ivoire N (%)	Ghana N (%)
Feasible employment or business opportunities	101 (67.3)	102 (66.2)
Could benefit from government policies	7 (4.7)	18 (11.7)
Could utilise what I learned abroad	115 (76.7)	127 (82.5)
My family members and relatives would accept me	28 (18.7)	47 (30.5)
My experiences and knowledge about abroad were useful	83 (55.3)	125 (81.2)
Didn't have positive expectations	3 (2.0)	4 (2.6)
Other	37 (24.7)	27 (17.5)

* More than one pre-coded response was possible.

The survey data shows that most respondents, particularly Ghanaians, believed their experience and knowledge about abroad would be useful in the home context. This was also confirmed by much of the qualitative information. A 45-year-old Ghanaian who worked for 14 years in senior positions for a multinational company in Gabon said:

> I often told people who were asking me – oh, why don't you go back over there, you have a very good job, you can still get a very good job because of your experience and the level you were at, and so on ... I say – well, it's a leap of faith. We all want to come in at a certain time. It may be one's first time, it may be naïve, it may be ideal, idealistic, but we all want to come and help our country. Because we've been outside, we believe that we've gained a lot and we have a lot to offer. That's what we believe, we may be totally wrong – but that's exactly what we believe and that's what really motivates us to come home.

Returning home can involve a gratifying challenge, but it also implies an important risk. This was stressed by a 45-year-old Ghanaian who had spent more than 10 years in Sweden:

> ... there is the desire to come back and be part of the system but ... there are also the risks, the threats for the individual. You may succeed or fail. Probably the chances of failure are greater than the chances of success ... My attitude is still positive, I think there's a lot to be done. My background is in Political Science, I have been doing work in the area of democracy, democratisation, policy studies, I have been teaching development ... and there are real issues to confront here. I mean this is a laboratory to test all those political theories and so on, because there's movement on the ground, there's change taking place, there are so many situations that we need to engage into to improve life, living conditions and so on. So there are challenges, really. But it's difficult, it's frustrating ... occasionally you can't do without scepticism which is good because it makes you think through your steps carefully to overcome the risks or the threats.

Although almost all respondents came back with at least one positive expectation, a fair share of them also had some major uncertainties and doubts. About one third of the returnees did not expect to find feasible job or business opportunities back home (Table 8-7). Also, only a very limited number thought they could draw benefits from government policies and a relatively small number believed they would be accepted by their family members and relatives.[4]

---

4 This wording was taken from the questionnaire used by the Centre for Asia Pacific Social Transformation Studies, University of Wollongong, Australia within the framework of a study of the return of skilled and business migrants to countries/regions of Bangladesh, China, Taiwan and Vietnam and of migration

In the questionnaire returnees were asked if before return they had sought any information about the situation in their home country, and from which sources they drew this information. From their responses it emerged that 91 per cent of the Ivorians and 73 per cent of the Ghanaians tried to get some information before they went back.[5] About 80 per cent of both groups were informed by friends or relatives, but whilst two thirds of the Ivorians got information from the media, only 28 per cent of Ghanaians did so. In contrast, nearly two thirds of Ghanaians assessed the situation back home during one of their own visits, whereas this was the case for only a third of the Ivorians. It is perhaps surprising that visits represented a more important source of information for Ghanaians than for Ivorians since, as was seen in the previous chapter, they visited their home country less often. From cross-tabulations it emerges, however, that in particular those who remained abroad longer than average were significantly more likely to have visited the home country to gather information before return (Tables 8-8 and 8-9). The same was true for migrants who returned because they expected to find better employment or business opportunities.

The government and its agencies were less significant sources of information; only one out of ten respondents said they had obtained information from these institutions. A 40-year-old returnee described at length how the return of highly-skilled migrants was promoted by the Ghanaian government in the mid-1990s:

> President Rawlings came to the US, he does it all the time when he goes to promote the country and tries to convince Ghanaians who are living up there to come back home and support the development of their country. So it was during one of his trips that he came to New York and I went to one of these lunches at Meryl Lynch and I happened to talk to some of the people that he came with, his delegation, and they had also heard about

---

based linkages between Australia and these countries/regions, meaning that family members and relatives would host/accommodate the returnee, and may not have been fully grasped by respondents.

5 The wording used in the two questionnaires may have influenced this difference between the two samples. The formulation in English was "Did you do any research to get information about Ghana before returning?" and in French this was translated a little more generically by "Vous êtes-vous informé sur la situation en Côte d'Ivoire avant d'y retourner?" The English wording was derived from the Asia-Pacific questionnaire.

Table 8-8 Cross-tabulation: obtained information about home country from visits by stayed abroad longer than average (Ghana)

Ghana	Stayed abroad longer than average		Total
Obtained information about home country from visits	**Yes**	**No**	
Yes	44	24	68
No	12	33	45
Total	56	57	113

Notes: Risk estimate 5.04; significance: 0.1%.

Table 8-9 Cross-tabulation: obtained information about home country from visits by stayed abroad longer than average (Côte d'Ivoire)

Côte d'Ivoire	Stayed abroad longer than average		Total
Obtained information about home country from visits	**Yes**	**No**	
Yes	35	17	52
No	31	54	85
Total	66	71	137

Notes: Risk estimate 3.59; significance: 1%.

me. So during the conversation they sort of told me that, or convinced me that, I should come back home and help. And at that time I wasn't too sure about coming back home, because obviously when you are living outside in America or in Europe, everything that you hear about Africa is so negative. You see the dark images, you see diseases, you see hunger. There's nothing on television in the rest of the world that you see about Africa, much more about Ghana, that is encouraging or positive. Oh yes, crime, you hear things like that. So after hearing this sort of message for 16 to 17 years, your brain is conditioned that – hey, I'm not going back

> there. I mean, I'm a Ghanaian, I have a good job, people are saying things about Ghana, you see it on TV, you read it in *Newsweek*, you see it on CNN, it's all negative … So with this frame of mind I'm saying to myself and to this person, why should I come back to Ghana, I'm happy here, I've got a life, I've got a kid. So this guy says you have to come to Ghana and see because if all of you guys would say the same thing, Ghana would never be where America is today. So I said okay, I'll come to Ghana and see if there are any opportunities and of course I mentioned it to my wife and she freaked out. She's like, hell – no, I am not going back to Africa! Oh my God we are gonna die, that sort of thing. That's the message that media feeds the rest of the world about Africa, so for me my first trip to Africa was an exploratory trip by myself to go and see whether this is really something that I can do.

Exploratory trips were organised by a number of migrants before they decided to return home. For many this represented a critical step in the planning and organisation of their own and their families' return. Another important step consisted in the mobilisation of resources to cover expenses related to the migrants' and their families' travel and relocation.

Mobilising Resources and Organising Return

Migrants who remained abroad longer were more likely to have invested more time in organising and mobilising resources for return. Table 8-10 shows that for almost two thirds of the Ivorians this took less than six months, whereas for two thirds of Ghanaians this took more than a year. Moreover it is interesting to note that those who expected the experiences and knowledge they had acquired abroad to be useful after return also took longer to organise their move.

A number of considerations regarding those who left the host country fairly unexpectedly were forwarded in the in-depth interviews. For instance, when asked whether his return occurred in a planned or rather unprompted manner, this 45-year-old Ghanaian who lived in the United States for 17 years replied:

> Very spontaneous. I wanted to come and I realised that there was no right time to come. I wanted to have some money before I make the move… to make sure that I ship my car to Ghana before I come, so that when I come to Ghana there is a car here … The time that I decided to come,

Table 8-10 Time spent planning and mobilising resources for return, by country and sex (%)

Duration	Côte d'Ivoire			Ghana		
	Male	Female	Total	Male	Female	Total
< 6 months	60.9	66.7	61.7	31.5	25.9	30.5
6-12 months	14.1	23.8	15.4	11.0	18.5	12.3
1-2 years	10.2	4.8	9.4	23.6	33.3	25.3
> 2 years	14.8	4.8	13.4	31.5	22.2	29.9
No response	–	–	–	2.4	–	1.9
TOTAL	100.0	100.0	100.0	100.0	100.0	100.0
Valid cases	(128)	(21)	(149)	(127)	(24)	(154)

> I had left both jobs that I was doing … and then I ran out of money … so at the time that I was leaving for Ghana I was practically broke and I tell this to many Ghanaians that when I touched down at the Kotoka International Airport I had 90 US Dollars on me. Fortunately for me I left with my brother, he had a second car and a driver that could take me around … it made the transition very, very easy. For many people who did not know they would come back … they don't even have a place where they can stay comfortably or a car to take them around. All those things were there for me, fortunately.

But there also are those who planned and organised their return well in advance:

> The first time I went back I had absolutely no idea that I would stay. I spent all that time preparing to come home… when I came home in 1977 I came with over 5000 books and a record collection of about 2000 LPs. I made that collection specifically because I wanted to come back home and I figured that the two things that would not be too available to me once I came back to Africa would be music and books… and when I was working I kept collecting bed sheets, everything that I figured I would need to make a living here. (58-year-old Ghanaian)

About half of the Ivorians and two thirds of the Ghanaians arranged their return by themselves. This suggests that in both cases individual initiative was paramount. For nearly a quarter of the Ivorians return was organised by a government sponsoring agency, reflecting the fact that many returned to become civil servants or to work in academia after having benefited from a scholarship. Only a few respondents in each sample indicated their family had arranged their return.

The fact that only a relatively small number said their employer had organised their return may in part be due to the fact that almost half of the returnees had in the meantime changed employer. It was found that not all the help promised by the employer actually materialised:

> Before I came I was told that – well, you wait for us, don't come now, we will prepare an office place for you, provide you with your car, your accommodation before you come. So when the green light was given for me to come, when I came there was no office, there was some old vehicle that they asked me to use, that was it. Foolish, I made a big mistake. My country, I made up my mind, I can't trust. They talked to me about it, I brought the kids along so I stayed in their guest house and, you cannot believe it, they made me pay for the expenses, the food, accommodation for the kids ... even though they promised that they were going to provide accommodation.

It is also not always easy to get a prospective employer to finance a migrant's move, as shown in the account of this 46-year-old Ghanaian who returned at his own expense:

> I started looking for a job ... whilst in Germany, but I didn't receive any appointment before I left. So the normal thing would have been for me to stay there until I got a job here before coming back. And I was hoping that I'd be offered a job before May '96, so I had told everybody I was leaving ... thinking that I'll have a job in Ghana. So I committed myself to leaving, and so I left. And when I came to Ghana, I came here and I said well I applied for a job here. They said well, you have a job here, so I started to work. I found out later that the reason why they didn't send me my job offer letter while I was there was that if they had, they would have had to buy me a ticket to come. Because once they recruit you outside they have to send you a ticket and pay for the shipping of your goods and other things which they didn't want to, they didn't have the money for it, but they couldn't tell me they didn't have the money for it, so the strategy was that if the chap wants to come, then he would come anyway.

In this and other cases where the migrant wants to go back but lacks the necessary resources, assistance from return incentive and recruitment programmes could become an important factor facilitating return.

Benefits from Return Incentive Programmes and Policies

As was seen in Chapter Two, considerable efforts and public money were invested in promoting return migration schemes. It therefore seemed important to assess their impact on the population under investigation. Returned migrants were first of all asked if, before returning, they were aware of any of such measures, a question to which about two thirds of the Ghanaians and three quarters of the Ivorians responded negatively (Table 8-11).

Among the returnees who participated in in-depth interviews only one had obtained assistance from the IOM. This 40-year-old Ghanaian, who studied for many years in the United States, explained how she obtained this form of aid:

> I called them and I said – listen I want to go back home, will you help? And I went through a series of interviews and they wanted to find out … through a rigorous assessment process what your qualifications were and then they bought me my tickets – I had two kids, my computers and everything, and even gave me a resettlement allowance. This is after they confirm that you really do intend to stay in your country.

In the case of students, the two governments favoured return indirectly through the award of scholarships comprising travel and other allowances to return home. They sometimes also solicited migrants who, in spite of an initial commitment, hesitated to come back home. This was the case of this 48-year-old Ivorian returnee who studied with a scholarship in France:

> The Ivorian government had sent a letter to the Embassy to say we have sent a student and we would like to know what he is doing, we request that he return. That is why the Embassy asked me to return. Well, I was a bit doubtful – should I go back, should I stay? What pushed me to return is the racism which started to become widespread.

Table 8-11 Return incentive programmes and policies, by country

Return incentive programmes and policies	Côte d'Ivoire N (%)	Ghana N (%)
Awareness of programmes/policies?		
Yes	40 (26.6)	56 (36.4)
No	110 (73.4)	98 (63.6)
Valid cases	(150)	(154)
Type of programmes/policies		
Government programme	20 (50.0)	8 (14.3)
IOM programme	4 (10.0)	28 (50.0)
General policy	10 (25.0)	6 (10.7)
Other	6 (15.0)	14 (25.0)
Valid cases	(40)	(56)
Received assistance?		
Yes	24 (60.0)	24 (42.9)
No	16 (40.0)	32 (57.1)
Valid cases	(40)	(56)
Type of assistance (more than one pre-coded response possible)		
Housing/housing allowance	3	1
Moving expenses	20	16
Subsidiary for children or spouse	4	–
Help finding a job	3	3
Other	5	13
How assistance facilitated return		
Lowered costs of return	5 (20.8)	1 (4.2)
Accelerated return	2 (8.3)	3 (12.5)
Other	8 (33.3)	9 (37.5)
No response	2 (8.4)	–
Valid cases	(24)	(24)

Table 8-11 cont'd

Return incentive programmes and policies	**Côte d'Ivoire N (%)**	**Ghana N (%)**
In what way could programmes/policies be rendered more attractive? (more than one pre-coded response possible)		
Help finding a good job	16	6
Extend funding base	1	9
Improve public information	1	8
Provide housing facilities	1	4
Introduce/maintain tax exemptions	1	4
Other	6	21
Don't know/no response	3	4

Table 8-11 reveals that, out of the 39 Ivorians and 56 Ghanaians who were aware of the existence of return incentive programmes and policies – in both countries 24 but proportionately more Ivorians than Ghanaians – drew some concrete benefits from them. The greatest share obtained financial aid to cover their moving expenses.

Other forms of assistance entailed housing allowances, subsidies for spouse or children and help to find a job. However, these last measures concerned no more than four respondents in each sample. Yet other forms of assistance, such as the provision of equipment or tax exemptions on equipment brought from abroad, were received by some of the respondents.

All the returnees who actually benefited from a return incentive programme or policy were asked in what way this had facilitated their return. The responses displayed in Table 8-11 suggest that the majority of the beneficiaries may have returned anyway, hence the measures only facilitated or accelerated return.

All the returned migrants who had heard about policies and programmes favouring return were asked in what way these measures issued by the government or other agencies could be improved to make them more attractive. The majority of the Ivorians who were asked replied that migrants should first of all be helped to find a good job in the home country. The responses of the Ghanaians were more evenly distributed between different propositions which ranged from specific interventions to more general policy recommendations. Several Ghanaians stressed the need to increase the funding base of return incentive programmes, so that more migrants would be able to derive some concrete benefits. Many Ghanaians also recommended improving public information on these return incentive programmes and policies, as they all too often go unnoticed. More specific suggestions included the provision to returned migrants of housing facilities and tax exemptions to bring back from abroad professional equipment and private goods at a reasonable price.

Summary of Findings

This chapter has looked at how the experiences of Ghanaian and Ivorian migrants affect, or are affected by, the dynamics of their return migration, in view of determining the influences of these return dynamics on their development potential. First of all it emerges that most of the participants in this study returned during periods of economic growth. This was especially the case with the Ghanaians, who were more likely to have been in employment abroad and therefore preferred to wait for better economic circumstances in their home country before they made the decision to go back. Ivorians returned more easily during economic recession because their main reason for return was that they had finished their studies. They had achieved the target that they themselves, their families or their employer had set for them, and could therefore go back. Ghanaians instead were more careful about the return home, mainly because of a paucity of professional opportunities there.

In general, migrants who returned because they had finished their studies were less likely to have transferred money home, either remittances or savings. This is because these migrants mainly focused on their educational aims and, if they worked, they did so only for a limited time. This type of migrant was also less likely to have acquired social capital whilst away. Their move back home did not require any particular decision-making, planning or organisation since it was part of an initial plan. They were, moreover, often constrained by their precarious residence status abroad. In contrast, deciding to return and preparing for such an event appeared somewhat more complicated for migrants who expected to find better business opportunities, as for these migrants there was more at stake (e.g. transfer and investment of financial resources; launch of a private business; set-up of an association). This is why this group was more likely to have visited the home country to gather information before returning home.

After having reached a higher stage in their career, migrants usually judged professional opportunities to be more attractive back home, where highly-skilled migrants have greater chances of accessing top levels of responsibility and authority. The existence abroad of a kind of "glass ceiling" hampering the migrants' career plans seems to represent a significant push factor for return. Many migrants returned hoping to get the recognition and respect they felt were appropriate for a person possessing their background, expertise and level of qualifications. Equipped with their foreign degree and work experience, they were ready to assume a special role in their home economies and societies. The great majority of all migrants felt that they could indeed utilise what they had learned abroad but, due to their longer presence in the host country(ies), more Ghanaians than Ivorians believed that their experience and knowledge gained abroad were useful.

Once back, most returnees were there to stay. But migrants who had lived and worked abroad longer were more likely to consider return as temporary, an issue that raises some concern. It may be that this kind of migrant has a greater propensity to re-emigrate. The majority of returnees had organised their return by themselves without any support. There was very little awareness of return incentive policies and programmes. Concrete benefits were drawn from these interventions by only one sixth of the two samples. The different forms of assistance have allowed some migrants to return home, but for the majority they have helped in accelerating return or lowered its costs, rather than being the key driving factor for return. Elite migrants returned because they felt the situation at home improved (or, in the case of Ivorians, after their studies) rather than because of return schemes facilitating such a move back home.

CHAPTER NINE

THE CHALLENGES OF READJUSTMENT AND REINTEGRATION BACK HOME

After return, migrants encounter a series of difficulties and hurdles in readjusting and reintegrating into their home contexts which can significantly affect their drive and ability to effect change back home. These challenges are the subject with in this chapter. It shows that the problems encountered by return migrants in readapting to the local working and living conditions are greatest in the first period after their return and then diminish. Despite these difficulties of reintegration return migrants had generally achieved their goals and were satisfied overall with their post-return situation. For some migrants, however, such challenges constitute a good reason to remain abroad or to re-emigrate after their return.

Migrants' and their Families' Experiences on Return

Whether or not returning migrants assume a developmental role is not only influenced by their experience abroad, but depends also on their circumstances after return. The opportunities or constraints that they face in different spheres affect their potential for change in various ways. These conditions also determine whether return migrants settle for good or decide to leave again. There are several reasons why migrants may become discouraged or frustrated and may even regret their migration or return.

Employment and Business Opportunities

An important aspect of the lives of the migrants who returned home was their professional situation. As was seen in the previous chapter, the reason that approximately one third of all surveyed respondents returned is that they expected to find better jobs or better business opportunities than they could find abroad. At least feasible employment and business opportunities were expected by about two thirds of the returnees before they returned home. However, such opportunities in the home country had changed very much since independence, as was stressed by this 48-year-old Ivorian university professor:

> What made Ivorians come back is that they had more opportunities than their fellows from other African countries, because Côte d'Ivoire was delayed with the training of its experts. In '46 there were only six Ivorians who had gone to university and at the beginning of the sixties there were still only a few. So for someone who had finished high school in 1972 there still were a lot of opportunities and I think a lot of Ivorians came back because they knew that they had a future. When the country started to have some problems, people no longer had enough opportunities, Ivorians have also started to remain abroad …

Before new recruitment into public administration was stopped due to structural adjustment programmes, most returnees were automatically reabsorbed into the civil service, especially those who had been sent abroad with a scholarship. This was the case for this 53-year-old Ghanaian, who said that he did not need to struggle at all, there was a job waiting for him upon return:

> My department sent me out to do a particular course where there was a weakness, so even before I came there was the need to come back to the department, because that was the reason why the department supported my candidature for a University of Ghana scholarship.

But times had changed in the private sector too, as shown by the account of this 60-year-old architect who returned home in 1970, after some studies in Italy, to set up his own firm:

> My integration did not cause any problems; I would even say that we were practically expected … We had the chance to come back regularly and to keep contacts, we were not completely out of touch. And then the country was led by people that we knew. At that time sometimes you had an assignment in a company even before you finished your studies or in the public administration … Now it's no longer the same. That's why many young people prefer to stay abroad and to work there, because in our countries it has become more difficult.

Several accounts revealed the importance of knowing the right people to find a good job after return. This strengthens the hypothesis that those who lose touch with home completely or stay away too long experience greater difficulties in finding a good job after return (Muschkin, 1993). But the "right" contacts are not always made or kept personally, as evidenced by this account of a 38-year-old Ivorian who returned after having finished his studies in the United States:

> When I returned it took me approximately 6 to 8 months to find a job. Well, it's due to my parents' contacts that it has been a bit easier for me than for others. I was able to use the contacts that my parents had with certain persons and so finally I found something.

Sometimes those who did not have the right connections got discouraged and frustrated, and even considered re-emigration. Such was the story of this 48-year-old Ivorian who returned to Paris:

> When I returned with my degree I was 31 years old and … I was told I was too old to enter the civil service … the other thing I was told was that my degree was not adapted to the local context … The fact that my degree was not recognised and also the lack of freedom – wherever I passed I had to know someone or to dash something [give a bribe] – is something that shocked me profoundly … The fact that your qualifications are not recognised and that you have to lick someone's boots to get on … You can be the most qualified person in Côte d'Ivoire, but if you're not the son of someone you will not be taken into consideration'.

Another slightly younger Ghanaian returnee also drew attention to this kind of obstacle:

> The most competent people sometimes have to depend on somebody else's good nature … because we are not a society that is built on meritocracy. It's a society that is built purely on old boyism and all those things, which are not achievement standards, they are not standards of excellence: you went to the same school, you are from the same tribe or you belong to the same club.

A considerable number of Ghanaians and to a lesser extent of Ivorians launched their own private businesses after return. Some had taken this step before they returned home, but the majority did so only afterwards.

Frequently returnees combined their personal business initiatives with their duties and responsibilities as an employee.[1] In particular, those working in the civil service were inclined to opt for this solution since they were earning too little in the public sector.

However, the most important reason why certain returnees wanted to launch their own firm is that they thought they could use what they had learned abroad and that there was a demand for the knowledge they had gained in the local context. Many of them were eager to apply the ideas they had brought back from overseas as, for example, this 40-year-old Ghanaian who undertook an exploratory trip back home in the mid-1990s:

> I was totally blown away with the opportunities that I saw in Ghana and in Africa. That reminds me of a little story which someone was telling me a little while ago, where there are two salesmen … they sell shoes, sneakers, whatever and their bosses send them to a remote area to try and go and sell sneakers. The first company's salesperson goes to the remote area and says – hey man, these guys there are not wearing shoes, so I'm not going there to sell them sneakers because there's no business there. So he comes back and the boss says – fine, we're not going there. Then there is the other company, the guy says – these people are not wearing shoes, this is where the business is. So the boss says – yeah, go get it. So the guy goes to that country and they make a ton of money. So, it's with the same mentality that I came to Ghana and I went to some countries in Africa and I realised that nobody is creating content about Africa on the internet, and I said – oh my God, this is a unique opportunity for me.

Becoming self-employed by setting up a private company is often the ultimate aim of a returning migrant (Black et al., 2003c; Callea, 1986). This was stressed by a 40-year-old Ghanaian who, after her return from the United States, launched a now well-established consulting company which offers management, financial and policy advisory services to public and private sector organisations and institutions:

> People have come back with different experiences and in fact most of the returnees that I'm aware of have come back to set up their own

1 Survey information was collected only regarding the primary activity of the respondents, but evidence from in-depth interviews suggests it is important to pay greater attention in the future to the phenomenon of double work commitments.

> businesses, and I think they have been relatively more successful setting up their businesses because ... I think you have an advantage when you've travelled and you've come back, you are willing to take on more risk, you are willing to push what you are doing ... I think certainly my attitude to work is probably different from [that of those who did not migrate]. If I don't get the information I want, I don't hesitate calling the Chief Executive of any organisation. In that way I think I get what I want ... I think it takes that aggressiveness to be able to survive here.

Of course, these narratives, like all those illustrated in this book, reflect the subjective point of view of the returnees. As such they cannot be taken at face value, but what is being stressed here is that becoming self-employed involves greater risks than being employed in a public or a private structure. Employment most often grants social security and it is preferred by migrants who desire to avoid the difficulties connected with becoming their own bosses.

In brief, the findings show that it was not only younger migrants who were more likely to have gone back to work in the private sector, but also those who first left when they were younger and who lived and worked abroad longer. Older migrants, particularly those with a Doctorate, who moved abroad mostly for educational purposes and returned quickly after their studies, were instead more likely to be employed in the public sector. More problems of adjustment to local working conditions were usually encountered by the first group of respondents.

Problems of Adjustment to the Local Working Conditions

In the questionnaire respondents were asked to specify the problems they faced after return in adjusting to the local working conditions. The answers displayed in Table 9-1 show first that the interviewed Ivorians generally reported encountering less problems than the Ghanaians, and second that for both groups of returnees the problems have diminished over time. In fact the number of returnees saying they were not facing any problem progressively increased from the time right after return to the time of the interview.

Ivorians generally encountered fewer problems than Ghanaians did after return in the workplace. When interviewed, many more of the former claimed they were no longer facing any problems. However, about twice as many Ivorians (41 per cent) as Ghanaians (21 per cent) said they did

Table 9-1 Problems of adjustment to local work conditions after return, by country and period (%)

Problems of adjustment	Côte d'Ivoire			Ghana		
	First	After some time	Now	First	After some time	Now
Many problems	36.2	14.8	10.7	31.2	16.2	11.7
Some problems	19.5	25.5	18.8	40.9	48.7	44.8
No problems	44.3	59.7	70.5	27.9	35.1	42.9
No response	–	–	–	–	–	0.6
TOTAL	100.0	100.0	100.0	100.0	100.0	100.0
Valid cases	(149)	(149)	(149)	(154)	(154)	(154)

not encounter any problem at any time. That fewer Ivorians met problems of adjustment to the local work conditions is not surprising, because they stayed and worked for a shorter period abroad. Their mentality and lifestyle were therefore less likely to have been affected by the migration experience.

Indeed, overall, respondents who stayed abroad longer than average and especially those who had worked abroad for extensive periods were more likely to have encountered problems of adjustment. Those who did not encounter any problems on return were also more likely to be working in the public sector, whereas those who were self-employed and had employees were much more likely to have dealt with problems of adjustment to the local working conditions since their return, especially amongst Ghanaians. These problems increased over time. For both Ghanaians and Ivorians by far the greatest problems derived from the need to readapt to the local work culture (Table 9-2).

Problems with the local "work attitude and approaches" were encountered most commonly, but far more by Ghanaian than Ivorian respondents, principally because they had lived and worked abroad longer. In-depth interviews reveal that returned migrants were often frustrated with the deficiencies in work ethics, professionalism, transparency and meritocracy. In particular they complained about poor time management, planning, organisation, productivity and standards of performance. Three

Table 9-2 Problems in the workplace, by country

Problems in the workplace*	Côte d'Ivoire N (%)	Ghana N (%)
Work attitude and approaches	43 (28.6)	109 (70.8)
Finding a good job	27 (18.0)	15 (9.7)
Relationship with collaborators	29 (19.3)	12 (8.2)
Physical work conditions	14 (9.3)	28 (18.2)
Heavy and slow bureaucracy	10 (6.7)	18 (11.7)
Socio-economic environment	7 (4.7)	14 (9.1)
Lack of local capacities	3 (2.0)	9 (5.8)
Other	24 (16.0)	41 (26.2)

* Responses given to an open-ended question.

quarters of the returned Ghanaians also had "difficulties with the work ethics and practices".[2]

Several returnees felt their experience abroad had made them more responsible and professional compared to the local standards. This was for instance the case of this 36-year-old Ghanaian returnee who was given some key assignments to manage some critical public services:

> I think the major problem I had and I still have is a professional one, because the work ethics I have been taught and used in England varied greatly from the work ethics in Ghana. Therefore I had to decide, and I'm still deciding, whether to apply that ethics. And that's what I tried to do initially. You do things in a certain way, you get to work at a certain time and people are late, you query them, you do your work properly. Or was I going to be more flexible, allow mistakes if it meant that the company was at risk, and then gain popularity for being so flexible.

The problems existing in both the public and the private sectors were portrayed as follows by a 45-year-old Ghanaian returnee:

2 Unfortunately this answer slipped out of the French translation of the questionnaire and thus no data regarding this specific issue is available for the Ivorian sample.

> I can go to a ministry where I'm supposed to have a meeting with somebody, let's say some director … he may be there, he may not be there. His support staff may also not be there. Or, if they are there, they may be sleeping on the job. I'm just saying that as an example … In the private sector, you find there's markedly, markedly more professionalism. If you go to most of the big banks now … you are not going to find that … you'll find more professionalism there, because I guess people can be hired and fired quite easily.

Several returnees also complained that things are often done too slowly and inefficiently. This 45-year-old Ghanaian explained the source of some of his greatest frustrations:

> The attitude to time just blew my mind … these are some of the things I don't think I can ever get used to, it still drives me crazy … These are some of the problems and just the pace of doing things. Things that normally take you hours can go on for two weeks. Somebody gets a bribe along the line, the system is so. The system doesn't work especially when you have been trained in New York for 15 years.

Bad governance and corruption were frequently mentioned in conjunction with problems related to the heavy and slow bureaucracy. Some of the respondents placed these issues in the wider socio-economic, political and cultural context. Some also recognised that many of these problems have intensified in connection with the general degeneration of the situation as, for example, this Ghanaian who, after return, established a private development consultancy firm:

> My frustration stems first of all from what I know used to happen here, not so much from what happens abroad. My frustration stems from comparing Ghana with Ghana; and I'm not that old, I'm 46 or something. I remember in these streets here every day the gutters would be cleaned, once a week the guy from the municipality would come and spray. You didn't notice mosquitoes that much. The fact that everybody is always sick with malaria, it wasn't the same … Things became a lot more difficult by the mid-seventies. So my frustrations stem from what I remember and it's easy to say – oh in America, London things are done like that. I know this is not London, not Rome, not Reykjavik, but what is important is that you see some progress instead of decline, and the decline is often everywhere.

More general problems such as the poor remuneration, limited benefits and the difficult working conditions were extensively referred to in certain in-depth interviews. The "poor physical conditions" existing in most of the workplaces were a source of concern for several of the returnees (Table 9-2). The lack of basic infrastructure and facilities such as water and power supply, telecommunications, roads and transportation represented a major constraint and hampered many returnees in their work. To this needs to be added the absence or obsolescence of professional equipment and the lack of up-to-date technology. On the other hand, bureaucratic procedures were just as cumbersome for both groups of respondents.

Some returnees also said they had difficulties in "finding a good job", generally meaning a well remunerated one, after return. It is not surprising that this problem was raised by many more Ivorians than Ghanaians considering that many more of the former were employed in the public sector where currently salaries tend to be lower than in the private sector. Cross-tabulations confirmed that Ivorians working in the public sector more often affirmed that they had a problem with their low income. A 53-year-old Ghanaian working in the university regretted that the conditions had deteriorated so much:

> Having left here for some years and having come back to find that things had so deteriorated to the extent that you had to do something to supplement your income ... At the time when we were students, we saw that the university lecturers are a class of people in an ivory tower; everything is fantastic about them and ... I came to realise that it is really not so as I originally thought.

A 45-year-old Ghanaian who launched a non-governmental organisation after return elaborated on this issue:

> Salaries in the universities really reduce you to bare necessities and even then you are not able to meet bare necessities. Now if you have a family and you are not thinking only about yourself and you've lived abroad, you also want to get good schooling for your kids, you are thinking for their future, their security and so on and you plunge them into this situation where education is in crisis and the health sector has a lot of problems, the institutions simply do not function.

In their search for good employment some returnees not only encountered the problem of low salary levels, but also had difficulties in finding a job that adequately matched their qualifications. Others were frustrated because they did not get promoted as, for example, this 56-year-old Ghanaian, who went to the United States to get a Masters degree:

> The major difficulty was … the fact that by the time you came back your colleagues would have moved up in terms of ranking because, you see over here, we don't regard further studies, further work, as part of your preparation for work with the organisation. So once you are not here when it comes to promotion, you are not considered. So depending on the number of years you spent abroad, you come back and find that your colleagues are promoted ahead of you and that can be annoying … When you have gone, made more efforts to acquire skills to come and help, you find that people who are complacent, sitting down, are rather going forward.

Another important kind of problem of adjustment is related to the difficulties returnees encountered in their "relationship with collaborators" in the workplace. The issue of the relations between returned migrants and non-migrants was dealt with in Chapter Six, but here the account of a 41-year-old Ivorian who returned from Germany can shed some further light on its complexity:

> There often is repulsion vis-à-vis those who stayed. I would even say that many of them have a certain inferiority complex, as many of those who went abroad have a superiority complex. They say to themselves – I know it better – whereas we may know a little more, but not necessarily better; and those who stayed here say – he has lived in Europe, he did this, he did that. There is a great, great problem of reintegration.

This returnee also stressed that non-migrants are often jealous of returned migrants because they did not get a chance to go abroad. They feel threatened, he said, and try to protect their position in the workplace. Here again, it needs to be stressed that this is only one side of the story, and that it would be interesting to know what non-migrants think about returnees.

Compared to the wealth of socio-psychological and organisational problems in the workplace the "lack of local capacities" was only rarely mentioned as a problem. However, this partly hinges on the way this response was formulated as it appears somewhat generic.

Many of the above-cited problems of adjustment were not sufficiently anticipated by migrants before their return, as shown in the account of this 45-year-old Ghanaian who returned to direct the law firm she had launched whilst she was away:

> When you come on vacation you really don't know – let's say, have a real pulse, have a real feeling for business, for how you can really work. You know people; that's true. But just integrating and getting into the system is much more than difficult. I think I came back with the expectation that well, here I am, I've got all this experience and I've gathered all this knowledge and wisdom that I guess people can use over here. But at the same time you have to remember that people had been here, a lot of my peers had been here ... a lot of them had stayed behind and had gone through a very, very bad time. And coming back in 1996... the situation in Ghana was much, much better ... those of my type who came back felt that finally the business process would be much, much better, which it was to a certain extent, but it was not as simple as I had thought. I had been used to working in what was more or less say a technologically advanced situation, where our secretaries and almost everybody was using computers and one of the things that I found when I came back was that the support staff, the level of support staff that I expected was not there.

Evidently there often is a considerable gap between the expectations of returning migrants and the realities they find on the ground. In part this is due to the fact that, as was seen before, a significant number of respondents never or only rarely visited their country of origin whilst they were overseas. But apparently even for those who undertook regular visits home it was not always easy to gain a thorough understanding of the evolving local working and living conditions.

Living Conditions and Difficulties of Re-adaptation

It was noted in the previous chapter that the longer migrants remain abroad and the fewer visits they made home, the more unrealistic tend to become their expectations. This results in a situation where they encounter difficulties when they need to readapt to the local work conditions. The same principle seems to apply to the difficulties they meet in readjusting to the local living conditions. Return migrants' concerns were predominantly linked to the "way services and facilities operate" (Table 9-3).

Table 9-3 General problems encountered after return, by country

Problems after return*	Côte d'Ivoire N (%)	Ghana N (%)
Difficulties with the way services/ facilities operate	82 (54.7)	121 (78.6)
Low income and difficulties making ends meet	65 (43.3)	54 (35.1)
Difficulties finding good employment	48 (32.0)	19 (12.3)
Problems with family and friends' expectations	61 (40.7)	58 (37.7)
Need to go back and live with parents/ family members	15 (10.0)	24 (15.6)
Problems readapting to the way of life	33 (22.0)	51 (33.1)
Problems setting up my own business	52 (34.7)	42 (27.3)
Difficulties with the work ethics and practices**	...	116 (75.3)
Other problems	16 (10.7)	18 (11.7)
No problem	5 (3.3)	6 (3.9)

* It was possible to give more than one pre-coded response.
** Unfortunately this question was not presented to the Ivorian sample.

Not only were returnees preoccupied with the poor quality of education and health services; they were also bothered by poorly working basic amenities such as power and water supply and communications. A 42-year-old Ghanaian who, after a few years, decided to go back to London because she missed the "day-to-day comfort factors" she had become used to in Europe, offered the following description:

> Here I drive my car, go to supermarket, park in one place, get everything I need from one shop and put it in my car and go home. That's the end of my shopping, and I have everything I need for one week or two weeks. In Ghana you get up in the morning, you go to the market, you buy your fresh vegetables and fruits there, you buy all your yams, your plantains there. Then you go to the butcher shop in town, you buy your meat there. Then you drive to another shop where you buy your dry goods and tin things and all this between the heat and the traffic and the noise, and it

> will take you three, four hours to finish your basic shopping. This is if you are not even looking for special things, just ordinary things. So everything took time, everything. If you phone someone you find the phone is not working, you turn on the taps sometimes and the water is not running, you are watching television or you are trying to feed your child and the lights go off, and that's it. So we tried to adjust, at a time we got a generator, this, that and the other, but you are still part of the infrastructure, and when there is a problem you are part of it.

Poor customer care was another problem that was very frequently mentioned during the interviews. The account of this 37-year-old Ivorian returnee constitutes one example:

> You go to the post office to buy some stamps and the person who you have to deal with, especially those who are older, does not even raise her head. She talks to you without looking at you, which means you don't even dare to talk to her because you are worried to disturb her. And that's a mentality that continues to persist. In Europe, in the West, you are told the customer is king. But here the principle is not applied … that elderly woman thinks that a younger person owes her respect. For her it's inconceivable that it is the customer who is king. It doesn't mean anything to her, it's nonsense. The younger people of my generation accept this more easily, because they have seen this abroad … they know how you are received at a post office in the United States.

A 43-year-old Ghanaian addressed the issue of poor services and customer care with an even stronger criticism:

> From the little to the big things, from the taxi driver who thinks he can be rude to a passenger, to a hotel where the bed sheets aren't changed … we have a society where we are very tolerant of less than satisfactory services. Our thinking is that that's okay … people don't complain about anything … the more people who have been abroad, who come back and demand what they were used to in England or in America or wherever they were, the more people do that, the more people here will see that maybe they are not abnormal, maybe when he says he wants a Coca-Cola, he wants a Coca-Cola, he doesn't want a Club-Cola … You don't ask questions as to whether the alternative is any good; you just bring it and assume that the person who is paying money is going to accept what you bring as an alternative. You get into a *tro-tro* [a local collective taxi] … and the mate

> who you are going to give money to at the end of the journey thinks he's doing you a favour by picking you up ... It's there in everything, from top to bottom, from the ministers of state to the Joe who is coming to weed your garden. They all act in the same way.

However, re-adaptation problems may also include several other issues. The account full of regrets of an Ivorian who, although he desired to stay abroad, was obliged to return from Canada after only seven years of absence, represents a relatively extreme example:

> When I arrived I no longer knew the city of Abidjan. I was only a school kid when I left and I came back much later as a grown-up man. I had assimilated certain behaviours, I thought everybody is good and, when people aren't, they tell you. But truly people in Africa are more hypocritical than the Chinese, and so it's been difficult for me. People give an appointment and don't respect it, people lie ... so it's been difficult for me who came from North America where when you say x it's x, you don't change ... Also, the food and water. Besides in Abidjan I cannot drink the tap water, and so I cannot go anywhere in Côte d'Ivoire because even from the plates from which I have to eat, I immediately get amoebas. And then I had no employment ... and I had to walk [a lot because I did not have the money for transportation], and when I walked I got wet to the bones since I came back during the winter, it was minus 30° in New York and when I get here it was plus 30°.

Similarly, a 37-year-old Ivorian returnee who lived overseas in Belgium for about ten years was struck by the great differences existing between the host and the home societies:

> During the years I lived in Europe I was no longer aware of the poverty in my country. There are things that are very shocking when you come back from Europe where social security is very effective, insurance, basic health care for all, the fact that everybody can go to school, can satisfy hunger. You end up believing that those are ordinary things and then when you go back, you realise that on the same planet there really is a huge gap that separates two environments.

Table 9-3 strikingly confirms in quantitative terms the relevance of the already verbally reported syndrome: the suffering of economic hardship due to "low incomes" which in turn depend upon the difficulties of "finding good employment"[3] and/or of "setting up own businesses". Perhaps, as a consequence, many respondents had "problems with family and friends' expectations" and had difficulties meeting the related demands. Some even reported housing problems and had had to go back to living with their parents or other family members. For example, a 53-year-old Ghanaian who returned to work as a civil servant and faced problems making ends meet, also had to resist family pressures:

> The aspirations of my parents, my people were extremely high. You've gone to the UK, gone to do a PhD, you are a lecturer at the University of Ghana, so the aspiration, the expectations from my people from the village were extremely high, and I couldn't meet these expectations. They were expecting so much from me as somebody who had come out of the family as a star. I realised that there was no way that I could meet the high expectation, so that frustrated me. I had no money, the salary wasn't enough, and the little money I had, my brother had smashed my car, so I had to use it to put the car back on the road. So I had nothing, I had to depend upon the University and that was where I saw that probably, if I had stayed on in England for a few more years, it would have been better.

Families and friends, and even the larger community, often demand not only financial assistance but also moral and material support. But another crucial problem is related to the expectations society places on returnees as far as their attitudes and behaviour are concerned. Women have to deal with the greatest pressures in this respect. A 51-year-old Ivorian university lecturer who lived with his wife abroad illustrated the way they both were forced to readapt to the local manners and customs:

> When we were in France my wife studied and me too, but as I was doing a Doctorate I had more time. Since I no longer had to attend classes I brought the children to school, I picked them up, and replaced her in the evenings in the kitchen so that she had enough time to study. I laid the table, we ate and I washed the dishes and this for many years. She was

3 Of course, amongst the élite expectations may be very high, and the definition of "good employment" might be much narrower than that accepted by most of the population.

> used to that and I also did it without any problem. And then we returned to Côte d'Ivoire and at a certain point my mother in law was ill and came to stay with us. One day she comes into the kitchen and sees me cooking and washing dishes – scandal – she screamed! Her daughter tried to explain – look, I'm busy with other things, but the old women said – if it's like that, I will do the cooking, I will wash dishes and all the rest, what do you think your parents in law will think if they saw him doing all this? … Since then I've lost the right to access the kitchen. When I go in that direction, my wife immediately asks me what I'd like and brings it. All that leads us back into common habits because it is expected that when Monsieur comes back home he is to sit in his long chair, read the newspaper, and someone may even help him to take off his shoes. It's the mentality of our parents, which they consider necessary: men should not care about tiny things in life.

Several problems were reported during in-depth interviews which had an important gender dimension. Some set special emphasis on the differences existing in gender relations abroad and back home. For example, for this 42-year-old Ghanaian who was interviewed in London where she had lived most of her life, returning home entails a sort of "culture shock" which she illustrated in great detail:

> Particularly when I got married I realised that there were many cultural differences that I did not appreciate very much at all. There were certain things that were normal for me and that were not normal for others; and certain others were normal for a typical Ghanaian woman and not for me. Some of my independence, shall we say, as a result of growing up outside of that culture, I found clashed a little bit with what was expected of me. There are a lot of attitudes. For example in Ghana people are very free to drop in and see you as they like when they are passing by, relatives you know; there is never any question of I'm phoning to see if you are there, if it is convenient for me to come, no, no, no, you can be lying there in bed but you have to invite the person and, no matter what you are doing, be hospitable. I found that very intrusive … And things like, hmm, it's very acceptable for men to go out, go drinking with their friends and its not so acceptable for women to do that. You go out with your husband when it's family things, christening, weddings, social events or whatever. But for you to go out by yourself to certain places or with other girls that is found a little unacceptable … and certain things like … men frequently in a Ghanaian, African context tend to be of quite polygamous nature,

> and society quite often does not condemn them. These days with AIDS and everything it doesn't exactly encourage them, but it's not really the condemnation you will get in the West … A lot of African women, Ghanaian women believe that as long as they are married and their husband comes home eventually, and they are Mrs whatever … it's okay … as long as the husband is not too late, as long it's not with somebody they know. You know, they are prepared to be accommodating and turn a blind eye, pretend they haven't seen it, and he continues to look after them, to look after his children … And with me it's like – this is wrong, this is awful, you should not stand for it, it's dangerous, it's wrong, it's undignified, it's not good.

That certain practices are difficult to re-accept for women who have lived abroad was also found in Asia (Iredale et al., 2002). An example in Ghana was a 37-year-old woman who reported problems after return with the way she dressed. Her stay in England had changed the way she thought and dressed, but wearing shorts was considered inadmissible for a director of a major government agency, as she had become. One day she was prevented from giving a lecture to people from a District Assembly because her skirt was considered too short. Another example is constituted by the experience of a 32-year-old Ivorian who returned to work in an international organisation. She stressed she had problems with expressing her views in the workplace:

> You terribly bother people when you say what you think … you are not expected to have your viewpoint. You bother the others also because you are much younger … I recently have had some African bosses … and as long as they were English-speaking Africans or Europeans they had a much greater open-mindedness … But what I realised is that with the French-speaking Africans you always have the age of their child, their nephew. Thus there always is this paternalism which makes it difficult to accept that you have a different point of view as for them that is contradictory. I noticed for example that if a young European, a young Belgian or Dutch, would express their views freely this was appreciated. But if I would do that there would be the opposite reaction. For them I do not make any contribution, I almost annoy them since, as a woman, I'm the girl who has the same age of their child. So I suffer from certain stereotypes, and I'm the loser. It's immediately perceived negatively although I am in a professional environment and these are neither my uncles nor my aunts. In brief, what they would accept from a Westerner

> as an open-minded attitude, as an input to the discussion, is immediately perceived as a annoying contradiction, and anyway, you will be seen as having a too innovative mindset, as being too emancipated, and as someone who has received a poor education from her parents.

Most participants in the survey encountered one or more general problems of readaptation after return. Only a very small number – 4 per cent of Ghanaians and 3 per cent of Ivorians – declared they had had no problems. This affected the way they looked upon their experiences before and after return as well as their plans for the future, as will be seen in the next section.

Satisfactions, Regrets and Plans for the Future

Despite readjustment problems a very high proportion of Ghanaians (94 per cent) did not regret their decision to return to their country of origin (Table 9-4). In the questionnaire they indicated that, if they could go back in time, they would still opt for returning home. However, almost half of these respondents declared that, if they could actually redo their lives, they would go about return differently. More than one third said they would come back earlier and one in five stated that they would organise their return better. Smaller proportions of respondents indicated they would have wanted to come back later, in order to earn and save more money or to gain more professional experience.

In contrast, among the Ivorians, over a quarter said that if they could go back in time, they would not have returned home. This is probably due to the fact that, as was seen in Chapter Four, Côte d'Ivoire was just experiencing its first serious political crisis at the time of the survey. In this case, slightly more than half of those who said they would still return home indicated they would do exactly as they had done in the past. Among those who declared they would do it differently, almost one third said they would make different personal decisions and about one in ten respectively said they would come back earlier, better organise return, acquire more work experience or follow different studies abroad. Only a very limited number of Ivorians said that they would have liked to come back home later than they actually did.

Across both groups, only a very marginal number of respondents (3 per cent) regretted their original migration, whereas two thirds said they would migrate in exactly the same way. Many of those who said they

Table 9-4 Questioning the decision to go abroad and to return, by country (%)

Decisions	Côte d'Ivoire	Ghana
If you could go back in time, would you make the same decision to return to your country of origin?		
No	27.5	5.2
Yes, I would repeat the same	42.3	52.6
Yes, but I would do it differently	30.2	40.9
Don't know	-	1.3
TOTAL	100.0	100.0
Valid cases	(149)	(154)
If you could go back in time, would you make the same decision to leave your country of origin?		
No	3.3	2.6
Yes, I would repeat the same	64.7	62.3
Yes, but I would do it differently	32.0	35.1
TOTAL	100.0	100.0
Valid cases	(150)	(151)

would act differently felt they would have gone to a different destination or made different study or career choices. Many Ivorians reported they would have preferred to move to an English-speaking country. Whereas one in five Ghanaians wished they had spent less time abroad, not a single Ivorian claimed the same. A small number of respondents also said they would plan their departure better.

Many migrants who participated in in-depth interviews and returned with the expectation of finding better professional opportunities did not regret their decision to return. This 40-year-old Ghanaian who earned several prestigious degrees overseas and launched her own consulting firm in Accra, for example, declared herself satisfied:

> The opportunities that I get here, I don't think I could ever get in the US. I mean I think you get [here] a lot of high-profile jobs ... you get a lot of very challenging responsibilities that I probably would never have the opportunity to get [abroad], or even if I did, I would be part of a group. I

> would never have had the opportunity at my age to lead key assignments … and so it's always been gratifying to have come back.

Similarly, a 46-year-old Ghanaian who opted for an academic career in the university felt that he had a much wider range of professional opportunities at home than abroad:

> When I look at some of my contemporaries, other Africans who were either in Germany or in the UK, or in the US at that time also doing their PhD, who I knew and who stayed and worked there … [and] I look at the things I do, the kinds of journals I publish in, compared to the kind of journals they publish in, the kind of money I can make, the kind of money they make, the kind of conference I go to, I find that I have much more opportunities than they have … Those in America are teaching in very small colleges, small colleges of very little significance, they are not likely to find jobs in large mainstream, well-established universities. So nobody gets to know their work, but because I'm coming from Africa, it's easier for me to go to Harvard and give them a talk and people will listen to me. If I came from a small college in the Midwest nobody is going to pay attention to me in the US … being in Africa has helped me … I don't think if I was living in the UK for example, as a Ghanaian academic, let's say teaching at London University, that it would be that easy for me to publish books. If I went to Macmillan and said I want to write a book on Ghana, they will say you live in the UK, how can you write a book on Ghana? But if I live in Ghana and do a book on Ghana they take it much more seriously.

But there are also a number of examples of returnees who had regrets. This 49-year-old Ivorian university professor clearly would act otherwise if he had to remake his life in current times:

> If today I had to make this decision, if I was a student today and I had a scholarship to study in the United States or in France, from there I would go directly to work for an international organisation. Even in my position today, if I manage to go to the US or elsewhere, I will try to work for UNDP, the ADB or I don't know. Because over there it is much more advantageous to be an international rather than a national officer. So my choice is clear.

Returned migrants were asked in an open-ended question in the survey about their plans for the future and to make a projection for the next three years, and next ten years. About a quarter of Ivorians and a little fewer Ghanaians indicated that it was their primary plan for the next three years to evolve in their career. Approximately one in five of all respondents were instead interested in setting up their own private businesses. An equal share of Ghanaians said they intended to continue with what they were already doing, whereas this was the case for only one in ten Ivorians. In contrast, a higher proportion of Ivorians planned to change occupation.

The plans that returnees had for the next ten years represented a coherent pursuit of those they nurtured in the shorter term. For about a third of the Ghanaians achieving a good standard of living back home mattered and for approximately a quarter of them the main objective was to retire and lead a calmer life. This is not surprising considering that the Ghanaian sample had an older age structure than the Ivorian one. For one Ghanaian in ten, the priority was to become self-employed (and many of them had already achieved that status when they were interviewed), or to contribute to the development of the home country. For Ivorians the objective of becoming self-employed was more important in the longer term; about one in five planned to launch a private firm in the coming ten years. Smaller proportions aimed to develop in their career or to retire, and only a few said they planned to ameliorate their social status and standard of living.

The Option of Re-Emigrating or Remaining Abroad

Return migrants were also asked if they planned to go abroad again and, if so, for what reasons. In the questionnaire the great majority of respondents – 87 per cent of Ivorians and 89 per cent of Ghanaians – declared that this was not part of their plans. Several of the returnees who gave in-depth interviews also stressed their firm intention to remain for good in the home country as did, for example, this 40-year-old Ghanaian:

> If you ask me to come back to America and you pay me US$5 million a year and take on a job [there] as opposed to staying in Africa and helping to emancipate my own people, I'll stay in Africa. I can tell you to take the US$5 million and go somewhere and find somebody else but I won't go. I'm here to stay.

At the time of the survey only about one in ten returnees were planning to go abroad again, and intended to do so in the coming five years. Yet cross-tabulations in the Ivorian sample show that returnees who had encountered many problems after return with regard to their professional conditions were more likely to plan a new departure.

Both Ivorians and Ghanaians had various reasons for intending to re-emigrate in the future. For the former these reasons were mainly connected to the profession and for the latter mostly for study purposes. A number of returnees had in fact failed to readapt back home and were no longer able to cope with the situation. This was the case of a 42-year-old Ghanaian expatriate who had lived most of her life in the United Kingdom and who described in great detail the reasons she had returned to live in London:

> One of the many, many reasons is that there life is just too hard. Just dealing with the basics it takes so much energy that it gives so little time to move up and move on, because you are spending so much dealing with the basics. I'm in the office I have got a paper to write, I have a meeting to deliver, I have a presentation to give. What am I doing? I'm phoning around trying to find water, people to go to my house and fill the water tank because it has run out of water, and I've got a child at home, one coming from school. Or I'm sitting there taking an interview for somebody for a position. I get a phone call, it's urgent. What is it? My girl who is with the child, we've run out of gas, so she can't cook the child lunch. Then I call my husband on his mobile asking him to take one of his workers to go and fill the gas cylinder and bring it back home so she can cook. Or to buy something on his way when picking my daughter up from school ... You have to plan all these basic things, whereas here I would just have to phone a takeaway, they would deliver to the house, you know, that's why you never come home and worry about it. The gas wouldn't run out here, because it's piped, you see. So you know water is clean, it's safe you don't have to think I should buy bottled water. I mean we buy bottled water here but we don't have to because you know the water is safe. In Ghana I wouldn't let my children drink the water from the tap because I don't know what is in there ... So these are all things which were inconvenient when we were there. In the third year that we were there, we had a very, very big power crises in Ghana and power was rationed very severely. It started off initially with you having power for 12 hours and then you would be cut off for 12 hours. Then eventually it moved to 24 hours on, 24 hours off. Then it became 12 hours on, 24 hours off. So, the fridge was, there was no point

> because by the time it got cold the power goes off again. We had to buy food everyday, cook it that day, eat it that same day. You had to boil water when the light came on and put into two or three flasks for the children, baby's milk and all other business. You had to iron your clothes as soon you had electricity for three days ahead, because you don't know when the electricity will come back. Wherever you are going you had to plan so far ahead. And then the heat, no fans, no air conditioning, the children would get rashes, heat rash… they were sick and it was in the night you couldn't even see their faces to see what was happening, to know if they are hot. You know, all these things became a problem. Our first child was very healthy, thank God, you know we really had very few problems with her. But the second one when she was born, it was a different story. She was fine for the first few months and then she would get a cold it would become a cough, it would become a chest infection, she will be wheezing like an asthmatic. We went to one doctor, to another doctor, to another doctor. One time I took her to the hospital because she was breathing very badly we got there they said she needs oxygen, we had to take her to the children's ward. This clinic was five minutes from our house, and we were very happy we bought that house because it was near the clinic. I took her to the children's ward they started to give her oxygen. After two minutes I realised that oxygen wasn't coming so I called the technician. He came and adjusted it. After two minutes the same thing happened. The second time I called him he said – ooh, the oxygen is finished and I said – well bring another one, and he said – this is all we have, and this child is suffocating. So, luckily they had given her an injection to help to relieve the pressure on her lungs. Otherwise she might have died just because of oxygen! It was those kinds of issues that really told us that it was time to leave.

The inefficiency and poor quality of basic services is certainly among the reasons why certain migrants opt to remain abroad. For a 45-year-old Ghanaian returnee the three main reasons some migrants do not return are:

> [Firstly] they have nowhere to stay when they come back. A lot of people just left here and from family homes. They've gone and they've set up a home there. Can you imagine you have to come back and stay with the family again? No, they can't! You find they send money down for people to build houses for them and the people spend the money and they didn't build the houses. So people don't come because they have nowhere to stay.

> Secondly because their children are installed … have made all friends. Maybe education is free or they are only paying a bit. Here they have to pay high fees to get the same level of education for their children … Thirdly, I think a lot of people have difficulty with the sanitation problems in this country. Because a lot of them left from the rural areas and maybe a lot of people who are abroad, I can't say that they are from the residential areas, no, no, they come from the village and small town and they were able to go to school abroad. They were not lucky to have passed their O and A levels and all that, they went to work, they call it hustling. Now they've made a little money and they are able to live in clean surroundings, they don't want to go back … they can't and part of it is because they have a complex about it, they don't want to be reminded of where they came from, they don't because they find it so disgusting compared to what they are used to now.

But there also other reasons why some migrants decide to stay abroad, as shown by responses of returnees to an open-ended question asking why some of their fellow compatriots had decided to remain abroad (Table 9-5). For most respondents the "better professional opportunities abroad" acted as the main deterrent of return. In several instances the better opportunities existing abroad also delayed return because migrants did not envision to return until they had saved enough money. In fact, "lack of savings or credit" was cited as a cause for which certain fellow compatriots stayed abroad. Of course, this posed more problems to migrants who planned to become self-employed. But savings were also considered important to bridge an initial period of unemployment or to secure suitable accommodation after return.

For Ghanaians the "higher standards of living abroad", including effective social services and possibly social security, were of particular importance, as was the fear that they would be unable to re-adapt to the local living conditions. During their long absence they might have changed significantly and could no longer imagine that they will be able to reintegrate back home, as a 47-year-old Ghanaian migrant in London stressed:

> I think they have lived in this system for so long that, like it or not, they are Europeans, they think like Europeans [laughter].

Or, on balance, they simply do not consider the conditions in their country of origin suitable enough to return home. But there also comes a time

Table 9-5 Reasons for remaining abroad, by country

Reasons for remaining abroad*	**Côte d'Ivoire N (%)**	**Ghana N (%)**
Better professional opportunities abroad	102 (86.0)	68 (44.2)
Higher standards of living abroad	35 (23.3)	89 (57.8)
Political/economic problems in country of origin	15 (10.0)	38 (24.7)
Difficult readaptation into home context	15 (10.0)	53 (34.4)
Incomplete studies/Lack of qualifications	29 (19.3)	17 (11.3)
Family reasons	16 (10.6)	30 (19.5)
Loss of permanent residence abroad	20 (13.3)	7 (4.5)
Lack of savings or credit	4 (2.6)	32 (20.8)
Too much pressure from family and friends at home	7 (4.6)	8 (5.2)
Other	13 (8.6)	23 (14.9)
No response	–	1 (0.6)

* Responses given to an open-ended question.

when migrants themselves feel that it is too late to make a major change in life such as the one involved with return migration:

> I have a friend who is a very, very good gynaecologist in New York, and runs a very, very good practice and makes a lot of money and every time I go to New York he gives me money to bring to his mother and he sends money regularly, and I said to him – why don't you have this same practice in Ghana and I'm quite sure you could make good money in Ghana, maybe not as much as now you are making, but yes very good money. And he says – well now I'm too old, I'm too old, if I had come to Ghana 15 years ago, yes I would have done it, but now I'm too old. So why didn't you do that 15 years ago? Well, I guess I wanted to see what was here. But the impression I get is he simply drifted, he never really made any conscious decisions about what he wanted to do with his life, and that's how I found many, many people. They don't go studying there and decide I want to live in the US by all means. They just find themselves drifting.

For Ivorians higher standards of living were also critical, though much less important than better professional opportunities. Few Ivorians mentioned the difficulties of re-adaptation as a problem, their emphasis was on the risk of losing their residence status and on family reasons. That in Europe migrants are able to draw benefits not only from appropriate social services but also from social security, often regardless of their occupational status and income level, was stressed by a 45-year-old man who had returned to Côte d'Ivoire:

> If you have achieved only a low educational level and you get here you cannot survive, you cannot find a job, and even if you get a job, you will not be respected. Overseas instead you are protected by a social safety net. You may be unemployed or you may only have a small job, you still have the right to get subsidies, health insurance and even your children are paid. So they too don't even consider going back. Here it's difficult for those who lack the necessary qualifications, because they will not find a good job. But abroad, even when you are a simple cleaner, society will take you in hand. Once you have a residency permit you have the right to get loans, you have all the rights, so you are fine there.

According to one third of the Ghanaians some other migrants had not returned because of the political and economic problems at home; they kept a negative perception of their country of origin, they said, and were lacking up-to-date information. In contrast, only one Ivorian in ten made this argument. A greater share of the Ivorians said that some migrants still needed to complete their studies, or they had failed to get their degree. Some of them, they stressed, were reluctant to return and to expose their failure back home. Others were also concerned about losing their residence status and rights abroad.

That return can become difficult when migrants have not succeeded whilst abroad was emphasised by King (2000). This was also stressed by a 56-year-old Ghanaian, for whom there were two main conditions for return:

> A job back home and a roof over your head, and probably how to move around. There was a programme that was started in the US and I think in Germany trying to get people to go back home. They'd say we would pay for your freight and transport. That's not enough! What's more important is a job where he is going to or something that he can do when he gets back immediately. It's not the transport or the fare, no, it is getting

> something to do when you get back home, because everybody knows you've gone to learn new things, so you are coming back to be even bigger than you used to be. So if you come back and you have no job, nowhere to stay, it means you have gone back instead of going forward, and that is humiliating enough for us.

Reasons related to the family included the aim of sending the children to school abroad, where there is a higher quality of education. But several returnees also stressed that some migrants stay away because of the high expectations and sometimes heavy pressures of their family and friends.

Summary of Findings

In this chapter it was seen that the readjustment and reintegration of returned migrants back home is often challenging and not always successful. Some returnees in fact do not manage to readapt to the local working and living conditions and thus opt to leave again. But many migrants also directly opt to remain abroad because, after several years absence, they fear that they will not be able to readjust and reintegrate back home. Or they believe that the socio-economic and political conditions in the country of origin are not yet suitable enough to take such an important step as returning home. Some evidence was provided that professional conditions at home are seen by returnees as the most significant barrier to return, although confirmation of this would require more extensive study of those who chose not to return.

In spite of these constraints, most respondents did not nurture any substantial regrets and the great majority planned to stay home permanently. This is perhaps not so surprising considering that the sub-category of those who returned but had re-emigrated in the meantime was excluded from the sample. What is interesting, though, is that migrants who returned with a greater development potential, because they acquired more different forms of capital abroad, were generally more challenged by problems after return. This could explain why this group more often considered return only as a temporary move, because some evidence suggests that re-emigration plans depend on problems encountered after return.

Although returnees felt employment and business opportunities in the home country had considerably decreased over time in both the public and the private sectors, many migrants believed they could forge a better career at home. They were significantly helped in this if they had good connections and knew the right people, whereas for those who lacked these assets it was often difficult to get good employment. Finding a good and well-paid job was seen as more difficult by Ivorians than by Ghanaians because the former were more frequently looking for employment in already-existing institutions and companies. The latter more frequently returned with the intent of becoming their own bosses and launching their own private enterprise. For many of them it was clear that they needed to take some risks and maintain a certain aggressiveness if they wanted to advance and make a difference by applying what they had learned abroad.

Migrants who launched their own businesses and had to manage employees encountered more problems of adjustment than employees working in the public sector. The biggest complaints of returnees were about work attitudes. Returning migrants do not necessarily anticipate the vast range of problems that they can face when they resettle back home. During holiday visits and even short business trips it is often difficult to develop a real sense of affairs and grasp the real day-to-day challenges.

Return migrants who stayed and worked abroad longer encountered greater problems in readjusting to the local working conditions as well as in readapting to the local living conditions. These problems also revealed an important gender dimension, which shed some light on why women may be more reluctant to return and more inclined to re-emigrate. For some women, returning home has involved a "culture shock" in terms of gender relations back home compared to abroad.

Chapter Ten

Assessing the Implications of Return Migration at Different Levels

This chapter assesses the impact of return migrants at different levels by dwelling on some significant, practical examples of change provoked at the micro, meso and macro levels. It shows that returned migrants were generally able to improve their personal position and to achieve their professional goals; and the evidence presented demonstrates that they were fairly satisfied with different aspects of their work. Returned migrants promoted various kinds of change in their social and family environment, and more importantly in the workplace. They also contributed to change in the public sphere, through community development initiatives and advocacy for example. But not all returnees embark on such positive initiatives and play a meaningful role back home. The discriminating factors include their occupational level, time since last return, personal attributes and the specific country context.

Improvements in the Personal Position of Returnees

Both objective and subjective indicators were used to assess the improvements that have occurred, through mobility and return, in the migrants' and their families' well-being. Interviewees were asked to establish whether, on balance, the migration experience had had more positive or negative effects for themselves and their immediate family members. Then they compared their current income level with the one they used to have abroad and also with that of other persons who work in a similar position at home. Overall they were relatively satisfied with their working conditions and also, more generally, with the overall living conditions back home.

Achievement of Objectives and Relative Income Levels

Almost all of the participants in the main survey considered that their migration experience has, on balance, produced more positive than negative effects for themselves and their immediate families. When asked if they saw themselves and their family better off now than before they first emigrated, three quarters of the respondents replied affirmatively. For some Ivorians, however, this improvement in income had little to do with their foreign experience. They said it was linked to their career path and the more advanced stage that they had in the meantime attained in their life-course. Before departure they were students and thus dependent on their parents; after return they were employed and had become financially autonomous.

A higher number of Ghanaians thought that their migration experience had allowed them to gain significant experience and to advance professionally. Many also believed that abroad they had been able to acquire more material resources than if they had stayed home. A 45-year-old Ghanaian returnee stressed this issue during her interview:

> I was making the money that I needed to be able to do certain things and even when you talk about it materially, there are a lot of things I could not have done if I had been here. Truly, I couldn't have gotten myself my own house, mortgage free, no way. With the monies that were being paid at that point in time there was no way that you could do that. I couldn't have set up my business, I could not, really. I could not have supported my family the way I have been able to and be comfortable at it. There's no way I could have done all that!

Two important indicators were used to assess the improvements that migration and return had brought about in the migrants' well-being. Returnees were asked, firstly, how their current annual income compared with that of other persons in their home country who had reached a similar position but had not migrated, and secondly, how it compared in real terms (i.e. referring to the standard of life they could afford) with the one they used to have abroad.

Table 10-1 displays responses to the first question. What we find is that most Ivorians felt their income was about the same as that of the average person in a similar position, whereas among Ghanaians, more believed it was above the average. Interestingly, a higher proportion of Ghanaians working in the public sector than those working in the private sector believed that their income was higher. This partly reflects the difference in the age structure of the two groups, and also that, compared to Ivorians, Ghanaians were more advanced in their careers. The majority of Ivorians affirmed they were earning about average mainly because most were occupied in the public sector where salary levels are generally less elastic, especially at lower grades of responsibility.

In general, returnees who had worked abroad longer seemed more likely to think their income is higher than that of others in a similar position, suggesting that foreign work experience is valued and rewarded in the local labour market. In this respect, it can be mentioned that Ghanaians, who considered the work experience and financial capital they acquired abroad as important for their work, were more likely to think that they were better off than others in terms of revenue.

Table 10-1 Perceived difference between current income and average income of other persons in a similar position, by country and sector of activity (%)

Difference	Côte d'Ivoire			Ghana		
	Private	Public	Total	Private	Public	Total
Much lower than average	7.4	3.1	4.7	6.3	14.8	6.3
Lower than average	7.4	8.3	8.0	13.4	11.1	13.4
About average	50.0	62.5	58.0	37.0	29.6	37.0
Higher than average	18.5	18.8	18.7	23.6	33.3	23.6
Much higher than average	13.0	5.2	8.0	14.2	11.1	14.2
No response	3.7	2.0	2.7	5.5	–	5.5
TOTAL	100.0	100.0	100.0	100.0	100.0	100.0
Valid cases	54	96	150	127	26	153

When returned migrants were asked to compare their current annual income with the one they were making abroad, only about one respondent in ten said this had not much changed. There was a great variation in the responses reflecting differences in their experiences abroad and back home.

Table 10-2 shows that approximately a third of the Ghanaians and half of the Ivorians were earning more than what they had earned abroad. However, a rather considerable share of both groups said that their earnings were much decreased since they returned home. Some returnees felt shocked when finding the huge gap between the salary they had earned abroad and the one offered back home, as for instance this 42-year-old Ghanaian woman:

> [In Accra] I was working in a very prestigious organisation. I had a very, very good senior job. I had access to easy loan, I was given all kind of benefits for rent advance, rent was subsidised, I had fuel provided, I had domestic allowances, my utility bills were paid for. I had a lot of things that most people don't get. But even with all of that… [we could not make it]. In the last month I was there I found that for the first time I received my pay and about ten days later it was finished. It had never happened that way before and I suddenly thought, if we hadn't made the decision to move [back to London], how on earth were we going to make it.

Table 10-2 Difference between current income and former income abroad, by country and sector of activity (%)

Difference	Côte d'Ivoire			Ghana		
	Private	Public	Total	Private	Public	Total
Much lower than before	29.6	29.2	29.3	25.2	57.7	30.7
Lower than before	5.6	18.8	14.0	26.8	11.5	24.2
Not much change	13.0	7.3	9.3	13.4	3.8	11.8
Higher than before	13.0	31.3	24.7	18.9	23.1	19.6
Much higher than before	38.9	12.5	22.0	12.6	3.8	11.1
No response	–	1.0	0.7	3.1	–	2.6
TOTAL	100.0	100.0	100.0	100.0	100.0	100.0
Valid cases	54	96	150	127	26	153

From cross-tabulations in the Ghanaian sample it was found that female respondents were almost three times less likely than male respondents to have improved their earnings after return. Moreover, female returnees felt discriminated against in the workplace, and not only from the point of view of income. A 37-year-old Ghanaian returnee, when asked what she missed most since her return, answered:

> The balance or equality between men and women, that is what I miss because we don't have that here … What I mean is you are not looked

> upon as a woman with so many constraints. Oh, you are a woman so you can't do the work that a man is doing. [Abroad] you are considered for your capacity, what you are able to produce, whether you are a woman or a man, you are considered on an equal footing and, if you do well, you are given what's your due. But here most of my [male] colleagues who like me have done a Masters are all now heads of departments, deputy directors, but I have not been given that opportunity because I'm looked upon as a woman, I have so many constraints. I have a child now and it's like – oh, her family life is gonna get in, I don't think she can do the work, so we are not going to give her that position.

From this evidence it is seen that women sometimes experience more difficulties in the workplace, as was also found by Iredale et al. (2002) in Asia. Cross-tabulations on the Ghanaian sample confirm that female respondents were usually less satisfied with their income and career opportunities. No very significant differences based upon gender were instead found regarding other aspects such as the level of their professional responsibilities.

Current Working Conditions

The satisfaction of returned migrants with their working conditions was explored in the questionnaire survey by asking them not only about their income but also about their career opportunities, responsibilities, relationships with colleagues, the organisational culture and management in their workplace. Their responses, set out in Tables 10-3 and 10-4, show that overall Ghanaians were more satisfied with their working conditions than Ivorians. Ghanaians derived the highest level of satisfaction from their professional responsibility, and Ivorians from the relationship they enjoyed with colleagues.

In both cases the lowest level of contentment was registered in relation with the current level of income, followed by the organisational culture and management in the workplace. However, a far larger share of Ghanaians than of Ivorians was either "very satisfied" or "satisfied" with their current income.[1] As was already seen above, this is because a

---

1 The findings that more than twice as many Ivorians than Ghanaians were not satisfied with their remuneration and that they generally were much more often "not satisfied" with different aspects characterising their working conditions are

greater share of Ivorian respondents was employed in the public sector and had attained only the lower occupational levels. In fact, self-employed Ivorians and those who had reached the very top of the employment hierarchy were usually more satisfied with their current income.

Also from Table 10-3 it can be seen that Ghanaians were far more satisfied in general than Ivorians. Satisfaction with the professional responsibility was often expressed by those employed in the private sector or by those who had launched their own firm. The same was true for those who gained more work experience abroad, through working for longer periods in training-related jobs.

It should be acknowledged that measuring satisfaction, especially cross-nationally, is not unproblematic. For instance, are the differences recorded really due to "objective" conditions such as career position or responsibility, or perhaps due to broader cultural traits. Could it be for instance that, for whatever reasons, Ghanaians are "innately" or "culturally" happier than Ivorians?

What is Most Appreciated and What is Missed Back Home

Despite the fact that many returnees earned less at home than they did abroad and were relatively dissatisfied with some of the working conditions, the findings show that many believed their overall quality of life had improved since they had returned. Recent developments in the home economy and society were especially and almost exclusively praised by Ghanaian respondents; this is not surprising considering that at the time of the interviews Côte d'Ivoire was undergoing a major political crisis. But what for instance this 39-year-old Ivorian, who came back after 24 years of absence, appreciated most was the greater real purchasing power he had acquired back home:

> The quality of life is better because, with an income equivalent to what I was making in France, I live much better here … You have a better

---

probably due in part to a translation error. In the original English version of the questionnaire the wording "not at all satisfied" was adopted, while in the French questionnaire the less extreme wording "not satisfied" was used. This may have resulted in more Ivorian respondents opting for this response, rather than for the alternative one (i.e., "less than satisfied").

Table 10-3 Degree of satisfaction of Ivorian and Ghanaian returned migrants with work-related aspects (%)

Work-related aspects	Degree of satisfaction						
	Very satisfied	Satisfied	Less than satisfied	Not satisfied	No response	Total	Valid cases
			Côte d'Ivoire				
Income	5.3	26.7	29.3	36.0	2.7	100.0	150
Career opportunities	9.3	36.7	21.3	28.0	4.7	100.0	150
Responsibility	13.3	51.3	16.7	16.0	2.7	100.0	150
Relationships with colleagues	14.0	62.0	17.3	2.7	4.0	100.0	150
Management	6.7	35.3	32.0	22.0	4.0	100.0	150
Organisational culture	8.0	34.0	31.3	23.3	3.3	100.0	150
			Ghana				
Income	12.3	42.9	27.3	15.6	1.9	100.0	154
Career opportunities	25.3	51.3	16.9	5.8	0.6	100.0	154
Responsibility	35.7	58.4	4.5	1.3	–	100.0	154
Relationships with colleagues	33.8	57.1	9.1	–	–	100.0	154
Management	23.4	51.9	22.1	1.9	0.6	100.0	154
Organisational culture	13.0	47.4	31.2	7.8	0.6	100.0	154

> quality of life not only because you earn more but also because you get more social recognition.

Several other returned migrants also stressed that there were many things that they could not afford abroad, but which were perfectly accessible back home. These included a big house or office, domestic help or a chauffeur, for example. In her interview, a 45-year-old Ghanaian returnee stressed this particular issue:

> I love to go on vacation and live in the hotels and drink my wine and eat good food, get room service and place my orders … I like to do that for ten days and then I just want to come home. And when I come home my house always looks so big compared to where I've been, and I have a cook … In Ghana you can afford all these things even on a small budget, you can afford a little extra comfort which you can't afford over there.

The account of a 50-year-old Ivorian manager also sheds light on leisure life which can act as a home pull-factor for migrants who are abroad:

> Here I have a certain quality of life, domestic help for example, which means that I have much more time. I also have plenty of space here. In Europe I could never live in such a big house with a garden … To have the same standing there, I really would need to have attained a much higher level. Here you get a very good quality of life for what you earn, in terms of space, ease, comfort. It's not the same in Europe.

The survey also captured what migrants spontaneously (based upon an open-ended question) said they appreciated most since their return (Table 10-4). Both Ivorians and Ghanaians praised most the warm nature of human relationships and the community-based lifestyle. Many respondents, especially Ivorians, also appreciated the proximity with family and friends.

Being close to family, relatives and friends was considered important for various reasons. Many returnees particularly valued the sense of "love" and "togetherness" that they could find only in the family sphere, as well as certain "family values" including mutual respect and reciprocal assistance. "Here you have people helping you at every stage of your life", a 36-year-old Ghanaian professional female returnee pointed out, with reference to the social support system existing back home and the

Table 10-4 What is most appreciated back home, by country

What is most appreciated back home*	Côte d'Ivoire N (%)	Ghana N (%)
Human relations/community-based life	91 (60.7)	50 (32.5)
Proximity with family/friends	87 (58.0)	31 (20.2)
Feeling home	20 (13.3)	21 (13.6)
Recent development	3 (2.0)	27 (17.5)
Less stress	6 (4.0)	31 (20.2)
Climate/environment/food	26 (17.3)	15 (9.7)
Professional opportunities/ability to make a contribution	2 (1.3)	23 (14.9)
More recognition and respect	–	32 (20.8)
Nothing	4 (2.7)	2 (1.3)
Other	17 (11.3)	28 (18.1)

* Responses given to an open-ended question.

help she gets from her family and relatives to raise her children. Another 37-year-old Ghanaian returnee responded:

> Ghanaians are very loving and friendly people. There's always somebody to listen to you, which I found very difficult abroad. [There] everybody is for himself and God for all. But here people look out for each other. That is one thing that I really appreciate. And also, another thing that I appreciate about Ghana is our family life, the extended family system. You get so much support from the extended family system.

Human relations impregnated by a strong sense of community were an important thing from which migrants were drawing benefits and gratification since their return. These are based on some commonly accepted values such as "solidarity" and "hospitality", as was emphasised by this 37-year-old Ivorian in his interview:

> It's mainly the visits. Here you can go and visit a friend at any time without calling ahead of time. It's not a problem at all. That's what I like, we visit

> each other when we don't have anything else to do. Here there is a greater sense of fraternity and friendship than over there.

The nature of these relationships was often summarised in two words – "human warmth" or "*chaleur humaine*" – a dimension that most returnees said was lacking in the West. This also included more relaxed, cordial and friendly relationships and an overall atmosphere where one could feel free from discrimination and racism and get back a sense of "belonging" and "being home". This last issue was raised not only in questionnaire interviews (see Table 10-4), but also during in-depth interviews – as for instance by this 49-year-old Ivorian who had lived in France, Spain and Mexico:

> What I appreciate most is not to feel like a foreigner anymore. Because abroad there is always one thing that makes you feel ill at ease, and that is when you feel extraneous with regards to the community. When I came back I found back that human warmth that I often missed abroad, especially in Europe. I appreciate being home, that nobody can tell me to leave, that in a certain sense I'm free to act, I've my references, I've kept my culture. It's a very great freedom when you do not have to pay attention to everything you do, because although you need to respect certain norms, it's your education and you know how you have to behave. But when you are abroad you have to pay attention about your behaviour twice as much as those who are born there since you are penalised everywhere. For all that you pay special attention to what you do. You are not completely free in your activities because you are a foreigner, and even more so due to the perception that Europeans have of a black person and the label they immediately stick on you.

Finally, what several returnees also said they appreciated back home was the pleasant climate, the natural environment including the sea, beaches and forests, and the local food. Many Ghanaians said that back home they were able to lead a much less stressful life than the one they had overseas.

But in the questionnaire survey returned migrants were also asked in an open-ended question what they missed most since they had returned home. The results of content analysis and classification, contained in Table 10-5, indicate most interestingly that, after effective services and infrastructure, what returnees – who had learned to live between two or more "worlds" – missed most was the lack of information and of intellectual stimulation. This was the most frequently mentioned issue of Ghanaians and the second most frequently cited topic for Ivorians.

Since access to information was considered an important factor, this issue together with media use was further explored in other parts of the questionnaire. When asked if they had access to a computer in the workplace, 93 per cent of the Ivorians and 98 per cent of the Ghanaians replied affirmatively and this shows that generally today the PC has become a *sine qua non* indicator of élite status. Yet only 64 per cent of the Ivorians compared to 90 per cent of the Ghanaians had access to the internet, which is apparently due to the fact that many more Ivorians were working in the public sector where up-to-date equipment is often lacking.

Table 10-5 What is missed most back home, by country

What is most missed back home*	**Côte d'Ivoire N (%)**	**Ghana N (%)**
Effective services/infrastructure	61 (40.7)	43 (27.9)
Access to information/intellectual stimulation	47 (31.3)	43 (27.9)
Choice of leisure/consumption goods	40 (26.6)	36 (23.4)
Administrative and institutional framework	32 (21.3)	17 (11.0)
Professional context/opportunities	21 (14.0)	22 (14.3)
Climate/environment/food	17 (11.3)	13 (8.4)
Friends/human relations	9 (6.0)	8 (5.2)
Nothing	14 (9.3)	1 (0.6)
Other	15 (16.6)	23 (14.9)

* Responses given to an open-ended question.

Returned migrants were moreover asked about their sources of information concerning the international arena. A first indicator was the readership of foreign publications which were read "very often" or "often" by more than half of the Ivorians and almost three quarters of the Ghanaians. Smaller shares read foreign-published books or foreign newspapers. That far more Ivorians than Ghanaians affirmed they used to read foreign scientific publications "very often" or "often" is certainly due to the fact that many more were working in academic institutions. Other indicators used were foreign television and radio programmes. A majority of both groups said they watched such television programme "very often" or "often", whilst the number listening to this kind of radio programmes was even more significant. In sum, it emerges forcefully that intellectual stimulation through continuing access to information from abroad represents a critical issue for most highly skilled returnees.

Another thing that many returned migrants said they missed most since they came back were of course effective services and efficient infrastructure. Complaints concerned the lack of particular kinds of facilities, typical of European welfare systems. Specific reference was made to social and financial services, transportation and communications. However, many returnees also said they missed the "orderly functioning of the system" they had known in the host country(ies). The absence of a wide choice of leisure activities and consumption goods, which highly skilled returnees were used to abroad, was regretted somewhat less.

Changes Promoted in the Social Environment and the Workplace

At the meso level attention was focused on the changes that returned migrants have brought about in their social environment and in the workplace. It appears that migrants provide financial and material support to their family and kin as well as to other people in need, but that the high expectations and demands on migrants' resources can hardly be completely satisfied. After return some of the respondents usefully intervened in their social environment by sensitising relatives, friends and others and promoting new attitudes and behaviour. Most important, however, many returning migrants assumed a role of "agents of change" in the workplace. It is here where they can best apply their foreign-acquired knowledge, skills and ideas and where they can provoke the most tangible progress. Let us take each of these arenas in turn: first kin and friends, then the workplace.

Supporting Family and Kin under the Pressure of their Expectations

Even though reciprocal obligations and responsibilities to relatives outside the nuclear family have diminished over time, returned migrants normally come under pressure from the expectations not only of their own family and kin, but also of friends, neighbours and people coming from the same village, tribe or clan. This is because they are seen as privileged people who were given a special opportunity to improve not only their own, and their family's lot, but also to help the community at large. A 49-year-old Ivorian returned migrant put it this way:

> When you arrive here the perception of your group is that you are the one who left to go and get water, you came back with water and you need to share the water. But at the same time you have returned with a rational mind thinking that it would be better to teach everyone how to become autonomous. People at the beginning don't understand that. They adopt an egalitarian approach which means that if there is someone who has a little more than the others he needs to share it with the others, and that represents a constraint because you cannot save and invest.

Similarly, a 42-year-old Ghanaian in London stressed that she and several other migrants found it more and more difficult to trust the recipients of their remittances:

> You have so many stories of people working hard here, making their money, doing three jobs. They send their money home to relatives or friends to start building their homes. These send them pictures, this is where the house has reached, this is the finished house. But they went and took pictures from other people's property and were sending these pictures to the people and in the meantime they had spent the money. And then you go back and they start – why are you being like that, you are lucky you live abroad, you are making all that money. I needed the money to pay for your uncle's operation or your father's this, this and that. What did you want us to do? You realise that you are actually causing people problems when you put money in their hands.

However, from the migrants' accounts it clearly emerges that helping others is not only a burden. It can be gratifying and also useful as it is an aspect of generosity as well as an essential feature of social and economic life. Because of the principle of reciprocity, givers deserve assistance in time of need and, even if the return payment is not immediate, it eventually comes (Nukunya, 1992). Furthermore, helping others also confers prestige, and allows donors to assume authority and power in the social environment; these are two important assets if migrants want to promote change after return. This aspect was stressed by a 51-year-old Ivorian who illustrated his somewhat contradictory feelings regarding the extended family:

> Here we are busy with the extended family which is also interesting. But there are moments where it is oppressive because you are obliged to settle all the problems of the extended family. When you arrive and you have been successful, the whole extended family relies on you to settle all their problems, especially financial problems. And since we are not paid well it becomes difficult to manage all that along with the little family that you have just created. And when you have a spouse like mine with whom you have lived in Europe, in a specific context, she feels this change. I'm less available for her now due to my activities for the party, the village, the ethnic community ... But what at times appears as a pressure of the family, is other times an inestimable support. When you have any difficulties here, if for example today people got to know that I had an accident, I would receive the visit of perhaps 100 or 200 persons, and that can be comforting because you appreciate that so many people know you and that you are useful.

Earlier it was seen that for somewhat less than two-thirds of all the returned migrants who participated in the survey the expectations of family and friends did not constitute any particular problem. This 57-year-old Ghanaian who studied in the United Kingdom belonged to this group:

> When a person comes back they feel he has got everything, he has made it, he has been abroad and they can worship him and they also expect so much from him. But I would say that I was lucky in the sense that my family was not demanding. In a sense my family was just waiting for me to succeed, you know. My father, my mother, my sisters, they all knew that it takes time to establish as a lawyer. But of course once you started succeeding you wanted to also be generous, not because my sisters were in want as such, but it showed that well this is a brother who always had something to spare and so you are generous to them. So I didn't face that

> kind of situation whereby people would be demanding to the extent that if you don't care you will even go back to Europe.

In-depth interviews revealed that those who were afflicted by this problem dealt with it in different ways. This 42-year-old Ghanaian who started his own firm after return said:

> The culture can be overwhelming and because you are back, you are an élite and therefore the extended family requirement can be onerous, intrusive ... The question is whether you have the capacity [to satisfy these demands], or if you believe it's so wrong that this is a bother. You need to have a strategy. In the first two years, in a sense I broke all the rules by not doing most of the cultural things that I was supposed to do such as funerals, "out-doorings" and whatever brings you closer in contact, but also lead to more responsibilities in society, because I felt I had very little capacity with regard to the money I had. I had something to do with it: the energy I had I had to focus it on my business, and if I began to dissipate it, I would have been less able to help in the future. So the question for me was whether to take the insults at the beginning and create an end which would be more sustainable so that I would be able to participate and help better later. And I guess I was lucky to have chosen that.

This 48-year-old Ivorian in Paris had also chosen an alternative solution to respond to his family's requests:

> I adopted another type of support when I was back home. I believe I have no money to give ... I prefer to go and negotiate with my brothers and sisters, we reflect together and develop joint projects, and then I help financing these projects based on my resources. But I do that as in a project, I expect them to reimburse me. So I helped them to set up a windmill, for example. Because in the past I used to give money, but I stopped as I realised that it did not work because it was never sufficient. When you give money you give the impression that you have unlimited amounts of it and that you can give money to everyone. But obviously you cannot give money to everyone, you can only give it to some and not to others. It is better to develop a project because you reflect together as to who will provide support and everybody has to make a contribution. My contribution usually consists in money, because I have access to credit here. But the others also contribute their parts. It's a joint project.

Altogether it seems that quite a lot of support is provided by migrants to family and kin as well as to other people after their return, compared to what they had provided whilst they were away. It is in fact much more difficult to decline the demands of those who are in need when one is living in the same context as an integral, active part of the community.

Sensitising Relatives and Friends and Promoting Behavioural Change

The financial and material assistance that returnees provide to others to enhance their well-being is only one way through which they try to foster change in their social environment. There are also other kinds of changes that they seek to promote in this context. In the survey returnees were asked in an open-ended question to provide some concrete examples on how they had used what they learned abroad to bring about change in family life.

Table 10-6 groups the returnees' answers into different categories. It shows that a few of them, mainly Ivorians, tried to limit the interference and demands of the extended family and made it clear that their attitude had changed. Several of them stressed that now they attributed more importance to their own nuclear family. Some also insisted on the fact that they lacked the time that is needed to entertain such an extended social network, saying that in practice they avoided as much as possible to participate in social events such as funerals, and limited the visits of relatives, friends and other people, especially unannounced visits, a conventional practice which they now found difficult to accept given their changed lifestyle.

The kind of contribution that was evoked most frequently by the respondents was the promotion of new attitudes and behaviour among family members and friends. Respondents said that they had emphasised the importance of education and provided advice on career issues, counselled on financial matters and introduced certain family members to new technologies (e.g. computers). In the questionnaire returnees provided several different examples. Some said they helped to enhance hygiene standards or family planning in the family and wider social environment. Others said they had taught their family members to be more responsible in managing their resources or to take new initiatives and strive for economic independence.

Table 10-6 Kinds of changes provoked in family life, by country

Changes in family life*	Côte d'Ivoire N(%)	Ghana N(%)
Promotion of new attitudes/ behaviour	53 (35.3)	24 (16.0)
Helping to solve problems/conflicts	9 (6.0)	17 (11.3)
Giving particular attention to children	13 (8.7)	11 (7.3)
Providing financial/material support	3 (2.0)	57 (38.0)
Limiting interference/demands	10 (6.7)	1 (0.6)
Other	18 (14.7)	7 (4.6)
None	61 (40.7)	93 (62.0)

* Responses given to an open-ended question.

Some respondents said they had helped to solve problems and conflicts and thus promoted greater family cohesion, by using constructive dialogue. Another thing that returnees mentioned quite frequently was that they paid particular attention to children and their needs. This meant not only that they spent more time with their children and personally cared for them rather than delegating most of the tasks to nannies or relatives; it also meant that they tried to provide their children with a higher quality of education and enabled them to gain a broader and more independent outlook. Some returnees highlighted that they allowed their children to speak their mind and to defend their viewpoint, a practice that is sometimes still found unacceptable by some local people.

When asked how he had applied what he had learned abroad in his family life, a 51-year-old Ivorian who returned from France to work in the university replied:

> The struggle that I led that has been successful is the one regarding the relationship between parents and children and the attitudes and behaviour regarding girls and women. I explain to other people that children should have the right to express themselves and to raise their concerns. Because here children are not supposed to do that; regardless of their age they have to be quiet. I had to struggle, to shock others … In the village they try to poison you because you are questioning the tradition and that is not permitted. But when at the family level you have a certain weight … they

> let you do. When my children go to the village they ask the grandfather questions and he said to me – since you've been to France your children are spoiled, it's bad, they ask too many questions: "Why do you do this? Why are you sitting there the whole day and grandmother is always busy working? You are lazy?" But now my parents have started to become more tolerant and things have improved. Even the villagers have started to grant more freedom to their children ... So that's an achievement of which I'm proud. I really feel I have succeeded at the level of my family and also at the level of my village.

This respondent went on to describe how his mother is now more regularly involved in discussions and decisions concerning her children and the entire household. This was not the case before he started to petition for her greater participation and to shock his parents with his Westernised attitudes and behaviour.

Other returnees stressed that their relationship with the people who work in their homes had changed. This emerged from the following accounts:

> Because of my experience, growing up in college and having to work for myself and going through hard times, when I see security guards in Ghana, garden boys and so on, I know what they are going through because I've been through the same things. So once again, it just humbles me and I talk to them, eat with them and sometimes my wife when she was here would say – why do you entertain the garden boy in the kitchen? You know he's a garden boy, he has to be outside. And I say – my goodness, he's a human being! What's your problem? He's a human being just like me and you. (40-year-old Ghanaian who owned a private firm)

Another returned migrant, a 37-year-old woman, explained that she now has a different way of dealing with the personnel working in her home. She said that compared to others she was providing food and clothes to their nanny and trying to get her into a trade. She stressed she often had tried to convince others that there is a need to ensure the welfare of these people.

Introducing Knowledge, Skills and New Ideas in the Workplace

In Chapter Six it was pointed out that migrants accumulated abroad, and transferred back home, various kinds of human capital which they consider important for their work, but that difficulties arise which can significantly hamper their efforts to promote meaningful change in their workplace. In spite of these difficulties, some concrete examples were cited of how they used what they had learned abroad to bring about change in their workplace. It must once more be mentioned that return migrants' accounts of their own contributions may be subjectively biased. They may be somewhat embellished or exaggerated, although not completely untruthful since their claims were as much as possible verified, by the field methodology adopted.

From Table 10-7 we can see that the most important contributions are made in the fields of: (a) improvement of organisational structures and management practices; (b) increase in work morale and productivity; and (c) development of technical know-how. There is, however, a significant difference between the two countries, firstly because Ghanaians were able to provide a greater number of examples than Ivorians, which suggests that they are more willing and capable of effecting change in the workplace. Secondly, Ghanaians provided far more examples of improvements they made in organisational structures and management practices, whereas Ivorians mentioned more examples where they contributed to the development of technical know-how. This in part is due to the fact that Ghanaians more often had launched a private enterprise.

The "development of technical know-how" was distinguished from the "introduction of new technology" because the first category was limited to improvements in technical processes which increase the productiveness of machines and eliminate manual operations. It mainly includes changes in information technology (e.g., the introduction of computers and increasing computerisation of operations). An example is provided by a Ghanaian who launched a new energy regulatory body and described how he introduced internet and intranet facilities in his offices. The use of this technology had allowed him and his staff to handle information exchanges much more effectively.

"Development of technical know-how" instead involved advances in technology made through the application of new scientific knowledge and empirical methods. Examples included the introduction of new techniques in the fields of research and teaching, administration and audit, marketing and human resources, banking and brokerage, environment and forestry,

Table 10-7 Kinds of contributions made in the workplace, by country

Kinds of contributions made in the workplace	Côte d'Ivoire N (%)	Ghana N (%)
Improvement of organisational structures/ management practices	44 (29.3)	79 (51.3)
Increase in work morale/productivity	61 (40.6)	71 (46.1)
Development of technical know-how	44 (29.3)	36 (23.4)
Training personnel (or students)	26 (17.3)	27 (17.5)
Introduction of new technology	8 (5.3)	20 (13.0)
Started new project/enterprise	19 (12.6)	17 (11.0)
Acts as a role model	9 (6.0)	21 (13.6)
Other	8 (5.3)	4 (2.6)
None	24 (16.0)	4 (6.5)

* Responses given to an open-ended question.

telecommunications and information technology. A 49-year-old professor who taught Geography at the University of Abidjan illustrated, for example, how he and his colleagues had played a leading role in the reform of the teaching curriculum by applying some of the approaches that had already been successfully experimented in France and the United States. "For those who never went abroad to study it was a real innovation, but for us it was not something completely new because we already had experienced that when we were overseas", he said.

A 53-year-old Ghanaian civil servant who studied Agricultural Sciences in the United Kingdom explained that what he learned abroad had allowed him to develop some new technical know-how in his workplace:

> When I went to do my PhD, I studied a particular organism and when I came back I was prepared to, you know, introduce this technology into the country. I was able to identify crops that are affected by this particular organism … and I also learned other techniques. So when I came back I was able to apply these techniques that I also have taught to my students and I guess I was able to influence their way of doing work.

A 39-year-old Ivorian who received specialised training in insurance brokerage in France was hired after return by one of the main private insurance companies in Abidjan. He also described the specific kind of change he had tried to promote in his field:

> When I arrived here I realised that there was a real need for new insurance products and that no response was being provided to these needs. There was for example a new product, called credit insurance, which was developing extremely fast in Europe, particularly in France as it is there where it was launched first. But here in Côte d'Ivoire too this type of product is needed, here where people have to secure their commercial goods and services. I said to myself, it's great, you have been trained in this and there also is the budget needed to develop this new product. You do not even need to search for customers because your customers are already there.

"Improvement of organisational structures and management practices" includes changes that returned migrants have promoted in the way communication occurs in the workplace, time is managed, decisions are made and executed. These efforts are usually targeted at increases in efficiency and productivity and include examples such as a clear definition of objectives, policies and procedures, reform of organisational structures, identification of performance targets, introduction of quality standards and appraisal systems, sound supervision and ongoing monitoring, strategic planning and respect of deadlines, rigorous management of resources and combating mismanagement and corruption. They also involve to some extent the motivation of personnel by satisfying as much as possible their basic needs (e.g., salary and benefits, working conditions, role and status, supervision and autonomy). For instance this 37-year-old Ivorian who worked for the Ivorian Chamber of Commerce reported:

> When I first arrived I got involved with management controls. They had a way of handling travel claims which I proposed to change in order to control the costs of field missions. Each time someone needs to travel he gets a per diem, a standard amount to cover his expenses. But it was not an easy task since before they used to give money in a very discretionary fashion based on the person who made the claim.

Another example was provided by a Ghanaian returnee who had managed one of the most important public hospitals in Accra:

> Changes that I have been involved with are changes in procurement, how things are bought, what procedures are used, the tendering system, stock control, as none of these existed there. You are sitting in your office and someone comes up and says we need a thousand needles and you think by yourself, but we have ordered a thousand last week, what is the usage rate, what are the doctors doing, which department is using them? We don't know but we need more. So I have introduced procedures for stock control. If you take a few things out and make a note of it, you can find out where the things are going, what is the rate of usage, when you need items you don't just get up and say I need thousand needles, there is a process that you should go through to give certain days advance notice to the entire procurement and supply management. I did a lot of changes in that. Then I did a lot on just motivation of staff … So it's personnel, procurement. Under personnel I also introduced some better methods in recruitment and then monitoring, monitoring staff performance. So these are some of the areas where I have made changes.

Examples of initiatives to increase the motivation of staff which did not pertain directly to their more basic human needs which emerged from the survey were classified under "increase in work morale and productivity". This category encompasses a variety of things ranging from increasing the participation of staff to improving teamwork through enhanced motivation, information, delegation and negotiation. Building a "culture of openness" encompassing a greater information exchange and an increased "sense of ownership", limiting the use of hierarchies and using a "participatory management style" involving staff in the decision-making process, enhancing "work ethics" and professionalism, strengthening relations with customers and clients, marketing services effectively and developing new business or activities are only some of the more specific examples.

When questioned whether he would operate in the same way if he had not been abroad, the Ghanaian who headed a major public commission and was quoted above replied:

> I would not. The exposure is very important. The way of doing things, knowledge, acquisition of knowledge is very important and valid. Because for instance you come to my office, it's quiet, everybody is doing his job. We put a security lock there, you don't have business here, you don't come in. If you don't have an appointment here you don't come here. That is the basic rule; we don't entertain visitors to the commission, no! If you have a

> visitor, you go downstairs. You don't bring the visitor into the offices. That is the regulation. We have flexible working hours … and everybody here has a computer, every single person at the commission has a computer, and we communicate because, as I mentioned, we do electronic posting.

The office was indeed quite impressive and the difference with similar public offices striking.

In Abidjan an Ivorian manager in his mid-40s described the differences that he felt existed between his attitudes and behaviour and the ones of most managers who never had been abroad:

> You see today I wear a tie because later I have to take part in a TV programme. Otherwise I hardly wear a tie and those are things that seem irrelevant, but here I have friends who are chief executives and who are always perfectly dressed, who all the time go around and drive in expensive cars, they always go to the most fancy places. This sometimes, I tell you frankly, bewilders me because I wonder how they manage to do that. Because when I see the amount of work that I need to accomplish to make my business grow, when I consider the concerns I have for example there are people who owe me lots of money, but they don't care, they sleep well anyway. In Europe that's impossible. When you owe someone money you cannot sleep well because there you get under pressures, you are obliged to pay. So I have permanent concerns as to how to pay my bills, to pay my personnel and since I started my staff was always paid. For me that is a top priority because it would be inconceivable for me to go around in expensive cars when my personnel is not paid. But here you have a lot of people who do that … So it's little things like that, a little something but I can see it, because when people come here they tell me – your company is different from the others, it's a company of "whites". That's what people love to tell me, and my collaborators as well.

The problems that returned migrants encounter in their efforts to promote change seem to be more important in the public sector because it is here where they said they find more resistance. Organisational structures are usually more complex in this sector and allow for less flexibility and creativity. A 36-year-old Ghanaian returnee who headed a major public service encountered some serious obstruction also because she was young and a woman in a position which usually would have been held by a senior male professional. She was able to achieve only limited results, for the following reasons:

> You have about 2,500 staff and about a thousand of these, or about 800 of these are … very senior people, you know, in their 60s, 50s and I'm in my 30s and a female. The people I'm supposed to manage have children older than me. And then half of them have wives who listen to what they say, so in the whole domain of their activities they haven't come across a young woman who tells them what to do. They are not familiar with that, you see. So if I was a man perhaps it would be easier.

But difficulties and obstacles can also be found in the private sector. The Ivorian returnee who worked in the private insurance company and was cited above admitted that he had to hold back at least temporarily, mainly because of the resistance he encountered in his workplace among superiors and colleagues:

> I have had some tremendous problems to implement my plan and it is still not working for different reasons. People focus so much on what they have been trained to do, that only little is invested in doing something for which they have not been trained. This without realising that, if you embark on something new, you will have the whole market for yourself.

To avoid some of the resistance and potential obstacles, several returnees have decided to launch their own private firm or to work as independent consultants.

Transformations Concerning the Socio-economic and Political Spheres

The creation of new businesses is generally assumed to be an engine of growth for the economy and this is certainly one of the main potential contributions made by returning migrants. They may also make changes in existing firms and industries, through the application of what they gained abroad in terms of knowledge, skills and ideas, as well as the contacts and networks they were able to create. The promotion of community development, mobilisation of civil society and public advocacy are some other contributions made by returned migrants. These processes are examined in turn.

The Creation of New Businesses

The contribution of returning migrants to the development of new small and medium-sized businesses has been the subject of some debate (Black et al., 2003). It is undeniable that self-employment represents an important option for some people in developing countries, not least for returning migrants who encounter difficulties in finding a good job in already-existing organisational structures.

Of the 60 Ghanaians and 26 Ivorians who declared in the questionnaire that they were self-employed, respectively 57 and 21 had formally set up a business. Although the size of the businesses created by returned migrants was relatively small – the median number of people they employed was ten in Ghana and six in Côte d'Ivoire – their activities showed that returnees, especially the younger ones, are quite enterprising and ready to embark on innovative ventures. A good example was the creation of a brokerage firm which took the leading role in the development of capital markets in Ghana. When asked what, among the things that he acquired abroad, had helped him most in this endeavour, one of the three founders, a 42-year-old Ghanaian who had studied at Columbia and Yale and had worked on Wall Street, replied:

> I really think it is confidence and comfort because as you work in the financial sector, especially on capital markets and related issues, people need to feel that you understand their language, their culture of performance, timeliness and execution and you have a "business ethics" that they would appreciate. And so that certainly helps when foreign portfolio managers come into town because they like to feel you can connect, I guess, more effectively.

Another Ghanaian in his mid-40s came back from the United States to launch a company specialising in the development of internet content on Ghana for individuals and businesses. He saw the need to portray a more positive image about Africa through the internet. He explained why he had embarked on this initiative:

> If we are not given the opportunity to be on Newsweek or CNN, at least the internet brings us one step closer to the rest of the world, for them to see that Africa is not what they think it is. So for me these are some of the reasons why I felt… this is an opportunity for me to help Africa get a better presentation than we see out there. When I was in America

> there were few websites on Ghana or Africa, and if you looked at who the webmaster or the creator of the website was, it was either some white student, Jewish student … It was negative images, wars, AIDS, corruption, everything. So on the internet I'm going to make my change, and since I started, I believe I was one of the very few people when I came in '95–'96 to start content in Africa by Africans … A website created by Ghanaians or an African, managed by an African, the information by an African and broadcast by an African.

An analogous initiative for radio and television was developed by a Ghanaian returnee of the same age who established a radio and television syndication and advertising company. The company produces some of the most sought-after scripts and productions in Ghana, including local sitcoms and even some comical stories about Ghanaians in the United States and Ghanaians who returned home.

> So I did a play and called it the "Saga of the Returnee" which is about a Ghanaian who has returned home with all the fire to change the nation and how he is gradually losing that fire. One question was what happens to, what is in the system that affects people so negatively that even when they have all the energy and they … want to reform somewhere or somehow along the line they lose their faith and they give it up. What's in the system, you know? So it's a 90-minute comedy. People just come and laugh. That too shocks them because for the first time they were there laughing and we were laughing at ourselves, but the same time we were thinking about the questions that I was raising about our attitudes, our culture, about our politics. To the Ghanaian audience it was so new and so strange that it became an instant hit.

It was not only the formal education that he had received overseas in film-making and public relations that helped him in his business ventures:

> I think that I have learned so much because the 15 years abroad were not all rosy at all. Before I got into jobs in public relations, I had to do [many unskilled and menial jobs] … It's all for the experience there you know, it's just with my interaction with people there that I was learning so much. I have learned more when I was out of school, than in school. Yes, if I had gone there without schooling, I would still have came back totally educated in terms of real life experiences, and I think that's the energy that I brought back that Ghanaians find so different in everything that I

> do. So I can confidently say that what I am now really has all its roots in the 15 years that I was in the States.

It was seen in Chapter Two that some migration scholars have drawn attention to the problem of "deskilling", meaning that certain migrants not only do not learn anything abroad but also even lose some of their previously acquired expertise (Al-Rasheed, 1992; Brydon, 1992). No significant evidence was derived from this study that the Ghanaian and Ivorian highly-skilled migrants interviewed encountered such a problem. Working in low-level jobs abroad made many of them more aware of different social realities and taught them not to take anything for granted, as shown for instance in the account of this 40-year-old Ghanaian:

> I lived in Manhattan, I had my own apartment and of course I was working in several jobs to pay my school fees and everything. It wasn't easy, so it actually strengthened me and made me a more responsible person, because like I said earlier on, if you don't pay your bills, you are on your own and there's nobody who's gonna fend for you. So you just had to support yourself and it made me a much stronger person. Before I left Ghana I was a little more sheltered, I had never gotten a job all my life; we had chauffeurs, drivers and now all of a sudden I had to fend for myself.

An example where the creation of a new business has also resulted in a considerable employment creation was provided by this 61-year-old Ivorian returnee who in 1978 started a food-processing plant which today employs more than 6,000 people:

> I come from a place where everyone used to be a fisherman, we only did small-scale fishing. Today this activity can no longer feed the growing population. We need to change, but that is not easy because the mentalities are deeply rooted. It's in this sense that I used to say we are like an engine … we make them understand that those fishing techniques are now obsolete and show them other methods that can be adopted. In my region we have many resources, mainly manioc and coconuts. With friends we have built up a factory that processes coconuts which today is still operational.

The survey revealed that only one in five business owners launched their activities before or upon their return. More than half of them started them some time after return. Most of the businesses were set up in the six to seven years preceding the survey. When asked if they had received assistance from government or other sources to support their work, a quarter of the Ghanaians – but only one Ivorian – said yes. Among these Ghanaians slightly less than half had obtained some financial support or a loan and a little more than a quarter of them had received some technical assistance. Other more marginal forms of assistance included support with personnel and the provision of facilities and equipment, or the granting of a research or business starting fund. Most of the assistance was received from governmental sources.

The findings confirm that becoming self-employed and launching a new business after return are not an easy task. It was already seen before that approximately one third of the respondents had problems with the start-up of their business. In the questionnaire, returnees who had embarked on such a venture were asked to rank a series of difficulties they might have encountered (Table 10-8). The responses show that the lack of capital and/or credit was ranked highest and that the marketing of products or services and the policies, laws or regulations were ranked least significant.

As it has become more and more difficult to find a good job back home, the migrants' lack of savings can increasingly hamper their return. This emerged, for example, from the account of this 33-year-old Ivorian migrant who was living in Paris:

> I would like to return home to put my talents at the disposal of my country but to do so I need to have enough savings. I already went there several times to explore the ground. I first went home on holidays and recently again to try to launch a new newspaper called *Le gratuit d'Abidjan*. But the problem is that I do not have enough money and that inevitably raises the problems of funding. The banks there do not lend money, practically they do not lend any money at all to people who have not got any guarantee and that makes it very difficult to obtain even a small loan.

Migrants who return with their own savings have of course an important advantage, as emerged from the account of this 40-year-old Ghanaian:

> It was savings that I made there that I invested in my company in Ghana, and monies that I made in Ghana ... My company didn't build like this. I started in a small, one-room office with a laptop and that's all. Over the years it moved on to two offices, three offices and now this is what it is, and we are moving into other offices now, so it's expanding. But I

Table 10-8 Ranking of difficulties encountered in setting up a business, by country (%)*

Main difficulties	Côte d'Ivoire						Ghana					
	Rank 1	Rank 2	Rank 3	Rank 4	Total	Valid cases	Rank 1	Rank 2	Rank 3	Rank 4	Total	Valid cases
Capital/credit	52.4	23.8	9.5	14.3	100.0	21	50.9	10.5	15.8	22.8	100.0	57
Qualified collaborators	23.8	23.8	23.8	28.6	100.0	21	22.8	31.6	29.8	15.8	100.0	57
Marketing of products/services	14.3	23.8	33.3	28.6	100.0	21	14.0	19.3	33.3	33.3	100.0	57
Policies/laws/ regulations	9.5	28.6	33.3	28.6	100.0	21	12.3	38.6	21.1	28.1	100.0	57

* Four pre-coded difficulties are ranked in order of importance with 1 being the most important and 4 the least important problem.

> started in a little backroom office with one laptop, very simple place, so the investment wasn't heavy, but a lot of determination and the fact that I've nowhere to go other than Ghana. That determination to be successful was all I got. I'd walk into anybody's office because there was no turning back. I had nowhere else to go, so with my laptop I'd walk into the chief executives', ministers' offices and I was scared of nobody.

There is no doubt that building a new business requires a great deal of determination and perseverance. Although the availability of good collaborators was not ranked highly by many respondents in the survey, some did note problems they had when they embarked on a joint business venture with someone who never lived abroad. This was the case of this 46-year-old Ivorian who had studied and worked in the United States:

> I came back and got associated with a friend, a local business person. Since we first met we decided to set up a small firm, but since I have been away for so many years, things had changed a lot and my perception of the local situation was no longer valid. The people had changed, the country had changed and the customs had changed as well. But I agreed to come back because the business was attractive. We then worked together, but I must admit that when I got here, I realised that the situation was not the one that I had expected. It was not good at all! If I had the choice I would never do it again. I would have come back differently because the mentality of our brothers who remained here and ours who went abroad is not the same. There really is a difference. The way we approach things, the way we do business, we manage a business is different, it's totally different. In short – my partnership did not work.

Similarly, although marketing of products and/or services and the general regulatory and policy framework were not ranked highly as problems, from key interviews it emerged that returnees could get quite disappointed with regard to the latter. An Ivorian migrant in his mid-40s who owned a private business in Paris said, for example:

> In '94 when there was the devaluation to those who were abroad I said – well, let us do something useful and set up a new business back home. There are some who asked for permissions, this and that. But as soon as you arrive with a potentially successful project the local authorities want to be involved, primarily to make money and then also to control the initiative. This is particularly the case if you do something in the field of

> information and communication, two sectors which are in expansion. So unless you involve them they will create serious difficulties and hamper your work.

This account leads us back to the problem of corruption which was raised by migrants both in the survey and in-depth interviews and was already addressed in the previous chapter.

Promoting Community Development and Mobilising Civil Society

The promotion of new businesses is only one of the contributions made by Ivorian and Ghanaian returned migrants back home. The questionnaire survey and the in-depth interviews allow a better grasp also of other kinds of socio-economic, cultural and political transformations that returnees try to provoke in their home contexts. These contributions were captured in particular through an open-ended question in which they were asked if they had managed to achieve any changes in the public sphere by using what they had learned abroad.

Table 10-9 sets out the answers to this question and shows that more than a third of the Ghanaians indicated that they were promoting some new community development initiatives. These interventions included the conception and design of various development activities, and sometimes more integrated projects, in the areas of education, health, water and sanitation, the mobilisation of funds and materials for these initiatives and the monitoring of their implementation. That the target beneficiaries of such interventions mostly are the rural home communities from which the migrants originate was also found in other African countries (Diarra, 1998; Diatta and Mbow, 1999; Grillo and Riccio, 2003; Russell et al., 1990).

Some concrete examples were illustrated in more detail by returnees during the in-depth interviews. An Ivorian professor, for example, had tried to mobilise the inhabitants of his home village to improve the supply of water in their locality. He said he had the right contacts abroad allowing him to find the necessary financial resources:

> I went to see my people to tell them that since we are on a hill the women suffer because they are obliged to walk down 2 km to fetch water and then carry it up the hill to the village. I had found a Spanish NGO which was ready to build a water tank and pump the water up automatically.

However, as shown by his ensuing account, it is not always easy to change long- established practices:

> The people did not like the idea, because I was reasoning like a European. They came and explained to me that if I wanted to implement this plan I needed to stop thinking like a European. I had to accept that some sacrifices be made for the water that will be pumped, because it would be bothered and some sacrifices were therefore needed to appease it. For them I was taking the problem that other way around, I did not start where I should have started.

According to this returnee, the only way to overcome this type of resistance was to instigate changes carefully and progressively by building upon what already existed:

> We encounter tremendous problems when we try to apply our experience, but to promote the idea of change we also need to take the experience of the people, I mean people's know-how, into consideration. This can only be done through building on what already exists. If you want to make a revolution, you will break your head.

Table 10-9 reveals that a relatively large number of Ghanaians claimed to play an active role in various community organisations and structures and to have assumed a leadership role and. The main purpose of these structures was to organise and mobilise the communities and to increase their participation in various development initiatives. Most often respondents referred to town development committees and other grass-root associations operating in both rural and urban areas.

Some returnees had taken such a leading role by becoming the members of the board of a private or public institution or an active member of a professional association. Others had taken the lead and launched a new association or organisation such as a sports, residents or professional association, or an NGO. A few examples where more informal networks were used by returnees to promote exchanges of ideas and experiences also emerged from some of the accounts, from this 45-year-old Ghanaian woman for instance:

> I used to have this group called Learning Group and I just decided, why don't we invite a group of people that we know and they can invite other people and give use a talk on one of these current issues, and it was done,

Table 10-9 Kinds of changes promoted in the public sphere, by country

Kinds of change promoted in the public sphere*	Côte d'Ivoire N (%)	Ghana N (%)
Supports new initiative/project	20 (13.3)	66 (42.9)
Advocates change	45 (30.0)	55 (35.7)
Set up association/ organisation	4 (3.3)	8 (5.2)
Helps building capacity	5 (4.0)	15 (9.7)
Plays leadership role	1 (0.6)	34 (22.1)
Involved in church activities	–	82 (14.3)
Other	13 (12.0)	14 (9.1)
None	80 (53.3)	30 (19.5)

* Responses given to an open-ended question.

> and it worked very well. There were arguments and the people were asking questions. Everybody contributed and at the end of it we had snacks and a drink and everybody would go home. Nobody told me to do that, I did that myself.

Returnees seem to be helped in their efforts to promote change by the fact that they are often looked upon as role models. In fact, several respondents specified that not only their relatives and friends, but also other persons including people living in their home village or town, would listen to them. A 49-year-old Ivorian professor explained why returnees like him were able to assume such an influential role:

> In the traditional context it's like between the urban and the rural dweller. The first is better considered and recognised since he comes from Abidjan and for many rural dwellers Abidjan is a myth with its lagoon, its sky scrapers like the Hotel Ivoire, its cathedral. It's a fascinating world you see, that dazzles and so when you go to a village and you say you come from Abidjan you are considered an advanced individual, a modern person. Because they have never left the village, they are stuck there and so you are considered someone really great, it's a bit like that. If you go to the village and you have been to Europe or to the United States or somewhere else and they are told that you come from there you are immediately seen as different. The year when I came back from France and went to the village the youth who were studying there considered me a bit like God ... they

> asked many questions about abroad, but they were afraid of getting too close to me because they said we cannot fool around with this person who has been to France. So, you see, it's a myth.

This issue which was already explored by N'Diaye (1969) in his study on West African students in France, was also illustrated by another Ivorian professor who used a humorous anecdote:

> We have a bit this myth of abroad. What comes from outside is considered better than what we have here ... you see this fabric for example, the cloth that is worn here, often its quality is better here compared to that of the fabrics produced in Togo or Nigeria. Yet, Ivorian women prefer to go and buy them in Togo and sell them here because they find the colours nicer, it's better. This in spite of the fact that often it is the Ivorian companies who go and drop their fabrics in Lome which Ivorian women would then buy and bring back here ... That's part of the myth of abroad. When you have studied in France or Canada and you return here you are considered better qualified than those who were trained here, that's clear. The proof is that today everyone who has enough money sends his children to study in the United States, in France or somewhere else.

Table 10-9 shows that a fairly high number of Ghanaians, but no Ivorians, took an active involvement in church activities. A contribution that was instead made by both groups of respondents was building local capacity through teaching activities or through on-the-job training. The 56-year-old Ghanaian who had launched a new energy regulatory body gave a concrete example:

> This is a new set-up that I've tried to put up by using my expertise from the US ... it is completely different from most institutions, but it is not easy because it's a new thing, there's no capacity, you have to build capacity, you have to change the orientation of people, you have to make sure that things are working properly, you want to develop some code of conduct in terms of standards of performance, and sometimes it is not accepted because that is not the culture of some people.

The extent to which these changes that were promoted by returned migrants in the public sphere were actually determined by their experience abroad was explored further during in-depth interviews. From the responses it emerged that if for some of them the two things were unequivocally related, for others the linkage was not that clear. A Ghanaian who after several years of studies and work overseas had been elected mayor after his return said:

> When I was mayor I realised that I had a whole approach to handling the public which was a little unusual in that I honestly believed that you can only move people if they are informed. In other words: you don't get far lying to the public. They'll find out and when they find out the result is worse than if you told them the truth. Now it sounds so pompous but it's something that I learned during that period when I was a student in America. When we were there, Nixon was, first Lyndon Johnson was credited with the "credibility gap", if you remember that phrase, when he was lying about Vietnam and the papers were becoming more and more investigative. I mean when I first went to America, American press was fairly gentle on its politicians. When I first went there, and I think certainly in my perception of America, the journalists' disaffection with politicians started with Lyndon Johnson's conduct of the Vietnam War, okay? And I was a student at that time and I was listening to radio, reading the newspapers and the idea that politicians should not lie and if they lied they'd be caught was firmly implanted in my mind. But I wasn't aware of it. It was only when I was placed in a situation where I had to explain policies, where I had to execute policies, that I realised how firmly this idea that you had to be accessible to the public, you had to be accessible to the press, you had to tell your story as close to the truth as possible, was implanted in my mind. It's only in that period that I realised how much I had been imbibed with all these ideas. So if you ask me what I learned in that period I think one of the most enduring lessons is what I just described.

Some other returnees stressed instead that their foreign experience had not necessarily had any major impact on their agency after return. This was the case of this 45-year-old Ivorian, for example:

> I think that my experience abroad did not change much for me because since I was young I participate in community activities, in associations, it's a vocation. So, going abroad has not changed anything fundamentally. There's still the same vocation. The only thing is that if my community would lead an activity at the international level, they would be better prepared. If today, for example, I would speak with an ambassador to help my village, he would listen to me more carefully; he would know that

> I have lived in Washington, that I worked at the IMF. Even if I'm from the village he would accord me a greater consideration and I would be better prepared to discuss with him and negotiate some help. If a hospital would need to be constructed he would be more confident.

Others instead emphasised the influence that the education which they had received from their parents had had on them and stressed that it was difficult to discern what exactly could be attributed to their foreign experience. This has already been stressed by Gmelch (1980).

Campaigning for Change and Influencing Policy-making

Since they go back to work in key positions in private and public sectors, returning highly-skilled migrants can play a critical role not only in the socio-economic and cultural arenas but also in the political sphere. The positions of authority and responsibility they occupy allow them to affect the course of events considerably and to effect meaningful changes back home. That returned migrants push for change at different levels and also get personally involved with political and institutional decision-making was confirmed by both survey and in-depth interviews.

This type of contribution was mentioned in the first place by a quite high proportion of returnees (see Table 10-9). Most of these respondents specified that they were making an effort to raise public awareness with regard to development. They also claimed that they influenced policy-making in different ways. The concrete examples provided show that returnees made a widespread use of the media including radio, television and the newspapers. More or less formal information and communication campaigns were promoted by them and concerned health, social, environmental and political issues. Different social fora were also used by them to talk about and to foster exchanges around specific issues such as HIV/AIDS, education, gender equity, worker protection, human rights, good governance and democracy.

Advocacy and awareness-raising initiatives often reached from the centre to the periphery as returnees conducted some of these activities in their home villages or towns. During a questionnaire interview a Ghanaian stressed, for example: "I try to encourage other women from my village to send their girls to school. They know it can be done because I'm the only female who has reached this high level of education, so they all look up to me. Most parents are getting serious about sending their girl child to school now". Another returned migrant indicated: "We publicly expose a lot of these religious charlatans who take money from the people". Another affirmed: "My concern for social justice compelled me to pursue a major case of corruption in a state-owned insurance company".

Further interesting elements emerged through in-depth interviewing. For example, the Ghanaian professor who was already quoted above because he had built an effective social network reaching far beyond national borders described:

> Whatever benefits I draw from my network I'm compelled to share with other people. But beyond that I'm involved in many social activities like the involvement in my church. Just before you came I was preparing a document for the bishop. I give talks at various functions, I spend a lot of time doing radio discussions, television discussions, I am very strongly involved in discussions of a political nature, while I don't belong to any political party I talk to politicians from all sides, you know, where I think they should be going. In my mother's village I have spent a lot of money on social infrastructure, an example being that last week I was there and they need a new market and they came to me to ask can you help us and I'm paying for half of the materials they are going to use. The hospital needs a water tank and they need to buy it and I say give me a month. So others benefit a lot, they may not benefit directly from the networks I've established, let's say being drawn into the network, but they get the spill-over benefits from whatever incomes I make. I also share my knowledge by giving them talks.

The institutions of advanced education have always represented an important arena for knowledge transfers because many migrants, especially those belonging to the older generation, decided to go back and teach students what they had learned abroad. For this 49-year-old Ivorian returnee, for instance, it was clear that this was the type of contribution he needed to make:

> Rightly or wrongly I thought I had acquired certain knowledge and that it was my duty to pass it on to others. Thus, a private enterprise offered me twice as much as the university but I have opted for the university, because I felt I was more useful there, I had something to transmit.

Some of the older migrants also decided to go back to work in the university because there they could best lead political activities and campaigned for a plural political system. The education sector has long remained the greatest source of opposition and protest against the government and a suitable ground for returnees to foster some of the democratic ideas they had brought back from overseas.

A 51-year-old Ivorian professor recalled for instance how he and other colleagues who had been involved in politically-oriented student movements in France had returned with the idea of creating a political opposition party back home. They had decided to deploy their initial efforts in the university context because they felt they needed to raise the awareness of the younger generations. The other reason was that they decided to use the teaching staff's trade union as a platform for their unofficial political action since a multiparty system was sanctioned only later in 1990. Another Ivorian university professor (49-year-old) also returned from France to found with other returnees one of the first opposition parties:

> We have contributed much to the experience of multiple political parties because we were the only ones who had seen how a democratic society works, how parties different from the one in power operate, and we reflected on how we could go about that here.

During a focused interview he illustrated in great detail how he had led the political opposition in his home town in the North of Côte d'Ivoire:

> When the multi-party system was introduced in 1990 I decided to run as a candidate in the legislative elections. In my village that was considered unacceptable. If someone else would have tried to do that he would have been eliminated. There would have been serious problems. When I first arrived the people applauded because they believed I was the candidate for the PDCI [the only legal party until then]. That was the only party they knew and so I had to explain that I did not belong to the PDCI, that I belonged to a party which is opposed to the PDCI. In certain villages that I visited people were waiting for me with sticks, but some others also came to see me with politeness, especially those who knew that I was the son of my father because he is very well-known in this region. So when they found out that I had been to France to study and that I returned home – I practically was the only one originating from there who had managed to become professor – they suddenly had much more consideration for me,

> even though they did not know me. However, I said to myself that I still needed to be very careful since they could have reacted negatively, they could have quickly poisoned me. Oh yes, just by giving me something to drink or by shaking my hand. Putting certain poisons in people's hands is a common practice there. Someone who knows the antidote puts poison in his hand and then comes to shake your hand. Then he leaves you and goes rapidly to cure himself, whereas you start to feel sick. You have simply been poisoned by a handshake. Or someone puts poison in your drink and since you are supposed to drink from the same calabash, the poison is introduced when it is your turn to drink. I know all those practices and thus I'm very careful.

He then went on to explain how he had mobilised the youth and women in the villages and helped them to organise themselves into co-operative structures to obtain funding from government and foreign sources and to start new income-generating activities. However, political debate and change were not only fostered by older-generation returned migrants. They were also promoted by some of those belonging to the younger generation. A 45-year-old Ghanaian migrant who returned to launch an NGO had tried to enhance the transparency of the legislative elections in Ghana by submitting a major project proposal to the concerned institutions:

> I felt I could put my skills to use which also involved organising civil society, groups trying to get them to prepare themselves to participate in economic policy-making, and they need the information to work with government officials, World Bank and [other institutions] … [With some colleagues] we sat together and said in December 2000 there would be elections, given that we've had two elections and knowing what had happened, it might be useful this time to start election monitoring early, so we are not just going to monitor voting, we also want to monitor the preparation towards the voting to the general elections, and that meant we wanted a new concept of monitoring, we wanted to look at the state institutions responsible for creating grounds for free, fair elections. We wanted to look at the political parties, we wanted to encourage a more issue-focused debate …

Although his NGO was not awarded the funding to carry out these activities, he and his colleagues were able to contribute to a general debate on how the electoral commission prepares the voter registration exercise and on the credibility of the elections. Another practical example of change in the political sphere is provided by the account of this 57-year-old lecturer and writer who, after his return from the United Kingdom, struggled against authoritarian rule in Ghana:

> My experiences also made me very human rights conscious you know, because certain things cannot just be done in Britain, and you just wonder why a person should brutalise and then get away with it. Why a government should think it is not accountable to its people, why a person should dare suppose that the rule of law does not stretch to him because he happens to be in power. I spoke about some of these things even when the military regime was there, I wrote in newspapers, I spoke on radio when I had the opportunity to be interviewed. They didn't like it, but I did what I could by way of some kind of public advocacy.

Returned migrants have harnessed the power of the media to advocate and promote socio-cultural change, and to a somewhat lesser extent political change, in their home contexts. A 43-year-old Ghanaian who started one of the most important private radio stations in Accra illustrated the type of contribution he was making:

> I'm very critical of things, from the grammar used in newspapers, to the type of newspaper stories, to the Government, anything that I think is worth criticism... I like to get people actually thinking. I'm critical of the acceptance in this country of certain bad standards of workmanship, a total lack of customer care, these things. I think those are positive contributions because once you start criticising things in a way that says this can be done better, it has been done better, it means there are people, perhaps one or two, who would listen and understand that in a customer-dominated society, the customer is king.

Altogether the changes and transformations that returned migrants had effected in the public sphere were more important than those promoted in the family context, but less significant than those provoked in the workplace. This is also confirmed by the fact that, as shown by Tables 10-6, 10-7 and 10-9, the number of concrete examples where returnees felt they had promoted change in the public sphere by using what they had gained abroad was greater than that of examples concerning the family but smaller than that regarding the workplace.

Conditions under which Return Migrants can Stimulate Change

In the previous sections of this chapter it was seen that return migrants can contribute in many very different ways to socio-economic, cultural and political change in their country of origin. Yet, not all returnees assume a role of development agents back home. Some may not be aware of their potential or unwilling to make an impact, others may be inadequately equipped or unable to make any meaningful contribution. This again raises the central question as to what the conditions are that allow returning migrants to stimulate development in their home societies and economies.

Several multivariate regression analyses were conducted to assess the factors affecting the migrants' aptitude to effect change at different levels. The most important factors, which have emerged from the preceding analysis, were used as key explanatory variables in three multi-model logistic regression analyses. Their purpose was to predict if return migrants bring any change in the workplace, the family environment and the public sphere. Each one of these dependent variables takes the value 1 if the respondent made at least one change/contribution in each specific context, and 0 if none was made.

Different sets of explanatory variables were introduced step-wise in each logistic regression analysis to see if any of them provided for a significant explanation of variance in each of the dependent variables (see Table 10-10 for the full listing). The first group of explanatory variables related to the post-return situation of migrants in the home country (Model 1). The second group, introduced in Model 2, is linked to the migrants' return. In Model 3 more explanatory variables were added with reference to their migration experience. A final group of explanatory variables was introduced in Model 4 which relate to the personal attributes of the migrants.

The results of the models' estimates based on the main survey data are presented in Tables 10-11, 10-12 and 10-13 The first table, concerning change in the workplace, shows that returnees working as legislators, senior officials and managers (ISCO1) were much more likely to have operated change in the workplace than those working at lower levels. The net effect of this variable on change in the workplace is very significant. Also, migrants who had returned five to nine years preceding the interview were more likely to have provoked change in this specific context: quite

Table 10-10 Operational definitions of explanatory variables used in logistic regression analysis of changes in the workplace, family environment and public sphere

Explanatory variables	Operational definitions
Model 1: Situation in home country	
Occupational level ISCO1 ISCO2	Different levels of occupation of the respondents were represented by three dummy variables: ISCO1, ISCO2 and ISCO3. Each has the value of 1 if the occupation of respondents falls into the defined categories and 0 if it is classified under another level. ISCO3 was the reference category.
Employment status Self-employed	The employment status of respondents takes value 1 if respondents were self-employed (with or without employees) and value 0 if they were employees.
Sector of activity Public sector	The sector of activity assumes value 1 if respondents were working in the public sector and 0 if they were working in either the private sector or for a mixed institution.
Size of workplace Small workplace	This variable takes the value of 1 if there were less than 30 full-time staff working in the respondents' workplace, and the value 0 if there were more than that number.
Model 2: Return back home	
Return intention Permanent	This variable assumes 1 if respondents said that they returned with the idea of staying home permanently, and value 0 if they returned only temporarily, or on an intermittent basis (i.e. to come and go).
Time since return Returned <5yrs Returned 5–9 yrs	The time since last return was entered into the model using three dummy variables. The first variable "Returned <5yrs" takes value 1 when respondents returned since less than 5 years and 0 if they returned since a shorter/longer period. The second variable "Returned 5–9 years" is value 1 when respondents returned since 5 to 9 years and 0 if otherwise. Respondents who returned longer than 10 years ago were the reference category.

Table 10-10 cont'd

Explanatory variables	Operational definitions
Model 3: Experience abroad	
Age at first emigration	
Age first migration <20yrs	The age at first migration is a variable which has the value of 1 if respondents initially emigrated when they were younger than 20 years and value 0 if they were older.
Duration of absence	The total duration of absence of respondents assumes increasing logarithmic values.
Worked abroad	This variable is 1 if respondents worked abroad and 0 if they did not.
Model 4: Personal characteristics of respondents	
Sex	Sex is a variable which has the value of 1 if respondents are males and 0 if they are females.
Age	Age is represented by three dummy variables. The first variable "Age39" has the value of 1 if respondents are aged 39 years or less and the value 0 if they are older. The second variable "Age50Plus" takes value 1 if respondents are 50 years or older. The reference group includes respondents aged 40 to 49 years.
Education	The variable "Education" can take different values based on the respondents' highest educational attainment: 1 "High school", 2 "Undergraduate", 3 "Masters or equivalent", 4 "Doctorate or equivalent" and 5 "Other".
Country of interview	This variable assumes the value of 1 if respondents are Ivorians and the value 0 when they are Ghanaians.

strongly so compared to those who had returned a shorter time before the interview, but less compared to those who had returned earlier. The other two statistically significant explanatory variables concern the sector of activity and size of the workplace. Returnees employed in the public sector were less likely to have effected change in the workplace, and this was the case also for those who were working in large rather than in small workplaces. However, the interpretation of these two variables requires more caution since in the last model their level of significance was below 5 per cent, meaning that their independent influence is diminished by

Table 10-11 Logistic regression coefficients of change in the workplace

Variables	Model 1 Beta	Model 2 Beta	Model 3 Beta	Model 4 Beta
Self-employed	.6827	.6809	.6422	.6535
Public sector	.4180*	.4703*	.4642*	.4791^
Small workplace	1.8047^	1,8573^	1.9288**	1.8534^
ISCO1	4.2728**	4.8401**	4.9423**	5.1067**
ISCO2	1.9686	1.9290	2.0544	2.1083
Permanent return	.4479	.4375^	.4278	.4218^
Returned <5 yrs		1.6248	1.4862	1.2655
Returned 5–9 yrs		2.8690**	2.7011*	2.5002*
Age first mig. <20 yrs			.7784	.7686
Duration of absence			1.0913	1.1089
Worked abroad			1.6487	1.6045
Education			.8080	.8231
Côte d'Ivoire				.9180
Age39				1.5005
Age50Plus				1.2418
Male				1.1338
No of observations=304				
R^2	12.3%	15.9%	17.2%	17.7%
ΔR		3.6%	1.3%	0.5%
Overall classification	80.59%	80.59%	81.25%	82.89%

Significance: **<1% *<5%, ^<10%.

the introduction of variables concerning the personal attributes of the returnees.

Relatively few variables were found to have a significant impact on the propensity to operate change in the family environment (Table 10-12). Self-employed returnees were more likely to have initiated such change, as were those who returned within the five years preceding the interview. The personal characteristics of the returnees was the variable which influenced most their likelihood to initiate change in this social

Table 10-12 Logistic regression coefficients of change in the family

Variables	Model 1 Beta	Model 2 Beta	Model 3 Beta	Model 4 Beta
Self-employed	1.9415*	2.0115*	2.0875*	1.4200
Public sector	1.0030	1.0877	1.1343	1.1720
Small workplace	.8584	.8309	.8648	.9361
ISCO1	.5398	.6002	.5212	.3178
ISCO2	.6780	.7136	.6564	.5189
Permanent return	.8746	.9411	.9228	.9419
Returned <5 yrs		1.8165^	1.7561^	2.2065*
Returned 5–9 yrs		1.3393	1.2594	1.3194
Age first mig. <20 yrs			.9139	1.0594
Duration of absence			.6756^	1.2329
Worked abroad			1.5482	1.6422
Education			1.3382	1.3535
Côte d'Ivoire				.2260**
Age39				.4350*
Age50Plus				1.0589
Male				1.1307
No of observations=304				
R^2	2.9%	4.5%	7.2%	19.1%
ΔR		1.6%	2.7%	8.9%
Overall classification	67.11%	67.11%	68.09%	90.10%

Significance: **<1% *<5% ^<10%

environment and those aged between 40 and 49 years were more likely to have undertaken such initiatives.

The country of origin was found to have the most significant independent influence on whether or not returnees promoted any change in the family (Table 10-12) or in the public sphere (Table 10-13). In both cases Ivorians were significantly less likely than Ghanaians to have effected change. But another factor that seems to influence the agency of returned migrants in the public realm is their age at first emigration. Those who were younger than 20 years when they first emigrated appear to have more

Table 10-13 Logistic regression coefficients of change in the public sphere

Variables	Model 1	Model 2	Model 3	Model 4
	Beta	Beta	Beta	Beta
Self-employed	1.9345*	1.9766*	2.0148*	1.3063^
Public sector	1.2249	1.3621	1.6539	1.9626
Small workplace	1.0600	1.0330	1.0861	1.183
ISCO1	1.7468	1.9331	1.6793	.9007
ISCO2	1.8531	1.9106	1.9668	1.5926
Permanent return	.9259	.9742	.9684	.9877
Returned <5 yrs		1.7257^	1.6523	1.4536
Returned 5–9 yrs		1.6733^	1.4691	1.1630
Age first mig. <20 yrs			1.0754**	1.3177
Duration of absence			.5160^	1.1863
Worked abroad			1.9993	2.1131^
Education			1.1593	1.1951
Côte d'Ivoire				.1139**
Age39				.7312
Age50Plus				1.0897
Male				1.9331^
No of observations=304				
R^2	2.7%	4.4%	9.8%	25.5%
ΔR		2.7%	5.4%	15.7%
Overall classification	64.14%	62.50%	62.50%	70.39%

Significance: **<1% *<5% ^<10%

chances to assume a developmental role in this particular context. Other factors related to the migrants' experience abroad, such as their duration of absence and if they worked abroad, turned out not to have any significant impact on the returnees' propensity to effect change within these models.

To estimate the relative incidence of different sets of variables, the difference in the R^2 values was computed. This calculation showed which of the different sets of variables helped more in explaining variations in the phenomenon under investigation. It showed that in the first models, concerning change in the workplace, the greatest amount of variation occurs with regard to factors related to the migrants' situation after return. This means that factors such as the occupational level of the returnees are more determinant for their change potential in the workplace than their experience abroad (e.g., duration of absence or whether they have worked abroad), suggesting that structural conditions are critical in this arena and can either constrain or enhance their change initiatives. This also explains why returnees who are their own bosses have more margin of manoeuvre.

The most important variations in the second and third series of models were instead recorded in relationship with the personal attributes of the returnees, especially their country of origin. The family and public sphere therefore appear less constraining environments, allowing returnees to act on their own accord without too many external influencing factors. The importance of the country of origin is however more difficult to explain. One possible reason is that, as was already mentioned, in Ghana there has been much more discussion about the return of highly-skilled migrants and their role in national development. This perhaps has raised the awareness of returnees and mobilised them in this direction.

Summary of Findings

This chapter has shown that migration is seen by those involved to have had many positive effects, not only for the migrants themselves but also for their families. Migrants attributed these improvements mainly to the remittances and savings they had transferred from abroad and to the education and work experience they had gained during their absence. They were generally earning less than before they returned home, but more than other people in similar positions who had never emigrated. The fact that their income was not as high as it had been abroad seemed not to bother them particularly, as long as they had good career prospects and got enough recognition and respect. Professional responsibility seemed to be what mattered most, whereas income was less of a concern because in real terms it had a fair value and also because respondents were quite motivated and determined to stay home. Those who did not possess these latter qualities had probably already re-emigrated; so in one sense the returnee sample did not cover the whole picture of return and possible re-emigration.

The assessment done at the meso-level has confirmed that some of the benefits deriving from migration are seen to trickle down to the migrants' extended families and communities. But since the demands and pressures are very high, migrants say they find it difficult to satisfy all requests. Financial and material support is provided by returnees not only on the grounds of the principles of solidarity and reciprocity, but also because this confers prestige and enables them to acquire the authority and power that are needed to assume a credible role as agents of change. The contributions made by returnees in the family environment consisted mainly in some efforts to change the attitudes and behaviour of relatives and friends.

Significant change was also promoted by returned migrants in their wider social environment and public sphere. This happened through the conception, funding and implementation of community development activities and projects mostly targeted at the returnees' rural home towns and villages. There was often awareness on their behalf that foreign ideas and values cannot be so readily introduced, but need to be changed and adapted to fit the local context.

However, the most important contributions reported by returnees were those in the workplace. These consisted in the introduction of new knowledge, skills and ideas and execution of some critical changes and reforms. Many practical examples were provided showing that returnees helped in improving organisational structures and management practices, increasing working morale and productivity and developing technical know-how. Some returned migrants moreover launched new businesses, thereby creating employment and providing useful services. Those who sought to play a meaningful role in the public sector seem to have encountered more psychological resistance and physical obstacles. But in spite of these difficulties many returnees reported that they were able to make an impact here too. Having accessed key positions of responsibility and authority, they were in a strategic position to use their foreign knowledge, skills and experience to influence policy-making and the adoption of new measures.

However, once again it needs to be acknowledged that all the evidence for these changes and innovations comes from the returnees' own statements. Simple observation – for instance of offices or of other work premises – plus some cross-checking with other key informants helped to validate the general character of respondents' and interviewees' statements, but the possibility of exaggeration and self-aggrandisement can certainly not be ruled out.

A series of multiple-step logistic regression analyses was performed to determine what makes some return migrants assume a developmental role in their home context while others do not. The findings suggest that change initiatives in the workplace mostly hinge on whether returnees have enough responsibility, authority and power, and enough time to get established in such top positions. Before having reached a certain stage, migrants seem more reluctant to embark on reforms because they first need to readapt to the local context and secure their employment or the viability of their firm.

The regression analyses also confirmed that there is a significant difference between the two countries as far as changes in the family environment and public sphere are concerned. Perhaps, this is due to the greater public debate which has occurred around the issues of "brain drain" and "brain re-gain" in Ghana. It may be that this has helped in strengthening the awareness of returning migrants as to their change potential and their need to contribute to development. This may have mobilised them accordingly in different realms, especially in the family and public spheres. However, no difference was detected between the two samples in terms of their contributions in the workplace. The promotion of change in this latter arena was mainly influenced by the conditions in the migrants' workplaces. In contrast, the personal attributes of the returnees' were found to be more significant determinants of whether they assume the role of development agents in the family or in the public sphere.

CHAPTER ELEVEN

MAIN CONCLUSIONS AND SOME WAYS FORWARD

The purpose of this last chapter is to summarise the most important results of this study. It discusses the main empirical findings in the light of the questions raised and the connected theoretical issues. Two questions were central to the research. The first one was whether highly-skilled, élite migrants have any impact on the development of their country of origin and, if so, what kinds of benefit stem from their return migration. The second question regarded the conditions that determine whether such migrants make any contribution and play an active role as agents of development in their country of origin. Hence the first and longer section of this chapter synthesises and interprets the research results in terms of their ability to answer these main questions. Key findings of the study are highlighted in *italics*. Thereafter some important policy implications are discussed. Finally, the strengths and weaknesses of this study are pointed out and a few issues that require more research in the future are outlined.

An Interpretation of the Results

At the outset of this book it was seen from the literature review that empirical findings from different parts of the world are rather inconclusive with regard to the development impact of return migrants in sending countries. One of the reasons why there is so little agreement is that hardly any distinction has so far been made in existing studies between highly-skilled and low or unskilled migrants. This research, focusing exclusively on highly-skilled migrants, suggests that it is important to introduce such a differentiation. It shows that these better prepared migrants have a good chance of acquiring abroad different forms of capital and, after return, often move into strategic positions allowing them to make a developmental impact. This confirms the assumption of Ghosh (2000b) and Cassarino (2004), who postulated that the aptitude of returning migrants and their degree of preparedness are key factors which condition their development impact once back home.

The research presented here also substantiates the notion that the consequences of international migration and return are multifaceted and manifest themselves at various levels. They need to be seen in each contextual setting, taking wider socio-economic, cultural and political circumstances in the home and destination countries into account. By focusing on Ghanaian and Ivorian highly-skilled migrants and assessing the implications of their return mobility, this study has contributed to strengthening the hitherto insufficient understanding of these processes in West Africa. This represents an important step forward since this region, characterised by worsening socio-economic conditions and increasing migratory movements, deserves a special focus when reflecting about ways to maximise the benefits of migration and to reduce its negative effects. Also, West Africa has so far been neglected by empirical studies focused specifically upon return migration.

In order to discover the underlying driving forces and intrinsic mechanisms of return migration, this study conceives return as a relevant step within a migration cycle which involves two countries with their respective development contexts. For this reason it proved a sensible choice to adopt not only a comparative approach for the research but to extend information gathering to four different countries, the two West African ones just mentioned and their two European ex-colonial countries of reference. This has produced a great wealth of data which proved useful to understanding the structural determinants of migration and return, related to the socio-economic and political conditions in the countries of origin and destination.

Furthermore, the adoption of a multi-method approach requiring the collecting of qualitative as well as quantitative evidence proved useful to comprehending migrants' decision-making and behaviour and to gaining a good grasp of personal and subjective aspects such as motivations, aspirations and values. The research showed that each migration and return experience has unique aspects, but is also determined by many different factors depending on external circumstances as much as on the person itself. Individual goals, preferences, expectancies and decisions are moreover influenced by interpersonal relationships and a complex set of social ties. Nevertheless, the main thrust of the analysis has been towards careful generalisation and thus reaches beyond the attentive consideration of the great variety of individual cases.

In the chapters presenting the research results it was seen that the migration and return experiences of the Ghanaian and Ivorian highly skilled who participated in this study are dissimilar in many respects. Their reasons for emigration, duration of absence and the activities they engaged in while abroad were all found to differ considerably. The extent to which these differences may be generalised, or are related to the nature of the not rigorously representative samples, is hard to determine. However, the dissimilar histories and development profiles of Ghana and Côte d'Ivoire seem to have produced diverse migration experiences and outcomes. In particular, differential migration effects appear to be linked to these two countries' colonial heritage and post-colonial development experiences.

Yet many similarities between the Ghanaian and Ivorian respondents were detected, too, especially by integrating qualitative and quantitative data and by employing multivariate analysis, a technique which has helped to address the problems related to sampling biases. The following discussion provides an encompassing interpretation of the key findings, from which some policy implications can be drawn. These findings reveal interesting patterns and dynamics but, as stressed throughout the book, they may only be extended with the necessary caution. This means that there remains much scope for future research.

The most important finding of this study is that the return of Ghanaian and Ivorian highly-skilled migrants does indeed have *a positive impact in their country of origin*. Whilst abroad these migrants acquire resources conferring on them a significant development potential in their home countries. Capital transferred by returning migrants constitutes a valuable asset in the local context and enables migrants to make a meaningful contribution to national and local development. The conditions under which migrants acquire abroad and transfer back home different kinds of capital were identified. How these resources are used was determined as well as what different kinds of contribution are made by highly skilled returnees. However, it proved more difficult to establish the conditions which make some return migrants more mobilised than others in terms of their developmental potential.

It is often claimed that return migration has only limited positive implications. The findings of this research contradict these claims, demonstrating that Ivorian and Ghanaian highly-skilled return migrants not only accumulated different forms of capital abroad which were of use to them and their countries, but also deployed these resources productively in different realms. Financial capital, when brought back in significant amounts, was invested in the creation of businesses which produced quite tangible impacts. Although these businesses were often relatively small scale, they contributed directly to the creation of employment, expansion of services and increases in production. But positive multiplier effects were also detected in relationship with building-related expenditures. Furthermore, human and social capital constituted critical foreign-gained resources of highly-skilled migrants which helped them to embark on innovative ventures or discerning reforms. The research shows that the impact of return migrants is very much conditioned by their skills, experience and attitudes, and thereby corroborates findings of previous empirical research which has distinguished differential return effects of highly-skilled and low- or unskilled migrants (Gmelch, 1987; Thomas-Hope, 1999).

A broad spectrum of contributions was made by return migrants in both private and public sectors. The initiatives vary significantly and so do their impacts, with examples ranging from the creation of a new government agency regulating the energy sector in Ghana, across the establishment of a food-processing industry creating many jobs in rural Côte d'Ivoire, to the set-up of a Ghanaian NGO promoting the cause of democracy and human rights or the launch of a brokerage firm contributing to the development of the Ghanaian stock exchange. But return initiatives are not always that spectacular. Many contributions are made by returnees on a day-to-day basis in their workplaces, families and social circles, as well as in the wider public sphere. After return, migrants provided much financial and material support to members of their family, kin and other relatives, and instigated a positive change in attitudes and behaviour in their closer social environment. It was also seen that in the public sphere their contributions included initiatives such as the start-up of new projects aimed at promoting community development in their rural home villages, various advocacy activities regarding issues of public interest and the development of different associations or organisations. Their high-level posts and assignments conferred on them the necessary visibility and respect and allowed them to influence policy initiatives more or less directly.

Two different kinds of consequences of migration and return can be distinguished: *implications for the welfare of migrants and their families*; and *impact on the development of the country of origin*. The first aspect was evaluated, as suggested by Gmelch (1980), by means of both objective and subjective indicators. It appears that, on balance, migrants were not only better off than before emigration, but also quite satisfied with their post-return situation. Foreign capital gains allowed return migrants to improve their situations and to lead successful careers. Human capital in the form of a foreign degree and/or work experience represented valuable assets for those who sought employment, and foreign-acquired savings and connections, that is social capital, proved useful resources for those who opted for self-employment. The combination of these micro- and meso-level results produced broader socio-economic transformations that favourably influenced more macro-level development.

The research confirmed that both the work-related success of return migrants and their impact on development in the home country are influenced by a variety of factors. The most critical are linked to the migrants' experiences abroad and to their experiences after return. These latter are directly conditioned by the evolving situations in the home country, whereas the former depend on such conditions more indirectly because they also reflect personal motivations and goals of the migrants. The findings show that when the macro conditions in the home country are not propitious, migrants are more inclined to stay abroad longer, with all that involves in terms of their foreign experience and related capital acquisitions.

In fact, with regard to migrants' experiences abroad, two factors assume particular importance: their *duration of absence* and, even more importantly, the *type of activities* they followed in the host country(ies). This finding is largely in line with theoretical predictions and corroborates the assumption of return migration scholars, such as Bovenkerk (1974) and Cerase (1974), who expected the migrants' length of absence to influence migration and return outcomes. But this research shows that whether migrants worked and the length of their work experience are of even greater significance. Elite migrants who worked abroad were found more likely to have accumulated financial and human capital, because they gained more exposure to different experiences and people and this made their experience richer and more diversified. Hence, highly-skilled migrants with relevant work experience have a greater "added value" than those who exclusively studied or worked for short periods. This finding is in line with those of Black and Castaldo (2009) showing that work experience abroad is the most significant factor influencing entrepreneurial by return migrants.

Most importantly, however, this research revealed that there may be an *optimal work duration* – approximately five years – during which the greatest benefits are derived in terms of human and financial capital accumulation. After that stage the acquisition of these two forms of capital becomes more or less constant. Also, there are clear signs that, starting from a certain point onwards, the chances increase that migrants will not return home or find it too difficult to readjust to the home-country context. There are several reasons why this may happen. Firstly, it was shown statistically that the longer migrants remain abroad, the more difficulties they encounter after return. Secondly, from the migrants' accounts it appeared that the longer migrants remain abroad, the harder it becomes for them to return since they may already be too settled. The longer highly-skilled migrants remain in the host country(ies), the more likely they are to get training-related jobs, earn a better income, own a house or apartment, have children in school, etc; all factors which make return more difficult. That is also why, for migrants who stay away longer, it takes more time to plan and organise return. Thirdly, it was seen that in some European countries – as, for example, the United Kingdom – the possibility is provided for immigrants to change their residence status after a few years, making it more permanent.

Whether, as pointed out by Cerase (1974), the *duration of absence* also affects the decision to return or stay abroad could not be assessed in this study. To answer this question it would have been necessary to compare return migrants and emigrants, an undertaking which was not one of the aims of the research. But some evidence was produced supporting the argument that if migrants stay abroad too little time they may not have acquired enough experience and if they stay away too long they may have experienced and changed so much that they encounter too many problems in readapting to the original home context. Difficulties faced after return can seriously undermine their efforts or result in their re-emigration, both occurrences that diminish the benefits of return migration. Yet, as Cerase (1974) suggested, post-return readjustment problems may be concomitant with innovative efforts and hence can also be seen as a valuable indicator of change brought about by return migrants. This research shows in fact that highly-skilled migrants who stayed and worked abroad longer, and thus returned with more capital resources and a greater development potential, needed to overcome more challenges and hurdles to readjust to the local working and living conditions. Furthermore it was found, in line with other studies (King, 2000), that problems of reintegration are greatest right after return and then progressively diminish. Despite the fact that no statistically significant association was found between returnees' problems and development impacts, information derived from in-depth interviews clearly suggests that such difficulties constitute an important obstacle for returnees to promote development.

The findings also corroborate those of other empirical studies showing that the way reintegration occurs depends largely on the *expectations and return motivations* of the migrants (King, 2000; Rogers, 1984). These were found to affect the satisfaction of migrants concerning their return move and also the way they dealt with constraints and opportunities after return. Evidence was generated showing that pull factors tend to prevail over push factors in return decision-making, in line with previous findings from other world regions (King, 2000). But it also showed that highly-skilled return migrants being "pulled" back home by expectations of better job and business opportunities and by beliefs that their foreign experience and knowledge would be useful, were more likely to make a positive impact.

In general, return decision-making appeared more strongly affected by changes in the conditions in the migrants' country of origin, than by programmes and policies designed to enhance return migration. In particular, highly-skilled migrants were attracted by *enhanced opportunities for professional advancement*, although an exception is represented by so-called "student migrants" (i.e., those who went abroad to get a degree and then quickly returned home). What incentivised many highly-skilled migrants to return were the possibilities in the home country allowing them to get to the top. But they also desired to engage in more gratifying activities involving more responsibility and power, gain more recognition and respect and overall feel more useful. Income mattered less, also because the costs of living back home were lower, and often the non-material quality of life was perceived to be higher.

The socio-economic and political environment in the country of origin is what most influences migration abroad and return, as well as the migrants' impact on development after return. This explains why so much heterogeneity between Ghana and Côte d'Ivoire was found. The *time of return* is a particularly significant factor determining the consequences of reverse mobility. The findings show that, depending upon circumstances, the return of highly-skilled migrants produces quite different outcomes, because opportunities and constraints in the home context change over time and across occupational realms. That is why it proved useful to compare the migration and return experiences of migrants originating from an anglophone and a francophone West African country as well as of migrants belonging to separate age-conditioned mobility cohorts.

The development implications of return migration were found to differ not only according to the *age of the migrants*, but also in relationship to their *activity regime after return*. The most important differences were found in this respect between the private and the public sector, and were based on the migrants' post-return *employment status*. In fact, the opportunities and constraints that arose for return migrants proved not to be the same in different sectors. It also seems that foreign capital acquisitions may be used more easily, and perhaps even more productively, in self-employment activities, an occupational option which was preferred by many returnees, in line with what was found by other empirical studies (for example, Black et al., 2003c; Arif and Irfan, 1997; Murphy, 1999).

The study revealed that amongst élite migrants, those opting for self-employment were usually the more dynamic or ready to take risks. They appeared more eager to make a development impact than migrants who had returned to work in the public sector. Returnees who were employed in the public sector were found less likely to have operated any change in the workplace as well as in the family environment and the public sphere. However, with regard to the workplace it can be argued that, since the self-employed were their own bosses, they probably had more latitude to effect change in the workplace compared to those who were employees.

This leads us on to consider the second main question addressed by this study: what are the conditions under which highly-skilled return migrants make a meaningful contribution in different realms? The findings show that *factors related to their situation after return are more significant than factors linked to their experiences abroad*. This suggests that no matter how much capital migrants acquire abroad and transfer back home, their development impact really hinges on whether they have any opportunity of deploying this capital constructively. It depends mostly on the situation to which they return and the extent to which the conditions in different spheres are conducive or obstructive. Another important factor revealed by the research is that much depends on the *time that has passed since return*. In the family and public spheres highly-skilled return migrants were more likely to have introduced changes in the first five years after return, but in the workplace they started making more lasting contributions only after that time.

Information from in-depth interviews suggests that this is mainly because, before embarking on change and development initiatives, *returnees need time to readjust and reintegrate into the home context*. They need to secure their employment or test the viability of their newly-established firms. But they also have to re-appraise the local context in the light of the changes that have occurred during their absence. Most importantly, however, the accounts of Ghanaian and Ivorian highly-skilled returnees show that today there is a growing awareness that foreign-acquired knowledge, ideas, skills and practices cannot so readily be introduced into the local context. To produce lasting changes which can enhance sustainable development, the migrants need to internalise what they have learned abroad and adapt it carefully to the specific needs and circumstances of the home country.

Conducting research with a specific focus on the highly skilled, élite migrants has helped in achieving rich and interesting insights because many of the migrants involved had devoted considerable reflection and critical thought to the issues of migration and return. The study has therefore drawn much benefit from their very active participation in the inquiry. However, it is interesting that the richness of the information provided was not the same in the two countries. From the interviews we can gather that *Ghanaians have devoted more thought to these issues than Ivorians*. This is mainly because of the larger significance that the "brain drain" has assumed in their country and the greater importance that policy-makers here have attributed to the need of promoting "brain re-gain". Thus, in fact, in 2001 an important "Homecoming Summit" was organised in Accra in order to enhance public awareness.

In Côte d'Ivoire, by contrast, interviewees had apparently reflected less on migration and return issues probably because many had spent relatively less time abroad and were mainly trained there in view of returning home. Ivorians were also more reluctant to provide personal information or information regarding their business initiatives, because of the recent coup d'état and political uncertainties. When interviewed, this might have somewhat biased their reports. Indeed the following contrasts can be drawn. On the one hand, Ghanaians, who also tend to be more aware of their potential role in development, may have exaggerated or embellished the contributions they were making in their accounts while, on the other hand, Ivorians, whose awareness about these issues appeared more limited, might in fact have made some practical contributions without thinking of mentioning them in interviews. This contrasting tendency may have amplified the differences that were found regarding the role played by these two groups of migrants after return. Yet, an unequal awareness of these two groups concerning the developmental role of highly-skilled migrants appears to be the more plausible explanation why Ghanaians were more likely than Ivorians to have effected change in the family environment or in the public sphere.

Policy Implications

As a premise to the presentation of some policy implications it seems important to reaffirm that in current times, characterised by accelerating globalisation and increasing human mobility, return to the home country can hardly be viewed as the conclusion of a migration cycle. It must rather be seen as one step in a sequence of possible multiple movements. Beyond the fact that higher-skilled migrants have a higher propensity to move because of their greater resources, this mobility is likely to increase even more in the future. One of the reasons is the relaxation of immigration policies concerning this particular group of migrants, because of the growing interest of industrialised countries in the North in tapping into these human resources. But if such a trend accelerates further and if migration policies make it possible for highly-skilled migrants to move back and forth more easily, benefits could also be derived by sending countries in the South because the freer circulation of these people will imply multiplied and increased multidirectional transfers of different forms of capital, including human, social and financial.

If highly-skilled migrants had greater freedom of movement and the choice to come and go as they like, greater benefits could be derived by all those involved in the migration, both the host and the sending countries, as well as the migrants themselves. This observation seems particularly relevant in the light of the findings of this study, which have shown that for highly-skilled migrants there might be an optimal work duration abroad. When, after some time in the host country, their human and financial capital accumulation becomes constant, and highly-skilled migrants remain under the constraint of a glass ceiling, they may well prefer to go back where they have more chances to unfold their potential, provided they can return abroad once more if necessary.

However, for return to occur – and to occur successfully – the right situation must exist in the country of origin. When professional opportunities are lacking and the working and living conditions are too unattractive, even return schemes have proved to have only limited impacts. Creating an appropriate policy framework and promoting better conditions for return should be made a priority to attract highly-skilled migrants back and facilitate their reintegration in the country of origin. There is little doubt that, if return migrants encountered fewer readjustment problems, migrants would be more willing to return and also not be tempted or forced to leave again.

This study has found that an important factor influencing the growth of personal well-being and the contribution to socio-economic development of return migration is represented by the migrants' foreign work experience. This finding suggests that programmes aimed at reversing the brain drain by facilitating the return of the highly-skilled migrants should be better targeted at migrants who, in addition to a higher degree, have acquired substantial professional experience abroad. One problem is that these migrants are usually more difficult to attract away from their higher salaries and better working and living conditions abroad. Another problem is that they are more likely to encounter problems after return and to become frustrated because they do not find the facilities and services they became accustomed to when living abroad. Yet it is this group of migrants who transfer larger amounts of financial and human capital when they return and who embody the greatest development potential. Their impact can be maximised when they are recruited back into the very top-level positions in the private and public sectors because, as it was seen, in these positions they are more likely to make a meaningful contribution.

The research has confirmed that in the workplace the relationship between returnees and non-migrants is often characterised by ambiguity, with the former being associated with modernity and innovation and the latter with tradition and preservation of the status quo. This interpretation is, of course, much too simplistic for it needs to be stressed that both have a critical and complementary role to play. While migrants had the opportunity to gain human and social capital abroad and to transfer it back home, non-migrants have in the meantime accumulated more "location-specific" social and human capital back home. Their knowledge and understanding of the local context are more thorough, whereas migrants have a broader frame of reference that is helpful in identifying innovative solutions. Based on these considerations it appears crucial to find ways to strengthen the relationship between returnees and "stayers" so that their development efforts can be combined. It is not only this relationship that needs strengthening, but also that between the return migrants themselves. There is scope for return migrants to combine forces especially in those cases when the resources of single person may not be sufficient to embark on certain ventures, such as, for example, the launch of a business or the organisation of a cooperative.

A particularly important measure that could facilitate return migration and enhance its positive implications is the creation of favourably flexible conditions in which returnees can more easily settle and establish their business ventures. This study has shown that the contributions made by return migrants through the promotion of new businesses are meaningful in many ways, but also that they encounter many challenges and obstacles. One aspect that therefore needs to be looked at by policy-makers is what needs to be done to support such initiatives and to ensure their endurance and longer-term impacts. Much more attention needs to be paid to producing more easy accessible, stable and favourable environments for investment in businesses and in creating support for entrepreneurship.

In the past some development programmes and policies have been too narrowly focused on assisting migrants in resettling back home, producing sometimes undesirable side-effects. Some projects, for example, have hired highly-skilled nationals from the diaspora based on higher salary scales than those applied locally. This has created local jealousies and contributed to undermining the relationship between returnees and non-migrants. Some of the latter felt that their fellow-compatriots who left when the country was going through difficult times should not necessarily be rewarded "just for coming back". Based on past lessons and, in particular, acknowledging that many highly-skilled migrants may decide not return home permanently, more attention is now being focused on how to involve the intellectual and business diaspora through short-term assignments in their country of origin or through the participation in virtual intellectual and business networks. Policy initiatives facilitating these arrangements are valuable and, in this perspective, it should be take into account that more highly-skilled migrants that one would think are ready to make "voluntary" contributions.

Finally, this study has confirmed that return migrants have made, and often subsequently maintain, useful contacts abroad which represent crucial assets which they use to develop new business and professional activities back home. Indeed, highly-skilled return migrants move in international circuits cultivating relationships and transnational social capital which help them to connect different worlds. In the present era of globalisation, based on their unique social background, life histories and personal achievements, return migrants elaborate new and probably more flexible world-views which have an impact not only on their professional life but also on their family life and the upbringing of their children. This raises further issues which, as will be argued in the next section, need to be addressed by future research.

Some Critical Observations and Directions for Further Research

Before some suggestions regarding future research are forwarded in conclusion, the main strengths as well as the weaknesses of this study need to be pointed out. At the methodological level, four intertwined strategic options characterise its rationale and research design. Among the strong points, firstly, is the choice of studying highly-skilled return migration as a phenomenon in its own right which must not be confounded with the migration experiences of the unskilled population. Secondly, there is the decision to compare two different countries in order to establish commonalities and differences regarding the experiences of migrating abroad, migrants' return and the transfer of resources and their experience back home. This has allowed the research to bring into focus a number of social, economic, political and cultural factors which condition the basic relationships between variables and help to appreciate the external validity of the results. Thirdly, there is the aim to overcome the micro-macro divide by bringing into focus crucial issues at the meso-level regarding mainly social networks and family relations. Fourthly, there is the adoption of a research approach which integrates qualitative and quantitative evidence collected during the successive phases of field work. This combination of options has yielded a very solid basis of empirical evidence and has enhanced a more realistic interpretation of the findings.

But, as is always the case, this study also has its limits, which have to be taken into account. Information about development initiatives was obtained directly from the actors who reported the achieved impacts. Hence, in testing the hypothesis that return migration fosters development on the basis of data collected by means of a questionnaire, self-assessment biases cannot be excluded. But gathering information also from a variety of additional sources has helped in overcoming these constraints and cross-validating results. It would have been good if the effectiveness of development-oriented behaviour of returnees in different realms could have been more carefully monitored and cross-checked. But doing this by means of interviews with superiors, colleagues or relatives would have caused logistical problems which, within the present research framework and timetable, could not be tackled. In addition, in future studies moving along the same lines, it may perhaps be useful to gather the viewpoints of a sample of non-migrants operating in comparable situations in order to ascertain their view or judgement of the role of return migrants in the development process.

Another possible shortcoming to be acknowledged is the lack of an analysis in terms of a social stratification paradigm of the phenomenon of élite return migration. Problems related to the definition of "éliteness" were dealt with early on in the book. However, an unanswered question remains: to what extent do highly-skilled returnees, bringing back additional human, financial and social capital, end up enjoying a kind of "enhanced-élite" or "super-élite" status whereby they further enhance the class structure of their home countries, and potentially exacerbate the social inequalities between the rich and the poor, the powerful and the powerless? Here one needs to highlight the tension between, on the one hand, return migration's capacity to stimulate broad-based development via investment in businesses that create employment and wealth or via influence on local or regional development policy-making and, on the other hand, a trend toward enhanced social polarisation, with returnees enjoying privileged status reinforced by their overseas capital and experience, and exerting this power to influence and exploit others for their own further benefit.

Performing a comparative, cross-country study of migration and return has helped in illuminating the specific conditions under which return migrants take on a role as development agents. The data suggest that the causal effects of migration and return vary considerably in the different country settings. However, as has been stressed before, due to the impossibility of drawing interviewees randomly, the two samples on which the research evidence is based cannot be considered strictly representative. Hence the findings, though capable of indicating differential trends, can only be interpreted and generalised with considerable caution. In order to partially overcome this limit and to corroborate the emerging causal effects, some multivariate regression analyses were performed. These have revealed the key predictors of highly-skilled return migrants' impact in their home country.

Also, it cannot go unmentioned that the respect that needed to be given to the issue of confidentiality has represented a certain constraint. In fact, because of problems of privacy, the life histories or biographical information which were collected could not be exploited fully. Since most of the respondents were working at very high levels and were generally well-known in their cities, their identity would all too easily have been exposed. In order to avoid this problem, the statements are presented without much information or comment regarding the source and in a quite fragmentary way. Thereby they have unfortunately lost some of their intrinsic interpretative value.

Finally, a special problem at the data-gathering level needs to be mentioned. It derives from the need to use identical research instruments in two linguistically different research contexts, a French-speaking and an English-speaking country. In fact, translation always entails some major difficulties even if careful attention is paid to the wording and to the different meanings, and even when the necessary pre-tests are performed, as was the case in this study.

In order to gain a better grasp of the multifaceted change potential of return migrants, future research should pay more attention to variables at the meso-level. In this study an approach focusing on this level was chosen with the scope of establishing hypothetical links between the more conventional macro and micro perspectives. Through this multi-level methodological approach the socio-economic, political and cultural characteristics of the areas of origin and destination could be linked with the psycho-social factors which influence migrants' attitudes and behaviours. Interfacing the macro- and the micro-level perspectives at the meso level, emphasis could be given to the migrants' interpersonal relationships and social ties and to the role of their families, kin and other social groupings which, as we have seen, help shape the migrants' opportunities and constraints into assuming a meaningful role after return. A special focus on the migrants' role in the workplace, in the family and more generally in civil society has shown that attention should not only be given to contributions that can be measured, but also to more intangible forms of change which constitute the necessary premises of lasting development. However, the multiple implications of return migration at the meso level and, in particular, the full benefits of social capital transfer, remain at present only partially assessed. These need to be further explored, based upon appropriate research designs and measurement instruments.

Further research might, in addition, consider also interviewing other members of the families in order to encompass their points of view regarding migration. In this study some effort, based upon in-depth interviews, was made in this direction by trying to talk with spouses. But naturally the problem of privacy increases if an attempt is made to reconstruct what may be called the "family dynamics". This assumes an even greater importance when we consider the important gender issues that have emerged from this research. In fact, women generally encounter more problems after return and are therefore more reluctant to return.

These gender concerns need to be further investigated in future research. Attention should also be focused on issues regarding children and how they are affected by migration and return.

The possibility clearly exists for extending the comparative dimension of the research to other African or developing-world countries. This research was deliberately set up to compare a francophone with an anglophone West African country, drawing on and contrasting their respective French and British colonial traditions. One could easily add to this small sample other countries with a Portuguese, Spanish, or other (or, indeed, no) colonial heritage. The scale factor might also be relevant here, countries with small populations and small foreign-educated highly-skilled migrants being contrasted with larger countries where, perhaps, indigenous élites educated through local university systems would be more powerful *vis-à-vis* foreign-educated élites. The cases of, say, Gambia and Cape Verde (where there are no local universities), as against Nigeria or South Africa, would be some examples.

In conclusion, it must be pointed out that, although transnational migration practices, where people move back and forth on an intermittent basis, were found to be far from highly developed in the country settings compared, in the future, within the context of globalisation, this phenomenon can be expected to expand in West Africa as elsewhere. The research methodology and instruments that were used in this study have already been conceived with an aim of capturing the increasing complexity and dynamics of contemporary intercontinental mobility in this region of the world. But these research methods and instrumentation will need to be further elaborated and adapted as migratory movements become even more frequent and multi-directional in the coming years.

Annexes

Annex One

Guide for Preliminary In-depth Interviews in Accra and Abidjan

Interview Guide Accra and Abidjan

The migrants' experience abroad
Please tell me why and how you first left your country to study or/and work abroad?
What is your educational and professional background? Please tell me about all your experiences before departure and then abroad?
What are the things that you learned abroad, if any?
How would you describe your lifestyle abroad? To what extent did this lifestyle differ from the one you had before in your own country?
Please tell me how your family situation evolved in the course of your migration experience?
How would you describe the relationship you had abroad with other compatriots, foreign or autochthonous people?
Which other linkages did you establish with your host country/ies (for example, married an autochthonous person, bought a house, invested in stocks, etc.)?
Which ties did you keep with your home country during your stay abroad?
How often did you visit your home country while abroad, and for what reasons?
Whilst abroad, what was your attitude towards return? Please tell me about your plans and feelings?

The return and transfer of resources
How much time did you originally intend to spend abroad? How long did you actually stay away from home?
Why did you return home? Who or what influenced most your decision to return?
How permanent or temporary do you consider your return?
To what extent did you pre-plan your exit/return, or did it/they occur spontaneously?

If you could go back, would you make the same decision? If no, why?
What do you think, why certain migrants decide to stay abroad?
The migrants' experience back home

- What has happened since you have came back home? How did you readapt and readjust upon return?
- What difficulties did you encounter upon return, if any?
- What were your expectations when you decided to come back?
- What do you miss most among the things you had whilst abroad?
- What do you appreciate most among the things you found back home?
- How useful do you find your experience abroad? Do you encounter any obstacles in utilising what you have learned abroad? If so, please tell me about these the obstacles?
- In your view, what is the difference between someone who has never moved and someone like you who has spend some time abroad?
- How are your degrees/diplomas and/or working experience judged in the local labour market?
- What were you able to accumulate in terms of savings? How did you invest this capital?
- Which linkages do you maintain with your host country(ies)? What is the purpose of these linkages? How do you nurture these contacts and relationships? How often do you return abroad to visit you host country/ies?
- What are your plans and prospects for the future? What would you like your children to do to succeed in life?
- What do you think is the potential role of return migrants in the development of their home societies and economies?

Annex Two
Questionnaire

INTERCONTINENTAL MOBILITY AND RETURN OF HIGHLY QUALIFIED NATIONALS TO GHANA AND CÔTE D'IVOIRE[1]

Research Project
co-ordinated by The University of Sussex (UK)
in collaboration with ISSER, University of Ghana and ENSEA, Côte d'Ivoire

Country ______________________________________

Date of Interview _________________________________

Start time of interview:_____________ End time of interview:_____________

Location of interview ______________________________

Respondent's serial number __________________________

Interviewer's initials ______________________________

Additional notes ____
____
____
____

1 Some items included in this questionnaire were used by the Centre for Asia Pacific Social Transformation Studies, University of Wollongong, Australia within the framework of a study of the return of skilled and business migrants to countries/regions of Bangladesh, China, Taiwan and Vietnam and of migration based linkages between Australia and these countries/regions. That study was funded by the Ford Foundation.

Introductory Remarks for Interviewers

The purpose of this study is to better understand the contemporary patterns and dynamics of international return migration of highly qualified African nationals to their country of origin and its implications. This is deemed necessary because very little is known regarding the return and re-integration of highly skilled people into their home societies and economies. The interview will take approximately one hour. Questions that will be asked will focus mainly on your experiences abroad, your decision to return and your experiences back home.

The information obtained from this study will be used for academic research and policy analysis purposes only. All information provided by you will be kept confidential.

Section 1 MIGRATION EXPERIENCE ABROAD

1.1 I would like to start in asking you to list in a chronological order the periods of your life that you have lived continuously abroad. Please limit your indications to periods *exceeding one year* and specify the country, from when to when you lived there, and the main reason of your stay *(Interviewer, show **Card 1**.)*
Please also indicate who made the decision for your departure. *(Interviewer, show **Card 2** for each country.)*

Foreign country(ies)	From	To	**Code for main reason**	**Decision to leave**
1.				
2.				
3.				
4.				

Card 1 **Main reasons**
1. Studies/Training 2. Work/Business 3. Join family member(s) 4. Refugee 5. Other (*Please specify*) *Choose only one*

Card 2 **Decision to leave**
1. Myself alone 2. Myself with spouse/partner 3. Together with other family member(s) 4. Others made the decision for me (*Please specify*) *Choose only one*

1.2 Did you do any studies abroad?
1. Yes
2. No (*skip to Q1.4*)

1.3 What is the highest education degree you achieved abroad?
1. High school and below
2. Vocational school
3. Bachelor or equivalent
4. Master or equivalent
5. PhD/Doctorate
6. None
7. Other (*Please specify*) ____________________

1.4 What is the highest degree you achieved in Ghana?
1. None/Primary
2. Basic Education (Middle/JSS)
3. Post Middle Certificate Tr. (Voc./Tec./Comm.)
4. Secondary ('O', 'A') or SSS
5. Post Secondary Diploma Tr. (Teacher/Tech.)
6. Bachelor or equivalent
7. Master or equivalent
8. Ph.D./Doctorate
9. Other (*Please specify*) ____________________

1.5 Did you work abroad?
1. No (*skip to Q1.10*)
2. Yes (*for those been to several countries*): In which foreign country(ies) did you
work? ____________________
____

1.6 Altogether, how many months/years did you work abroad? __________ months/years

1.7 What kinds of work did you do abroad? Please list all :
____
____
____
____

1.8 Did you practise any jobs abroad which were *not related* to your training?
1. Yes
2. No

1.9 How many months/years did you work in occupations *related* to you training? ____________________ months/years

1.10 Looking back, how did you feel during your stay(s) abroad? (*Interviewer, show **Card 3**.*)

Foreign country(ies)	Code for feeling
1.	
2.	
3.	
4.	

Card 3 **Feeling**
1. Nobody paid any attention to me
2. Rejected
3. As a tolerated guest
4. As a welcome guest
5. As if I were a national
Choose only one

1.11 Have you been an active participant in any association, club or movement while abroad?
1. No
2. Yes (*Please specify which ones*)________________________________
____

1.12 Did you own a house or apartment abroad?
1. Yes
2. No (*skip to Q1.14*)

1.13 Do you still own a house or apartment abroad?
1. Yes
2. No

1.14 What about your current resident status abroad? (*Interviewer, show **Card 4**.*)

Foreign country(ies)	Code for Current status
1.	
2.	
3.	
4.	

Card 4 **Current status**
1. Never had permanent resident status
2. Lost permanent resident status
3. Still keep a permanent resident status
4. Have obtained citizenship
Choose only one

1.15 What is your current resident status here in Ghana?
1. Permanent resident status (including local citizenship)
2. Temporary resident status (visitor's visa/business visa, etc.)

1.16 How often did you visit your home country during your stay(s) abroad? *(Interviewer, record frequency for each period abroad)* ________________

____

____

Section 2. DECISION-MAKING ABOUT RETURN

Interviewer, for those with several returns: Now let us talk exclusively about your *last return.*

2.1 When was your most recent move to Ghana after a stay abroad exceeding one year?
_________month _______year

2.2 On what basis did you return at that time?
1. Permanent
2. Temporary
3. Intermittent (come and go)

2.3 Was your last return influenced by any of the following? *(Interviewer, show **Card 5**.)*

Card 5 **Reasons for return**

1. Termination of studies
2. Government policies or programs favouring return
3. Family reasons
4. Expectation of better job opportunities
5. Expectation of better business opportunities
6. Difficulties in getting a good job abroad
7. Had to return, no other choice (expiration of working permit, etc.)
8. To receive due recognition and respect
9. Other reasons (*Please explain)* ______________________________

____

____

Can choose more than one

2.4 Who made the decision for your return? *(Interviewer, show **Card 6**)*

Card 6 **Decision for return**
1. Myself alone 2. Myself with spouse/partner 3. Together with other family member(s) 4. Others made the decision for me (*Please specify*) ____________________
Choose only one

2.5 For how long before actual return occurred did you plan and mobilise resources for return?
1. Less than 6 months
2. 6 to 11 months
3. 1 to 2 years
4. More than 2 years

2.6 Did you know any Ghanaian friends or family members who had returned before you returned home?
1. Yes
2. No

2.7 Which of the following best describe your expectations before your return? *(Interviewer, show **Card** 7)*

Card 7 **Expectations**
1. Feasible employment/business opportunities 2. Could benefit from government policies 3. Could utilise what I learned abroad 4. My family members and relatives in Ghana would accept me 5. My experience and knowledge about abroad were useful 6. Didn't have positive expectations 7. Other expectations. (*Please explain*) ____________________ ____________________ ____________________
Can choose more than one

2.8 Did you do any research to get information about Ghana before returning?
1. Yes
2. No (*skip to Q2.10*)

2.9 What were your main information sources? *(Can choose more than one.)*

1. Friends or relatives
2. Newspapers, TV, or other media
3. Information provided by government and its agencies
4. My own trips to Ghana
5. Other sources (*Please specify*) ____________________

____

2.10 When you decided to return, what was your spouse/partner's reaction? Was she/he supportive?

1. Yes
2. No
3. Neutral (or indifferent)
4. Did not have any spouse/partner

2.11 Which of the following best describes the reaction of your friends abroad to your return? *(Choose only one.)*

1. All were supportive
2. Most of them were supportive
3. Some of them were supportive
4. All were neutral (indifferent)
5. All were not supportive or tried to dissuade me
6. Other (*Please specify*) ____________________

Section 3. RETURN BACK HOME

3.1 With whom did you return to Ghana? (Choose only one)

1. By myself alone
2. With spouse/partner only
3. With all my immediate family [2]
4. With others. (*Please specify*) ____________________

3.2 When you made the decision to return, were you aware of any incentive (facilitating) programs or policies issued by the Government or other institutions?

1. Yes
2. No (*skip to Q3.8*)

---

2 *Immediate family* only includes spouse or partner and own or adopted children. *Extended family* also includes parents, siblings, cousins, aunts and uncles, other relatives, close friends, etc.

3.3 What were these programs? (*Interviewer, please ask information on these programs as detailed as possible*)

____

____

____

3.4 Did you receive any assistance from the program(s) mentioned above?

1. Yes
2. No (*skip to Q3.7)*

3.5 If you received any assistance, which of the following have you received? *(Indicate all those which apply)*

1. Housing/housing allowance
2. Moving expenses
3. Subsidiary for children or spouse
4. Help finding a job
5. Other assistance. (*Please explain*) ________________________

   ____

3.6 In what way do you think the government incentive/recruitment program(s) facilitated your return?

____

____

____

____

3.7 In what ways do you think the existing incentive/recruitment programs may become more attractive to those who have not returned from abroad?

____

____

____

3.8 Who arranged your return? *(Choose only one)*

1. Current employer
2. Government sponsoring agency/Receiving institute (*skip to Q3.11*)
3. Myself (*skip to Q3.11*)
4. My family members or relatives (*skip to Q3.11*)
5. Others. (*Please specify*) (*ex. spouse's employer*) ________________

   ____

3.9 Did the employer offer you (or your spouse/partner) anything in addition to your salary before your return?

1. Yes
2. No *(skip to Q3.11)*

3.10 What did the employer offer to you (or your spouse/partner) and did you receive it?

____

____

____

____

3.11 After your return have you had any problems in adjusting to the working conditions in Ghana?

Problems	**At the beginning**	**After some time**	**Presently**
Many problems			
Some problems			
No problems			

(*Interviewer, if* ***no problems*** *in all periods, skip to Q3.13*)

3.12 What were the problems related to your work?

____

____

____

____

____

3.13 To the best of your knowledge about other Ghanaian nationals who remain abroad, what are the main reasons why they have not returned?

____

____

____

Section 4. WORKING CONDITIONS

4.1 Which of the following describes your present employment status? *(Choose only one)*
1. Employee
2. Self-employed without employees
3. Self-employed with employees
4. Other. (*Please specify*) ________________________________

4.2 How do you describe your present workplace? *(Choose only one)*
1. Government department
2. University or research institution
3. Non-government organisation (NGO)

4. Business (trading, banking/finance, insurance, consulting, etc)
5. Services (communication, transportation, tourism, etc.)
6. Industry (manufacturing, construction, etc.)
7. Other type. (*Please specify*) ______________________________

4.3 How large is your workplace/business in terms of full-time staff? *Please include **all** full-time employees*__________

Interviewer, Q4.4 – Q4.9 ***for Self-employed with or without employees only.***

4.4 When did you start and register your own business/ professional activity?	Month	Year
Start		
Registration		

4.5 Please rank the following factors in terms of the amount of difficulties they caused you in setting it up. (*Interviewer, show* ***Card 8***.)

Card 8	**Areas**
____	Starting capital/Credits
____	Qualified collaborators
____	Marketing products/Services
____	Policies/Laws/Regulations
Rank from 1 to 4 in order of importance	

4.6 *Interviewer, for Self-employed with employees only*. Do you provide computer access to your employees?
1. Yes
2. No. *Please specify why not?*______________________________

4.7 *Interviewer, for Self-employed with employees only*. Do you provide internet access to your employees?
1. Yes
2. No. *Please specify why not?*______________________________

4.8 Have you received any assistance from government agencies or other sources to support your work?
1. No (*skip to Q4.13*)
2. Yes. (*Please, specify the source)*____________________________
____

4.9 If you have received assistance, have you received any of the following? *(Indicate all that apply)*
1. Research fund/business starting fund
2. Bank loan/financial support
3. Personnel support
4. Facility/equipment
5. Technical assistance
6. Other support. (*Please specify*) ________________________________

Interviewer, Q4.10 – Q4.12 ***for Employees only.***

4.10 As an employee, have you changed your employer since your last return?
1. No
2. Yes (*Please tell me how often and why*) ____________________________
____

4.11 Does your workplace supply computer access for you?
1. Yes
2. No. *Please specify why not?*___________________________________

4.12 Does your workplace supply internet access for you?
1. Yes
2. No. *Please specify why not?*___________________________________
____

Interviewer, the next questions ***for all respondents.***

4.13 How satisfied are you with the following aspects of your current working condition? (*Interviewer, show* ***Card 9****.*)

Aspects of working condition	Code for satisfaction
1. Income	
2. Career opportunities	
3. Responsibility	
4. Relationship with colleagues	
5. Management	
6. Organisational culture	

Card 9 **Satisfaction**
1. Very satisfied 2. Satisfied 3. Less than satisfied 4. Not at all satisfied *Choose only one*

4. 14 Are you able to consult/use up-to-date information or equipment in your field (e.g. books, scientific journals, lab facilities, etc.) ?
1. Ready access
2. Limited access
3. No access

4.15 Is there any among the following which you have gained abroad, and how important are they to your current work/business in Ghana? *(Interviewer, show **Card 10**)*

Resources	**Gained abroad**	**Code for importance**
Work experience		
Knowledge and skills		
Network		
Financial capital		
Others. (*Please specify*) ______ ______		
None		

Card 10
Importance

1. Very important
2. Important
3. Fairly important
4. Not important

Choose only one

4.16 Do you consider the way you work particularly different as compared to the one of colleagues who have not lived abroad?
1. No, not really
2. Yes, very much
3. Yes, to some extent
4. If yes, please specify ______________________________

____

____

____

4.17 Have you tried to introduce and apply any new procedures/methods/ ideas in your workplace?
1. Yes
2. No (*skip to Q4.20*)

4.18 How frequently is the application of these procedures/methods/ideas causing difficulties or tensions with your colleagues?
1. Very often
2. Often
3. Occasionally
4. Rarely
5. Never (*skip to Q4.20*)

4.19 In which ways do these difficulties or tensions manifest themselves?
____
____
____
____
____

4.20 How frequently do you feel discomforted for being unable to apply some of your expertise and skills?
1. Very often
2. Often
3. Occasionally
4. Rarely
5. Never

4.21 How many hours do you work on an average working day?
____________________hours

Section 5. LIVING CONDITIONS

5.1 What is your marital status?
1. Single (*skip to Q 5.11*)
2. Married/Cohabitation
3. Separated
4. Divorced (*skip to Q 5.11*)
5. Widow/widower (*skip to Q 5.11*)

5.2 Is your spouse/partner currently living with you in Ghana?
1. Yes
2. No

5.3 Where was your spouse/partner born? __________ Region in Ghana
__________ Foreign Country

5.4 What is/are her/his current citizenship(s)? ____________________

5.5 What is the level of education of your spouse/partner?
1. None/Primary
2. Basic Education (Middle/JSS)
3. Post Middle Certificate Tr. (Voc./Tec./Comm.)
4. Secondary ('O', 'A') or SSS
5. Post Secondary Diploma Tr. (Teacher/Tech.)
6. University. (*Please specify*) ____BA/BS ____MA ___ PhD./Doctorate
7. Other (*Please specify*) ______________________________

5.6 What is the occupational status of your spouse/partner?
1. Homemaker
2. Student
3. Employee
4. Self-employed without employees
5. Self-employed with employees
6. Others (*Please specify*) ____________________________

5.7 What is your spouse/partner's profession? (*ex. economist*)
____

Interviewer, for those who have indicated homemaker or student in Q5.6, skip to Q5.10.

5.8 What is her/his current type of work? (*ex. teaching*)
____

5.9 What is her/his current position? (*ex. professor/lecturer*)
____

5.10 Has your wife/husband lived abroad for a period *exceeding one year*?
1. No
2. Yes. Please specify where she/he has lived?_______________

5.11 How many children do you have?_______________________

5.12 Where are they currently living? ____________________

5.13 Do you have any school going age children?
1. Yes. *Please specify how many*: __________ children.
2. No (*Skip to Q5.15*)

5.14 How many are going to the following schools
_____ Private school in Ghana. (*Please specify*) ____ GIS ____ Foreign School ___ Other private schools
_____ Public school in Ghana
_____ School abroad
_____ Other school (*Please specify*) ____________________

(*If all children are in school going age, skip to Q5.17*)

5.15 Do you have any children going to university?
1. Yes. *Please specify how many*: ________ children.
2. No (*Skip to Q5.17*)

5.16 How many are going to university

_______ Here in Ghana

_______ Abroad

5.17 What is your current accommodation?

1. House
2. Flat/Apartment
3. Other (*Please, specify*) ________________________________

5.18 How many bedrooms are there in your house/flat? ________________ bedrooms

5.19 Do you or your immediate family own the following? (*Can choose more than one*)

1. House/Flat
2. Car
3. Personal computer
4. None

5.20 How does your current annual income compare in real terms (standard of life you can afford) with the one you enjoyed abroad? *(Choose only one)*

1. Much lower than before
2. Lower than before
3. Not much change
4. Higher than before
5. Much higher than before

5.21 How does your current annual income compare with that of other people here in Ghana who have reached a similar position? *(Choose only one)*

1. Much lower than average
2. Lower than average
3. About average
4. Higher than average
5. Much higher than average

5.22 Does your consumption pattern (expenditures for clothes, leisure, travel, education of children, etc.) differ from that of people in similar positions who have never lived abroad?

1. No
2. Yes. In what respects does it differ? (*Please specify*)

____

____

5.23 Do you enjoy any of the following social benefits here in Ghana?
(Indicate all that apply)
1. Subsidised medical service/medical insurance
2. Pension program
3. Children or family allowance
4. Subsidised housing
5. Other benefits. (*Please specify*) ______________________
6. No benefit

5.24 What problems or difficulties have you experienced since your return? (*Interviewer, show* ***Card 11.***)

Card 11 **Problems/Difficulties**

1. Had difficulties finding a good employment
2. Had a low income and difficulties in making ends meet
3. Had to go back and live with parents and other family members
4. Had problems readapting to way of life
5. Had difficulties with the way services/facilities operate
6. Had problems with family and friends' expectations
7. Had problems setting up my own business
8. Had difficulties with the work ethics and practices
9. Other. (*Please, specify*) ______________________
10. No problem

Indicate all that apply

Section 6. TRANSFER OF RESOURCES

6.1 Are there special skills and ideas, knowledge and experience you gained abroad that have shown particularly useful to you in your present position?
1. Yes. (*Please explain*) ______________________
____
____
____
2. No. *(Please explain*) ______________________
____
____
____

6.2 Can you give me some concrete examples on how you used what you have learned to contribute to bring about change ?
(a) in work environment ______________________________

(b) in family life ______________________________

(c) in public sphere (community, society) ______________________________

6.3 Do your colleagues ask you for your advice?
1. Very often
2. Often
3. Occasionally
4. Rarely
5. Never

6.4 When you were abroad, did you send remittances to your family members?
1. On a regular basis
2. Occasionally
3. No (*skip to Q 6.7*)

6.5 How were the remittances used? (*Can choose more than one*).
1. Upkeep of spouse/partner and children
2. Upkeep of parent(s) and siblings
3. Financing of projects
4. Savings
5. Other uses (charity, donations, etc.) (*Please specify*) ______________

6.6 How did you transmit the remittances? (*Can choose more than one*).
1. Individual bearers
2. Banks
3. Post/Courier
4. Personally
5. Other (*Please specify*) ____________________

6.7 Did you accumulate any savings abroad?
1. Yes
2. No (*skip to Q 6.10*)

6.8 How much savings did you bring back to Ghana upon your last return?
1. No savings
2. <US$10,000
3. $10,000–$50,000
4. >$50,000

6.9 Which of the following best describes your major expenditures/investments upon your last return? (*Interviewer, show* ***Card 12.***)

Card 12 **Expenditures/Investments**
1. Housing related expenditure (building material/purchasing a house/flat)
2. Durable consumption goods (furniture, freezer/fridge, etc.)
3. Electronic appliances (computer, video, etc.)
4. Providing support to other family members
5. Investment in business
6. Investment in stock market
7. Other expenditures. (*Please specify*) ____________________
Indicate all that apply

6.10 Do you see you and your family much better off now than before you went abroad?
1. Yes. (*Please explain*) ____________________
2. No. (*Please explain*) ____________________

6.11 What type of contacts abroad have you kept since you returned? (*Choose only one*)
1. Personal
2. Professional
3. Both
4. None (*skip to Q6.13*)

6.12 In what way do you keep these contacts? (*Can choose more than one*)
1. By postal mail
2. By telephone/fax
3. By email
4. Through visits
5. Other way. (*Please specify*) ____________________

6.13 How often do you read any foreign publications since your return? (*Interviewer, show* ***Card 13.***)

Foreign publications	**Code for frequency**
1. Magazines	
2. Newspapers	
3. Scientific journals	
4. Books	
5. Other ____________	

Card 13	**Frequency**
1. Very often	
2. Often	
3. Occasionally	
4. Rarely	
5. Never	
Choose only one	

6.14 How often do you watch foreign TV programs since your return? (*Interviewer, show* ***Card 13.***)
1. Very often
2. Often
3. Occasionally
4. Rarely
5. Never

6.15 How often do you listen to foreign radio programs since your return? (*Interviewer, show* ***Card 13.***)
1. Very often
2. Often
3. Occasionally
4. Rarely
5. Never

Section 7. OVERALL PERCEPTIONS AND RETURN MIGRATION

7.1 What do you miss most here in Ghana among the things that you had abroad?

____

____

____

7.2 What do you appreciate most among the things you found back home upon your return?

____

____

____

7.3 Overall, has your stay abroad had more positive or negative implications for the wellbeing of:

Wellbeing of	**Positive Implications**	**Negative Implications**	**Other**
1. Yourself			
2. Spouse/Partner			
3. Children			

7.4 If you could go back in time, would you make the same decision to leave your country?
1. No
2. Yes, I would repeat what I did
3. Yes, but I would do it differently. (*Please specify*) ________________

____

7.5 If you could go back in time, would you make the same decision to return to your country?
1. No
2. Yes, I would repeat what I di
3. Yes, but I would do it differently. (*Please specify*) ________________

____

7.6 What do you see yourself doing in three and ten years time?
In three years:

____

____

____

In ten years:

____

____

____

7.7 Are you planning to go abroad again to settle there?

1. Yes (*Please explain **when** do you plan to leave and **why***) ____________

   ____

   ____

2. No (*Please specify*) ________________________________

   ____

7.8 Do you agree or disagree with the following statements? (*Interviewer, show **Card 14**.*)

Statements	**Code for Opinion**
1. Living abroad weakens the sense of responsibility toward members of the extended family	
2. Having a Western type education is important for my children	
3. Wives should have the same career opportunities as their husbands	
4. A person's plan to move abroad must be discussed among all relatives	
5. My children should know their home country early enough to feel at home in this country	
6. Someone who remains abroad can nevertheless help develop his home country. (*Interviewer, with Codes 1 and 2, please ask to specify how*) ______________________________ ______________________________ ______________________________ ______________________________ ______________________________	

Card 14 **Opinion**
1. Strongly agree 2. Agree 3. Undecided 4. Disagree 5. Strongly disagree
Choose only one

Section 8. PERSONAL CHARACTERISTICS

8.1 Interviewee's gender:
1. Male
2. Female

8.2 In which year were you born? __________ year

8.3 Where were you born? __________________________Region in Ghana
_______________ Foreign Country

8.4 What is/are your citizenship(s)? ___________________________________

8.5 What is your profession? (*ex. economist*) ____________________________

8.6 What is your current type of work? (*ex. teaching*)
____

8.7 What is your current position? ex. (*professor/deputy director*)
____

8.8 What is/was your father's occupation? (*ex. farmer, minister, teacher*)
____

8.9 Has your father ever lived abroad?
1. Yes. *Where* and *what* were his main activities abroad?
____
2. No

	Brother(s)	Sister(s)
8.10 How many brothers and sisters do you have? Please indicate only those who have the same mother and the same father.		
8.11 How many of your brothers and sisters are currently living abroad?		

8.12 What is your religious affiliation?
1. Catholic
2. Methodist
3. Presbyterian
4. Anglican
5. Other Christian
6. Islam
7. Traditional
8. No religion
9. Other______________________________

8.13 How many languages do you speak? Please list them in order of proficiency

____

8.14 Which of these language(s) did you learn abroad?

____

Annex Three

Guide for In-depth Interviews in London and Paris

Interview Guide London and Paris

Experiences abroad

Please tell me why and how you first left your country to study or/and to work abroad?

Could you list in a chronological order the periods of your life exceeding one year during which you have lived abroad and specify the country(ies)?

What is your educational and professional background? Please tell me about all your study and work experience before going abroad and since you are here.

How did your family situation evolve before and after you settled here? Where are your husband/wife and children (if any) and what do they do?

Can you describe your present lifestyle? In what respect does it differ from the one you had back home?

Do you own a house/flat here?

What type of professional and/or personal contacts have you made here, if any?

What kind of ties do you keep with your home country, if any (personal/professional linkages)?

Do you send back any remittances? If yes, how much and on what basis? How are these remittances used?

How often do you visit your home country, and for what reasons?

Are you an active participant in any association, club or movement? If yes, in which one(s)?

What are the things that you have learned abroad, if any? How useful do you find your experience abroad?

Return decision-making

What are your feelings and plans regarding return?

How much time did you originally intend to spend abroad?

If planning to return,
When do you plan to return and what are the main reasons?
For how long have you been planning to return?
On what basis do you intend to return (permanently, temporarily, intermittent)?
Do you expect to get any form of assistance for your return? If yes, which kind and from what sources?
What do you expect to find upon return? What are your personal and professional expectations?
What problems and obstacles do you expect to encounter upon return?
Do you plan to take back any savings? If yes, how much and how do you intend to invest these savings?
If planning to stay abroad,
Why do you plan to remain abroad?
What are the main problems and constraints regarding return?
Who makes the decision for your return?
What is your spouse/partner's and children's attitude towards return?
Do you know any persons who have already returned? If yes, how are they doing back home?
What do you think, why certain/other migrants decide to stay abroad?

Perceptions, plans and contributions
What do you miss most among the things you had in Ghana?
If you could go back in time, would you make the same decision to leave your country?
What are your plans and prospects for the future?
What would you like your children to do to succeed in life?
What do you think is the potential role of return migrants in the development of their home societies and economies?
What role could you personally play for the development of your home country?
How can someone who remains abroad help develop his home country?
What is/was your father's occupation? Has he lived abroad for more that a year? If yes, where and for what reason(s)?
In which year were you born?

Only for those who have already been back for a period exceeding one year

Experience back home

- Why did you decide to return to your home country?
- What were your expectations before return?
- How did you readapt and readjust upon return?
- What problems and difficulties did you encounter upon return, if any, in both the professional and the personal sphere?
- Have you tried to apply something that you have learned abroad? If yes, what obstacles and constraints did you encounter if any?
- In your view, what is the difference between someone who has never moved and someone like you who has lived abroad?

Annex Four

Odds Ratios and their Significance for Selected Cross-tabulated Variables

Cross-tabulated variables	Ghana		Côte d'Ivoire	
	Risk estimates	Significance Fisher's Exact Test	Risk estimates	Significance Fisher's Exact Test
Worked abroad* Sent remittances regularly	15.11	.001	–	–
Worked abroad longer than average* Sent remittances regularly	2.95	.002	–	–
Stayed abroad longer than average* Returned with > US$50,000 savings	20.14	.000	2.12	.054
Worked abroad longer than average* Returned with > US$50,000 savings	9.63	.001	2.32	.038
Worked abroad longer than average* Returned with US$10–50,000	–	–	5.49	0.43
Stayed abroad longer than average* Returned with < US$10,000 savings	.35	.002	–	–
Worked abroad longer than average* Returned with < US$10,000 savings	.35	.002	–	–
Stayed abroad longer than average* Returned with no savings	3.87	.067	–	–
Obtained/kept citizenship* Returned with no savings	4.12	.032	–	–
Moved first to Europe* Works somewhat differently from colleagues who never lived abroad	2.38	.023	–	–
Moved first to Europe* Works very differently from colleagues who never lived abroad	.50	.061	–	–
Only studied abroad* Worked abroad less than average	2.09	.000	–	–

Cross-tabulated variables	Ghana		Côte d'Ivoire	
	Risk estimates	Significance Fisher's Exact Test	Risk estimates	Significance Fisher's Exact Test
Only studied abroad* Worked abroad longer than average	–	–	.11	.000
Worked abroad* Stayed abroad longer than average	–	–	13.31	.000
Moved first to Europe* Highest degree obtained abroad: Doctorate	.127	.000	–	–
Moved first to North America* Highest degree obtained abroad: Doctorate	10.66	.000	–	–
Moved first to Europe* Highest degree obtained abroad: Masters	–	–	.43	.056
Moved first to North America* Highest degree obtained abroad: Masters	.453	.037	2.32	.061
Moved first to North America* Worked abroad longer than average	2.73	.007	–	–
Moved first to North America* Migrated more than once	0.48	.071	0.27	.035
First emigration at age <25 years* Worked abroad longer than average	3.11	.001	2.35	.018
Undergraduate studies abroad* Worked abroad longer than average	3.55	.022	2.80	.075
First emigration at age <25 years* Worked abroad in training-related jobs longer than average	2.62	.005	2.02	.045

Note: Risk estimates were only included in the table when significance tests were below 0.1%, 1% and 5% and, in some exceptional cases, when significance was below 1%.

Cross-tabulated variables	Ghana		Côte d'Ivoire	
	Risk estimates	Significance Fisher's Exact Test	Risk estimates	Significance Fisher's Exact Test
Never permanent resident status* Worked abroad	.049	.000	.15	.007
Stayed abroad longer than average* Never permanent resident status	.049	.000	.15	.000
Stayed abroad longer than average* Kept permanent resident status	6.66	.000	–	–
Stayed abroad longer than average* Acquired/kept local citizenship	8.87	.000	9.31	.000
Worked abroad longer than average* Never had a permanent resident status	.067	.000	.09	.000
Worked abroad longer than average* Kept permanent resident status	4.00	.001	3.99	.004
Lost permanent resident status* Worked longer than average	–	–	–	–
Worked abroad longer than average* Acquired/kept local citizenship	13.67	.000	11.35	.000
Acquired/kept local citizenship* One or more transilient moves	1.31	.003	–	–
Kept permanent resident status* More than one return move	4.41	.074	–	–
Acquired/kept local citizenship* More than one return move	–	–	2.55	.85
Obtained/kept citizenship* More than one transilient move	1.31	.003	–	–
Moved first to North America* Kept permanent resident status	2.01	.091	–	–
Stayed abroad longer than average* Felt like a national abroad	–	–	2.26	.069
Worked abroad longer than average* Felt like a national abroad	2.67	.041	2.79	.015
Owned a house/apartment abroad* Felt like a national abroad	3.26	.013	–	–

Cross-tabulated variables	Ghana		Côte d'Ivoire	
	Risk estimates	Significance Fisher's Exact Test	Risk estimates	Significance Fisher's Exact Test
Never had a permanent residency status* Felt like a national abroad	–	–	.32	.006
Lost permanent resident status* Felt like a national abroad	–	–	3.30	.014
Worked abroad* Visited home frequently during last stay abroad	–	–	4.00	.066
Reason for return: termination of studies* Sent remittances	–	–	.40	.017
Reason for return: termination of studies* Sent remittances regularly	.167	.002	–	–
Reason for return: termination of studies* Kept professional and personal contacts abroad	.283	.009	–	–
Expectation: Better business opportunities* Returned with >US$50,000 savings	3.27	.035	–	–
Stayed abroad longer than average* Temporary return	3.83	.013	3.59	.034
Acquired/kept local citizenship* Temporary return	4.73	.005	4.13	.019
Married* Temporary return	–	–	2.80	.036

Cross-tabulated variables	Ghana		Côte d'Ivoire	
	Risk Estimates	Significance Fisher's Exact Test	Risk Estimates	Significance Fisher's Exact Test
Works somewhat differently from colleagues who never lived abroad* Temporary return	3.48	.029	.25	.091
Works very differently from colleagues who never lived abroad* Temporary return	–	–	3.28	0.62
Only studied abroad* Received support from all friends for return	5.27	.029	4.13	.006
More than one return* Received support from all friends for return	3.09	.086	–	–
Stayed abroad longer than average* Obtained information about home country from visits	5.04	.000	3.59	.001
Expected feasible employment/ business opportunities* Obtained information about home country from visits	2.86	.022	–	–
Employed in public sector* Problems in making ends meet	–	–	1.97	.050
Sex: Female* Income higher than that earned abroad	.352	.067	–	–
Sex: Female* Satisfaction with income	.35	.019	–	–
Sex: Female* Satisfaction with career opportunities	.44	.080	–	–

Bibliography

Adepoju, A. 2003 "Migration in West Africa", *Journal for International Development* 46 (3), 37–41

Adepoju, A. 2000 "Recent Trends in International Migration in Sub-Saharan Africa", *International Social Science Journal* 165, 383–94

Adepoju, A. 1998 "Linking Population Policies to International Migration in Sub-Saharan Africa", in R. Appleyard (ed.) *Emigration Dynamics in Developing Countries, Volume I: Sub-Saharan Africa*, Aldershot: Ashgate, 301–37

Adepoju, A. 1995a "Emigration Dynamics in Sub-Saharan Africa", *International Migration* 33 (3/4): 315–91

Adepoju, A. 1995b "Migration in Africa: An Overview", in J. Baker and T.A. Aina (eds) *The Migration Experience in Africa*, Sweden: Nordiska Afrikainstitutet, 87–108

Adepoju A. 1994 "Preliminary Analysis of Emigration Dynamics in Sub-Saharan Africa", *International Migration* 32 (2), 197–216

Adepoju, A. 1991a "South-North Migration: The African Experience", *International Migration* 29 (2), 205–23

Adepoju, A. 1991b "Binational Communities and Labor Circulation in Sub-Saharan Africa", in D.G. Papdemetriou and P.L. Martin (eds) *The Unsettled Relationship: Labor Migration and Economic Development*, Westport: Greenwood Press, 45–64

Agunias, D.R. 2006 *From Zero-Sum to a Win-Win Scenario? Literature Review on Circular Migration*, Washington DC: Migration Policy Institute

Ahmed, I. 2000 "Remittances and their Economic Impact in Post-war Somaliland", *Disasters* 24 (4), 380–89

Al-Rasheed, M. 1992 "Political Migration and Downward Socio-economic Mobility: The Iraqi Community in London", *New Community* 18 (4), 537–49

Amin, S. 1967 *Le développement du capitalisme en Côte d'Ivoire*, Paris: Editions de Minuit

Ammassari, S. 2008 "The Development Potential of Different Capital Transfers by Ghanaian and Ivorian Return Migrants", in R. Bardouille et al. (eds) *Africa's Finances: The Contribution of Remittances*, Newcastle: Cambridge Scholars Publishing

Ammassari, S. 2005 "The Development Impact of Returning Migrants", in Eliminating Extreme Poverty: South-South Cooperation and the Millennium Development Goals (MDGs), special edition of *Cooperation South*, New York: UNDP

Ammassari, S. 2003a "Gestion des migrations et politiques de développement: optimiser les bénéfices de la Migration internationale en Afrique de l'Ouest", Rapport Provisoire, October, Geneva: ILO

Ammassari, S. 2003b "From Nation-building and Entrepreneurship: The Impact of Élite Return Migrants in Côte d'Ivoire and Ghana", paper presented at the International Workshop on Migration and Poverty in West Africa, 13–14 March, University of Sussex

Ammassari, S. 1994 "Internal Migration, Population Distribution and Development Policy", *IDS Discussion Paper* 342, Brighton: Institute of Development Studies

Ammassari, S. 1991 "Immigration into Germany: Dimensions, Problems of Measurement, Social Policies, and Perspectives", unpublished thesis submitted to the University of Rome "La Sapienza"

Ammassari, S. and R. Black 2001 "Harnessing the Potential of Migration and Return to Promote Development: Applying Concepts to West Africa", *IOM Migration Research Series* 5, Geneva: IOM

Anarfi, J. and S. Kwanke 2003 Migration from and to Ghana: A Background Paper, *DRC on Migration, Globalization and Poverty Working Paper* C4, Brighton: University of Sussex

Amondji, M. 1988 *Côte d'Ivoire: la dépendance et l'épreuve des faites*, Paris: Harmattan

Anwar, M. 1979 *The Myth of Return: Pakistanis in Britain*, London: Heinemann

Appleyard, R. (ed.) 1998 *Emigration Dynamics in Developing Countries, Volume I: Sub-Saharan Africa*, Aldershot: Ashgate

Appleyard, R. 1995 "Emigration Dynamics in Developing Countries", *International Migration* 33 (3/4), 293–314

Appleyard, R. 1992 "International Migration and Development – an Unresolved Relationship", *International Migration* 30(3/4), 251–66

Appleyard, R. 1989a "Migration and Development: Myths and Reality", *International Migration Review* 23 (3), 486–505

Appleyard, R. (ed.) 1989b *The Impact of International Migration on Developing Countries*, Paris: OECD

Appleyard, R. (ed.) 1988 *International Migration Today, Volume I: Trends and Prospects*, Paris: UNESCO

Arditti s, S. 1991 "Targeted Reintegration of Expatriate Brains into Developing Countries of Origin: The ECC-IOM Experience in Central America", *International Migration* 33 (1), 371–88

Ardittis, S. 1985 "The Assisted Return of Qualified Migrants to their Countries of Origin: The UNDP and ICM Multilateral Programmes", *International Migration for Employment, Working Paper*, Geneva: ILO

Arif, G.M. 1998 "Reintegration of Pakistani Return Migrants from the Middle East in the Domestic Labour Market", *Pakistan Development Review* 37 (2), 99–124

Arif, G.M. and M. Irfan 1997 "Return Migration and Occupational Change: The Case of Pakistani Migrants Returned from the Middle East", *Pakistani Development Review* 36 (1), 1–37

Arowolo, O.O. 2000 "Return Migration and the Problem of Reintegration", *International Migration* 38 (5), 59–82

Asamoa, A.K. 1996 *The Syndrome of Primary Contradiction and Development: The Ghanaian Experience*, Accra: Ghana Universities Press

Asiedu, A.B. 2003 "Some Benefits of Migrants Return Visits to Ghana", paper presented to International Workshop on Migration and Poverty in West Africa, 13–14 March, Brighton: Sussex University

Athukorala, P. 1990 "International Contract Migration and the Reintegration of Return Migrants: The Experience of Sri Lanka", *International Migration Review* 24 (2), 323–46

Attafi, A. 1994 "The Brain Drain – Theoretical Framework and Hypotheses", *Canadian Journal for Development Studies* 15 (1), 89–99

Assimeng, M. 1999 *Social Structure in Ghana: A Study in Persistence and Change*, Tema: Ghana Publishing Corporation

Awusabo-Asare, K. 1995 "Factors in International Return Migration in Ghana", in K.A. Twum-Baah et al. (eds) *Migration Research Study in Ghana, Volume 2, International Migration*, Accra: Ghana Statistical Service, 156–73

Bailey, K.D. 1987 *Methods of Social Research*, New York: The Free Press

Baker, K. 1992 "The Changing Geography of West Africa", in G. Chapman and K. Baker (eds) *The Changing Geography of West Africa*, London: Routledge, 80–113

Baker, J. and T.A. Aina (eds) 1995 *The Migration Experience in Africa*, Sweden: Nordiska Afrikainstitutet

Bakewell, O. 2008 "Keeping them in their Place: The Ambivalent Relationship between Development and Migration in Africa", *Third World Quarterly* 2 (7), 1341–58

Bakewell, O. and H. de Haas 2007 "African Migrations: Continuities, Discontinuities and Recent Transformations", in P. Chabal et al. (eds) *African Alternatives*, Leiden: Brill, 95–118

Bardouille, R. 2008 "International Migration and Remittances in Africa", in R. Bardouille et al. (eds) *Africa's Finances: The Contribution of Remittances*, Newcastle: Cambridge Scholars Publishing

Bardouille, R., M. Grieco and M. Ndulo (eds) (2008), *Africa's Finances: The Contribution of Remittances*, Newcastle Upon Tyne: Cambridge Scholars Publishing, 97–115

Barro, I. et al. 2003 "Etude sur le transfert d'argent des émigrés au Sénégal et les services de transfert en microfinance", Rapport final, Genève: BIT

Barros, L. et al. 2002 "L'Immigration irrégulière subsaharienne à travers et vers le Maroc", *Cahiers de Migrations Internationales*, 54F, Genève: BIT

Bathily, H. 2003 *Etude nationale sur le codéveloppement*, Rapport provisoire, Bamako: BIT

Batista, L. and P.C. Vicente 2007 "Brain Drain or Brain Gain: Evidence from an African Success Story", *IZA Discussion Paper* 3035, Bonn: IZA

Bennell, P.S. and M. Godfrey 1983 "The Professions in Africa: Some Interactions between Local and International Markets", *Development and Change* 14 (3), 372–402

Beine, M., F. Docquier and H. Rapoport 2001 "Brain Drain and Economic Growth: Theory and Evidence", *Journal of Development Economics* 64 (1), 275–89

Bernard, H.R. and L. Comitas 1978 "Greek Return Migration", *Current Anthropology* 19 (3), 658–59

Bhagwati, J.N. (ed.) 1976 *The Brain Drain and Taxation: Theory and Empirical Evidence*, Amsterdam: North-Holland Publishing Company

Bhargava, A. and F. Docquier 2006, "HIV Pandemic, Medical Brain Drain and Economic Development in Sub-Saharan Africa", *Report*, World Bank, Washington DC

Bilsborrow, R.E. et al. 1997 *International Migration Statistics. Guidelines for Improving Data Collection Systems*, Geneva: ILO

Bilsborrow, R.E. et al. (eds) 1984 *Migration Surveys in Low Income Countries: Guidelines for Survey and Questionnaire Design*, London: Croom Helm

Black, R. et al. 2003a “International Migration, Remittances and Poverty: The Case of Ghana and Côte d'Ivoire”, paper prepared for the World Bank, Sussex Centre for Migration Research

Black, R. et al. 2003b *Transnational Migration, Return and Development in West Africa*, Final Research Report, Sussex Centre for Migration Research, Brighton: SCMR

Black, R. et al. 2003c “Migration, Return and Small Enterprise Development in Ghana: A Route out of Poverty?', paper presented at the International Workshop on Migration and Poverty in West Africa, 13–14 March, University of Sussex

Black, R. and Tiemoko, R. 2003 “Migration, Return and Impact in West Africa”, paper for the Study on Structural Determinants in the West African Economy prepared for the Secretariat of the Sahel and West Africa Club, Sussex Centre for Migration Research

Blaud, C. 2001 *La Migration pour études*, Paris: Harmattan

Blion, R. 2001 “Economies et transferts migratoires, révélateurs des contradictions entre politiques et pratiques migratoires”, in R. Blion and I. Rigoni (eds), *D'un Voyage à un autre, Des voix de l'Immigration pour un développement pluriel*, Paris: Karthala, 95–114

Blion, R. 1995 “Les Burkinabé de Côte-d'Ivoire entre “intégration' et circulation migratoire”, *Mondes en Devéloppement* 23, 81–91

Blion, R. and I. Rigoni (eds) 2000 “D'un Voyage à un autre, Des voix de l'Immigration pour un développement pluriel”, Paris: Karthala, 95–114

Blion, R. and V. Verrière 1998 *Epargne des Migrants et outils financiers adaptés, Rapport final*, Paris: Ministère de l'Emploi et de la Solidarité

Boahen, A. 2000 *Ghana: Evolution and Change in the Nineteenths and Twentieth Centuries*, first published in 1975, Accra: Sankofa Educational Publishers

Böhning, W.R. 1984 *Studies in International Labour Migration*, London: Macmillan

Böhning, W.R. 1975 “Some Thoughts on Emigration from the Mediterranean Basin”, *International Labour Review* 111 (3), 251–77

Bottomore, T. 1993 *Elites and Society*, 2nd edn (first published in 1964), London: Routledge

Bourdieu, P. and L. Wacquant 1992 *An Invitation to Reflexive Sociology*, Chicago: University of Chicago Press

Boussaid, L. 1998 “The Brain-Drain and Developing Countries”, *Migrations Société* 10 (56), 65–71

Bovenkerk, F. 1982 "Why Returnees Generally do not Turn out to be 'Agents of Change'", in W.F. Stinner et al. (eds) *Return Migration and Remittances: Developing a Caribbean Perspective*, RIIES Occasional Papers 3, Washington DC: Smithonian Institution

Bovenkerk, F. 1974 *The Sociology of Return Migration: A Bibliographic Essay*, Publications of the Research Group on European Migration Problems 20, The Hague: Martinus Nijhoff

Boyd, M. 1989 "Family and Personal Networks in International Migration: Recent Developments and New Agendas", *International Migration Review* 23 (3), 638–70

Boyle P. et al. 1998 *Exploring Contemporary Migration*, New York: Longman

Bredeloup, S. 1995 "Sénégalais en Côte d'Ivoire, Sénégalais de Côte d'Ivoire", *Mondes en Développement* 23 (91), 13–29

Brettell, C.B. 2000 "Theorizing Migration in Anthropology. The Social Construction of Networks, Identities, Communities and Globalscapes", in C.B. Brettell and J.F. Hollifield (eds) *Migration Theory. Talking Across Disciplines*, New York: Routledge

Brewer, J. and A. Hunter 1989 *Multimethod Research: A Synthesis of Styles*, London: Sage Publications

Brossard, L. 2003 "Peuplement et Migration en Afrique de l'Ouest: une crise régionale en Côte d'Ivoire", *Afrique Contemporaine* 206, 151–66

Brown, S.S. 2006 "Can Remittances Spur Development? A Critical Survey", *International Studies Review* 8 (1), 55–76

Brown, M. 2002 "Intellectual Diaspora Networks: Their Viability as a Response to Highly Skilled Emigration", in R. Fibbi and J.B. Meyer (eds) *Diasporas, développement et mondialisation, Autrepart/Les Cahiers de sciences humaines* 22, 167–68

Brydon, L. 1992 "Ghanaian Women in the Migration Process", in S. Chant (ed.) *Gender and Migration in Developing Countries*, London: Belhaven, 91–108

Brydon, L. 1979 "Women at Work: Some Changes in Family Structure in Amedzofe-Avatime, Ghana", *Africa* 49 (2), 97–111

Brydon, L. and W.T.S. Gould 1984 "International Migration of Skilled Labour within Africa: A Review and Agenda for Future Work", *Liverpool Papers in Human Geography*, 17, Liverpool: University of Liverpool

Cabrillac, B. 2000 "Les aspects économiques et financiers de la crise ivoirienne", *Afrique Contemporaine: Dossier Côte d'Ivoire*, 38–44

Caldwell, J.C. 1969 *African Rural-Urban Migration: The Movement to Ghana's Towns*, Canberra: Australian National University Press

Callea, S. 1986 "Different Forms, Reasons and Motivations for Return Migration of Persons who Voluntarily Decide to Return to their Countries of Origin", *International Migration* 23 (1), 61–71

Cassarino, J.P. 2004 "Theorising Return Migration: The Conceptual Approach to Return Migrants Revisited", *International Journal on Multicultural Studies* 6 (2), 253–79

Cassarino, J.-P. 2000 *Tunisian New Entrepreneurs and their Past Experiences of Migration in Europe: Resource Mobilization, Networks and Hidden Disaffection*, Aldershot: Ashgate

Castles, S. 2008 "Development and Migration – Migration and Development: What Comes First?", Social Science Research Council Conference Migration and Development: Future Directions for Research and Policy, 28 February–1 March, New York, revised paper 14 April 2008

Castles, S. 2007 "Twenty-first Century Migration as a Challenge to Sociology", *Journal of Ethnic and Migration Studies* 33

Castles, S. 2004 "The Factors that Make and Unmake Migration Policies", *International Migration Review* 38, 852–84

Castles S. and R.D. Wise (eds) 2008 *Migration and Development: Perspectives from the South*, Geneva: IOM

Castles, S. and G. Kosack 1973 *Immigrant Workers and Class Structure in Western Europe*, London: Oxford University Press

Carrington, J. and Detragiache, E. 1999 "How extensive is the Brain Drain?", *Finance and Development*, 36 (2), http://www.imf.org/external/pubs/ft/fandd/1999/06/carringt

Cerase, F.P. 1974 "Migration and Social Change: Expectations and Reality. A Study of Returned Migration from the United States to Italy", *International Migration Review* 8 (2), 245–62

CERPOD 1995 *Enquête Ivoirienne sur les Migrations et l'Urbanisation 1993*, Rapport National Descriptif, Bamako: CERPOD

Chant, S. and Radcliffe, S. 1992 "Migration and Development: The Importance of Gender", in S. Chant (ed.) *Gender and Migration in Developing Countries*, London: Belhaven, 1–29

Chilivumbu, A. 1985 *Migration and Uneven Rural Development in Africa: The Case of Zambia*, Lanham: University Press of America

Chiswick, B.R. 2000 "Are Immigrants Favourably Self-Selected? An Economic Analysis", in C.B. Brettell and J.F. Hollifield (eds) *Migration Theory. Talking Across Disciplines*, New York: Routledge

Choldin, H.M. 1973 "Kinship Networks in the Migration Process", *International Migration Review* 7 (2), 163–75

Cissé, M. 1993 "Un pari: créer un centre de santé", *Hommes et Migrations* 1165, 30–32

Condé, J. 1989 "Measures to Encourage Return Migration and Reintegration of Returned Migrants in their Home Country", in R. Appleyard (ed.) *The Impact of International Migration on Developing Countries*, Paris: OECD, 323–32

Condé, J. et al. 1986 *South-North International Migrations, a Case Study: Malian, Mauritanian and Senegalese Migrants from Senegal River Valley to France*, Paris: OECD

Connell, J. et al. 1976 *Migration from Rural Areas*, Dehli: Oxford University Press

Cordell, D.D. et al. (eds) 1996 *Hoe and Wage: A Social History of a Circular Migration System in West Africa*, Boulder: Westview Press

Crook, R. 1990 "State, Society and Political Institutions in Côte d'Ivoire and Ghana", *IDS Bulletin* 21 (4), 24–34

Dahya, E. 1973 "Pakistanis in Britain, Transients or Settlers?", *Race* 14 (3), 241–77

Danso, K. 1995 "The African Brain Drain: Causes and Policy Prescriptions", *Scandinavian Journal of Development Alternatives* 14 (1–2), 249–64

Das, M.S. 1979 "Brain Drain Controversy and African Scholars", *Issue* 8 (4), 27–30

Daum, C. 2000a Liens entre Migration et développement: des points de repère, *Migrations Société* 67, 51–2

Daum, C. 2000b *Typologie des Organisations de solidarité internationale Issues de l'Immigration*, Compte-rendu final, Groupe de recherches et d'études migrations et transformations sociales

Daum, C. 1997 "Immigrés acteurs du développement: une médiations sur deux espaces", *Hommes et Migrations* 1206, 31–42

Daum, C. 1994 "Ici et là-bas, Immigration et développement: Les associations des immigrés ouest-africains en France", *Migrations Société* 6 (32), 99–110

Daum, C. 1993 "Quand les immigrés construisent leur pays", *Hommes et Migrations*, 1165: 13–7

Da Vanzo, J. 1981 "Microeconomic Approaches to studying Migration decisions", in G.F. De Jong and R.W. Gardner (eds) *Migration Decision Making*, 90–129

David, P. 2000 *La Côte d'Ivoire*, Paris: Karthala

Davidson, B. 1977 T*he Growth of African Civilisation: A History of West Africa 1000–1800*, first published in 1965, Harlow: Longman

Decraene, P. 2000 "L'éviction du Président Konan Bédié: une revue des faits", *Afrique Contemporaine: Dossier Côte d'Ivoire*, 3–8

De Haan, A. 2000 "Migration and Livelihoods: Case Studies in Bangladesh, Ethiopia and Mali", *IDS Research Report* 46, Brighton: IDS

De Haan, A. and B. Rogaly 2002 "Migrant Workers and their Role in Rural Change", *Journal of Development Studies* 38 (2), 37–58

De Haas, H. 2008 "Migration and Development: A Theoretical Perspective", *IMI Working Papers* 9, Oxford: International Migration Institute

De Haas, H. 2007 "Remittances, Migration and Social Development, A Conceptual Review of the Literature", *Social Policy and Development Programme Paper No. 34*, Geneva: United Nations Research Institute for Social Development

De Haas, H. 2006a "Turning the Tide? Why 'Development instead of Migration' Policies are Bound to Fail", *IMI Working Paper 2*, Oxford: International Migration Institute

De Haas, H. 2006b *Engaging Diasporas: How Governments and Developing Agencies Can Support Diaspora Involvement in the Development of Origin Countries*, a Study for Oxfam Novib, Oxford: International Migration Institute

De Jong, G.F. and J.T. Fawcett 1981 "Motivations for Migration: An Assessment and a Value-expectancy Research Model", in G.F. de Jong and R.W. Gardner (eds) *Migration Decision Making. Multidisciplinary Approaches in Microlevel Studies in Developed and Developing Countries*, New York: Pergamon Press

Dembele, Y. 1993 "Un an après, où en sommes-nous?", *Hommes et Migrations* 1165, 37–38

DeWind, J. and J. Holdaway (eds) *Migration and Development within and Across Borders: Research and Policy Perspectives on Internal and International Migration*, Geneva: IOM

Diarra, H. 1998 "Associations d'immigrés et développement: le point sur deux decennies d'Intervention", *Hommes et Migrations* 1214, 74–85

Diatta, M.A. and N. Mbow 1999 "Releasing the Development Potential of Return Migration: The Case of Senegal", *International Migration* 37 (1), 243–66

Diombera, M. 1993 "Pour une meilleure communication entre icie et là-bas", *Hommes et Migrations* 1165, 28–29

Docquier, F. 2005 "Brain Drain and Inequality across Nations", *IZA Discussion Paper* 2440, Bonn: Institute for the Study of Labour

Docquier, F. and A. Marfouk 2006 "International Migration by Educational Attainment 1990–2000)" in C. Özdenand M. Schiff (eds) *International Migration, Remittances and the Brain Drain*, Washington DC: World Bank and Palgrave Macmillan

Docquier F. and H. Rapoport 2008 "Brain Drain and Human Capital Formation in Developing Countries: Winners and Losers", *The Economic Journal* 118 (528), 631–52

Docquier, F. and A. Marfouk 2004 "Measuring the International Mobility of Skilled Workers 1990–2000", *Policy Research Working Paper Series WPS3381*, Washington DC: World Bank

Dozon, J.-P. 2000 "La Côte d'Ivoire au peril de l''ivorité': Genèse d'un coup d'Etat", *Afrique Contemporaine* 193, 13–23

ECA 2006a *International Migration and the Achievement of MDGs in Africa*, International Symposium on International Migration and Development, Turin, Italy, 28–30 June, Population Division Department of Economic and Social Affairs, United Nations Secretariat, UN/POP/MIG/SYMP/2006/04

ECA 2006b *International Migration and Development: Implications for Africa*, Addis Ababa: Economic Commission for Africa

Edward Taylor, J. et al. 2005 "Remittances, Inequality and Poverty: Evidence from Rural Mexico", *Department of Agricultural and Resource Economics Working Papers*, 05–003, http://repositories.cdlib.org/are/arewp/05–003

Ellerman, D. 2003 "Policy Research on Migration and Development", *World Bank Policy Research Working Paper* 3117, Washington DC: World Bank

Esser, H. 1988 *Aspekte der Wanderungssoziologie: Assimilation und Integration von Wanderern, Ethnischen Gruppen und Minderheiten. Eine Handlungstheoretische Analyse*, Darmstadt: Luchterhand

Fadé, M. 1993 "Un impératif: la Formation", *Hommes et Migrations* 1165, 33–36

Faist, T. 2000 *Volume and Dynamics of International Migration*, Oxford: Oxford University Press

Faist, T. 1997 "The Crucial Meso-Level", in T. Hammar et al. (eds) *International Migration, Immobility and Development*, Multidisciplinary Perspectives, Oxford: Berg, 187–217

Fall, A.S. 2003 "Enjeux et défis de la Migration internationale de travail ouest-africaine", *Cahiers de Migrations Internationales* 62F, Genève: BIT

Fall, M. 1987 *Des Africains noirs en France: des tirailleurs sénégalais aux Blacks*, Paris: Harmattan

Fauré, Y.A. and J.F. Medard 1982 *Etat et bourgeoisie en Côte d'Ivoire*, Paris

Fawcett, J.T. 1989 "Networks, Linkages and Migration Systems", *International Migration Review* 23 (3), 671–80

Fibbi, R. and J.-B. Meyer 2002 "Introduction. Le Lien plus que l'essence", in R. Fibbi and J.B. Meyer (eds) *Diasporas, développement et mondialisation*, Autrepart/Les Cahiers de sciences humaines, 22, 5–21

Findlay, A. 1990 "A Migration Channels Approach to the Study of High Level Manpower Movements: A Theoretical Perspective", *International Migration* 28 (1), 15–22

Findlay, A. and J. Salt 1989 "International Migration of Highly-skilled Manpower: Theoretical and Developmental Issues", in R. Appleyard (ed.) *The Impact of International Migration in Developing Countries*, Paris: OECD

Findlay, A.M. and E. Stewart 2002 "Skilled Labour Migration from Developing Countries: Annotated Bibliography", *International Migration Papers* 55, Geneva: ILO

Findley, S.E. 1995 "Migration and Family Interactions in Africa", in A. Adepoju (ed.) *The African Family in the Development Process*, London: Zed Books, 109–38

Findley, S.E. and S. Sow 1998 "From Season to Season: Agriculture, Poverty and Migration in the Senegal River Valley", in R. Appleyard (ed.) *Emigration Dynamics in Developing Countries, Volume 1: Sub-Saharan Africa*, Aldershot: Ashgate, 69–144

Fischer, P.A. et al. 1997 "Interdependencies between Development and Migration", in T. Hammer et al. (eds) *International Migration, Immobility and Development. Multidisciplinary Perspectives*, Oxford: Berg, 91–132

Freund, C. and N. Spatafora 2005 "Remittances: Transaction Costs, Determinants, and Informal Flows", *World Bank Policy Research Working Paper* 3704, Washington DC: World Bank

Gammeltoft, P. 2002 "Remittances and Other Financial Flows to Developing Countries", Expert Working Paper prepared for the Centre for Development Research Study: Migration-Development Links: Evidence and Policy Options, Copenhagen: CDR

Gardiner, R.K.A. 1968 "Africa", in W. Adams and H. Rieben (eds) *L'exode des cerveaux*, Lausanne: Centre de Recherches Européennes, 222–31

Ghana Statistical Service 1995 *Migration Research Study in Ghana, Volume 2 International Migration*, Accra: Ghana Statistical Service

Ghosh, B. 2000a "Introduction", in B. Gosh (ed.) *Return Migration. Journey of Hope or Despair?*, Geneva: IOM/UN, 1–5

Ghosh, B. 2000b "Return Migration: Reshaping Policy Approaches", in B. Gosh (ed.) *Return Migration. Journey of Hope or Despair?*, Geneva: IOM/UN, 181–226

Ghosh, B. 1992 "Migration-Development Linkages: Some Specific Issues and Practical Policy Measures", *International Migration* 30 (3/4), 423–52

Glaser, W. 1978 *The Brain Drain. Emigration and Return*, UNITAR Research Report 22, London: Pergamon Press

Glick-Schiller, N. et al. 1995 "From Immigration to Transnational Migration: Theorizing Transnational Migration", *Anthropological Quarterly* 68 (1), 48–63

Glick-Schiller, N. et al. (eds) 1992 *Toward a Transnational Perspective on Migration*, New York: New York Academy of Science

Gmelch, G. 1987 "Work, Innovation, and Investment: The Impact of Return Migrants in Barbados", *Human Organization* 46 (2), 131–40

Gmelch, G. 1980 "Return Migration", *Annual Review of Anthropology* 9, 135–59

Gmelch, G. 1979 "Irish Return Migration: The Socio-demographic Characteristics of Return Migrants", *Papers in Anthropology* 20 (1), 155–66

Gould, W.T.S. 1988a "Government Policies and International Migration of Skilled Workers in Sub-Saharan Africa", *Geoforum* 19 (4), 433–45

Gould, W.T.S. 1988b "Skilled International Migration: An Introduction", *Geoforum* 19, 381–85

Gould, W.T.S. 1974 "International Migration of Labour within Africa: A Bibliographical Review", *International Migration Review* 8 (3), 347–65

Grey-Johnson, C. 1986 "Measures to Facilitate the Return and Reintegration of Highly Skilled Migrants into African Countries", *International Migration* 23 (1), 197–211

Grillo, R. and B. Riccio 2003 "Translocal Development: Italy-Senegal", paper presented to International Workshop on Migration and Poverty in West Africa, 13–14 March, Brighton: Sussex University

Grubel, H.G. and A. Scott 1977 *The Brain Drain: Determinants, Measurement and Welfare Effects*, Waterloo: Wilfrid Laurier University Press

Gubert, F. 2002 "Do Migrants Insure Those who Stay Behind? Evidence from the Kayes Area (Western Mali)", *Oxford Development Studies* 30 (3), 267–87

Gundel, J. 2002. "The Migration-Development Nexus: Somalia Case Study", *International Migration* 40 (5), 255–81

Gurak, D.T. and F. Caces 1992 "Migration Networks and the Shaping of Migration Systems", in M. Kritz et al. (eds) *International Migration Systems: A Global Approach*, New York: Oxford University Press, 150–76

Gustafsson, B. and N. Makounen 1994 "The Importance of Remittances for the Level and Distribution of Economic Well-being in Lesotho", *Journal of International Development* 6 (4), 373–97

Hammer T. et al. 1997 *International Migration, Mobility and Development. Multidisciplinary Perspectives*, Oxford: Berg

Handloff, R.E. 1988 *Côte d'Ivoire: A Country Study*, Washington DC: Library of Congress

Harris, J.R. and M.P. Todaro 1970 "Migration, Unemployment and Development: A Two-sector Analysis", *American Economic Review* 60, 126–42

Hatton, T.J. and J.G. Williamson 2003 "What Fundamentals Drive World Migration?', *Wider Discussion Paper 2003/23*, Helsinki: UNU/WIDER

Hermele, K. 1997 "The Discourse on Migration and Development", in Hammar et al. (eds) *International Migration, Immobility and Development. Multidisciplinary Perspectives*, Oxford: Berg, 133–58

Hernandez-Coss, R. 2006 "The Impact of Remittances: Observations in Remitting and Receiving Countries", discussion paper prepared for the G24 XXIII Technical Group Meeting, Singapore, 13–14 September

Hoffmann-Nowotny, H.-J. 1973 *Soziologie des FremdenarbeiterProblems: Eine theoretische und empirische Analyse am Beispiel Schweiz*, Stuttgard: Ferdinand Enke

Ilahi, N. 1999 "Return Migration and Occupational Change", *Review of Development Economics* 3 (2), 170–86

ILO 2003 *Tendances Mondiales de l'Emplois*, Genève: BIT

ILO 2002 *Initiative pour une politique de gestion des migrations en Afrique. Une contribution pour le NEPAD, Secteur de la Protection Sociale*, Ouagadougou: ILO

IMF 2002 *Balance of Payments Statistic Yearbook*, Washington DC: International Monetary Fund

INS 2000 *Premiers résultats définitifs du RGPH-98*, Abidjan: Institut National de la Statistique

IOM 2008a *World Migration 2008, Managing Labour Mobility in the Evolving Global Economy*, Geneva: IOM

IOM 2008b *Return Migration: Challenges and Opportunities*, International Dialogue on Migration 2008, 96th Session, MC/INF/293, http://iom.int/jahia/webdav/shared/shared/mainsite/microsites/IDM/workshops/Return_Migration_challenges_120208/MC_INF_293_Return_Migration.pdf

IOM 2003 *World Migration 2003, Managing Migration. Challenges and Responses for People on the Move*, Geneva: IOM

IOM 1991 *Ninth IOM Seminar on Migration: South-North Migration*, Geneva: IOM

Iredale, R. 2001 "The Migration of Professionals: Theories and Typologies", *International Migration* 39 (5), 7–26

Iredale, R. 1999 "The Need to Import Skilled Personnel: Factors Favouring and Hindering its International Mobility", *International Migration* 37 (1), 89–123

Iredale, R. et al. 2002 *Return Skilled and Business Migration and Social Transformation*, Wollongong: Centre for Asia Pacific Social Transformation Studies

Johry, K.N. 1995 "Human resource Development and Migration of Trained Manpower", *Journal of Scientific and Industrial Research* 54 (4), 243–48

Jonkers, K. 2008 "A Comparative Study of Return Migration Policies Targeting the Highly Skilled in Four Major Sending Countries", MIREM Project, Migration de Retour au Maghreb, Analytical Report, MIREM-AR 2008–05, Florence: European University for Advanced Studies

Kabki, M. et al. 2003 "'Wo benan⊠ a ⊠y⊠ bebree': The Economic Impact of Remittances of Holland-based Ghanaian Migrants on Rural Ashanti", paper presented to International Workshop on Migration and Poverty in West Africa, 13–14 March, Brighton: Sussex University

Kambiré, P. 1994 "Réseaux et stratégies migratoires entre le Burkina Faso et la Côte d'Ivoire, Histoire de vie d'un Migrant", *Itinéraires Notes et Travaux* 42, Genève: IUED

Kane, A. 2001 "Diaspora villageoise et développement Local en Afrique: le cas de Thilogne association développement", *Hommes et Migrations* 1229: 32–35

Kaplan, D. 1997 "Reversing the Brain Drain: The Case for Utilizing South Africa's Unique Intellectual Diaspora", *Science, Technology, and Society* 2 (2), 58–78

Kapur, D. 2001 "Diasporas and Technology Transfer", *Journal of Human Development* 2 (2), 265–86

Kapur, D. and J. McHale 2005 *Give us the Best and Brightest: The Global Hunt for Talent and Its Impact on the Developing World*, Washington DC: Center for Global Development

Kazi, S. 1991 "Returning Migrants and their Re-integration: The Experience of Other Countries", *Economic Review* 22 (5), 39–42

Keita, A. 1996 La problématique de l'émigration des Soninké de Kayes (Mali): quelques aspects des problèmes sociaux du développement Rural intégré, *Notes et Travaux* 35, Centre Sahel/Université Laval, Québec: Université Laval

Kessy, M.K. 1998 *Culture africain et gestion de l'entreprise moderne*, Abidjan: Editions CLE

King, R. 2000 "Generalizations from the History of Return Migration", in B. Ghosh (ed.) *Return Migration. Journey of Hope or Despair?*, Geneva: IOM/UN, 7–55

King, R. 1996 "Migration in a World Historical Perspective", in J. van der Broeck (ed.) *The Economics of Labour Migration*, Cheltenham: Edward Elgar, 7–76

King, R. 1986 "Return Migration and Regional Economic Development: An Overview", in R. King (ed.) *Return Migration and Regional Economic Problems*, London: Croom Helm, 1–37

King, R. 1978 "Return Migration: A Neglected Aspect of Population Geography", *Area* 10 (3), 175–83

King, R. et al. 1983 "Return Migration: A Review of the Literature", *Discussion Papers in Geography* 19, Oxford: Oxford Polytechnic

Kipré, P. 1992 *Histoire de la Côte d'Ivoire*, Abidjan: Editions Ami

Korner, H. 1997 "The Brain Drain from Developing Countries – an Enduring Problem", *Intereconomics* 32, 26–30

Koser, K. 2000 "Return, Readmission and Reintegration: Changing Agendas, Policy Frameworks and Operational Programmes", in B. Ghosh (ed.) *Return Migration, Journey of Hope or Despair?*, Geneva: IOM/UN, 57–99

Krane, R.E. 1976 "Effects of International Migration upon Occupational Model, Acculturation and the Labour Market in Turkey", in *Manpower Mobility Across Cultural Boundaries: Social, Economic and Legal Aspects. The Case of Turkey and West Germany*. Social, Economic and Political Studies of the Middle East 16, 161–204

Krane, R.E. 1973 "The Effects of Cyclical International Migration upon Socio-economic Model", *International Migration Review* 7 (4), 427–36

Kutznetsov, Y. (ed.) 2006 *Diaspora Network and the International Migration of Skills: How Countries can Draw on their Talent Abroad*, Washington DC: World Bank

Lachaud, J.-P. 2002 "Envois de fonds, inégalité et pauvreté au Burkina Faso", *Revue Tiers Monde* 160, 793–827

Laczko, F. 2008 "Migration and Development: The Forgotten Migrants", in J. DeWind and J. Holdaway (eds) *Migration and Development within and Across Borders: Research and Policy Perspectives on Internal and International Migration*, Geneva: IOM

La Verle, B. 1994 *Ghana: A Country Study*, Washington DC: Library of Congress

Lavigne Delville, P. 1991 *La rizière et la valise. Irrigation, Migration et stratégies paysannes dans la vallée du fleuve Sénégal*, Paris: Syros Alternatives

Lee, E.S. 1966 "A Theory of Migration", *Demography* 3 (1), 47–57

Lepore, S. 1986 "Problems Confronting Migrants and Members of their Families when they Return to their Countries of Origin", *International Migration* 23 (1), 95–128

Lewis, A.W. 1954 "Economic Development with Limited Supplies of Labour", *The Manchester School of Economic and Social Studies*, 22 (2)

Lewis, G.J. 1982 *Human Migration. A Geographical Perspective*, London: Croom Helm

Libercier, M.-H. and H. Schneider 1996 *Migrants. Partners in Development Co-operation*, Paris: OECD

Lincoln, Y.S. and Guba, E.G. 1985 *Naturalistic Inquiry*, Beverley Hills: Sage Publications

Lipton, M. 1982 "Rural Development and the retention of the Rural Population in the Countryside of Developing Countries", *Canadian Journal of Development Studies* 3 (1), 11–37

Lipton, M. 1980 "Migration from Rural Areas in poor Countries: The Impact on Rural Productivity and Income Distribution", *World Development* 8 (1), 1–24

Logan, B.I. 1992 "The Brain Drain of Professionals, Technical and Kindred Workers from Developing Countries: Some Lessons from Africa–US Flow of Professionals (1980–1989)", *International Migration* 30 (3/4), 289–312

Logan, B.I. 1990 "An Assessment of the potential application of the Transfer of Knowledge through Expatriate Nationals (TOKTEN) Programme in Sub-Saharan Africa", *Applied Geography* 10, 223–26

Looney, R.E. 1990 "Macroeconomic Impacts of Worker Remittances on Arab World Labour Exporting Countries", *International Migration* 28 (1), 25–45

Losch, B. 2000 "La Côte d'Ivoire en quête d'une nouveau project national", *Politique Africaine* 78, 5–25

Lowell, L.B. and S.G. Gerova 2004 *Diasporas and Economic Development: State of Knowledge*, Washington DC: Institute for the Study of International Migration

Lowell, L.B. 2002a "Some Developmental Effects of the International Migration of Highly Skilled Persons", *International Migration Papers 46*, Geneva: ILO

Lowell, L.B. 2002b "Skilled Labour Migration from Developing Countries: Annotated Bibliography", *International Migration Papers 56*, Geneva: ILO

Lowell, L.B. and A. Findlay 2002 "Migration of Highly Skilled Persons from Developing Countries: Impact and Policy Responses. Synthesis Report", *International Migration Papers 44*, Geneva: ILO

Mabogunje, A.L. 1970 "Systems Approach to a Theory of Rural–Urban Migration", *Geographical Analysis* 2, 1–17

MacDonald, J.S. and L.D. MacDonald 1964 "Chain Migration, Ethnic Neighbourhood Formation and Social Networks", *Milbank Memorial Fund Quarterly* 42, 82–97

Mahroum, S. 2001 "Europe and the Immigration of Highly Skilled Labour", *International Migration* 39 (5), 27–43

Mahroum, S. 2000 "Highly Skilled Globetrotters: Mapping the International Migration of Human Capital", *R and D Management* 30 (1), 23–32

Maimbo, S. 2008 "Remittances and Financial Sector Development in Conflict-affected Countries: Lessons from Somalia and Afghanistan", in R. Bardouille et al. (eds) *Africa's Finances: The Contribution of Remittances*. Newcastle: Cambridge Scholars Publishing

Makinwa-Adebusoye, P.K. 1995 "Emigration Dynamics In West Africa", *International Migration* 23 (3/4), 435–68

Makinwa-Adebusoye, P.K. 1992 "The West African Migration System", in M.M. Kritz et al. (eds) *International Migration Systems: A Global Approach*, New York: Oxford University Press ,63–79

Marchal, B. and G. Kegels 2003 "Health Workforce Imbalances in Times of Globalisation: Brain Drain or Professional Model", *International Journal of Health Planning and Management* 18, 89–101

Massey, D.S., J. Arango, G. Hugo, A. Kouaouci, A. Pellegrino and J.E. Taylor 1998 *Worlds in Motion: Understanding International Migration at the End of the Millennium*, International Studies in Demography, Oxford: Clarendon Press

Massey, D.S., J. Arango, G. Hugo, A. Kouaouci, A. Pellegrino and J.E. Taylor 1993 "Theories of International Migration: A Review and Appraisal", *Population and Development Review* 19 (3), 431–66

Mayr, K. and G. Peri 2008 "Return Migration as Channel of Brain Gain", *NBER Working Paper No. 14039*, Cambridge: National Bureau of Economic Research

McCormick, B and J. Wahba 2003 "Return International Migration and Geographical Inequality: The Case of Egypt", *Journal of African Economies* 12, 500–32

McLaughlan, G. and J. Salt 2002 *Migration Policies Towards Highly Skilled Foreign Workers*, Report to Home Office, London: University College

Mesnard, A. 2004 "Temporary Migration and Capital Market Imperfections", *Oxford Economic Papers* 56, 242–62

Meyer, J.-B. 2001 "Network Approach versus Brain Drain: Lessons from the Diaspora", *International Migration* 39 (5), 91–110

Moreno-Fontes Chammartin, G. 2002 "La féminisation des migrations internationales", *Travailleurs et travailleuses Migrants, Education Ouvrière 2002/4* 129, Genève: BIT, 43–53

Mundende, D.C. 1989 "The Brain Drain and Developing Countries", in R. Appleyard (ed.) *The Impact of International Migration on Developing Countries*, Paris: OECD, 183–95

Muschkin, C.G. 1993 "Consequences of Return Migrant Status for Employment in Puerto Rico", *International Migration Review* 27 (1), 79–102

Murphy, R. 2000 "Return Migration, Entrepreneurship and Local State Corporatism in Rural China: The Experience of Two Counties in South Jiangxi", *Journal of Contemporary China* 9 (24) 231–47

Murphy, R. 1999 "Return Migrant Entrepreneurs and Economic Diversification in Two Counties in South Jiangxi", *Journal of International Development* 11 (4), 661–72

Nada, A.H. 1991 "Impact of Temporary International Migration on Rural Egypt", *Cairo Papers in Social Science* 14 (3), Cairo: American University Cairo Press

Nambiar, A.C.K. 1998 "In Search of Green Pastures: Myths and Reality of Gulf Migrant Workers", *Manpower Journal* 33 (4), 39–48

Nédélec, S. 1998 "Une expérience originale d'aide à la création de micro entreprise pour les Migrants", *Hommes et Migrations* 1214, 91–93

Ndiaye, N. 2000 "Le phénomène de la fuite des cerveaux et le programme de retour de personnel qualifié mis en oeuvre par l'OIM en Afrique", paper presented to IOM–UNECA Brain Drain Meeting, Addis Ababa, 22–24 February, Geneva: International Organisation for Migration

N'Diaye, J.-P. 1969 *Élites africaines et culture occidentale: assimilation ou résistance?*, Paris: Présence Africaine

Nukunya, G.K. 1992 *Tradition and Change in Ghana: An Introduction to Sociology*, Accra: Ghana University Press

Nyberg-Sørensen, N. et al. 2002a "The Migration-Development Nexus: Evidence and Policy Options", *IOM Migration Reseach Series* 8, Geneva: IOM

Nyberg-Sørensen, N. et al. 2002b "State of the Art Overview: The Migration Development Nexus. Evidence and Policy Options", hhtp://www.cdr.dk/resthemes/conflict/migdevfinal/htm

Obia, G.C. 1993 "Brain Drain and African Development: A Descriptive Framework for Deriving Indirect Benefits", *Journal of Third World Studies* 10 (2), 74–97

OECD 2008 *International Migration Outlook*, Sopemi 2008 Edition, Paris: OECD

OECD 2007 *International Migration Outlook*, Sopemi 2007 Edition, Paris: OECD

OECD 2002 *International Mobility of the Highly Skilled*, Paris: OECD

OECD 2000 *Globalisation, Migration and Development*, Paris: OECD

Ojo, K.O. 1990 "International Migration of Health Manpower in Sub-Saharan Africa", *Social Sciences and Medicine* 31 (6), 631–38

Ouattara, I. 1999 *Profil de la Pauvreté 1998*, Abidjan: Institut National de la Statistique

Ouattara, I. 1997 *Profil de la Pauvreté en Côte d'Ivoire 1993 et 1995*, Abidjan: Institut National de la Statistique

Oucho, J.O. 1995a "International Migration and Sustainable Human Development in Eastern and Southern Africa", *International Migration* 33 (1), 31–54

Oucho, J.O. 1995b "Emigration Dynamics of Eastern African Countries", *International Migration* 33 (3/4), 301–42

Özden, C. and M. Schiff (eds) 2006 *International Migration, Remittances and the Brain Drain*, Washington DC: World Bank and Palgrave Macmillan

Page, J. and S. Plaza 2006 "Migration, Remittances and Development: A Review of the Global Evidence." *Journal of African Economies* 15 (2),245–336

Panos 2000 "Dossier: Les immigrés, acteurs du développement Nord-Sud?", *Migrations Société* 67, 33–128

Papademetriou, D.G. 1991 "Migration and Development: The Unsettled Relationship", in D.G. Papdemetriou and P.L. Martin (eds) *The Unsettled Relationship: Labor Migration and Economic Development*, Westport: Greewood Press, 213–20

Papademetriou, D.G. and P.L. Martin (eds) 1991 *The Unsettled Relationship: Labor Migration and Economic Development*, Westport: Greewood Press

Parant, M. 2000 "Echecs et illusions des politiques d'aide au retour", *Hommes et Migrations* 1223, 52–56

Petek-Salom, G. 2002 "Peut-on encore parler de politique de réinsertion?' *Hommes et Migrations* 1236, 53–58

Petit, A. 2002 "L'ultime retour des gens du fleuve Sénégal", *Hommes et Migrations* 1236, 44–52

Piore, M.J. 1979 *Birds of Passage: Migrant Labor and Industrial Societies*, New York: Cambridge University Press

Pires, J. 1992 "Return and Reintegration of Qualified Nationals from Developing Countries Residing Abroad: The IOM Experience", *International Migration* 30 (3/4), 353–75

Pond, B. and B. McPake 2006 "The Health Migration Crisis: The Role of Four Organisation for Economic Co-operation and Development Countries", *The Lancet* 367/9520, 1448–55

Portes, A. 2008 "Migration and Social Change: Some Conceptual Reflections", keynote address to the conference on *Theorizing Key Migration Debates*, 1 July, Oxford University

Portes, A. (ed.) 1995 *The Economic Sociology of Immigration: Essays on Networks, Ethnicity and Entrepreneurship*, New York: Sage

Portes, A. and J. Walton 1981 *Labour, Class, and the International System*, New York: Academic Press

Puy-Denis, P. 1994 *Le Ghana*, Paris: Karthala

Quartey, P. 2006 *The Impact of Migrant Remittances on Household Welfare in Ghana*, Final Report submitted to the African Economic Research Consortium, Nairobi: AERC

Quiminal, C. 2002 "Retours contraints, retours construits des émigrés maliens", *Hommes et Migrations* 1236, 35–43

Quiminal, C. 1993 "Transformations villageoises et regroupement familial", *Hommes et Migrations* 1165, 18–22

Quiminal, C. 1991 *Gens d'ici, gens d'ailleurs: migrations Soninké et transformations villagoises*, Paris: Christian Bourgois Editeur

Quiminal, C. and M. Timera 2002 "1974–2002, les mutations de l'Immigration ouest-africaine", *Hommes et Migrations* 1239, 6–18

Ratha, D. et al. 2008a "Outlook for Remittance Flows 2008–2010, Growth Expected to Moderate Significantly, but Flows Remain Resilient", *Migration and Development Brief No. 8*, Washington DC: World Bank

Ratha, D. et al. 2008b "Beyond Aid: New Sources and Innovative Mechanisms for Financing Development in Sub-Saharan Africa", *Policy Research Working Paper* 4609, Washington DC: World Bank

Ratha, D. 2007 "Leveraging Remittances for Development", *Policy Brief, June 2007*, New York: Migration Policy Institute

Ratha, D. and Z. Xu 2008 *Migration and Remittances Factbook*, Washington DC: World Bank

Ratha, D. 2003 "Workers' Remittances: An Important and Stable Source of External Development Finance', in World Bank, *Global Development Finance 2003, Striving for Stability in Development Finance, Analysis and Statistical Annex*, Washington DC: World Bank

Ranis, G. and J.C.H. Fei 1961 "Theory of Economic Development", *The American Economic Review* 51 (4), 533–51

Ricca, S. 1989 *International Migration in Africa: Legal and Administrative Aspects*, Geneva: ILO

Robin, N. 1996a *Atlas des migrations ouest-africaines vers l'Europe, 1985–1993*, Paris: Eurostat/ORSTOM

Robin, N. 1996b "La multipolarisation de la Migration Sénégalaise", in E. Ma Mung (ed.) *Mobilités et investissements des émigres: Maroc, Tunisie, Turquie, Sénégal*, Paris: Harmattan, 48–64

Rodriguez, E.R. 1998 "International Migration and Income Distribution in the Philippines", *Economic Development and Cultural Change* 46 (2), 329–50

Rogers, R. 1984 "Return Migration in comparative Perspective", in D. Kubat (ed.) *The Politics of Return: International Return Migration in Europe*, New York: Center for Migration Studies 277–99

Rose, A.M. 1970 "Distance of Migration and Socio-economic Status of Migrants", in C.J. Jansen (ed.) *Readings in the Sociology of Migration*, London: Pergamon Press, 85–92

Russell, S.S. 1992 "Migrant Remittances and Development", *International Migration* 30 (3/4), 267–87

Russell, S.S. et al. 1990 "International Migration and Development in Sub-Saharan Africa", *World Bank Discussion Papers* 101, Washington DC: World Bank

Sakka, D. et al. 1999 "Return Migration: Changing Roles of Men and Women", *International Migration* 37 (4), 741–63

Saloutos, T. 1956 *They Remember America: The Story of Repatriated Greek Americans*, Berkeley: University of California Press

Sami, M. and de Guchteneire, P. (Eds)(2006 "Transnational Knowledge through Diaspora Networks, Special Issue", *International Journal on Multicultural Studies* 8 (1)

Sander, C. and S.M. Maimbo 2005 "Migrant Remittances in Africa: A Regional Perspective", in S.M. Maimbo and D. Ratha (eds) *Remittances: Development Impact and Future Prospects*, Washington DC: World Bank

Saxenian, AL. 2005 "From Brain Drain to Brain Circulation: Transnational Communities and Regional Upgrading of India and China", http://people.ischool.berkeley.edu/~anno/Papers/scid-2005.pdf

Sindzingre, A. 2000 "Le contexte économique et Social du changement politique en Côte d'Ivoire", Afrique Contemporaine: Dossier Côte d'Ivoire 27–37

Sjaastad, L. 1962 "The Costs and Returns of Migration", *Journal of Political Economy* 70, 80–93

Skeldon, R. 1997 *Migration and Development: A Global Perspective*, Harlow: Longman

Smith, L. and V. Mazzucato 2003 "Houses, Businesses and Urban Livelihoods: The Influence of Transnational Networks on Economic Activities in Accra, Ghana", paper presented to International Workshop on Migration and Poverty in West Africa, 13–14 March, Brighton: Sussex University

Smith, M.P. and L.E. Guarnizo (eds) 1998 *Transnationalism From Below*, New Brunswick: Transaction Publishers

Solimano, A. 2001 "International Migration and the Global Economic Order: An Overview", *Policy Research Working Paper* 2720, Washington DC: World Bank

Solimano, A. 2008 *The International Mobility of Talent: Types, Causes, and Development Impact*, Oxford: Oxford University Press

Solimano, A. 2006 "The International Model of Talent and its Impact on Global Development: An Overview", *Serie macroeconomía del desarrollo*, 52, Santiago: UN. http://www.andressolimano.com/articles/Migration/Intl_Model_Overview_aug06.pdf

Stahl, C.W. 1991 "South-North Migration in the Asia-Pacific Region", *International Migration* 23 (2), 163–94

Stahl, C.W. 1989 "Overview: Economic Perspectives", in R. Appleyard (ed.) *The Impact of International Migration on Developing Countries*, Paris: OECD, 361–87

Stahl C.W. (ed.) 1988 *International Migration Today, Volume 2: Emerging Issues*, Paris: UNESCO

Stahl, C.W. 1983 "Labour Migration and Economic Development", *International Migration Review* 16 (4), 869–99

Stalker, P. 2000 *Workers Without Frontiers, The Impact of Globalization on International Migration*, Geneva: ILO

Stark, O. et al. 1998 "Human Capital Depletion, Human Capital Formation, and Migration: A Blessing in a 'Curse'", *Economic Letters* 60 (3), 363–67

Stark, O. et al. 1997 "A Brain Gain with a Brain Drain", *Economic Letters* 55 (2), 227–34

Stark, O. 1991 *The Migration of Labour*, Cambridge: Basil Blackwell

Stinner, W.F. et al. (eds) 1982 *Return Migration and Remittances: Developing a Caribbean Perspective*, Washington DC: Smithonian Institution

Stone, W. and J. Hughes 2002 "Social Capital: Empirical Meaning and Measurement Validity", *Research Paper*, 27, Melbourne: Australian Institute of Family Studies

Strachan, A.J. 1980 "Government Dponsored Return Migration to Guyana", *Area* 12 (2) 165–69

Sutton, C. and S. Makiesky 1975 "Migration and West Indian racial and Ethnic counciousness", in H.I. Safa and B. du Toit (eds) *Migration and Development*, The Hague: Mouton, 113–44

Tall, M.S. 2003 "Les émigrés sénégalais et les nouvelles technologies de l'information et de la communication", *Technologie, entreprise et société, Document de programme* 7, Genève: UNRISD

Tall, M.S. 1994 "Les investissements immobiliers à Dakar des émigrants sénégalais", *Revue Européenne des Migrations Internationales*10 (3), 137–51

Tansel, A. 1997 "Schooling Attainment, Parental Education, and Gender in Côte d'Ivoire and Ghana", *Economic Development and Cultural Change* 45 (4), 825–56

Taylor, J.E. 1999 "The New economics of Labour Migration and the Role of Remittances in the Migration Process", *International Migration* 37 (1), 63–87

Taylor, E. 1976 "The Social Adjustment of Returned Migrants to Jamaica", in F. Henry (ed.) *Ethnicity in the Americas*, The Hague: Mouton, 213–30

Thomas-Hope, E. 1999 "Return Migration to Jamaica and its Development Potential", *International Migration* 37 (1), 183–207

Tiemoko, R. 2003 "Migration, Return and Socio-economic Change in West Africa: The Role of Family", paper presented to International Workshop on Migration and Poverty in West Africa, 13–14 March, Brighton: Sussex University

Todaro, M.P. 1976 *International Migration in Developing Countries: A Review of Theory*, Geneva: ILO

Todaro, M.P. 1969 "A Model of Labor Migration and Urban Unemployment in Less Developed Countries", *American Economic Review* 59, 138–48

Touré, M. 2000 "Immigration en Côte d'Ivoire: la notion de 'seuil tolérable' relevé de la xénophobie", *Politique Africaine: Côte d'Ivoire, la tentation ethnonationaliste*, Paris: Karthala, 75–93

Traoré, S. and P. Bocquier 1998 "Synthèse Régionale, Réseau Migration et Urbanisation en Afrique de l'Ouest (REMUAO)", *Etudes et Travaux du CERPOD* 15, Bamako: CERPOD

Twum-Baah, K.A. et al. 1995 *Migration Research Study in Ghana: International Migration*, Accra: Ghana Statistical Service

UNICEF 2001 *La situation des enfants dans le monde*, New York: UNICEF

UN Economic and Social Council 2006 "Counting Immigrants and Expatriates in OECD Countries: A New Perspective", paper submitted by the Organization for Economic Co-operation and Development (OECD) to Seminar on Population and Housing Censuses, 54th plenary session, Paris, 13–15 June, Economic Commission for Europe Statistical Commission, Conference of European Statisticians, ECE/CES/2006/SP/15

United Nations 2009a "UN Data Country Profiles", Côte d'Ivoire. http://data.un.org/CountryProfile.aspx?crName=C%C3%B4te%20d%27Ivoire

United Nations 2009b "UN Data Country Profiles, Ghana", http://data.un.org/CountryProfile.aspx?crName=Ghana

UN Population Division 2009 "Trends in Migrant Stocks: The 2005 Revision", http://esa.un.org/Migration

UN Population Division 2002 *International Migration Report 2002*, ST/ESA/SER.A/220, New York: United Nations

UN Secretariat 1986 "The Meaning, Modalities and Consequences of Return Migration", *International Migration Review* 23 (1), 77–93

UN Statistics Division 2002 "Millennium Indicators", http://millennium indicators.un.org/

Van Hear, N. 2002 "Sustaining Societies Under Strain: Remittances as a Form of Transnational Exchange in Sri Lanka and Ghana", in N. Al-Ali and K. Koser (eds) *New Approaches to Migration: Transnational Communities and Transformation of Home*, London and New York: Routledge, 202–23

Verrière, V. 2001 "Heurs et malheurs d'une ressources tant convoitée. Exemples empruntés au Sénégal, au Maroc et à la Turquie", in R. Blion and I. Rigoni (eds), *D'un Voyage à un autre, Des voix de l'Immigration pour un développement pluriel*, Paris: Karthala, 115–28

Weber, M. 1949 *The Methodology of the Social Sciences*, trans. and ed. E.A. Shils and H.A. Finch (first published 1904–07), New York: Free Press of Glencoe

Weil, P. 2002 "Towards a Coherent Policy of Co-Development", *International Migration* 40 (3), 41–55

WHO 2006 "Working together for Health", *The World Health Report 2006*, Geneva: WHO

Wickramasekara, P. 2003 "Options politiques de réponse à la Migration des compétences: rétention, retour et circulation", *Perspectives des Migrations du Travail* 5F, Genève: BIT

Wolpert, J. 1966 "Behavioural Aspects of the Decision to Migrate", *Papers of the Regional Science Association* 15, 159–69

World Bank 2003 *Global Development Finance 2003, Striving for Stability in Development Finance, Analysis and Statistical Annex*, Washington DC: World Bank

World Bank 2003b *World Economic Outlook*, Washington DC: World Bank

World Bank 2002a "Gender Statistics", http://genderstats.worldbank.org/

World Bank 2002b "Country Data Profiles", http://devdata.worldbank.org/external/

World Bank 2002c "Health, Nutrition, and Population Statistics", http://devdata.worldbank.org/hnpstats/

World Bank 2001 "Country at a Glance", http://www.worldbank.org/data/

World Bank 2000 "Entering the 21st Century", *World Development Report 1999/2000*, New York: Oxford University Press

World Bank 2009a "Côte d'Ivoire at a Glance", devdata.worldbank.org/AAG/civ_aag.pdf

World Bank 2009b "Ghana at a Glance", devdata.worldbank.org/AAG/civ_aag.pdf

World Bank 2008 *Migration and Remittances Factbook 2008*, Washington DC: World Bank

World Bank 2006 *Global Economic Prospects: Economic Implications of Remittances and Migration*, Washington DC: World Bank

Yatéra, S. et al. 2000 *Les investissements économiques des Migrants dans leur pays d'origine, Synthèse de l'étude réalisée par Migrance Africaine/Programme Solidarieté Eau*, Bamako: FSP Codéveloppement Mali

Zachariah, K.C. et al. 2000 "Socio-economic and Demographic Consequences of Migration in Kerala", *Working Paper* 303, Kerala: Centre for Development Studies

Zachariah, K.C. and H. Condé 1980 *Demographic Aspects of Migration in West Africa*, Paris: OECD

Zlotnik, H. 2003 "Migrants' Rights, Forced Migration and Migration Policy in Africa", paper prepared for the Conference on African Migration and Urbanization in Comparative Perspective, 4–8 June, Johannesburg, South Africa

Zolberg, A. 1964 *One Party Government in the Ivory Coast*, Princeton; University of Princeton Press